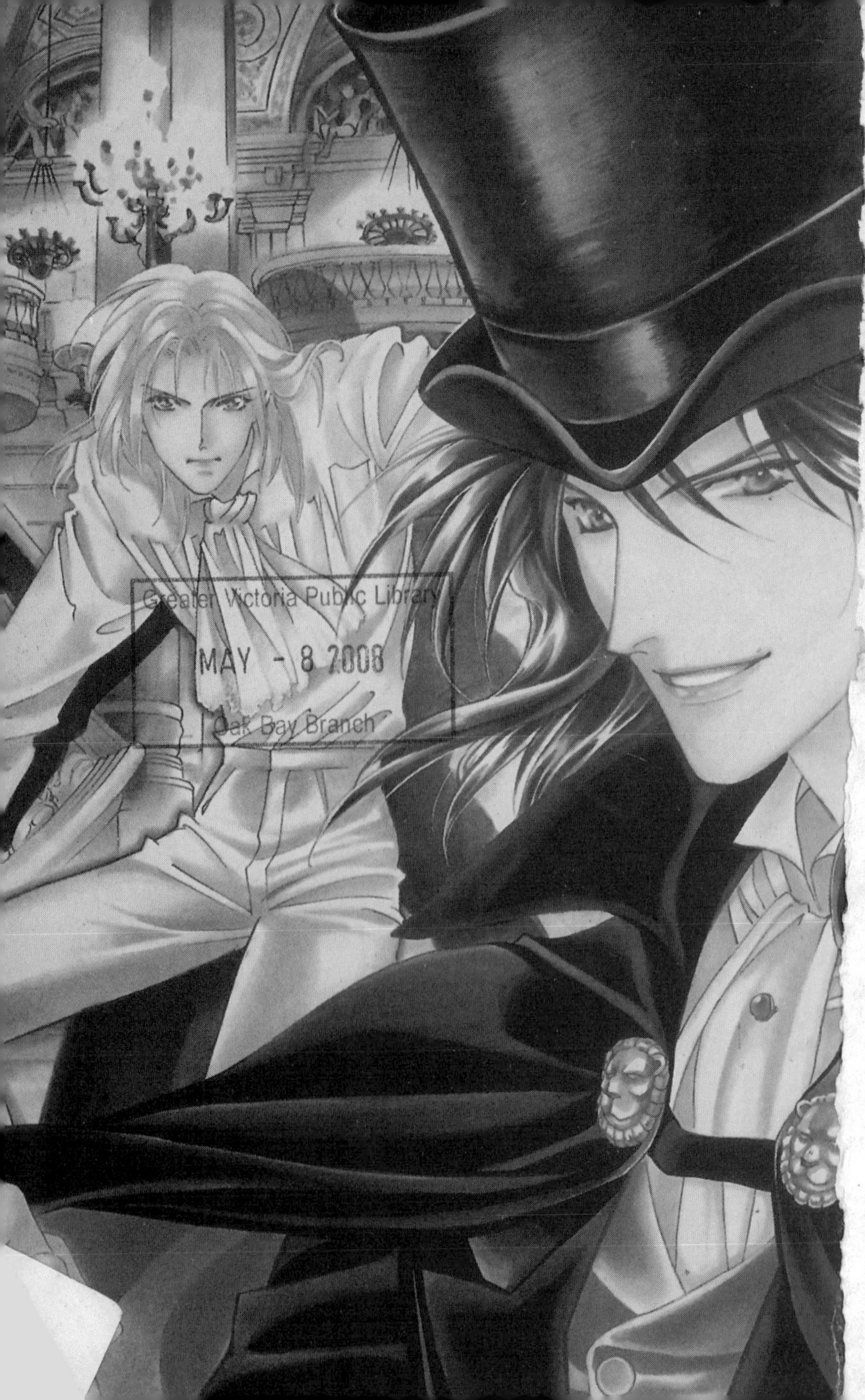

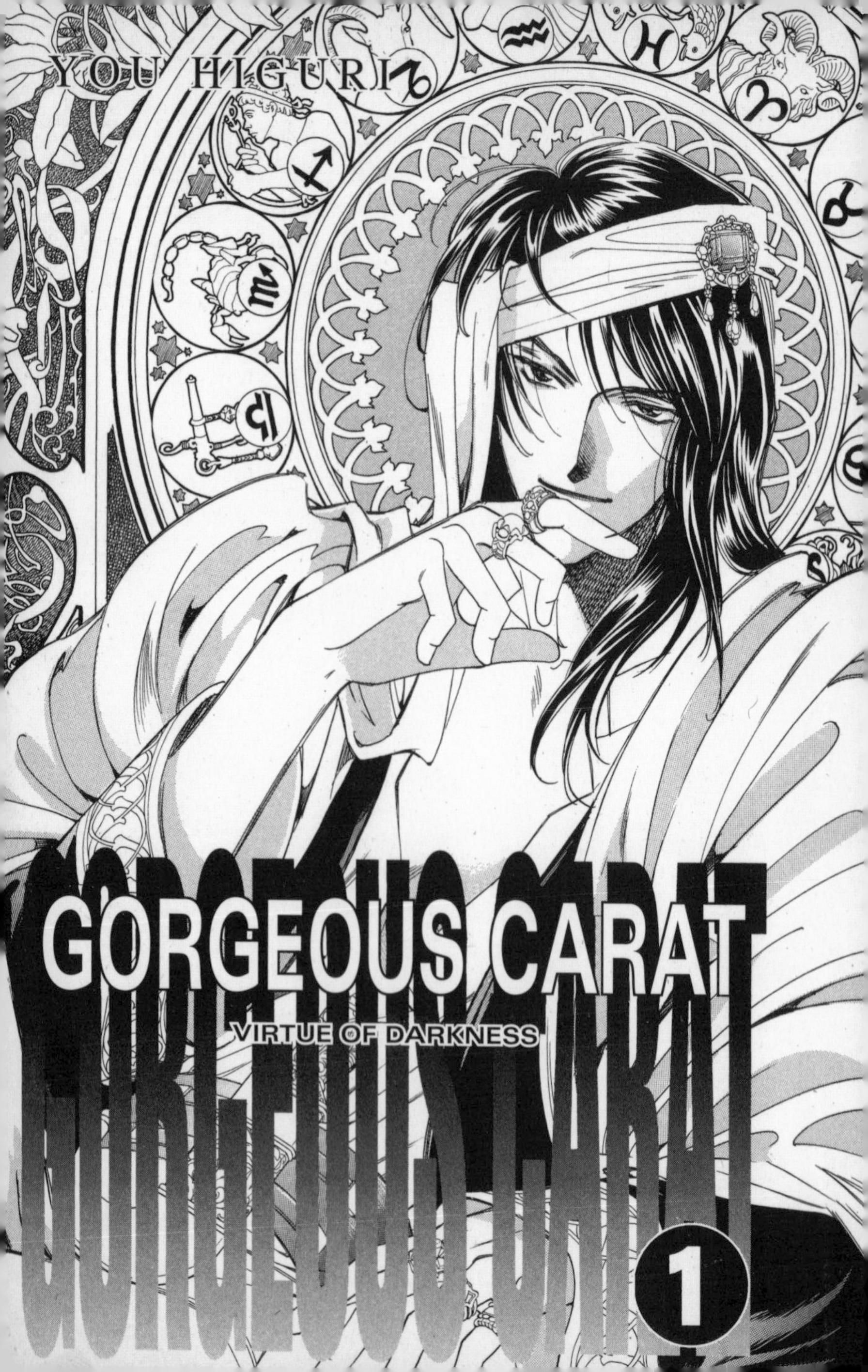
YOU HIGURI
GORGEOUS CARAT
VIRTUE OF DARKNESS
GORGEOUS CARAT
1

GORGEOUS CARAT
Virtue of Darkness

❶

CONTENTS

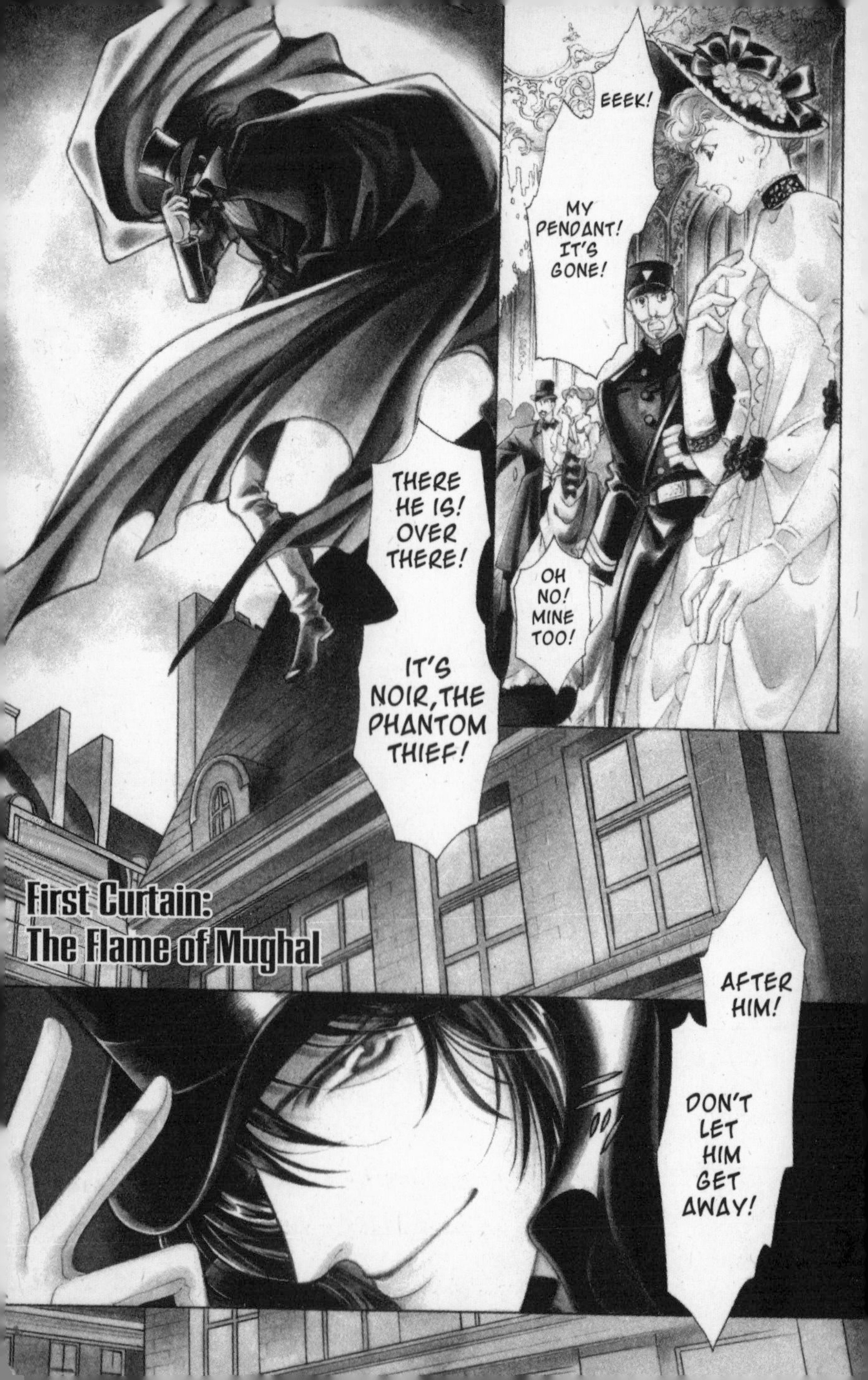
EEEK!
MY PENDANT! IT'S GONE!
OH NO! MINE TOO!
THERE HE IS! OVER THERE!
IT'S NOIR, THE PHANTOM THIEF!
First Curtain: The Flame of Mughal
AFTER HIM!
DON'T LET HIM GET AWAY!

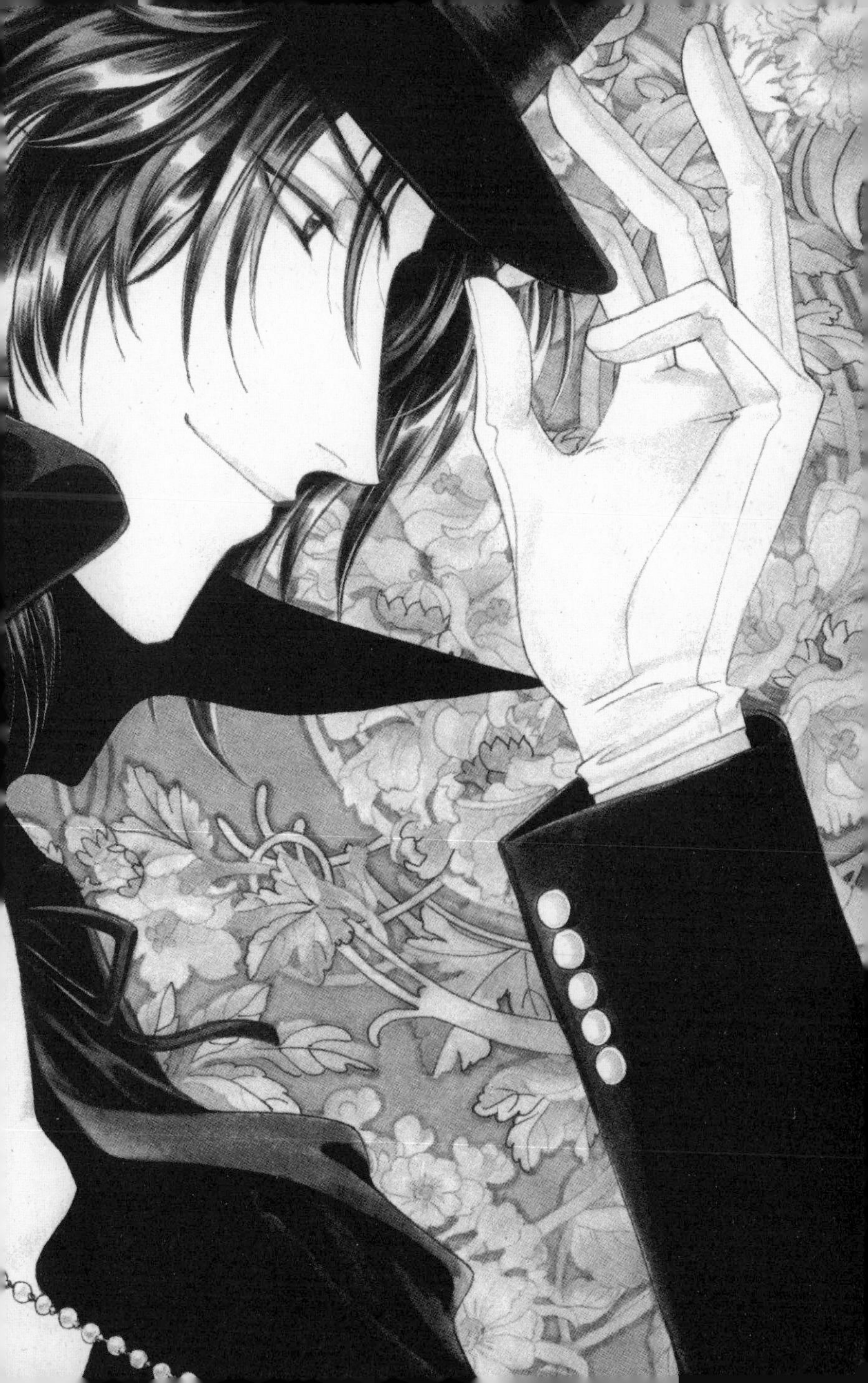

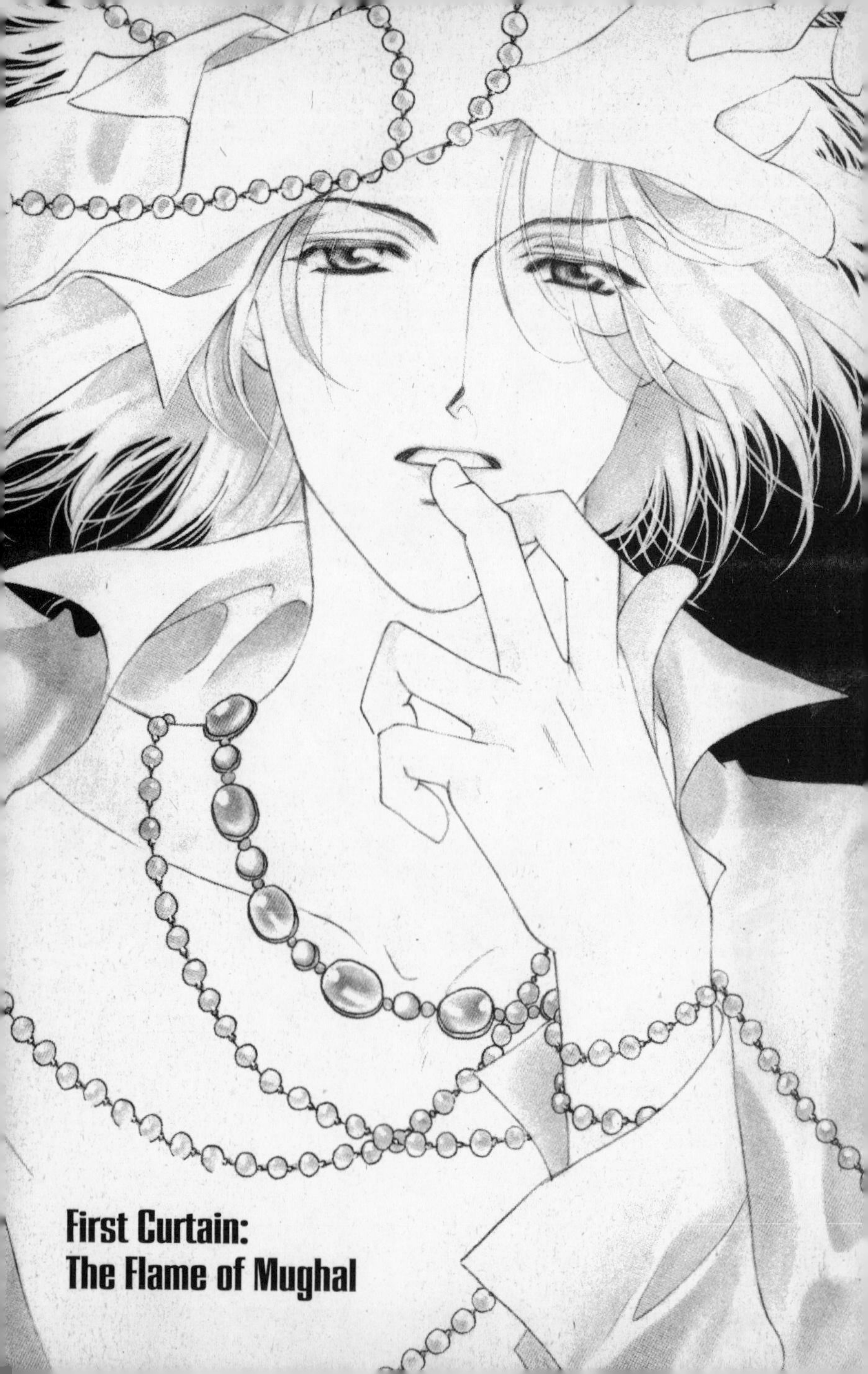

First Curtain: The Flame of Mughal

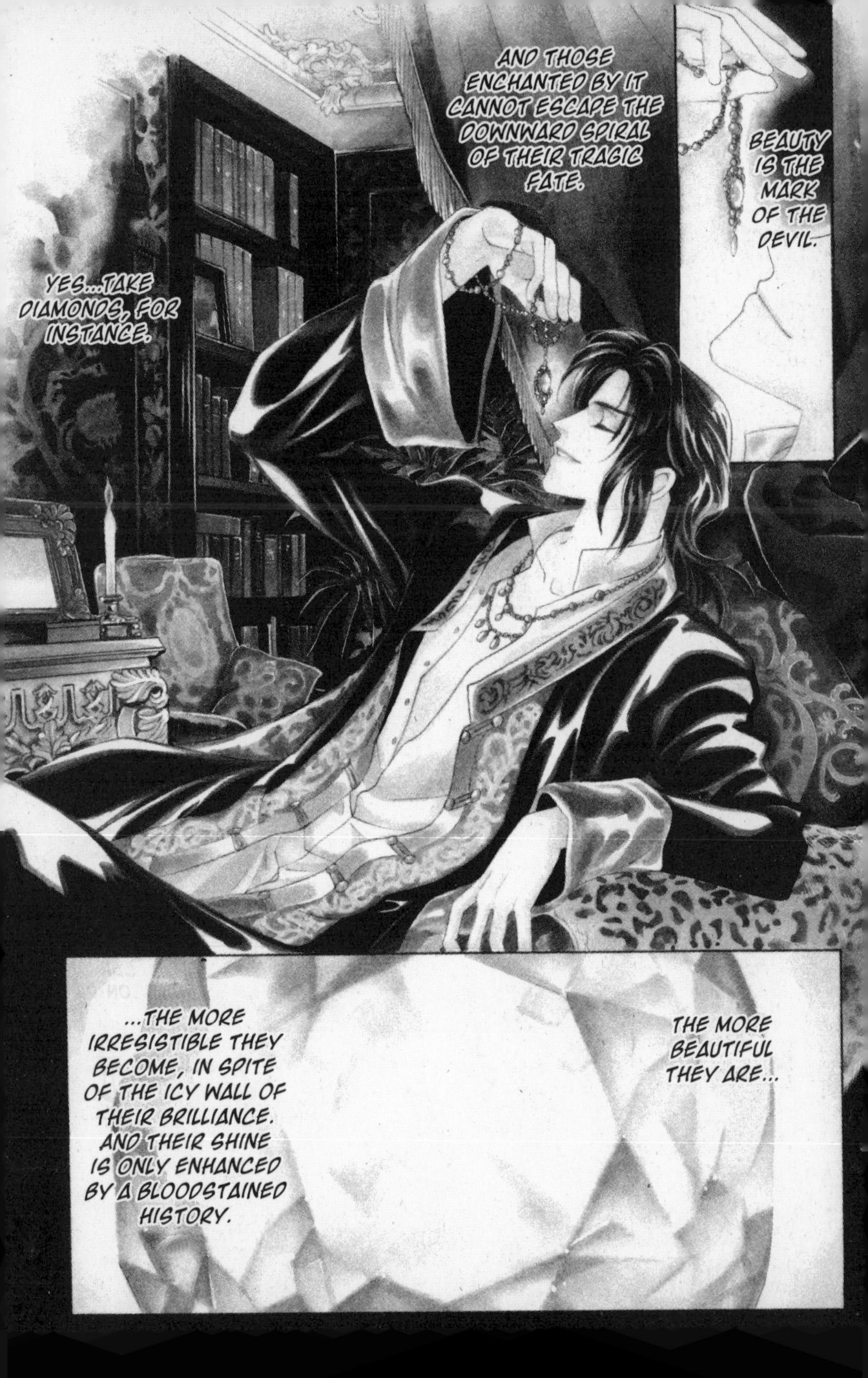
BEAUTY IS THE MARK OF THE DEVIL.
AND THOSE ENCHANTED BY IT CANNOT ESCAPE THE DOWNWARD SPIRAL OF THEIR TRAGIC FATE.
YES...TAKE DIAMONDS, FOR INSTANCE.
THE MORE BEAUTIFUL THEY ARE...
...THE MORE IRRESISTIBLE THEY BECOME, IN SPITE OF THE ICY WALL OF THEIR BRILLIANCE. AND THEIR SHINE IS ONLY ENHANCED BY A BLOODSTAINED HISTORY.

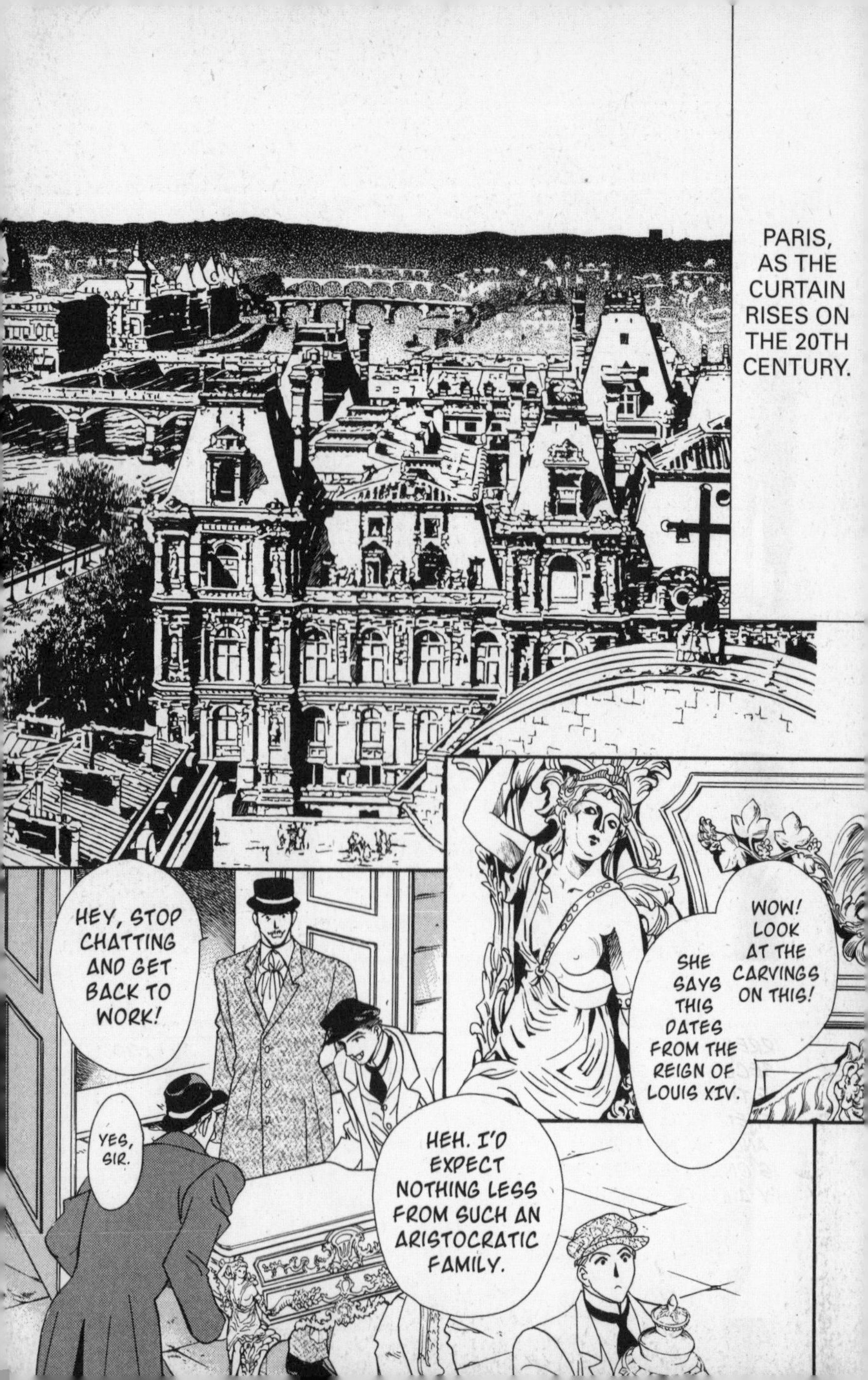
PARIS, AS THE CURTAIN RISES ON THE 20TH CENTURY.
WOW! LOOK AT THE CARVINGS ON THIS!
SHE SAYS THIS DATES FROM THE REIGN OF LOUIS XIV.
HEY, STOP CHATTING AND GET BACK TO WORK!
YES, SIR.
HEH. I'D EXPECT NOTHING LESS FROM SUCH AN ARISTOCRATIC FAMILY.

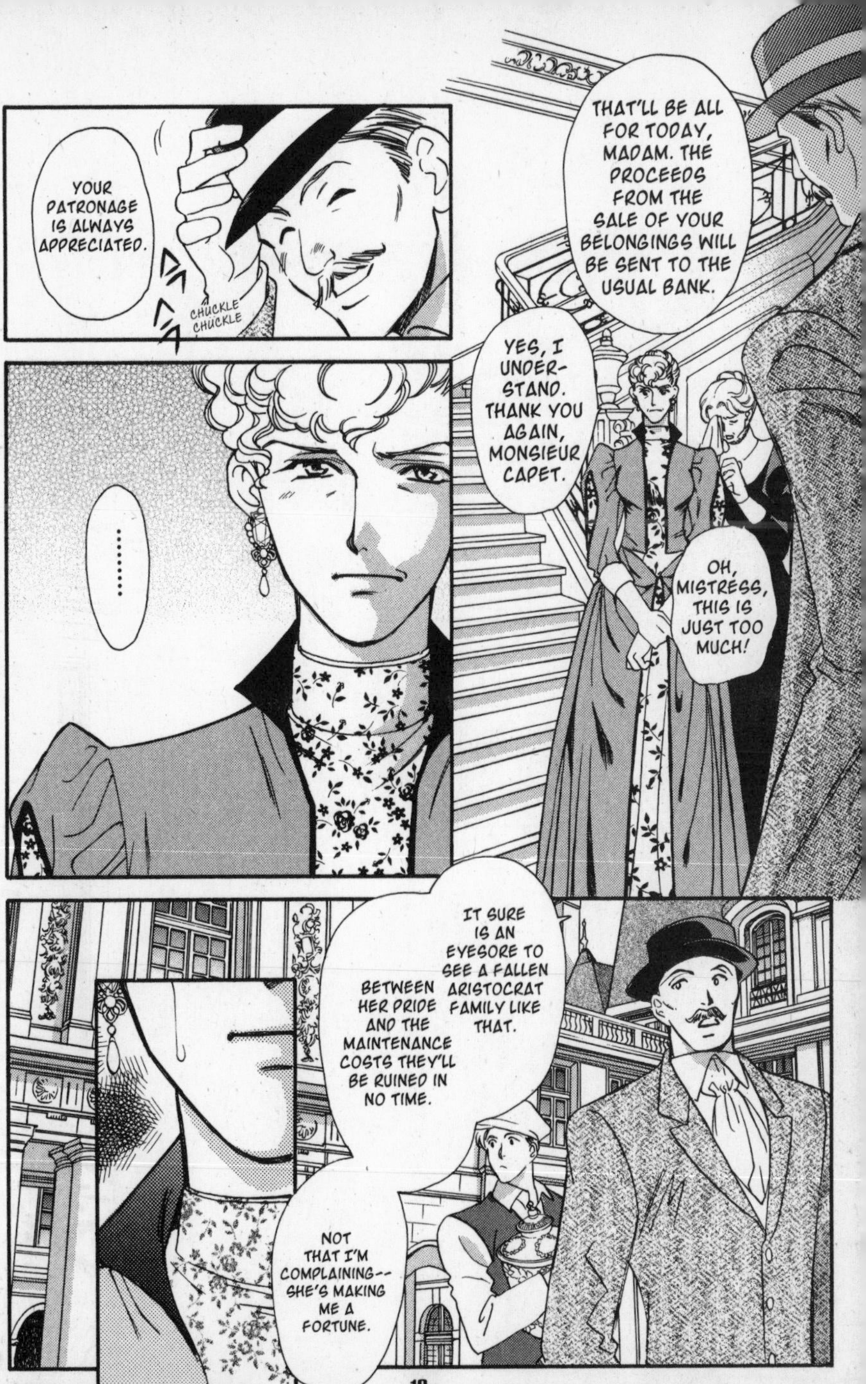
THAT'LL BE ALL FOR TODAY, MADAM. THE PROCEEDS FROM THE SALE OF YOUR BELONGINGS WILL BE SENT TO THE USUAL BANK.
YES, I UNDER-STAND. THANK YOU AGAIN, MONSIEUR CAPET.
OH, MISTRESS, THIS IS JUST TOO MUCH!
YOUR PATRONAGE IS ALWAYS APPRECIATED.
CHUCKLE CHUCKLE
......
IT SURE IS AN EYESORE TO SEE A FALLEN ARISTOCRAT FAMILY LIKE THAT.
BETWEEN HER PRIDE AND THE MAINTENANCE COSTS THEY'LL BE RUINED IN NO TIME.
NOT THAT I'M COMPLAINING--SHE'S MAKING ME A FORTUNE.

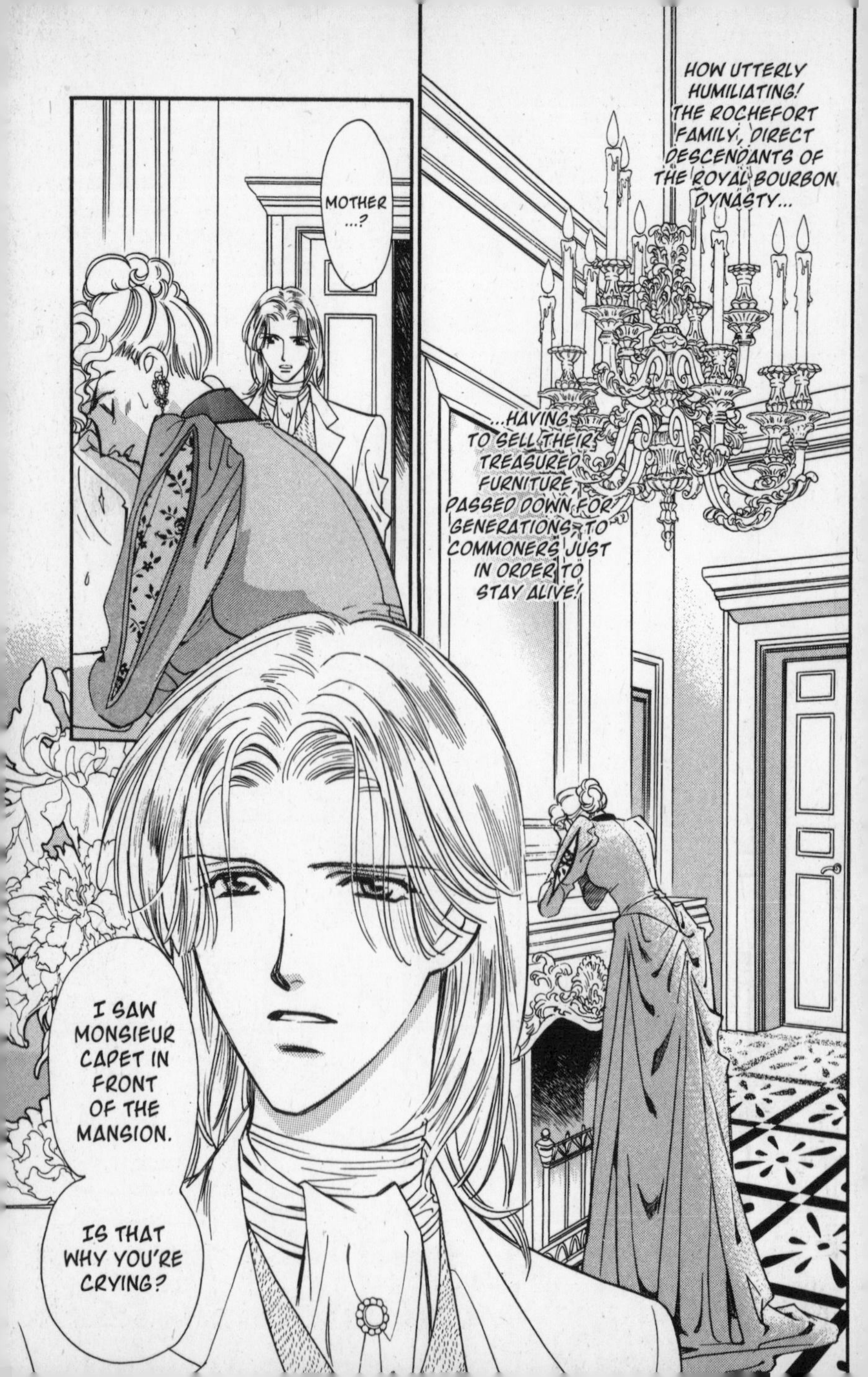
HOW UTTERLY HUMILIATING! THE ROCHEFORT FAMILY, DIRECT DESCENDANTS OF THE ROYAL BOURBON DYNASTY...
...HAVING TO SELL THEIR TREASURED FURNITURE, PASSED DOWN FOR GENERATIONS, TO COMMONERS JUST IN ORDER TO STAY ALIVE!
MOTHER ...?
I SAW MONSIEUR CAPET IN FRONT OF THE MANSION.
IS THAT WHY YOU'RE CRYING?

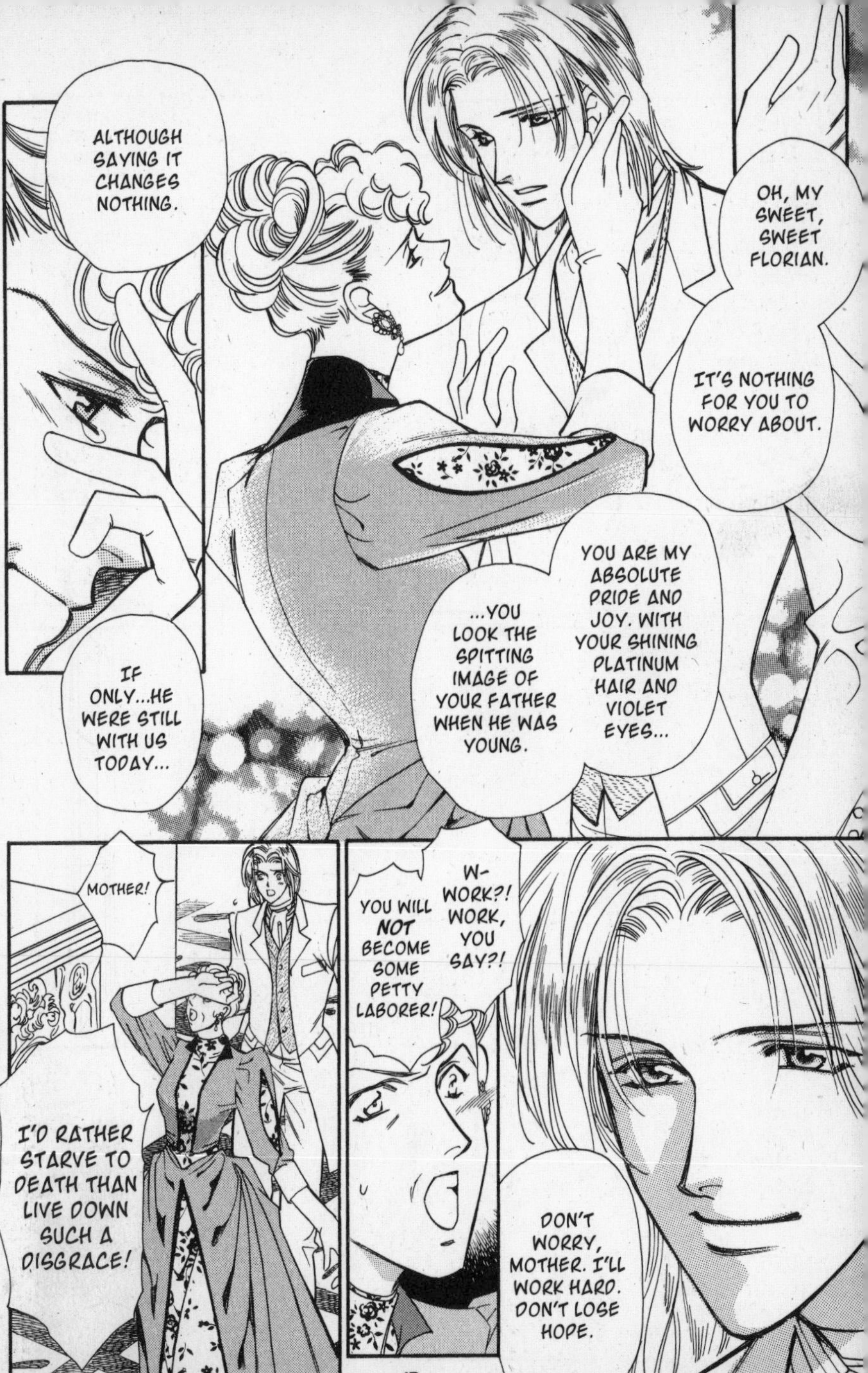
OH, MY SWEET, SWEET FLORIAN.
IT'S NOTHING FOR YOU TO WORRY ABOUT.
YOU ARE MY ABSOLUTE PRIDE AND JOY. WITH YOUR SHINING PLATINUM HAIR AND VIOLET EYES...
...YOU LOOK THE SPITTING IMAGE OF YOUR FATHER WHEN HE WAS YOUNG.
IF ONLY...HE WERE STILL WITH US TODAY...
ALTHOUGH SAYING IT CHANGES NOTHING.
DON'T WORRY, MOTHER. I'LL WORK HARD. DON'T LOSE HOPE.
W-WORK?! WORK, YOU SAY?!
YOU WILL **NOT** BECOME SOME PETTY LABORER!
MOTHER!
I'D RATHER STARVE TO DEATH THAN LIVE DOWN SUCH A DISGRACE!

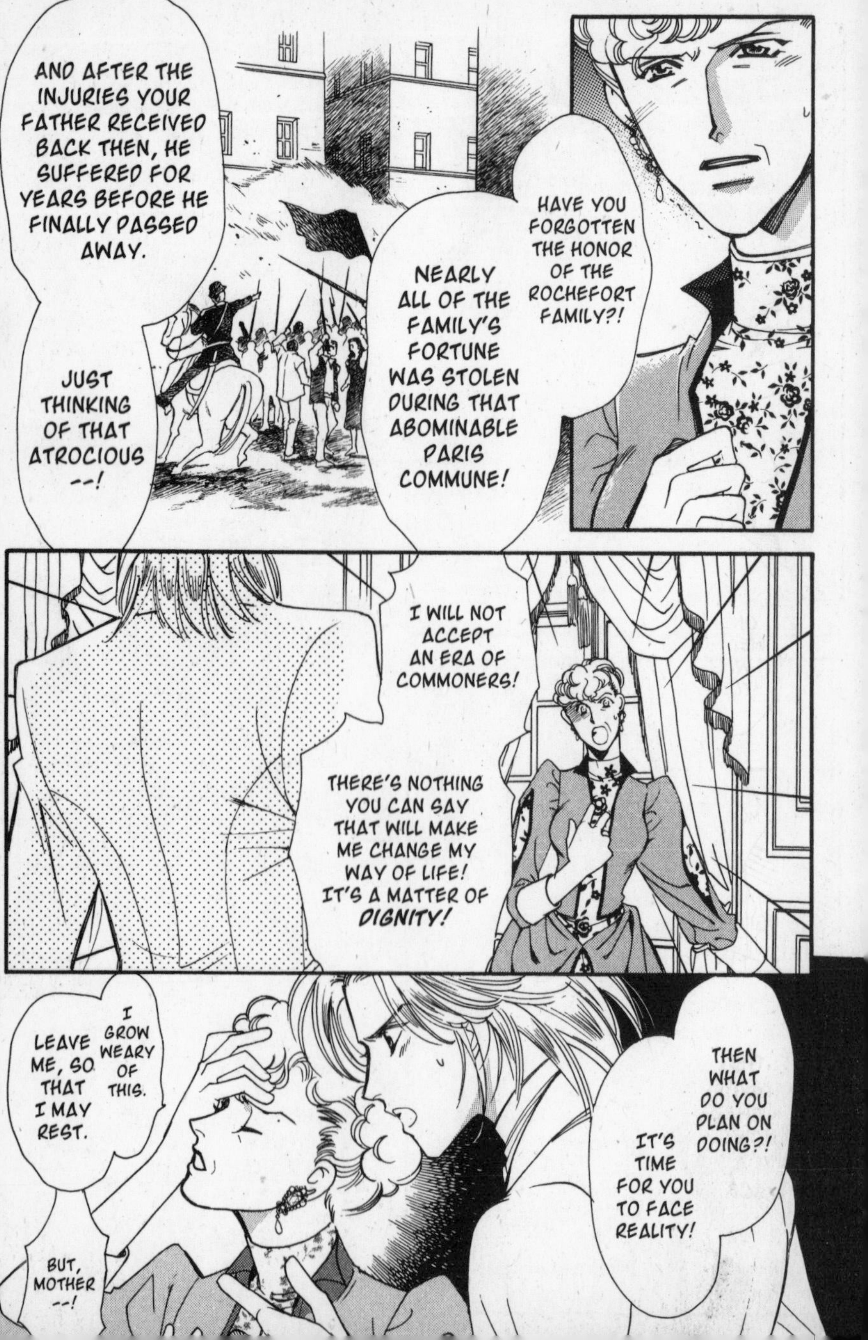
HAVE YOU FORGOTTEN THE HONOR OF THE ROCHEFORT FAMILY?!
NEARLY ALL OF THE FAMILY'S FORTUNE WAS STOLEN DURING THAT ABOMINABLE PARIS COMMUNE!
AND AFTER THE INJURIES YOUR FATHER RECEIVED BACK THEN, HE SUFFERED FOR YEARS BEFORE HE FINALLY PASSED AWAY.
JUST THINKING OF THAT ATROCIOUS --!
I WILL NOT ACCEPT AN ERA OF COMMONERS!
THERE'S NOTHING YOU CAN SAY THAT WILL MAKE ME CHANGE MY WAY OF LIFE! IT'S A MATTER OF *DIGNITY!*
THEN WHAT DO YOU PLAN ON DOING?!
IT'S TIME FOR YOU TO FACE REALITY!
I GROW WEARY OF THIS.
LEAVE ME, SO THAT I MAY REST.
BUT, MOTHER --!

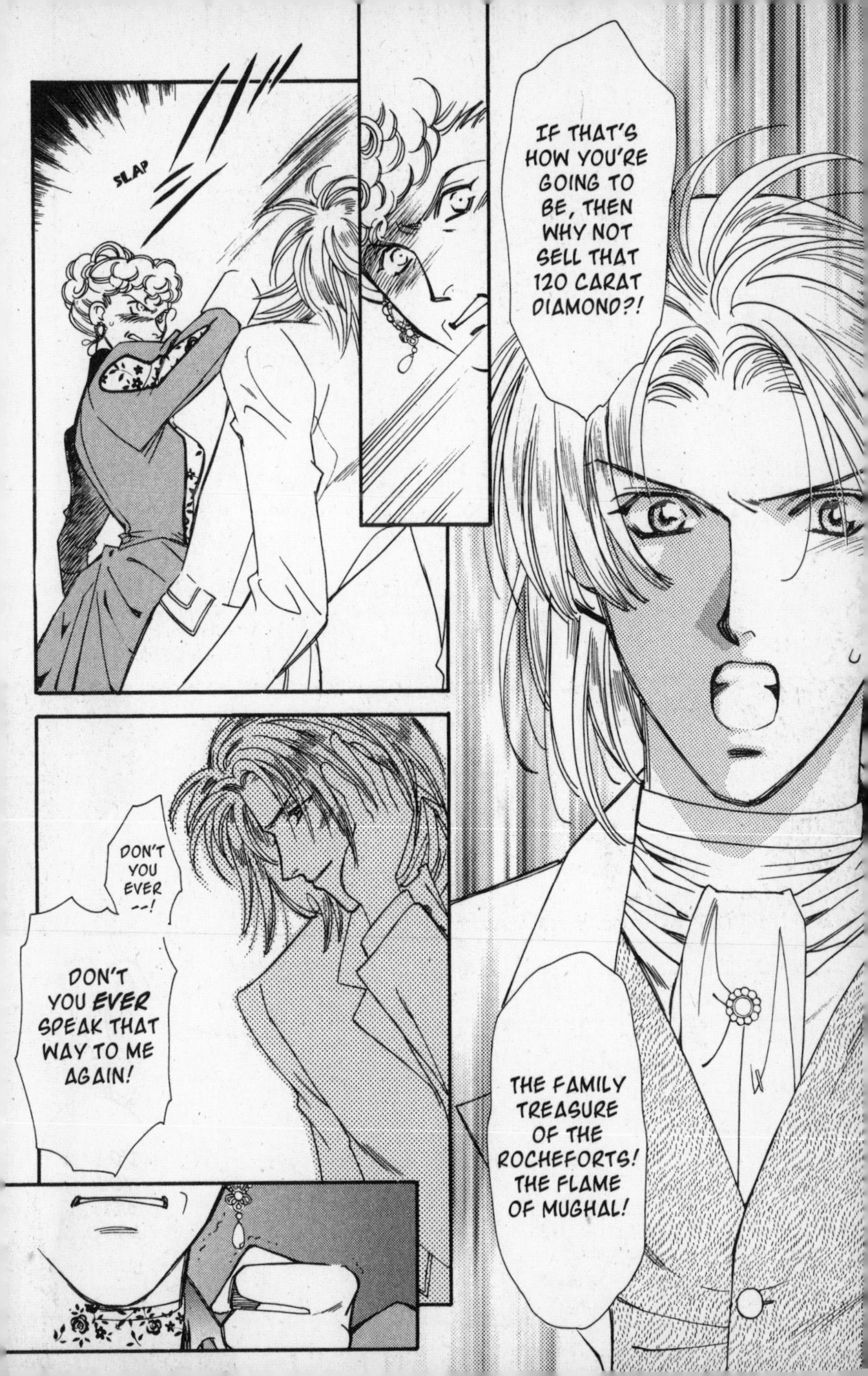
IF THAT'S HOW YOU'RE GOING TO BE, THEN WHY NOT SELL THAT 120 CARAT DIAMOND?!
THE FAMILY TREASURE OF THE ROCHEFORTS! THE FLAME OF MUGHAL!
SLAP
DON'T YOU EVER --!
DON'T YOU *EVER* SPEAK THAT WAY TO ME AGAIN!

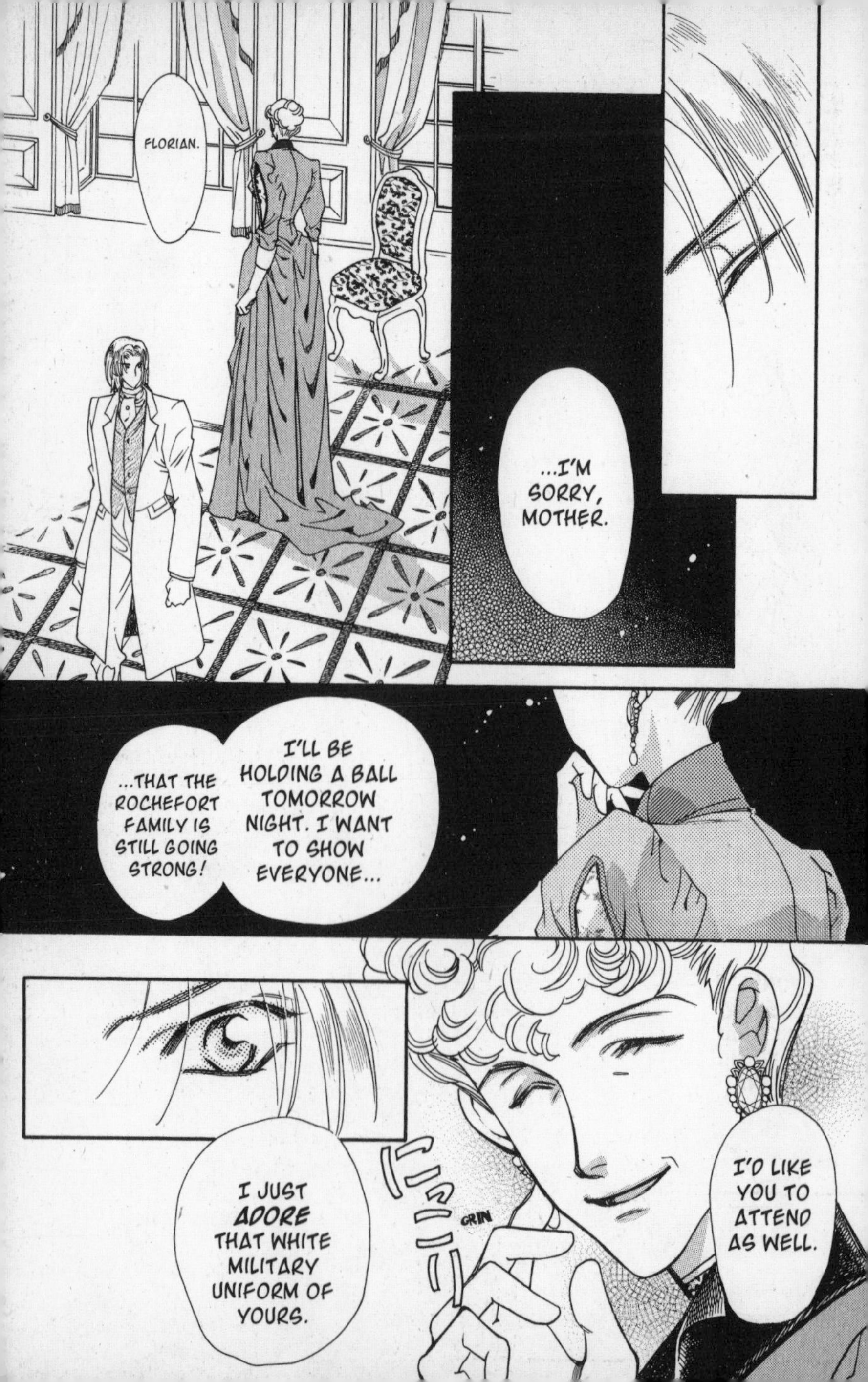
...I'M SORRY, MOTHER.
FLORIAN.
I'LL BE HOLDING A BALL TOMORROW NIGHT. I WANT TO SHOW EVERYONE...
...THAT THE ROCHEFORT FAMILY IS STILL GOING STRONG!
I'D LIKE YOU TO ATTEND AS WELL.
GRIN
I JUST ADORE THAT WHITE MILITARY UNIFORM OF YOURS.

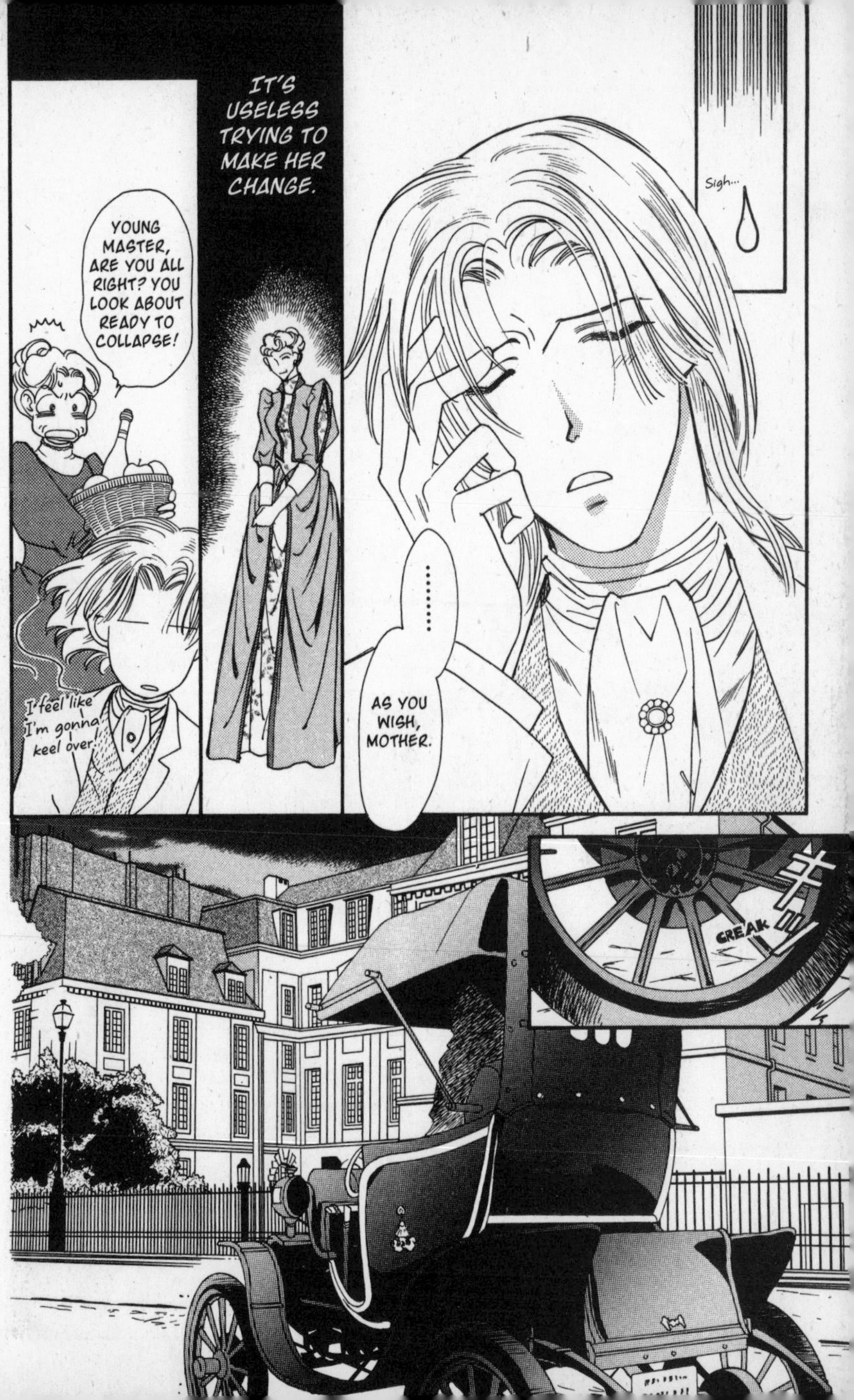
Sigh...
......
AS YOU WISH, MOTHER.
IT'S USELESS TRYING TO MAKE HER CHANGE.
YOUNG MASTER, ARE YOU ALL RIGHT? YOU LOOK ABOUT READY TO COLLAPSE!
I feel like I'm gonna keel over.
CREAK

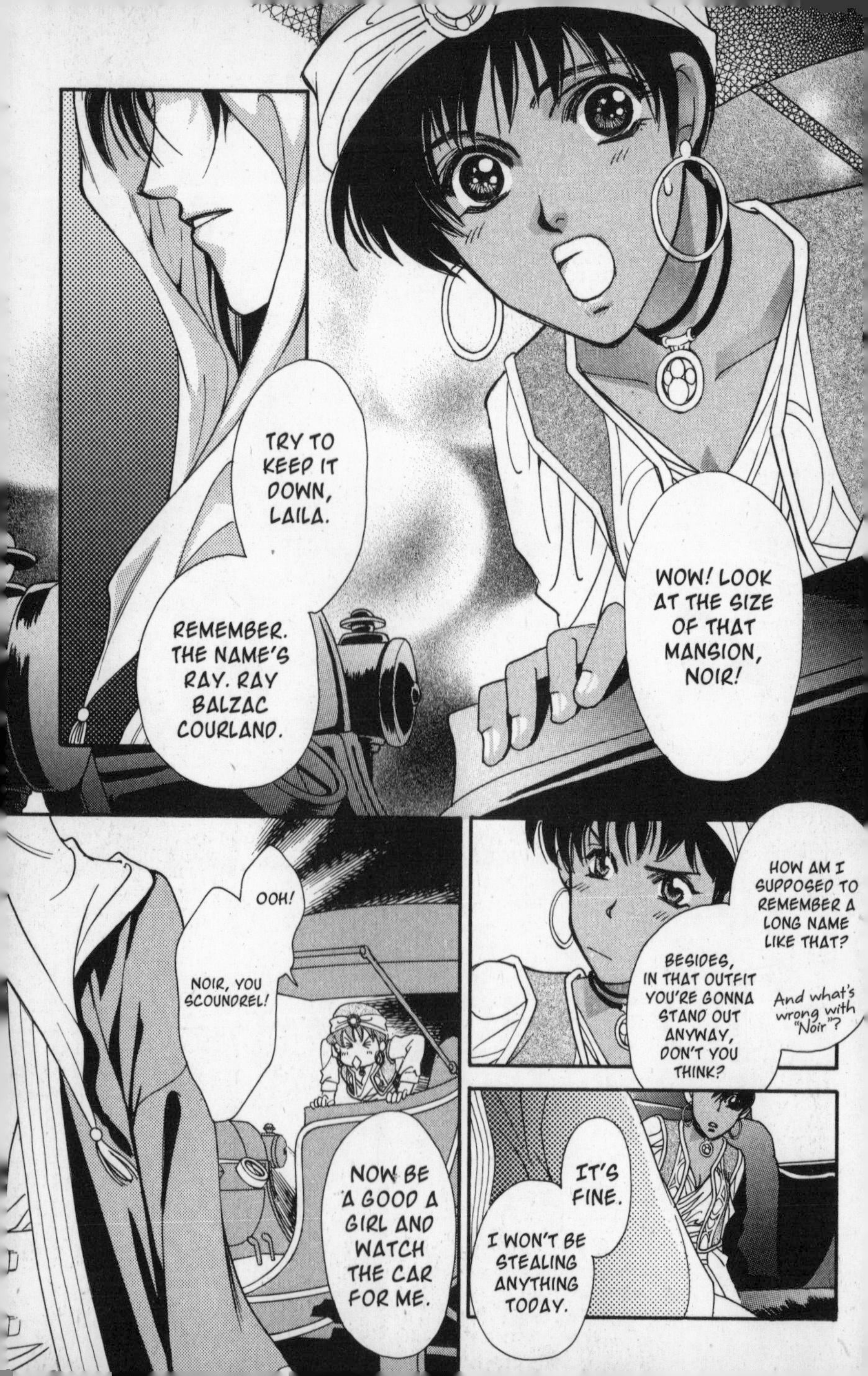
WOW! LOOK AT THE SIZE OF THAT MANSION, NOIR!
TRY TO KEEP IT DOWN, LAILA.
REMEMBER. THE NAME'S RAY. RAY BALZAC COURLAND.
HOW AM I SUPPOSED TO REMEMBER A LONG NAME LIKE THAT?
And what's wrong with "Noir"?
BESIDES, IN THAT OUTFIT YOU'RE GONNA STAND OUT ANYWAY, DON'T YOU THINK?
IT'S FINE.
I WON'T BE STEALING ANYTHING TODAY.
OOH!
NOIR, YOU SCOUNDREL!
NOW BE A GOOD A GIRL AND WATCH THE CAR FOR ME.

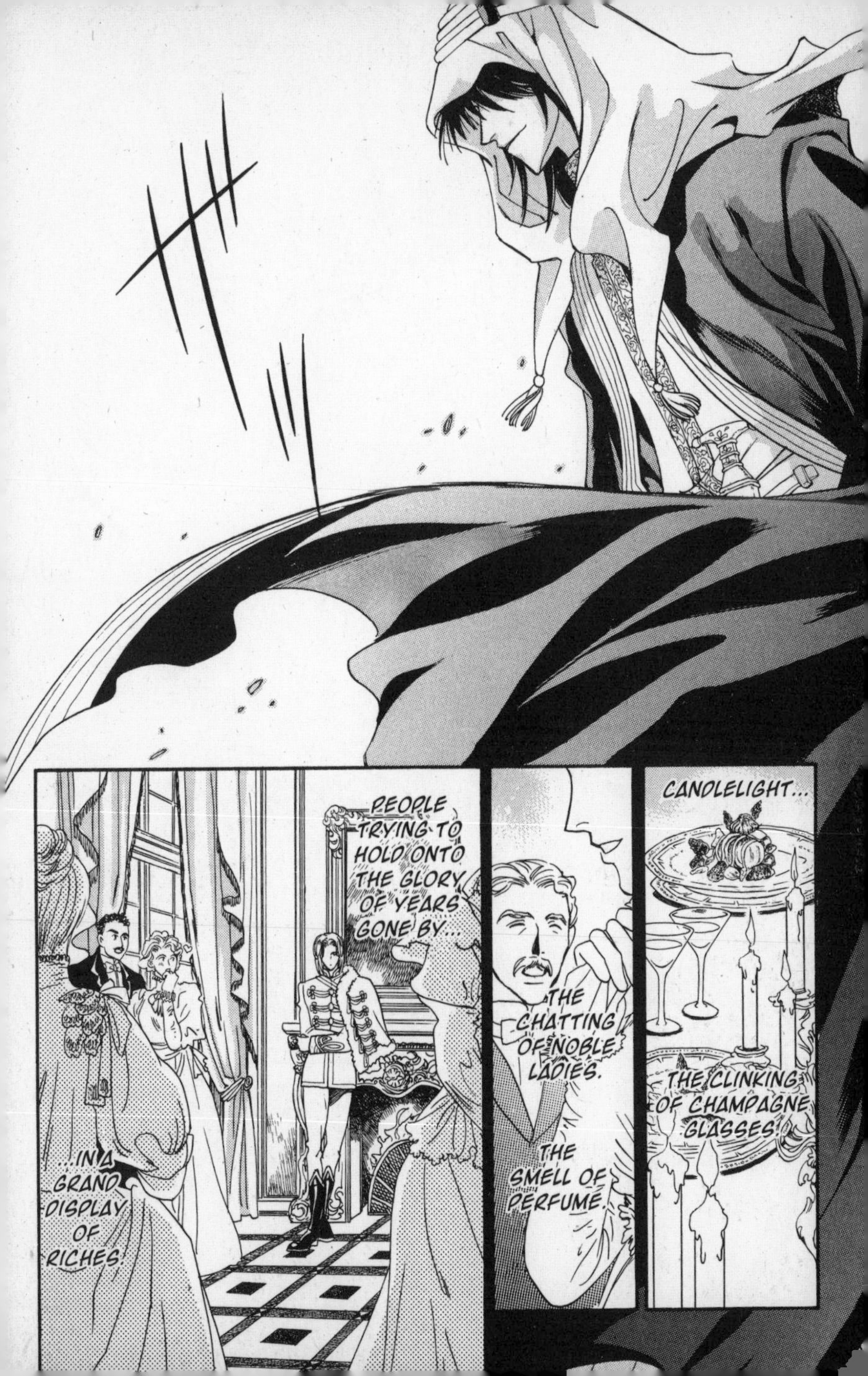
CANDLELIGHT...
THE CLINKING OF CHAMPAGNE GLASSES.
THE CHATTING OF NOBLE LADIES.
THE SMELL OF PERFUME.
PEOPLE TRYING TO HOLD ONTO THE GLORY OF YEARS GONE BY...
...IN A GRAND DISPLAY OF RICHES.

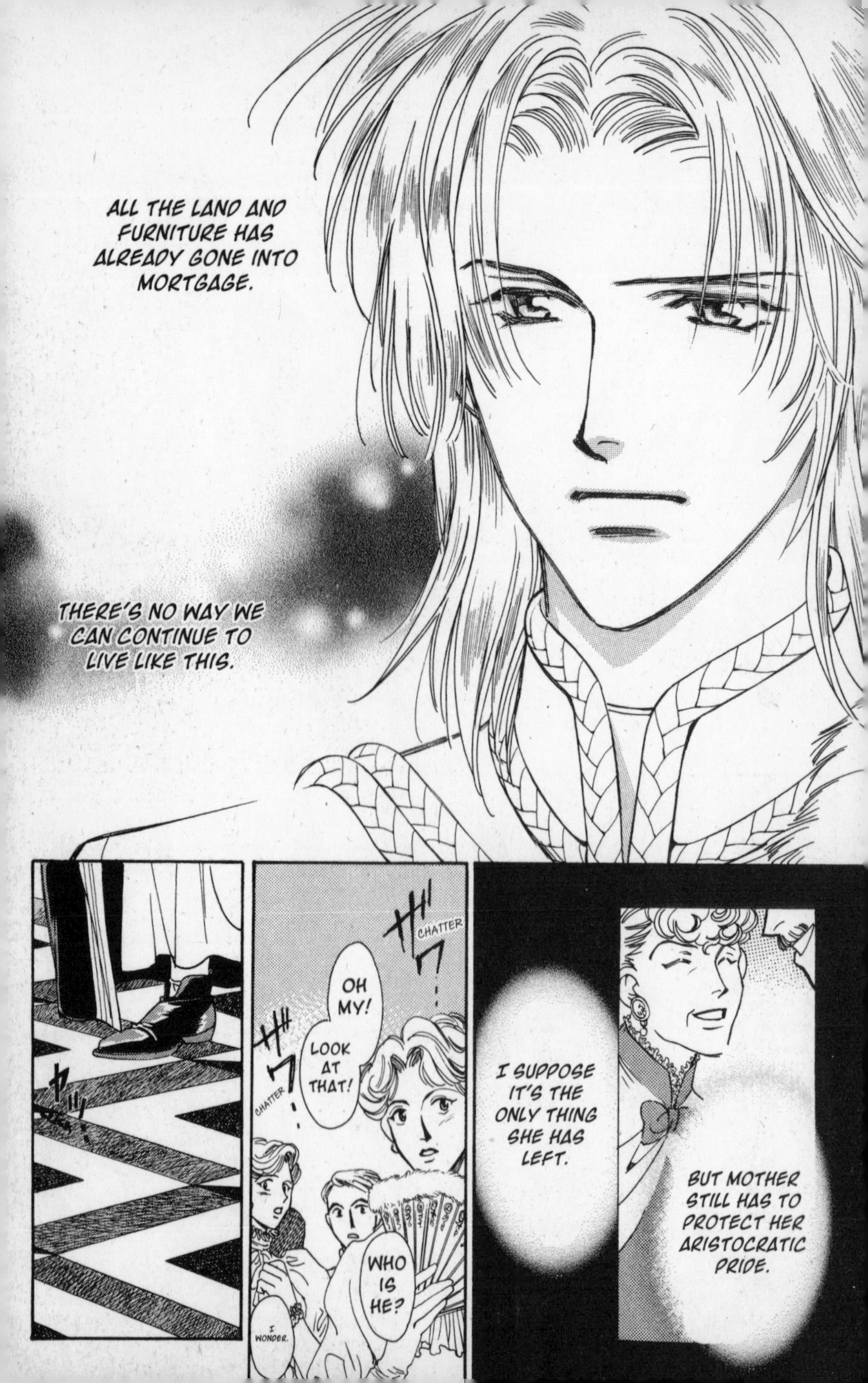
ALL THE LAND AND FURNITURE HAS ALREADY GONE INTO MORTGAGE.
THERE'S NO WAY WE CAN CONTINUE TO LIVE LIKE THIS.
BUT MOTHER STILL HAS TO PROTECT HER ARISTOCRATIC PRIDE.
I SUPPOSE IT'S THE ONLY THING SHE HAS LEFT.
ザワ
CHATTER
OH MY!
LOOK AT THAT!
ザワ
CHATTER
WHO IS HE?
I WONDER.

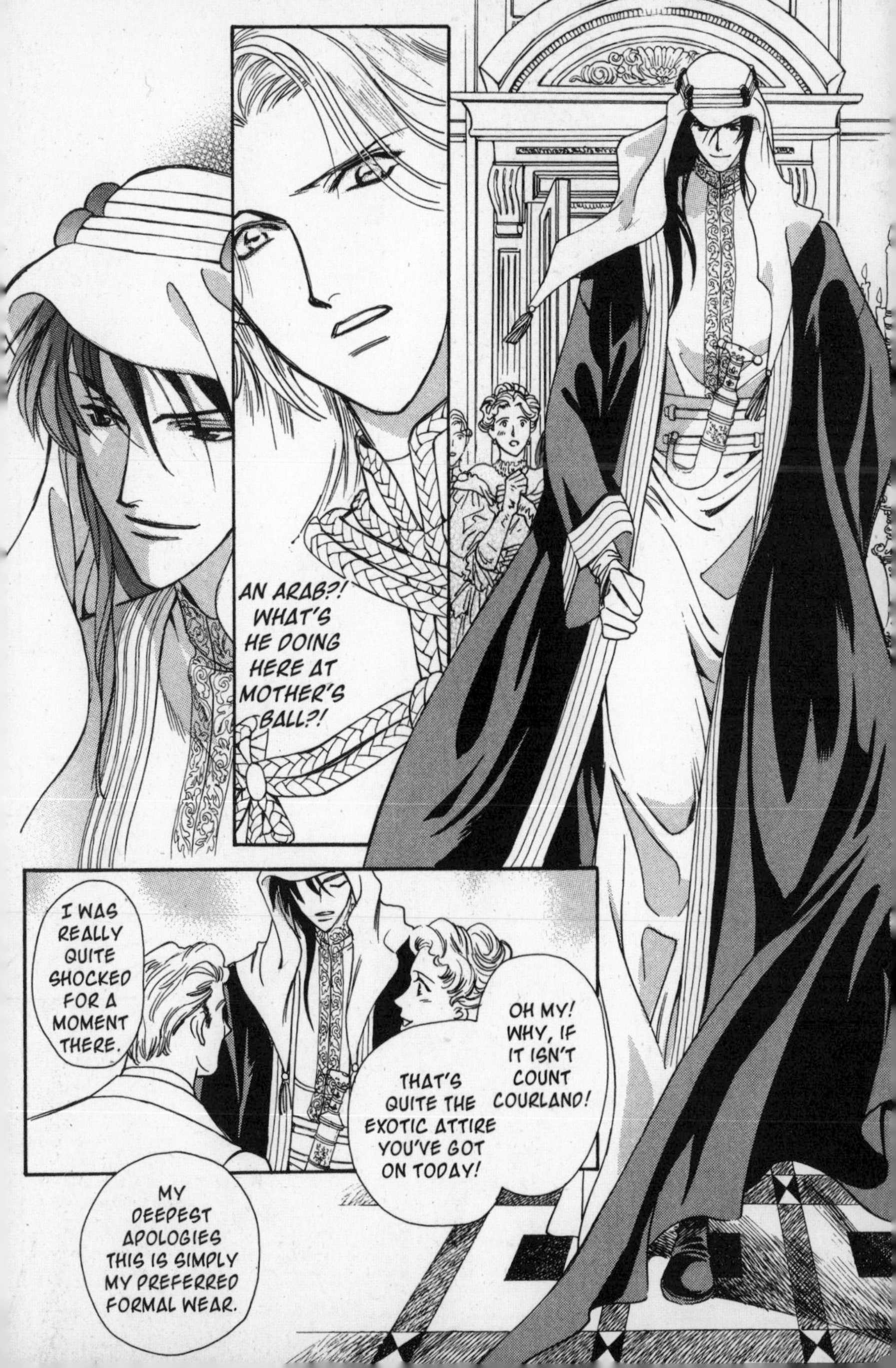
AN ARAB?! WHAT'S HE DOING HERE AT MOTHER'S BALL?!
OH MY! WHY, IF IT ISN'T COUNT COURLAND!
THAT'S QUITE THE EXOTIC ATTIRE YOU'VE GOT ON TODAY!
I WAS REALLY QUITE SHOCKED FOR A MOMENT THERE.
MY DEEPEST APOLOGIES THIS IS SIMPLY MY PREFERRED FORMAL WEAR.

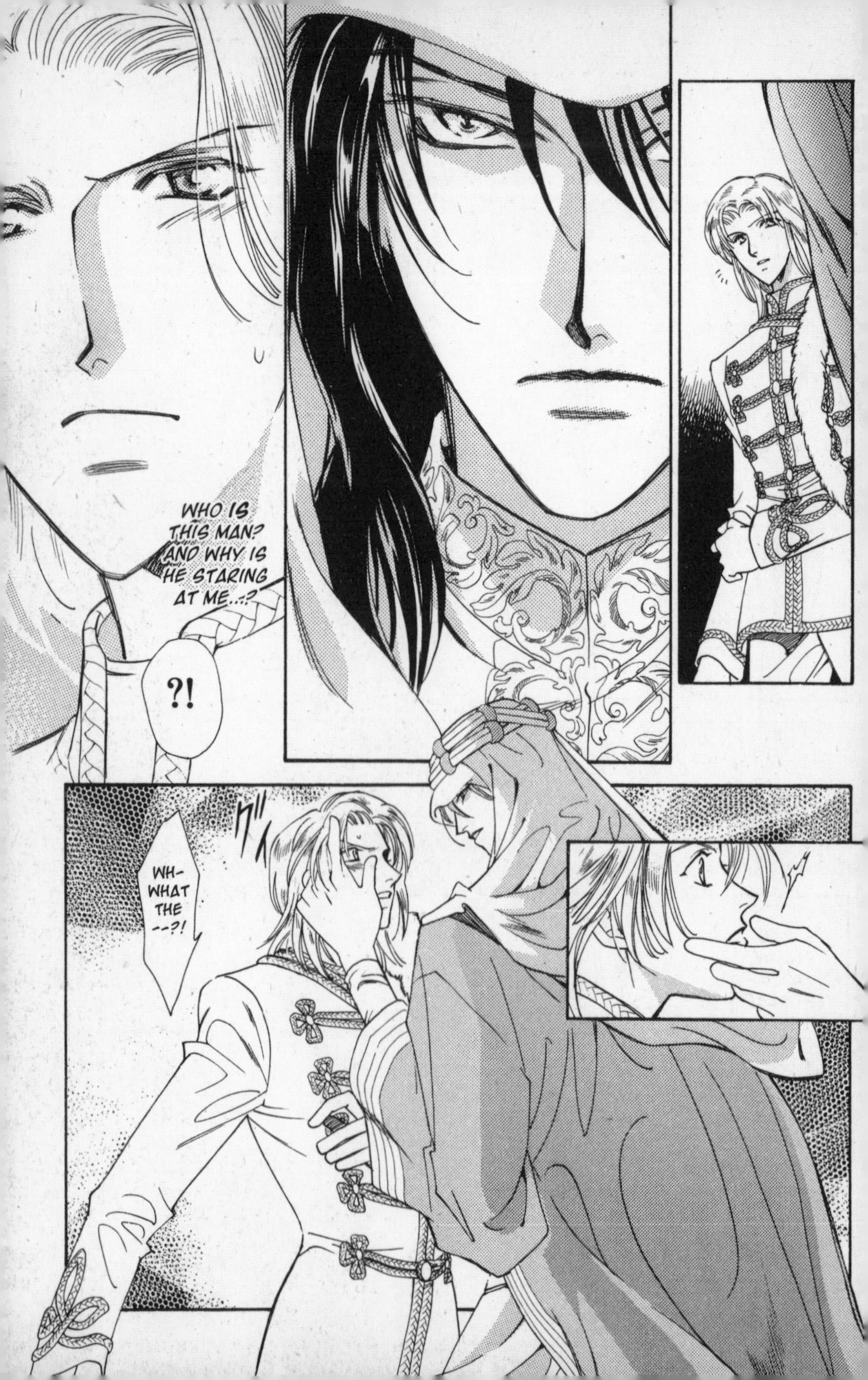
WHO IS THIS MAN? AND WHY IS HE STARING AT ME...?
?!
WH- WHAT THE --?!

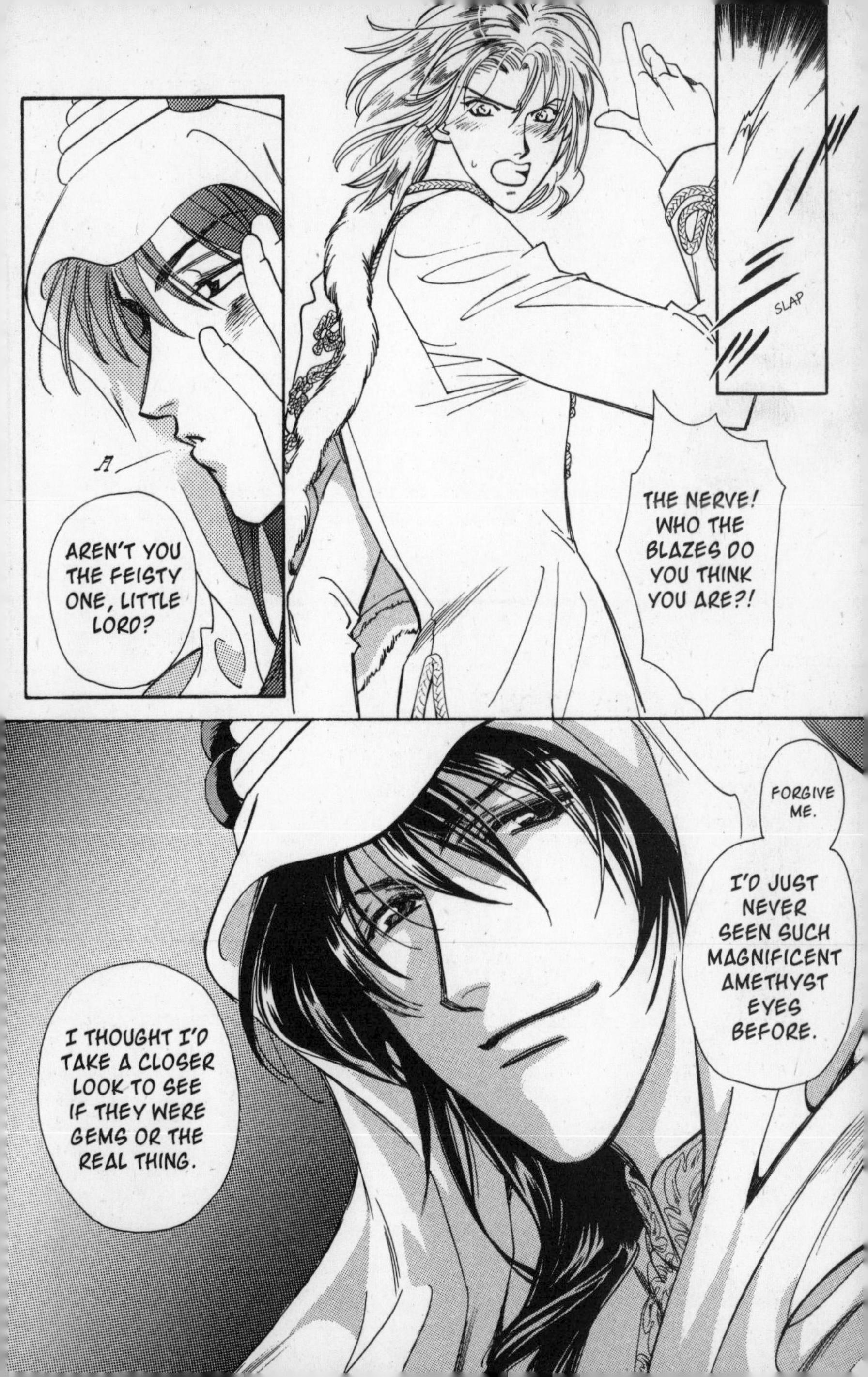
SLAP
THE NERVE! WHO THE BLAZES DO YOU THINK YOU ARE?!
AREN'T YOU THE FEISTY ONE, LITTLE LORD?
FORGIVE ME.
I'D JUST NEVER SEEN SUCH MAGNIFICENT AMETHYST EYES BEFORE.
I THOUGHT I'D TAKE A CLOSER LOOK TO SEE IF THEY WERE GEMS OR THE REAL THING.

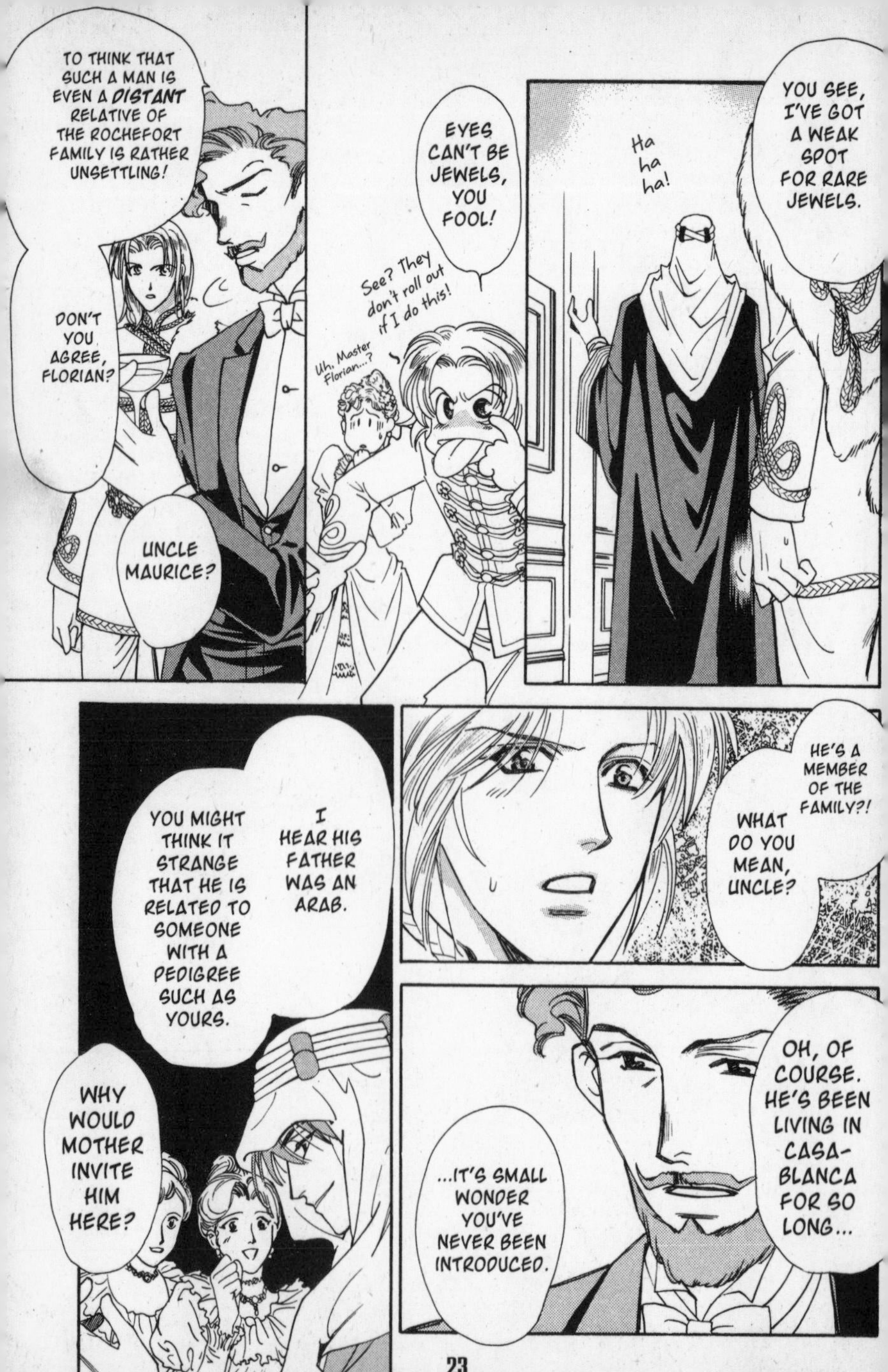
YOU SEE, I'VE GOT A WEAK SPOT FOR RARE JEWELS.
Ha ha ha!
EYES CAN'T BE JEWELS, YOU FOOL!
See? They don't roll out if I do this!
Uh, Master Florian...?
TO THINK THAT SUCH A MAN IS EVEN A *DISTANT* RELATIVE OF THE ROCHEFORT FAMILY IS RATHER UNSETTLING!
DON'T YOU AGREE, FLORIAN?
UNCLE MAURICE?
HE'S A MEMBER OF THE FAMILY?!
WHAT DO YOU MEAN, UNCLE?
OH, OF COURSE. HE'S BEEN LIVING IN CASA-BLANCA FOR SO LONG...
...IT'S SMALL WONDER YOU'VE NEVER BEEN INTRODUCED.
I HEAR HIS FATHER WAS AN ARAB.
YOU MIGHT THINK IT STRANGE THAT HE IS RELATED TO SOMEONE WITH A PEDIGREE SUCH AS YOURS.
WHY WOULD MOTHER INVITE HIM HERE?

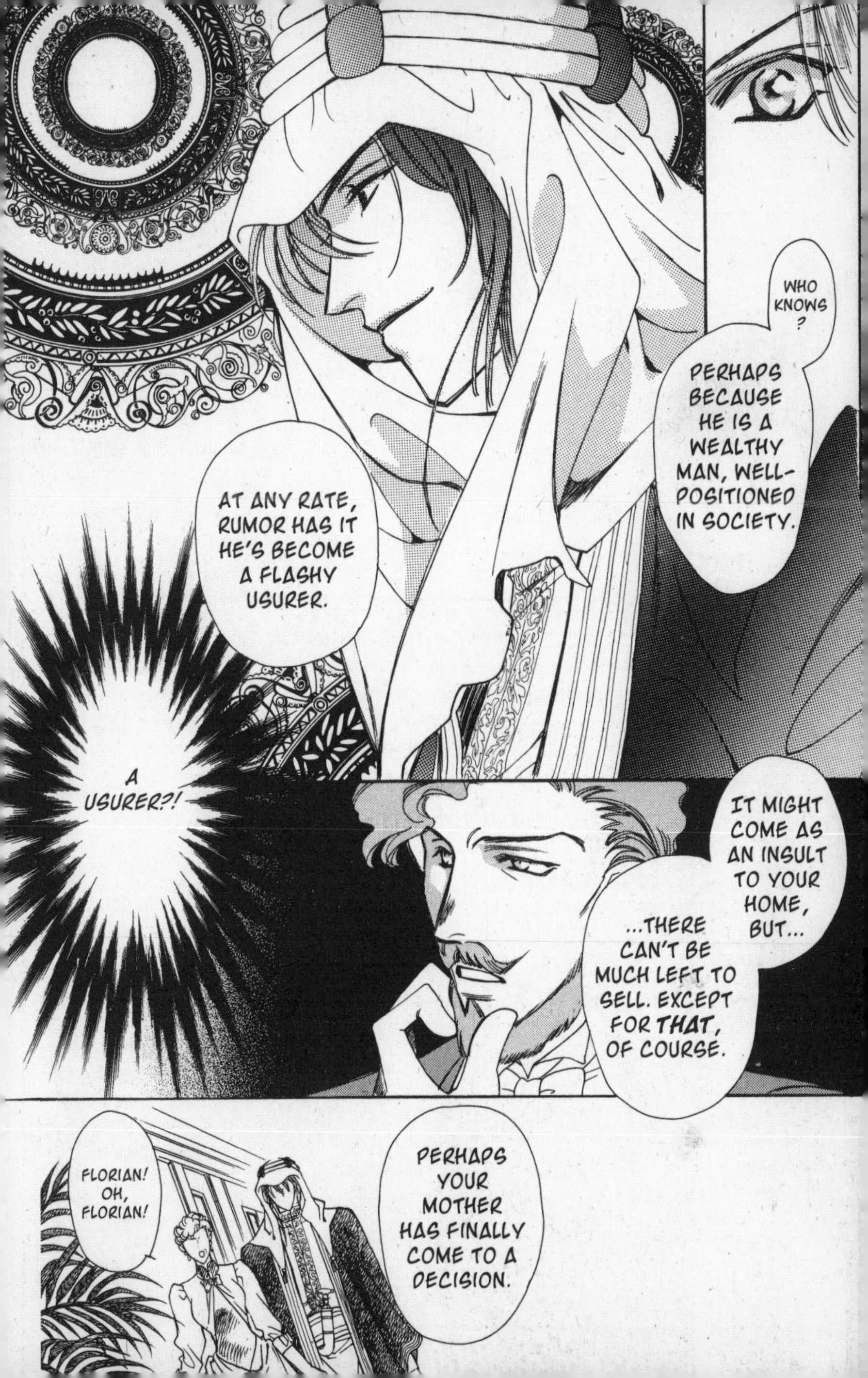
WHO KNOWS?
PERHAPS BECAUSE HE IS A WEALTHY MAN, WELL-POSITIONED IN SOCIETY.
AT ANY RATE, RUMOR HAS IT HE'S BECOME A FLASHY USURER.
A USURER?!
IT MIGHT COME AS AN INSULT TO YOUR HOME, BUT...
...THERE CAN'T BE MUCH LEFT TO SELL. EXCEPT FOR **THAT**, OF COURSE.
PERHAPS YOUR MOTHER HAS FINALLY COME TO A DECISION.
FLORIAN! OH, FLORIAN!

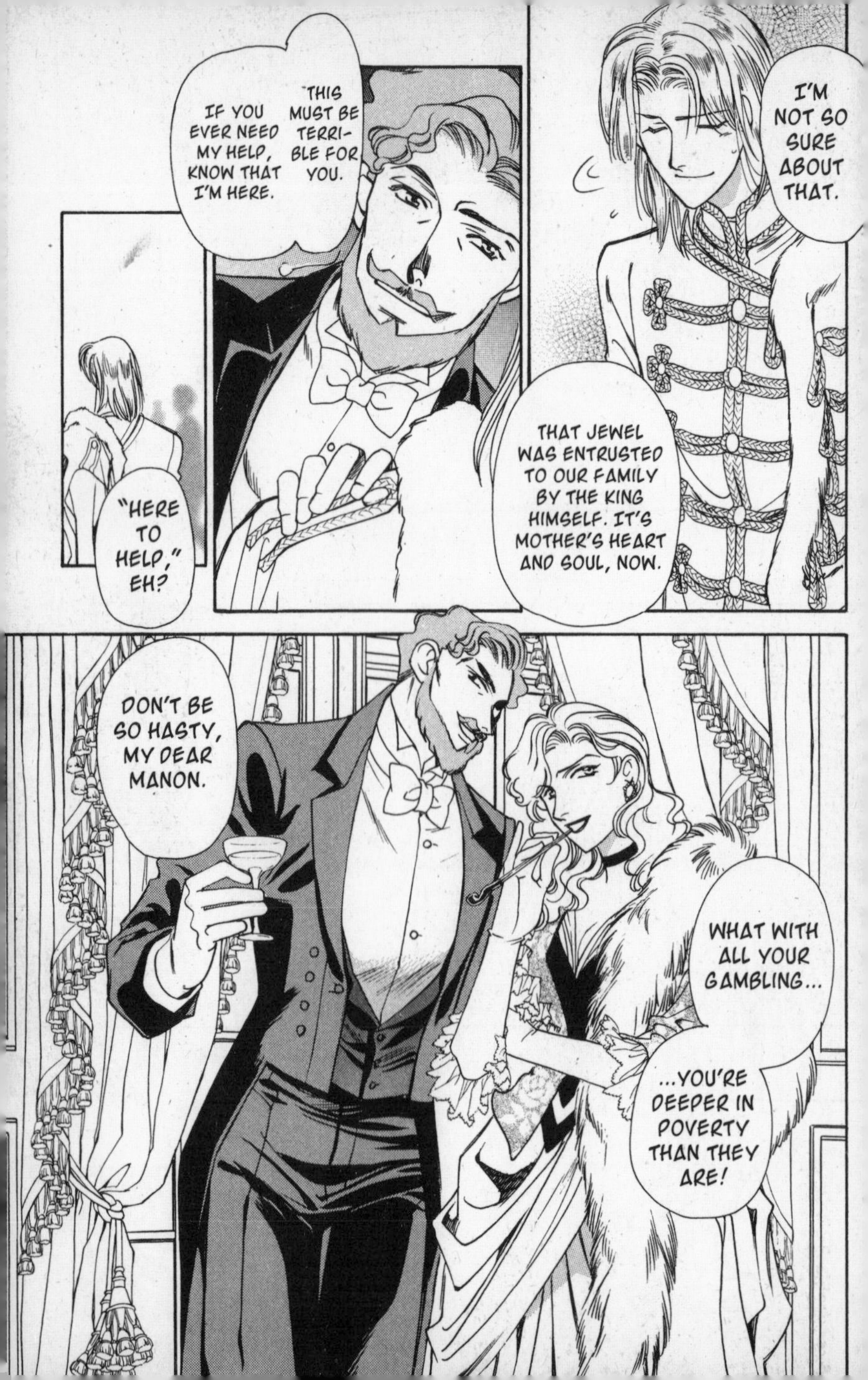
I'M NOT SO SURE ABOUT THAT.
THAT JEWEL WAS ENTRUSTED TO OUR FAMILY BY THE KING HIMSELF. IT'S MOTHER'S HEART AND SOUL, NOW.
THIS MUST BE TERRI-BLE FOR YOU.
IF YOU EVER NEED MY HELP, KNOW THAT I'M HERE.
"HERE TO HELP," EH?
WHAT WITH ALL YOUR GAMBLING...
...YOU'RE DEEPER IN POVERTY THAN THEY ARE!
DON'T BE SO HASTY, MY DEAR MANON.

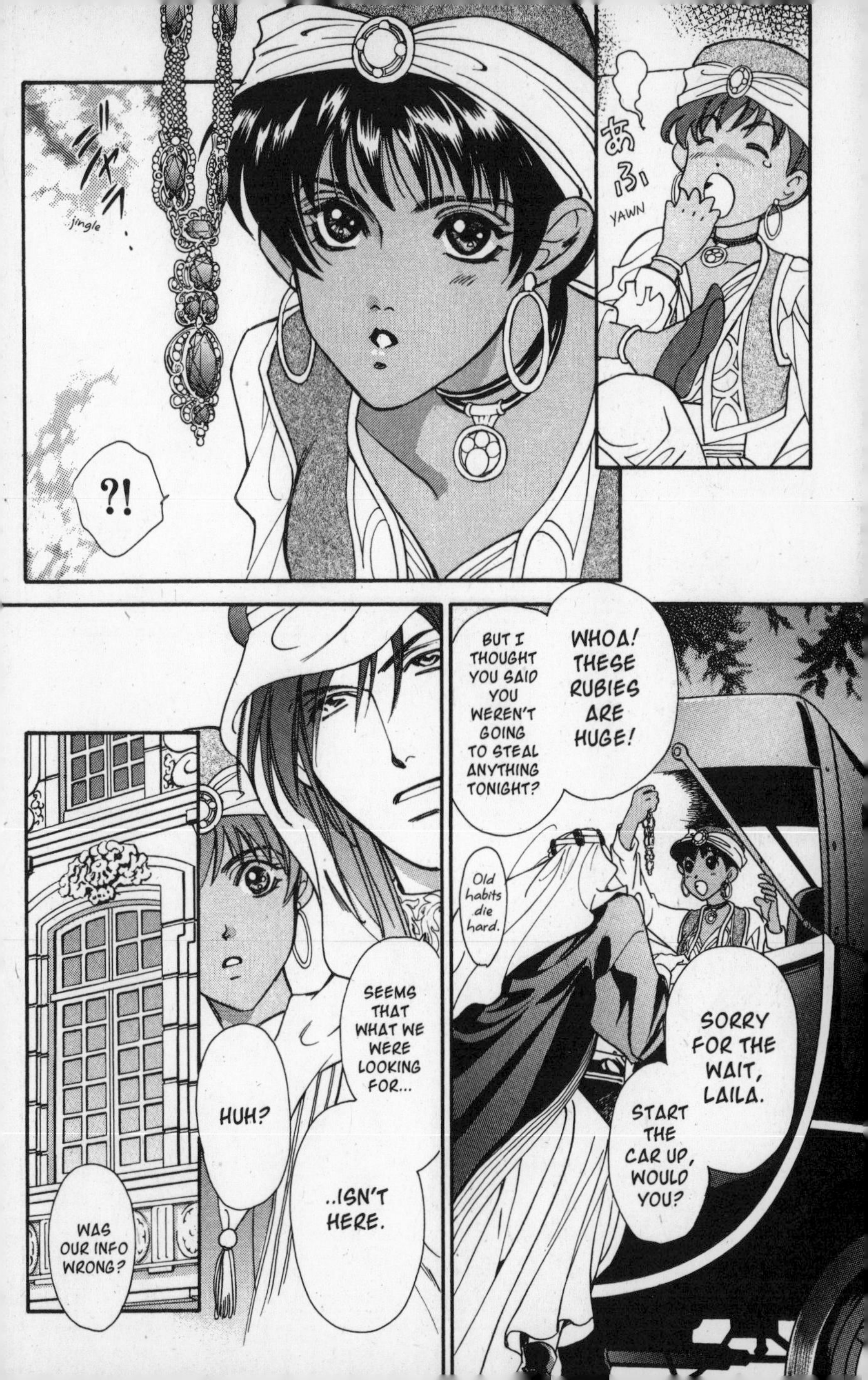
あふ
YAWN
jingle
?!
WHOA! THESE RUBIES ARE HUGE!
BUT I THOUGHT YOU SAID YOU WEREN'T GOING TO STEAL ANYTHING TONIGHT?
Old habits die hard.
SORRY FOR THE WAIT, LAILA.
START THE CAR UP, WOULD YOU?
SEEMS THAT WHAT WE WERE LOOKING FOR...
HUH?
..ISN'T HERE.
WAS OUR INFO WRONG?

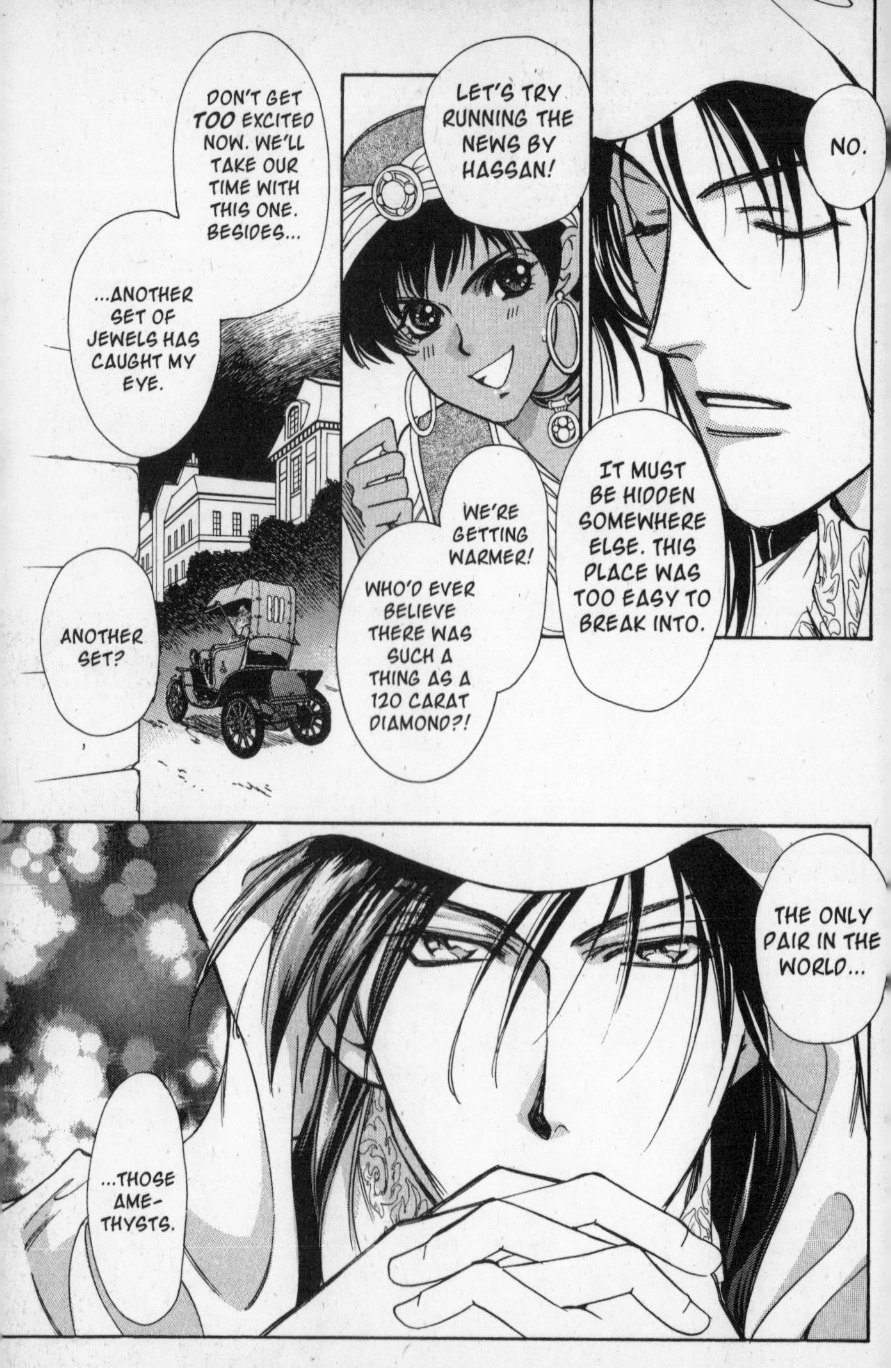
NO.
IT MUST BE HIDDEN SOMEWHERE ELSE. THIS PLACE WAS TOO EASY TO BREAK INTO.
LET'S TRY RUNNING THE NEWS BY HASSAN!
WE'RE GETTING WARMER!
WHO'D EVER BELIEVE THERE WAS SUCH A THING AS A 120 CARAT DIAMOND?!
DON'T GET *TOO* EXCITED NOW. WE'LL TAKE OUR TIME WITH THIS ONE. BESIDES...
...ANOTHER SET OF JEWELS HAS CAUGHT MY EYE.
ANOTHER SET?
THE ONLY PAIR IN THE WORLD...
...THOSE AME-THYSTS.

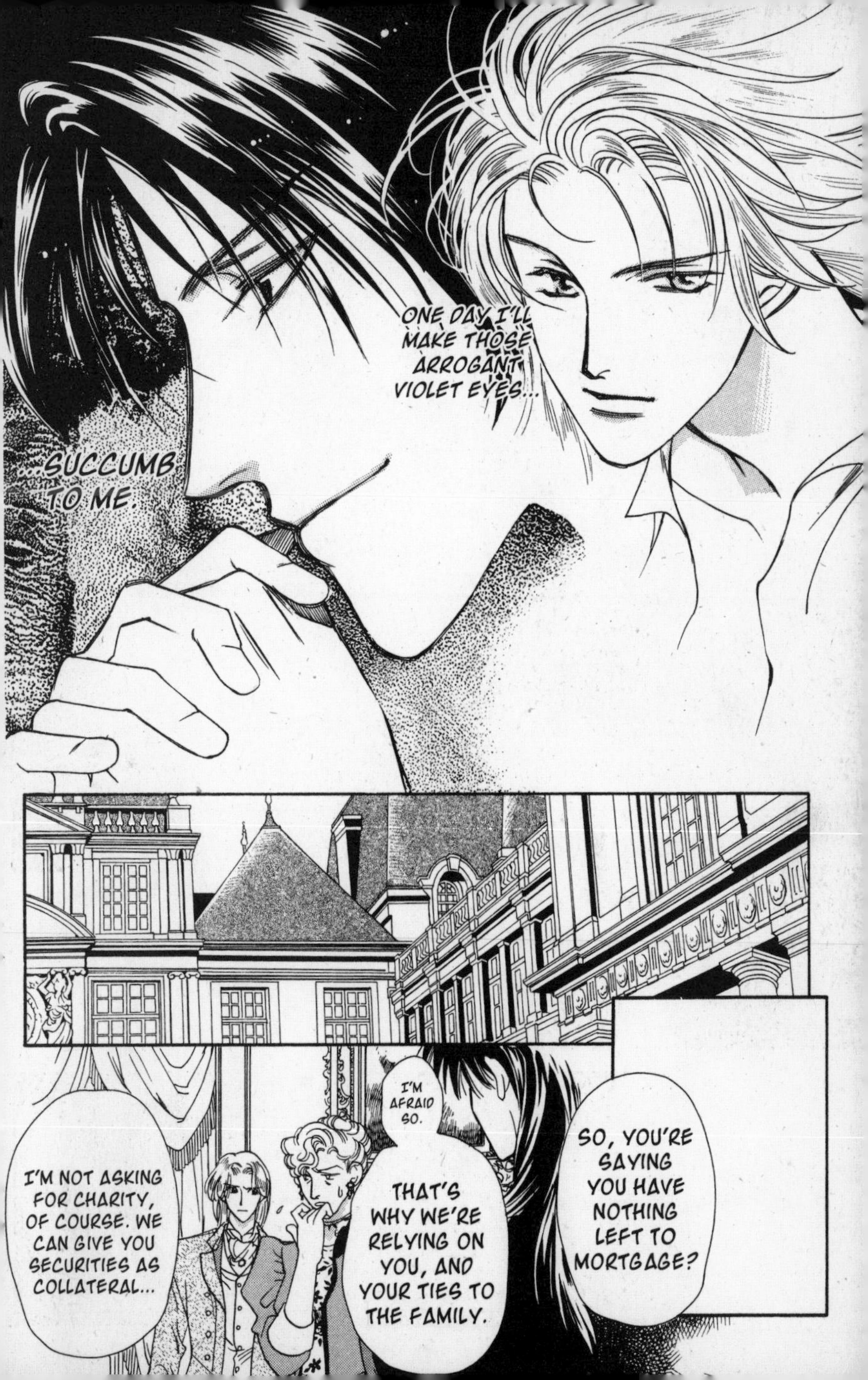
ONE DAY I'LL MAKE THOSE ARROGANT VIOLET EYES...
...SUCCUMB TO ME.
SO, YOU'RE SAYING YOU HAVE NOTHING LEFT TO MORTGAGE?
I'M AFRAID SO.
THAT'S WHY WE'RE RELYING ON YOU, AND YOUR TIES TO THE FAMILY.
I'M NOT ASKING FOR CHARITY, OF COURSE. WE CAN GIVE YOU SECURITIES AS COLLATERAL...

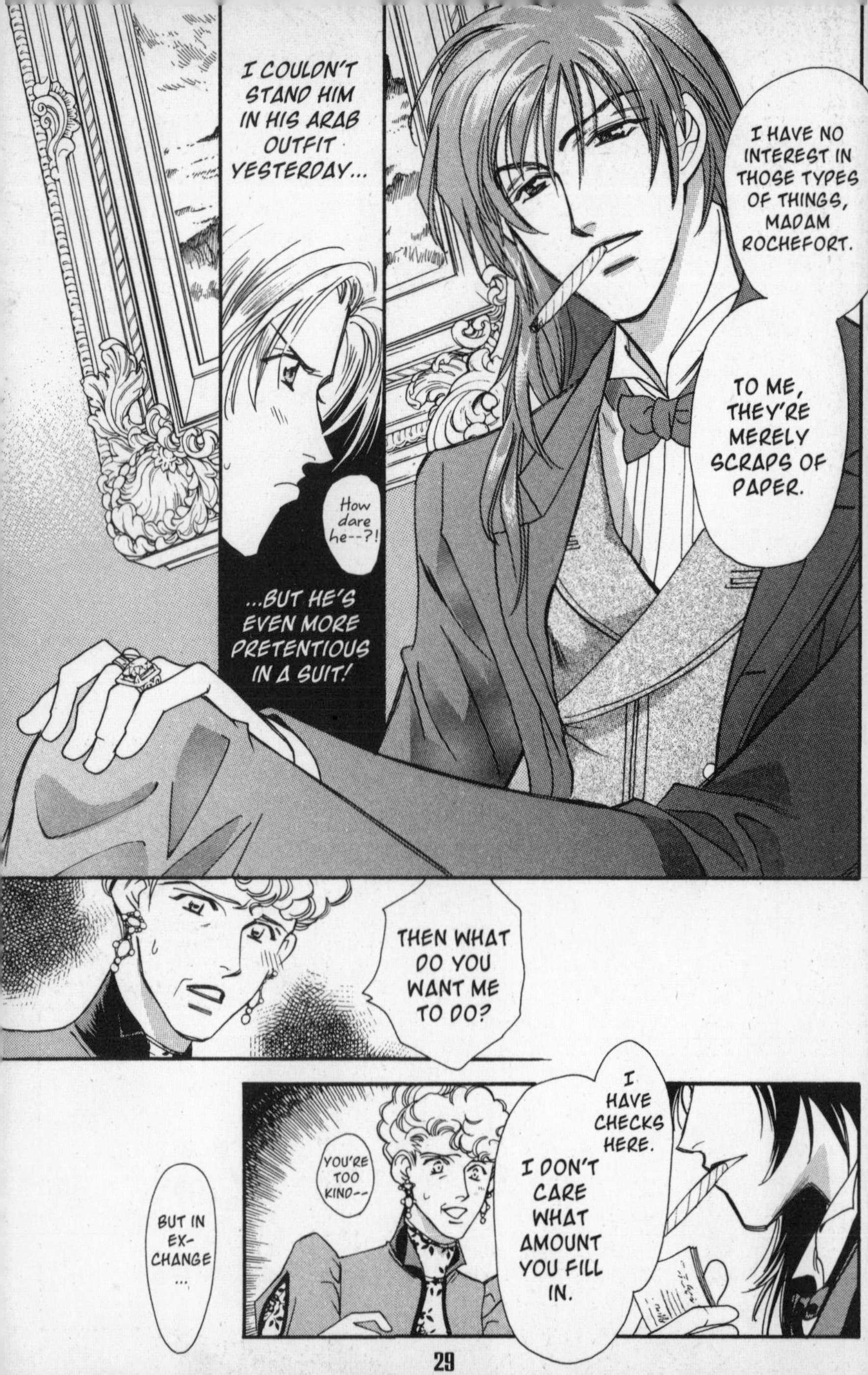
I HAVE NO INTEREST IN THOSE TYPES OF THINGS, MADAM ROCHEFORT.
TO ME, THEY'RE MERELY SCRAPS OF PAPER.
I COULDN'T STAND HIM IN HIS ARAB OUTFIT YESTERDAY...
How dare he--?!
...BUT HE'S EVEN MORE PRETENTIOUS IN A SUIT!
THEN WHAT DO YOU WANT ME TO DO?
I HAVE CHECKS HERE.
I DON'T CARE WHAT AMOUNT YOU FILL IN.
YOU'RE TOO KIND--
BUT IN EX-CHANGE...

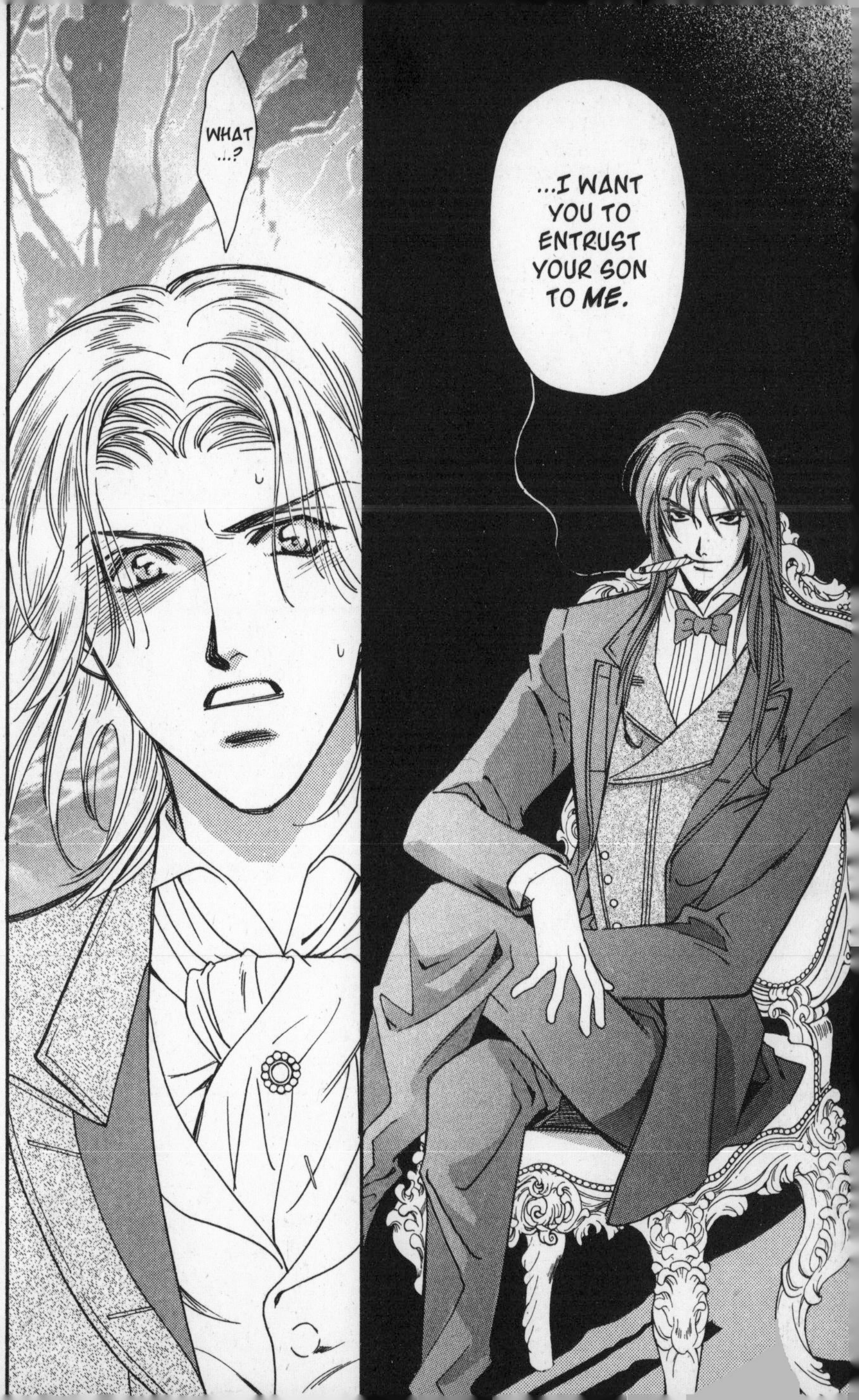
...I WANT YOU TO ENTRUST YOUR SON TO ME.
WHAT ...?

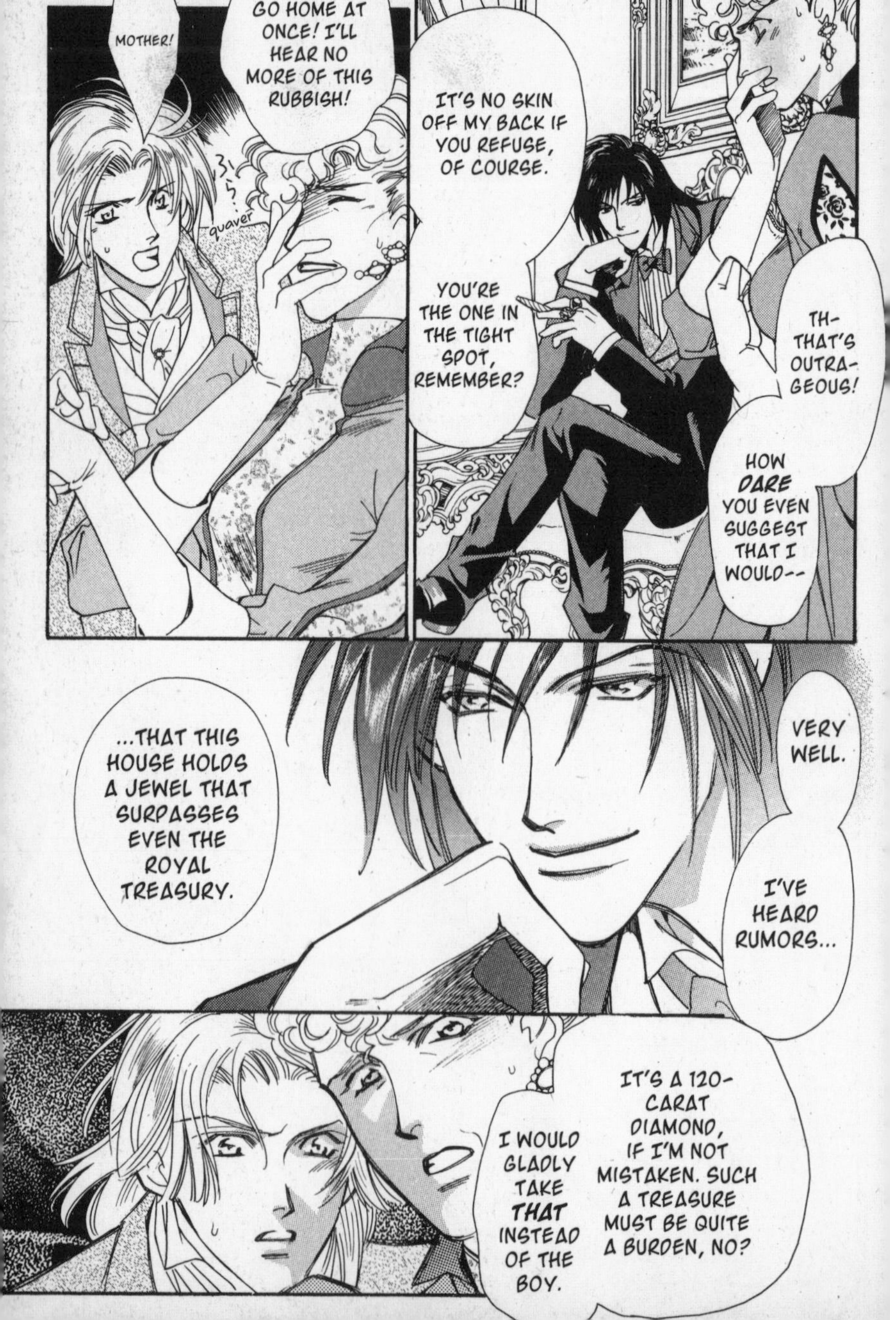
IT'S NO SKIN OFF MY BACK IF YOU REFUSE, OF COURSE.
YOU'RE THE ONE IN THE TIGHT SPOT, REMEMBER?
TH-THAT'S OUTRAGEOUS!
HOW DARE YOU EVEN SUGGEST THAT I WOULD--
GO HOME AT ONCE! I'LL HEAR NO MORE OF THIS RUBBISH!
MOTHER!
ふら…
quaver
VERY WELL.
I'VE HEARD RUMORS...
...THAT THIS HOUSE HOLDS A JEWEL THAT SURPASSES EVEN THE ROYAL TREASURY.
IT'S A 120-CARAT DIAMOND, IF I'M NOT MISTAKEN. SUCH A TREASURE MUST BE QUITE A BURDEN, NO?
I WOULD GLADLY TAKE THAT INSTEAD OF THE BOY.

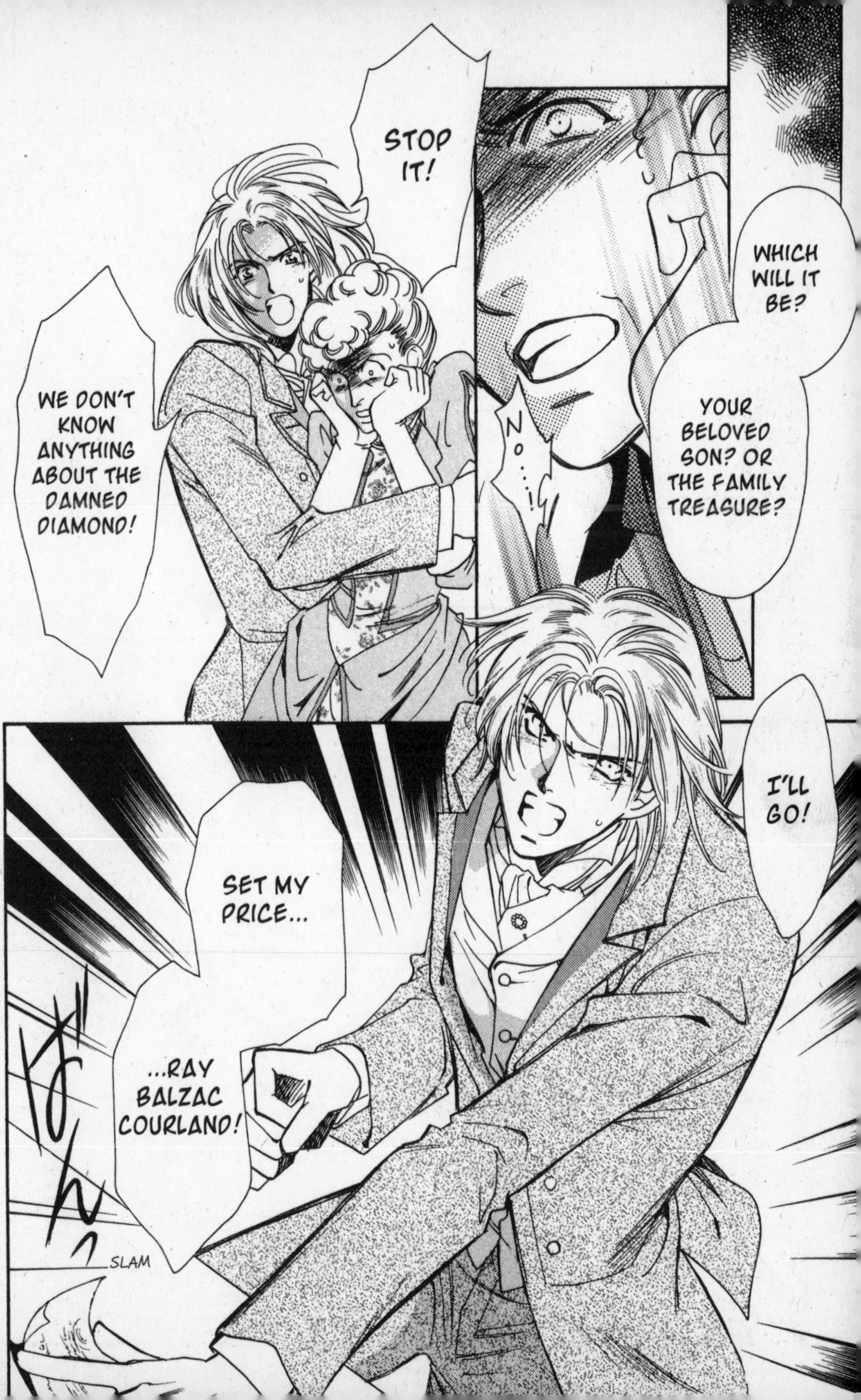
WHICH WILL IT BE?
YOUR BELOVED SON? OR THE FAMILY TREASURE?
No...!
STOP IT!
WE DON'T KNOW ANYTHING ABOUT THE DAMNED DIAMOND!
I'LL GO!
SET MY PRICE...
...RAY BALZAC COURLAND!
SLAM

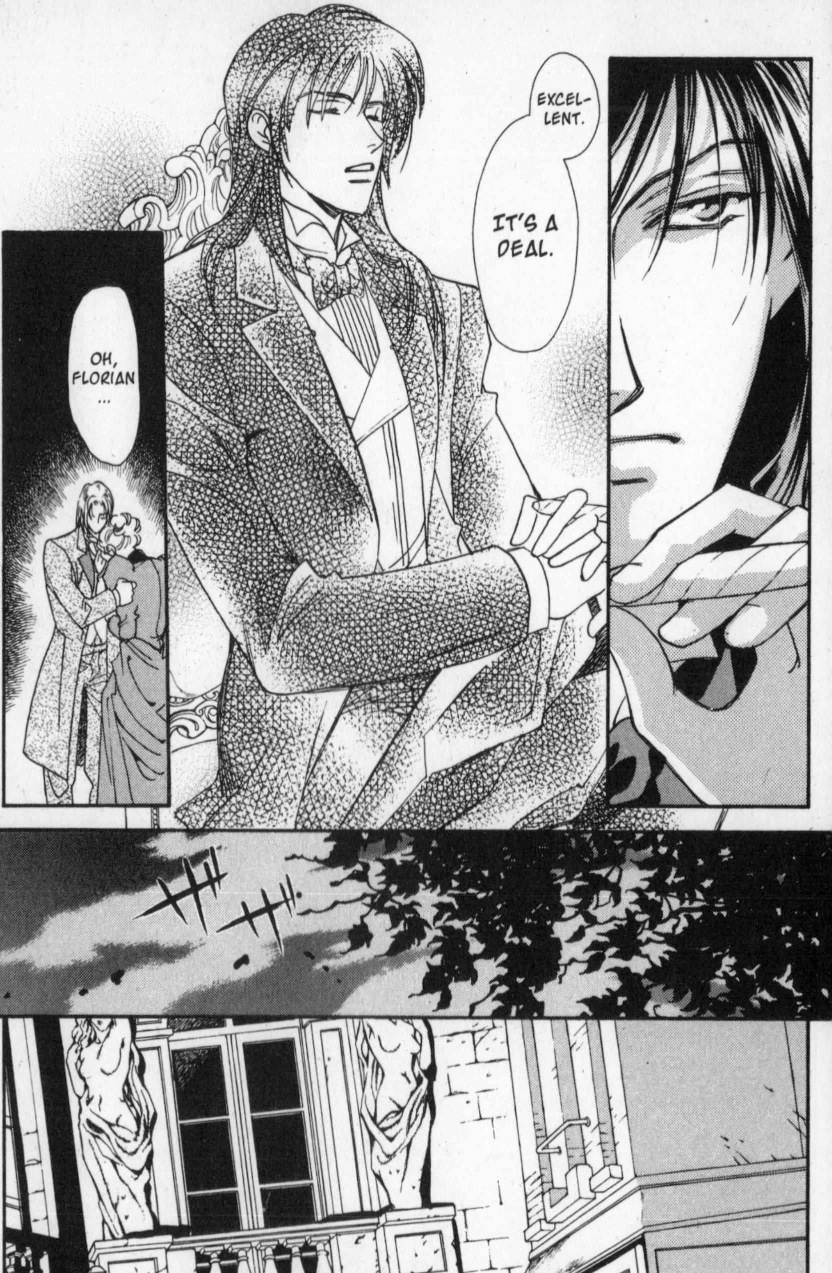
EXCEL-LENT.
IT'S A DEAL.
OH, FLORIAN ...

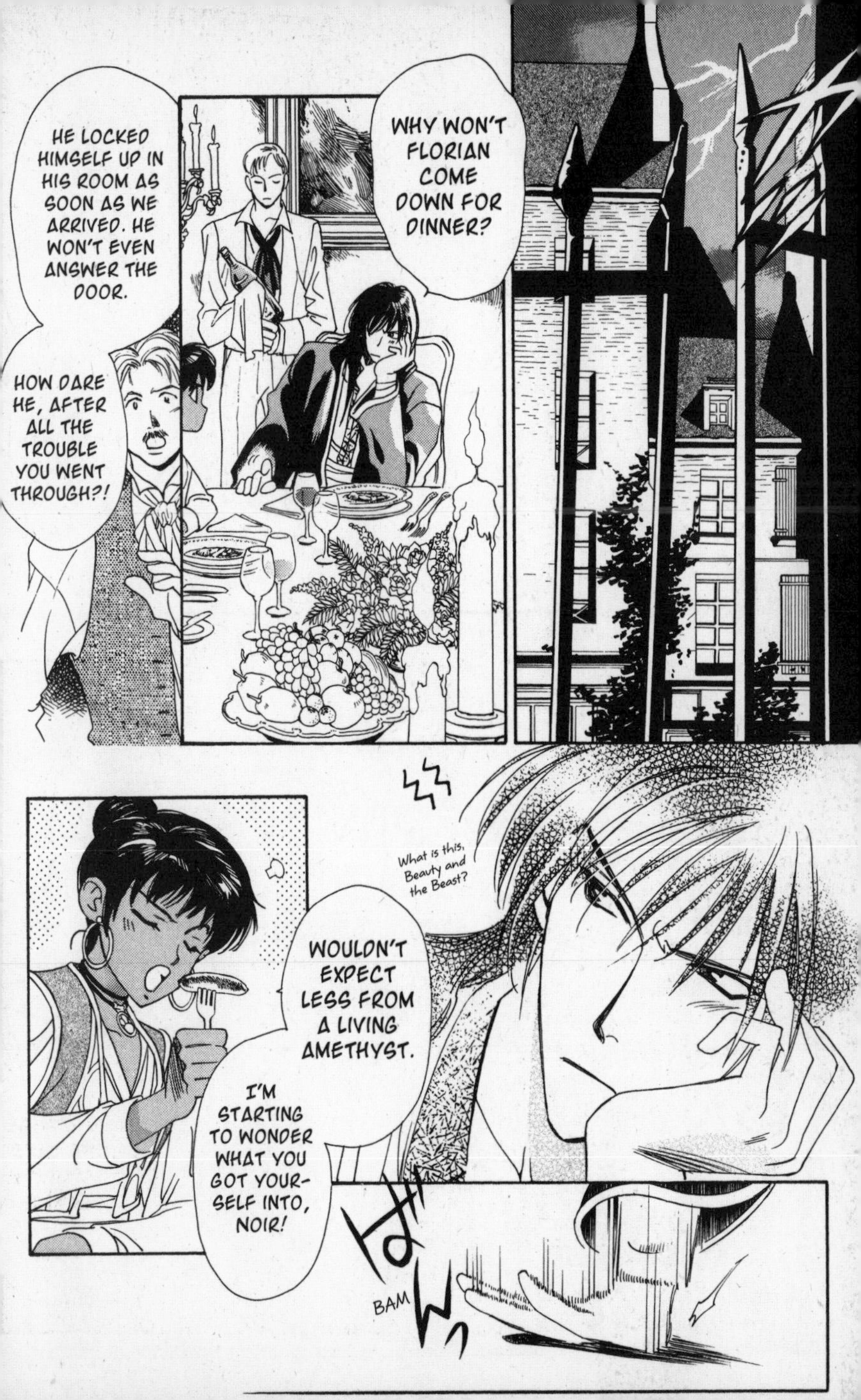
WHY WON'T FLORIAN COME DOWN FOR DINNER?
HE LOCKED HIMSELF UP IN HIS ROOM AS SOON AS WE ARRIVED. HE WON'T EVEN ANSWER THE DOOR.
HOW DARE HE, AFTER ALL THE TROUBLE YOU WENT THROUGH?!
What is this, Beauty and the Beast?
WOULDN'T EXPECT LESS FROM A LIVING AMETHYST.
I'M STARTING TO WONDER WHAT YOU GOT YOURSELF INTO, NOIR!
BAM

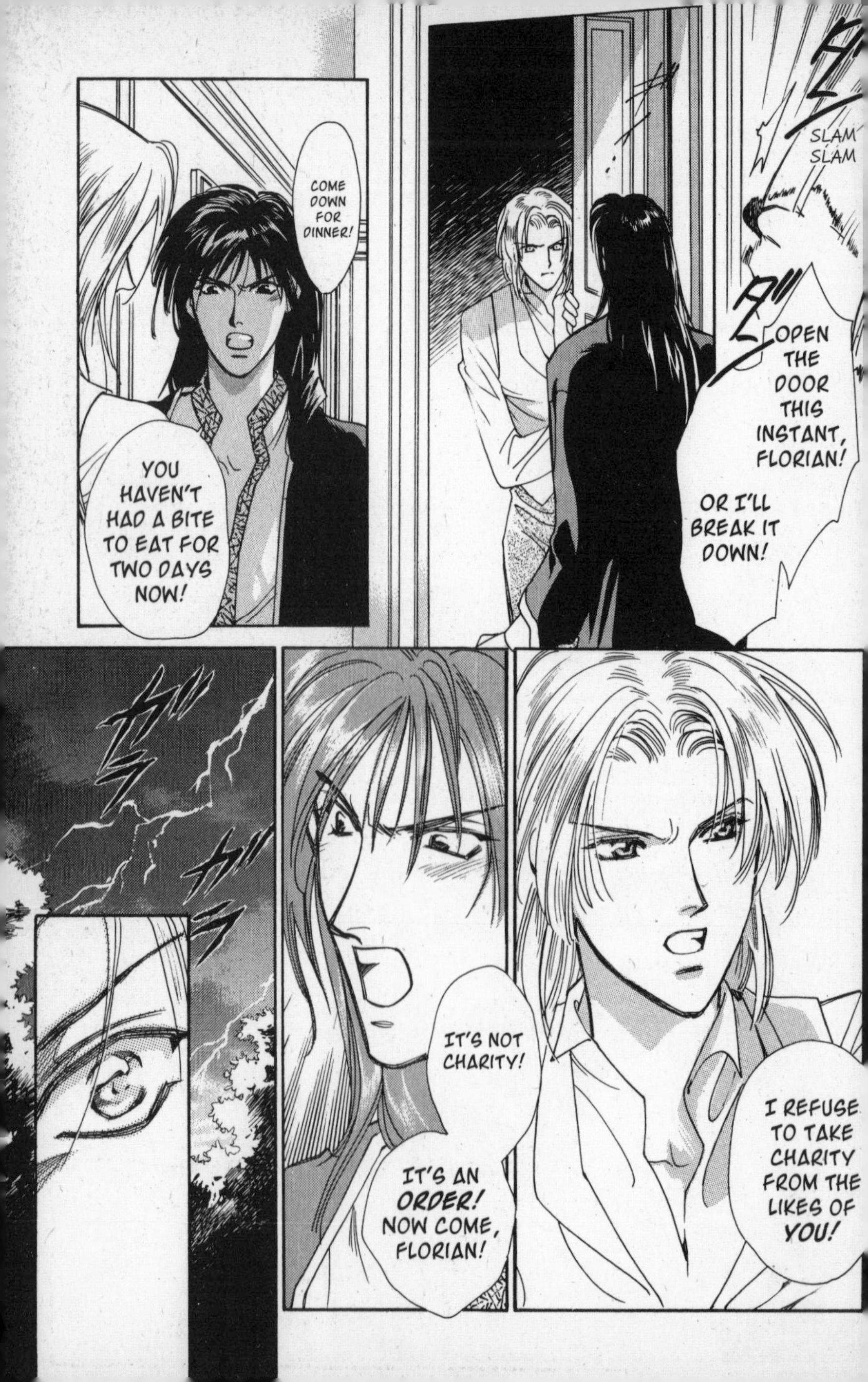
SLAM SLAM
OPEN THE DOOR THIS INSTANT, FLORIAN!
OR I'LL BREAK IT DOWN!
COME DOWN FOR DINNER!
YOU HAVEN'T HAD A BITE TO EAT FOR TWO DAYS NOW!
I REFUSE TO TAKE CHARITY FROM THE LIKES OF *YOU!*
IT'S NOT CHARITY!
IT'S AN *ORDER!* NOW COME, FLORIAN!

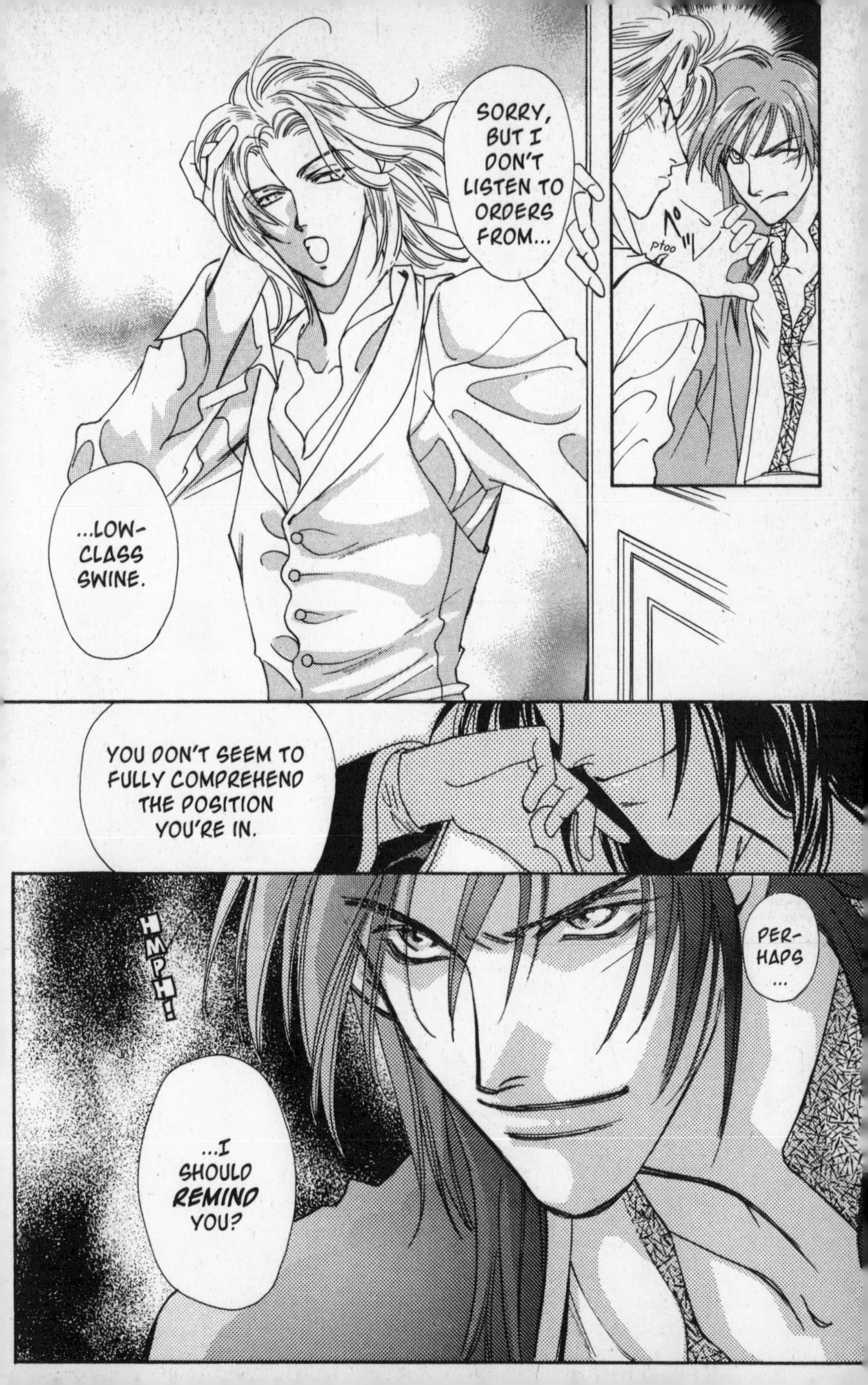
ptoo
SORRY, BUT I DON'T LISTEN TO ORDERS FROM...
...LOW-CLASS SWINE.
YOU DON'T SEEM TO FULLY COMPREHEND THE POSITION YOU'RE IN.
PER-HAPS...
HMPH!
...I SHOULD REMIND YOU?

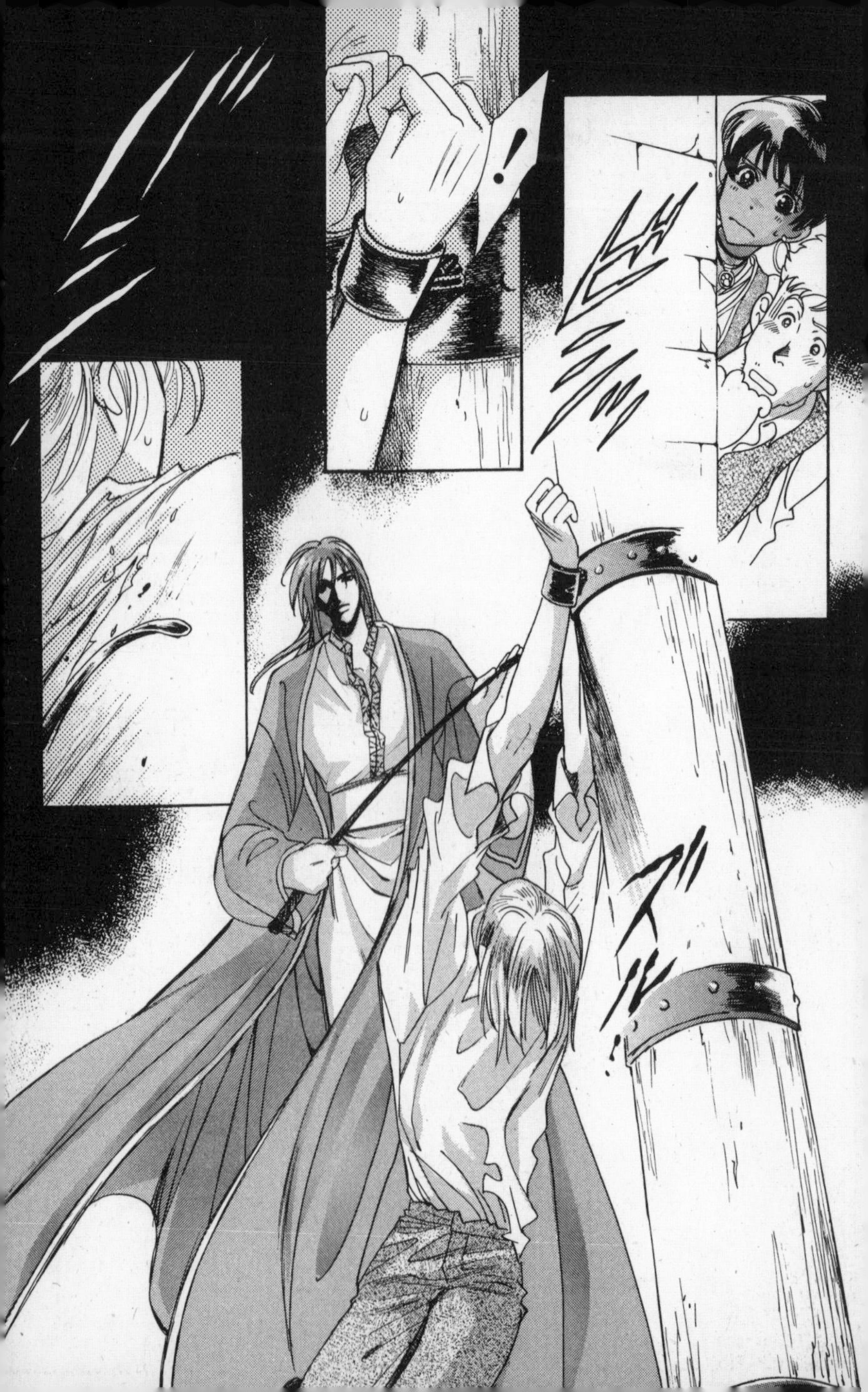
!

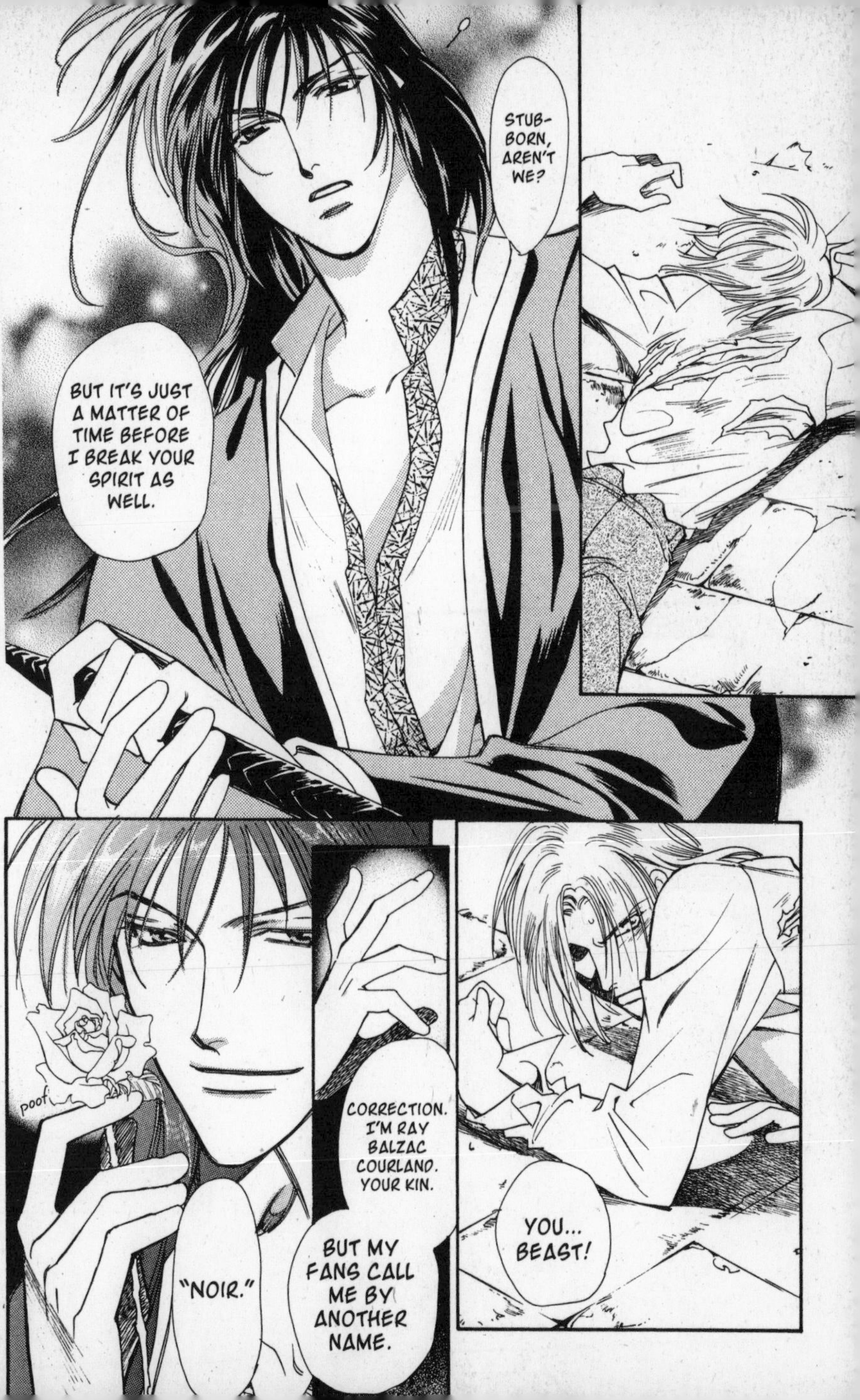
STUB-BORN, AREN'T WE?
BUT IT'S JUST A MATTER OF TIME BEFORE I BREAK YOUR SPIRIT AS WELL.
YOU... BEAST!
CORRECTION. I'M RAY BALZAC COURLAND. YOUR KIN.
BUT MY FANS CALL ME BY ANOTHER NAME.
poof
"NOIR."

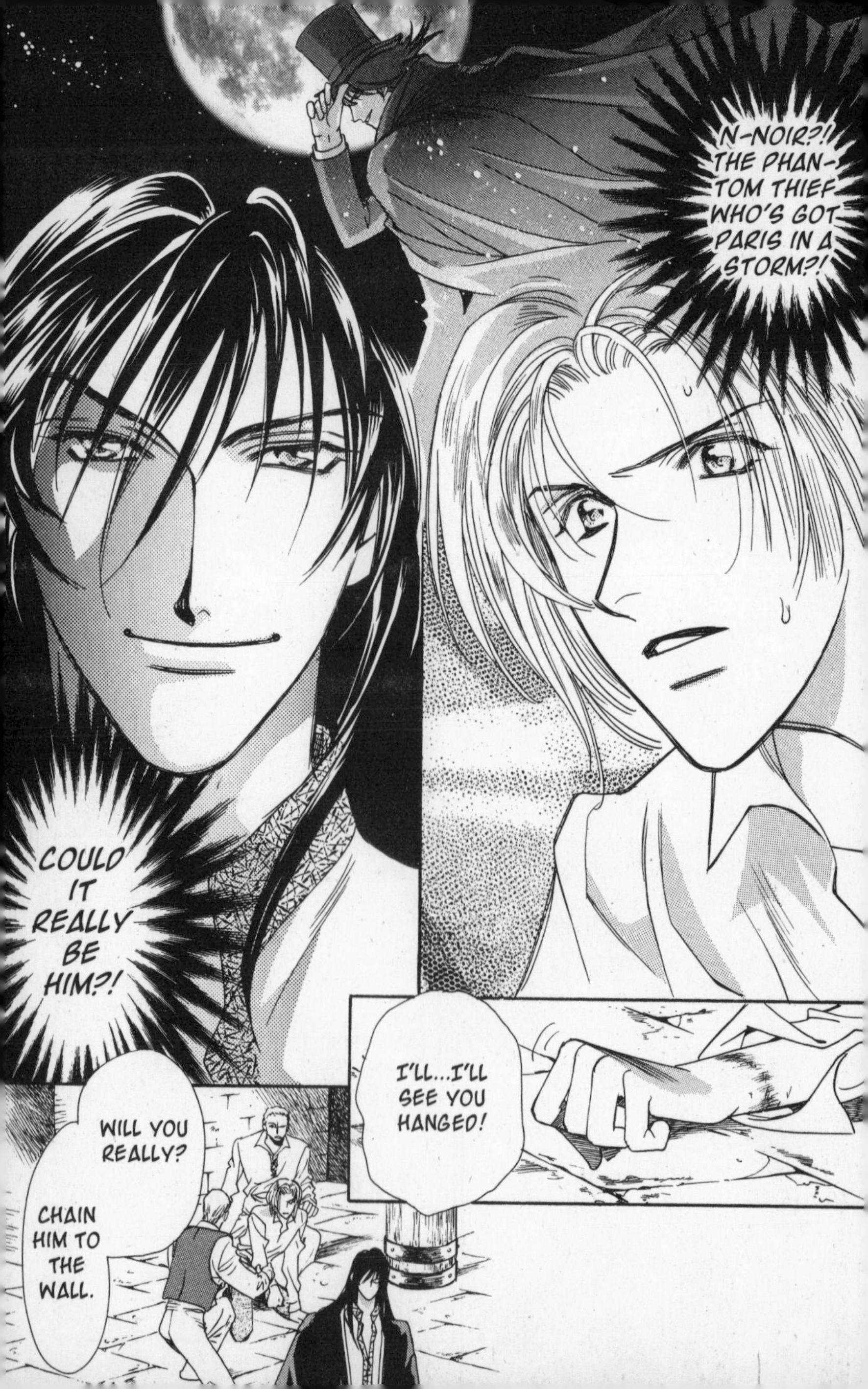
N-NOIR?! THE PHANTOM THIEF WHO'S GOT PARIS IN A STORM?!
COULD IT REALLY BE HIM?!
I'LL...I'LL SEE YOU HANGED!
WILL YOU REALLY?
CHAIN HIM TO THE WALL.

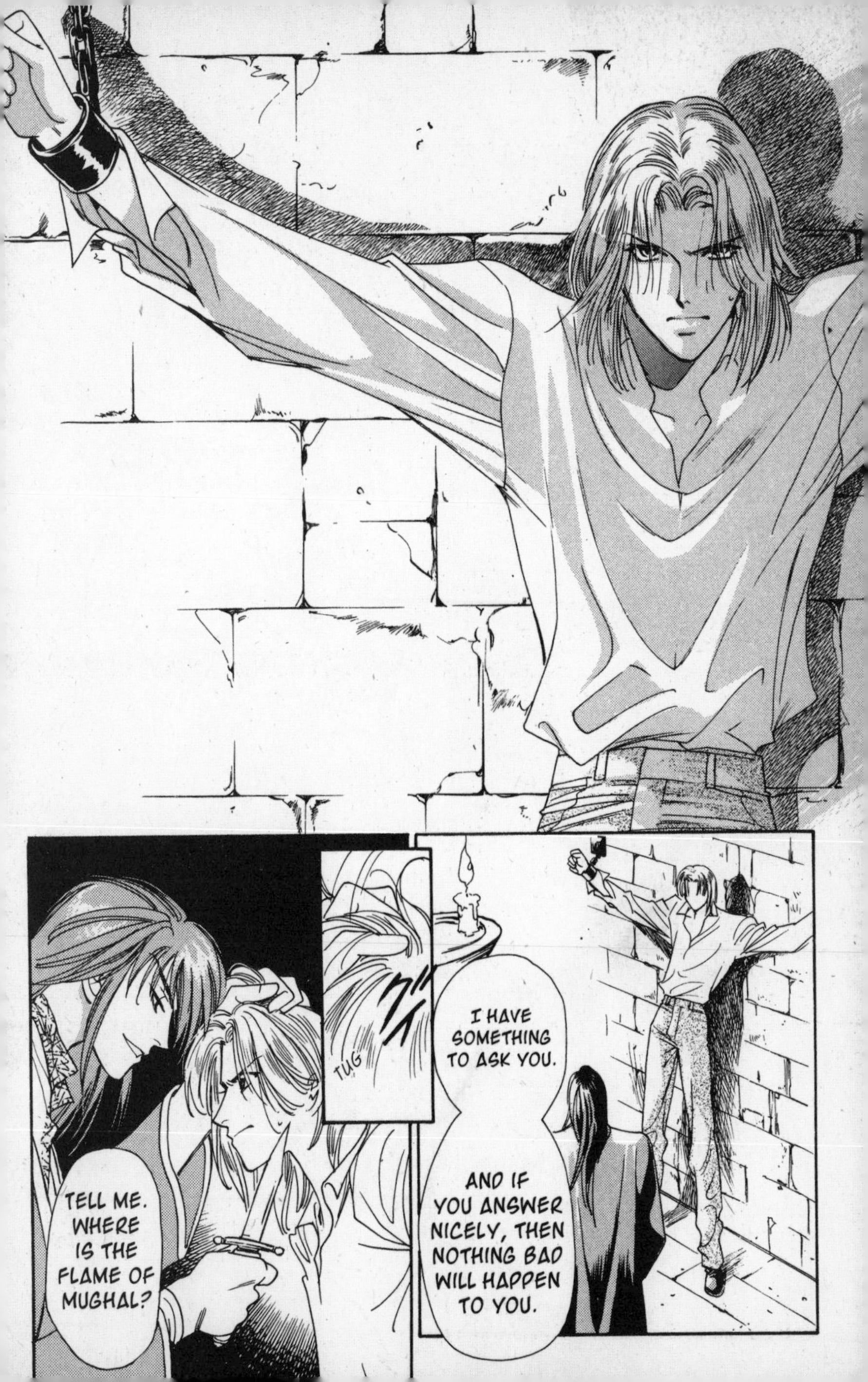
I HAVE SOMETHING TO ASK YOU.
AND IF YOU ANSWER NICELY, THEN NOTHING BAD WILL HAPPEN TO YOU.
TUG
TELL ME. WHERE IS THE FLAME OF MUGHAL?

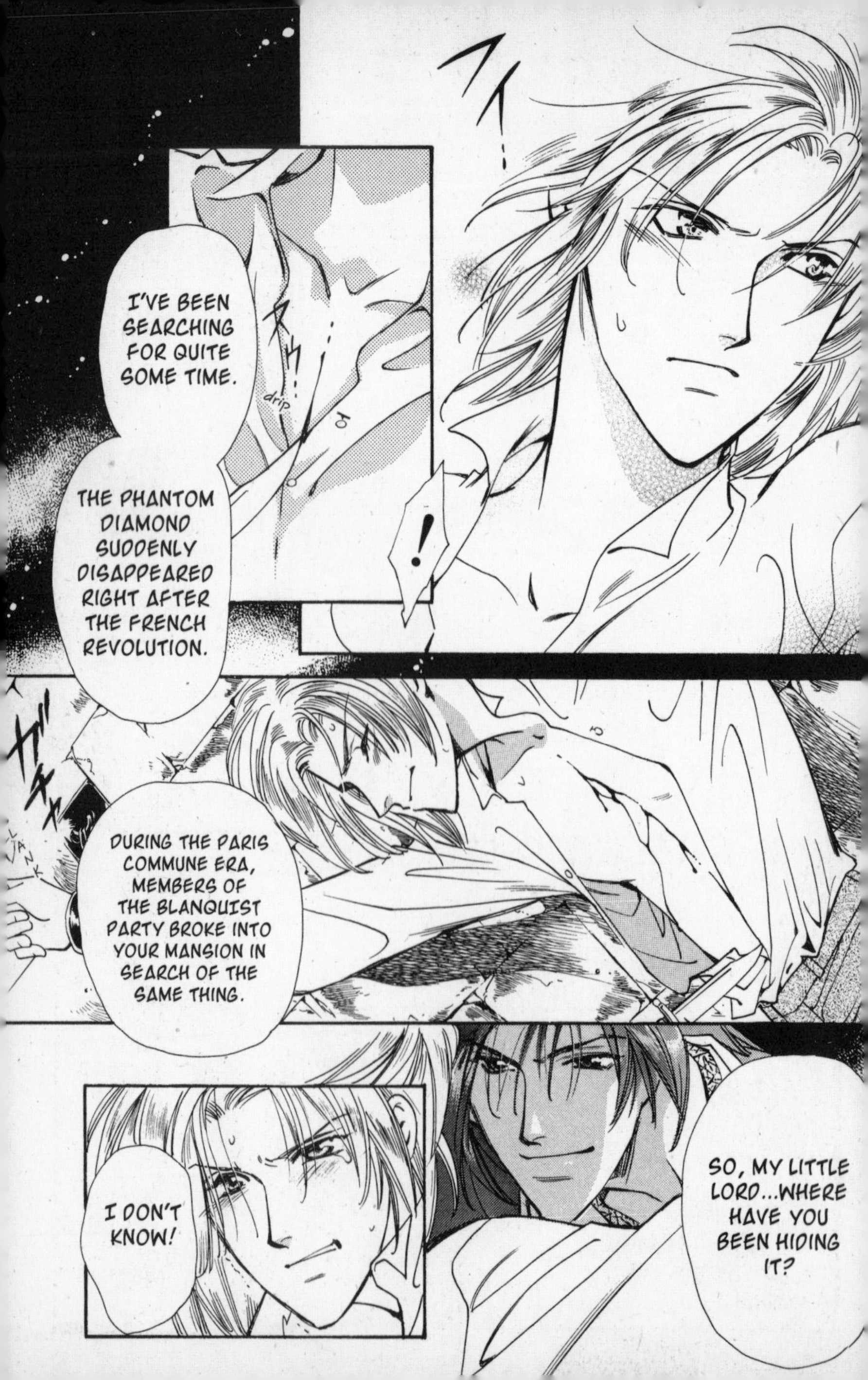
drip
I'VE BEEN SEARCHING FOR QUITE SOME TIME.
THE PHANTOM DIAMOND SUDDENLY DISAPPEARED RIGHT AFTER THE FRENCH REVOLUTION.
DURING THE PARIS COMMUNE ERA, MEMBERS OF THE BLANQUIST PARTY BROKE INTO YOUR MANSION IN SEARCH OF THE SAME THING.
SO, MY LITTLE LORD...WHERE HAVE YOU BEEN HIDING IT?
I DON'T KNOW!

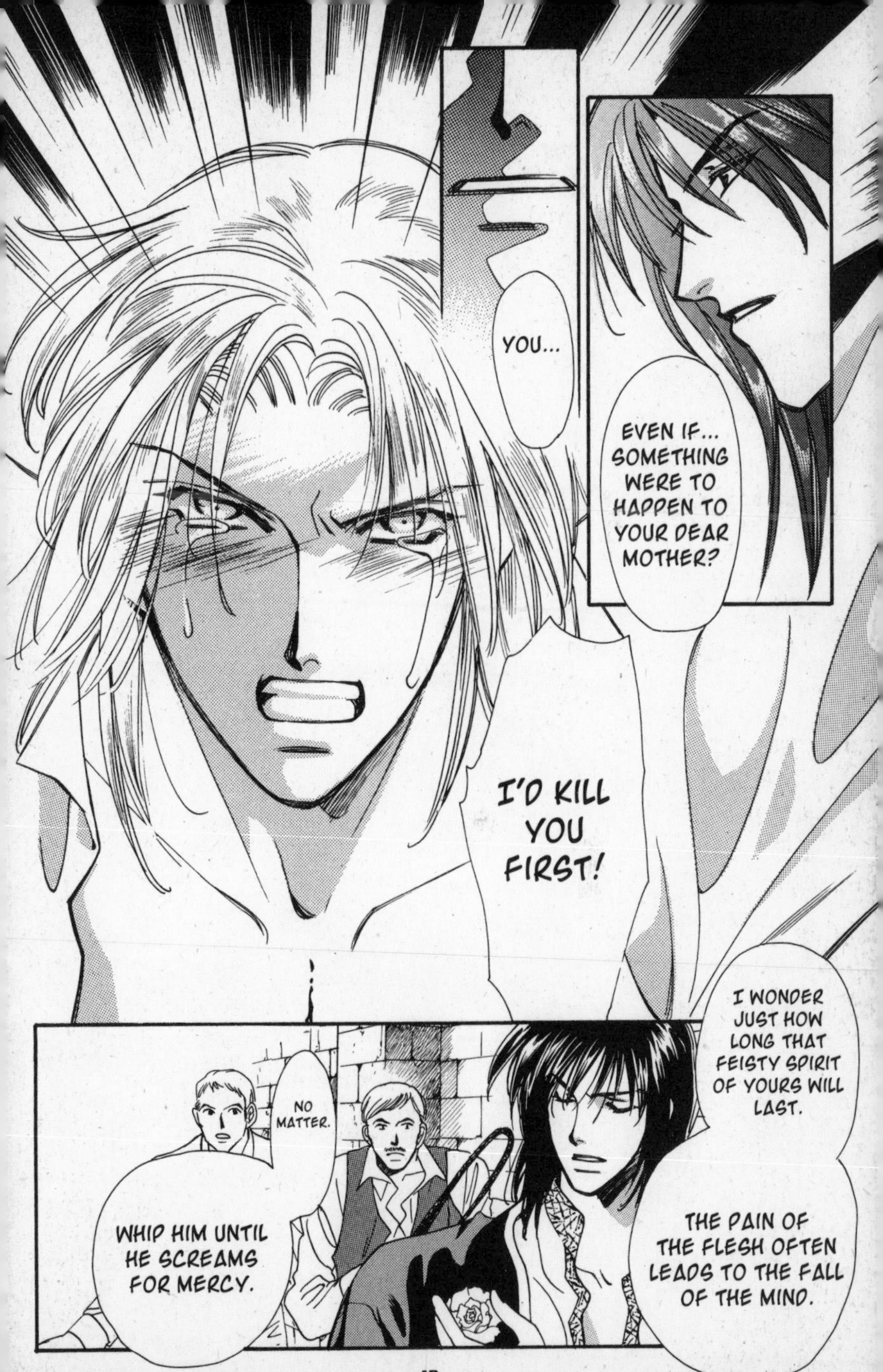

EVEN IF... SOMETHING WERE TO HAPPEN TO YOUR DEAR MOTHER?
YOU...
I'D KILL YOU FIRST!
I WONDER JUST HOW LONG THAT FEISTY SPIRIT OF YOURS WILL LAST.
THE PAIN OF THE FLESH OFTEN LEADS TO THE FALL OF THE MIND.
NO MATTER.
WHIP HIM UNTIL HE SCREAMS FOR MERCY.

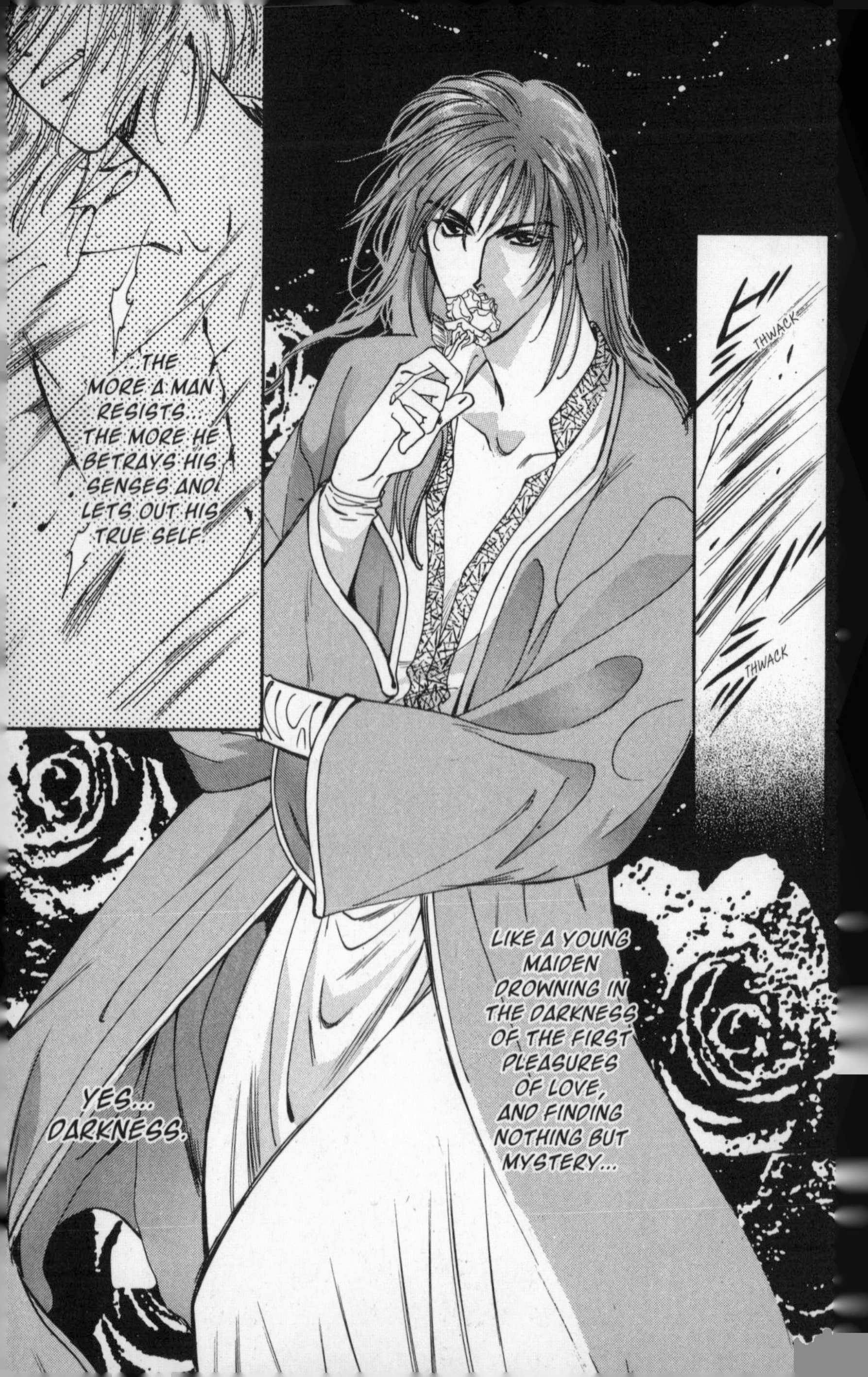
THWACK
THWACK
...THE MORE A MAN RESISTS, THE MORE HE BETRAYS HIS SENSES AND LETS OUT HIS TRUE SELF.
LIKE A YOUNG MAIDEN DROWNING IN THE DARKNESS OF THE FIRST PLEASURES OF LOVE, AND FINDING NOTHING BUT MYSTERY...
YES... DARKNESS.

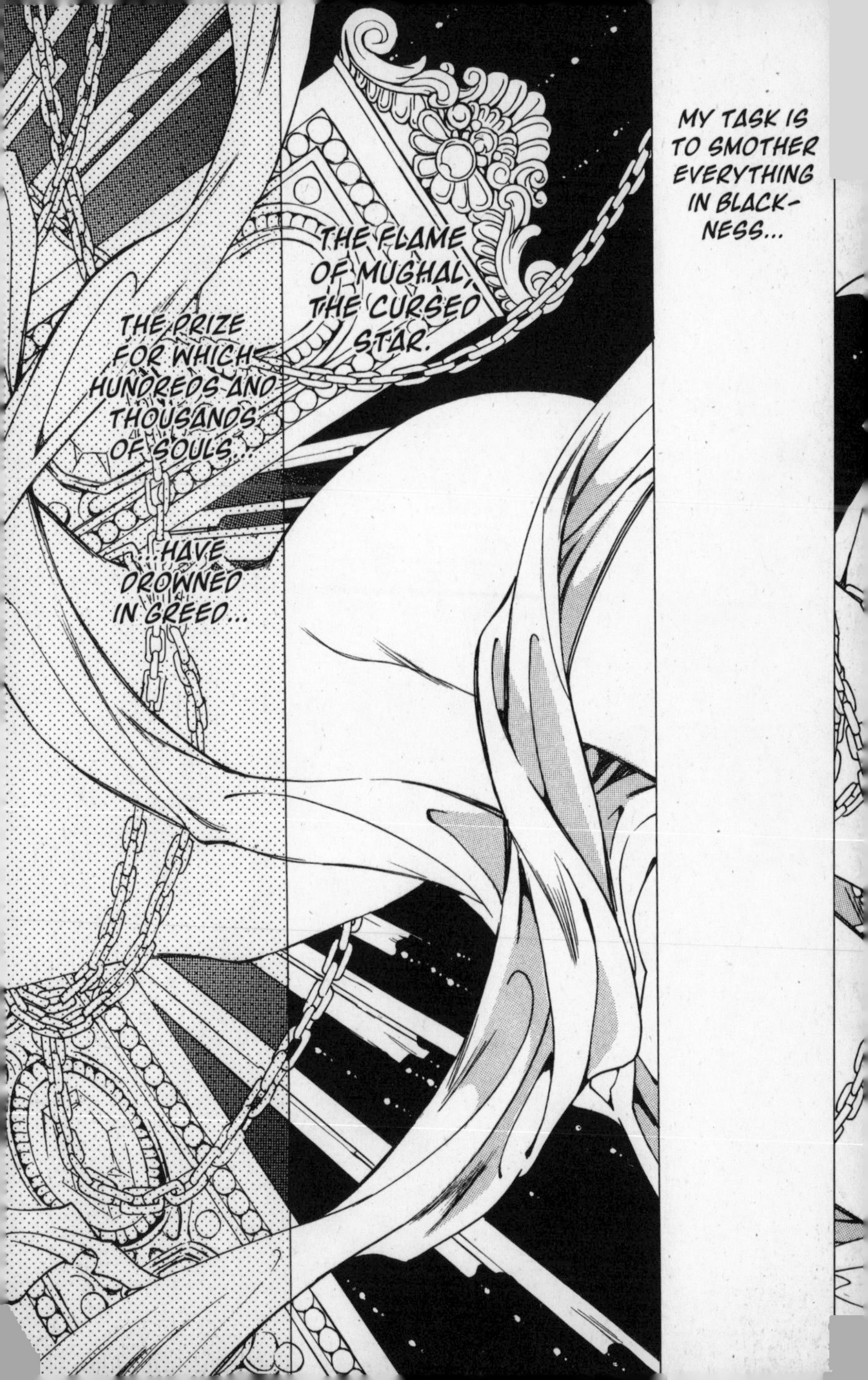
MY TASK IS TO SMOTHER EVERYTHING IN BLACK-NESS...
THE FLAME OF MUGHAL, THE CURSED STAR.
THE PRIZE FOR WHICH HUNDREDS AND THOUSANDS OF SOULS...
...HAVE DROWNED IN GREED...

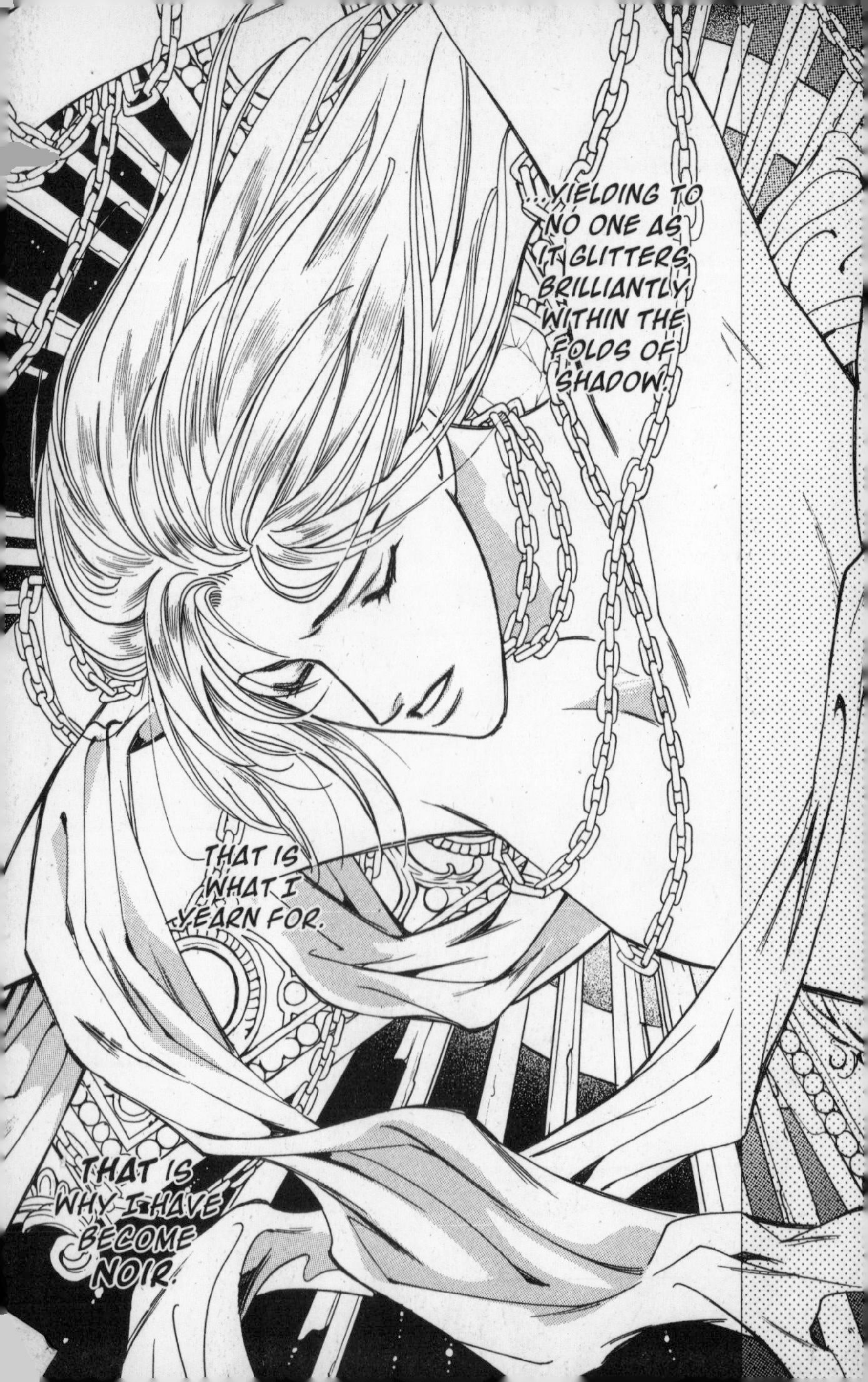
...YIELDING TO NO ONE AS IT GLITTERS BRILLIANTLY WITHIN THE FOLDS OF SHADOW.
THAT IS WHAT I YEARN FOR.
THAT IS WHY I HAVE BECOME NOIR.

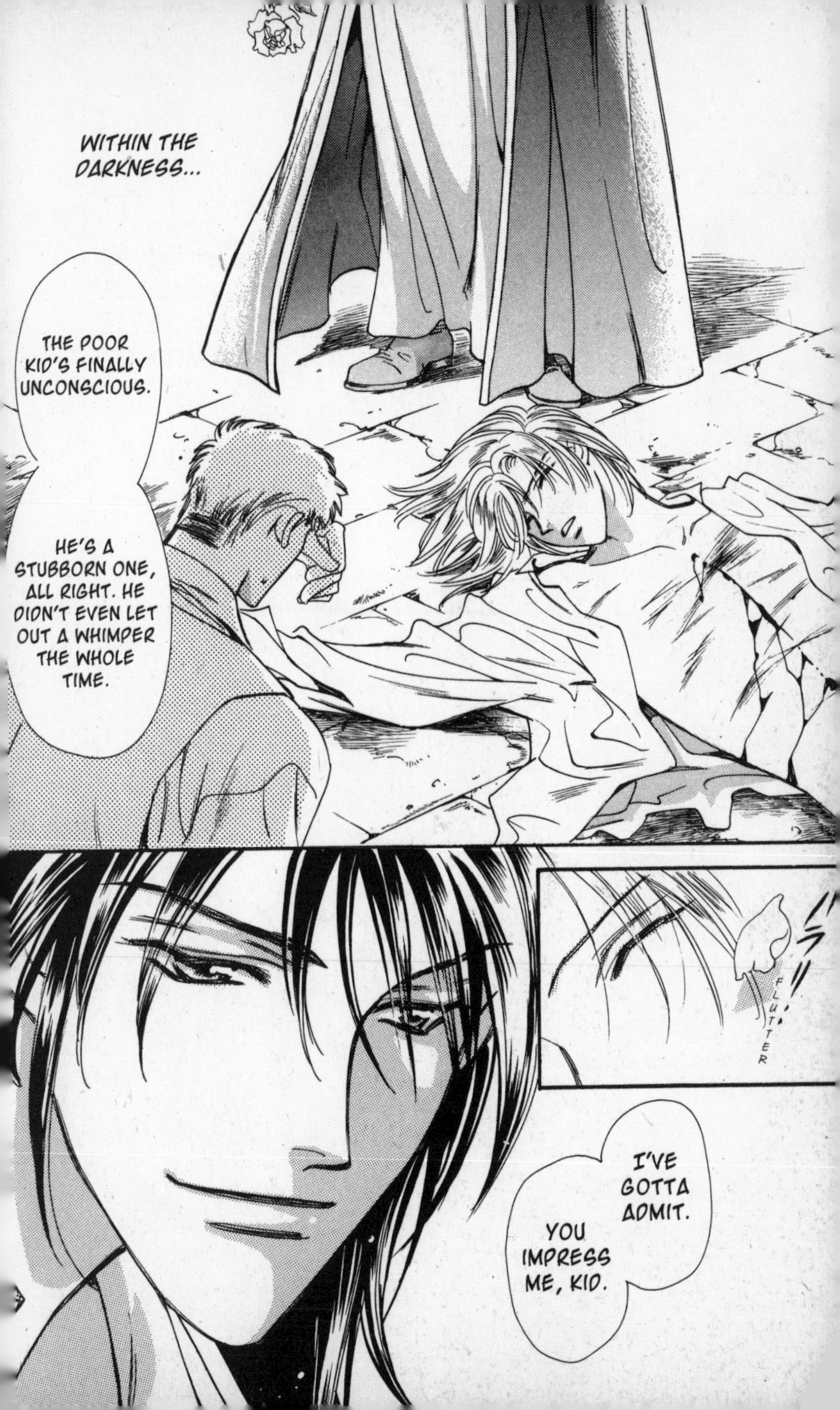
WITHIN THE DARKNESS...
THE POOR KID'S FINALLY UNCONSCIOUS.
HE'S A STUBBORN ONE, ALL RIGHT. HE DIDN'T EVEN LET OUT A WHIMPER THE WHOLE TIME.
FLUTTER
I'VE GOTTA ADMIT.
YOU IMPRESS ME, KID.

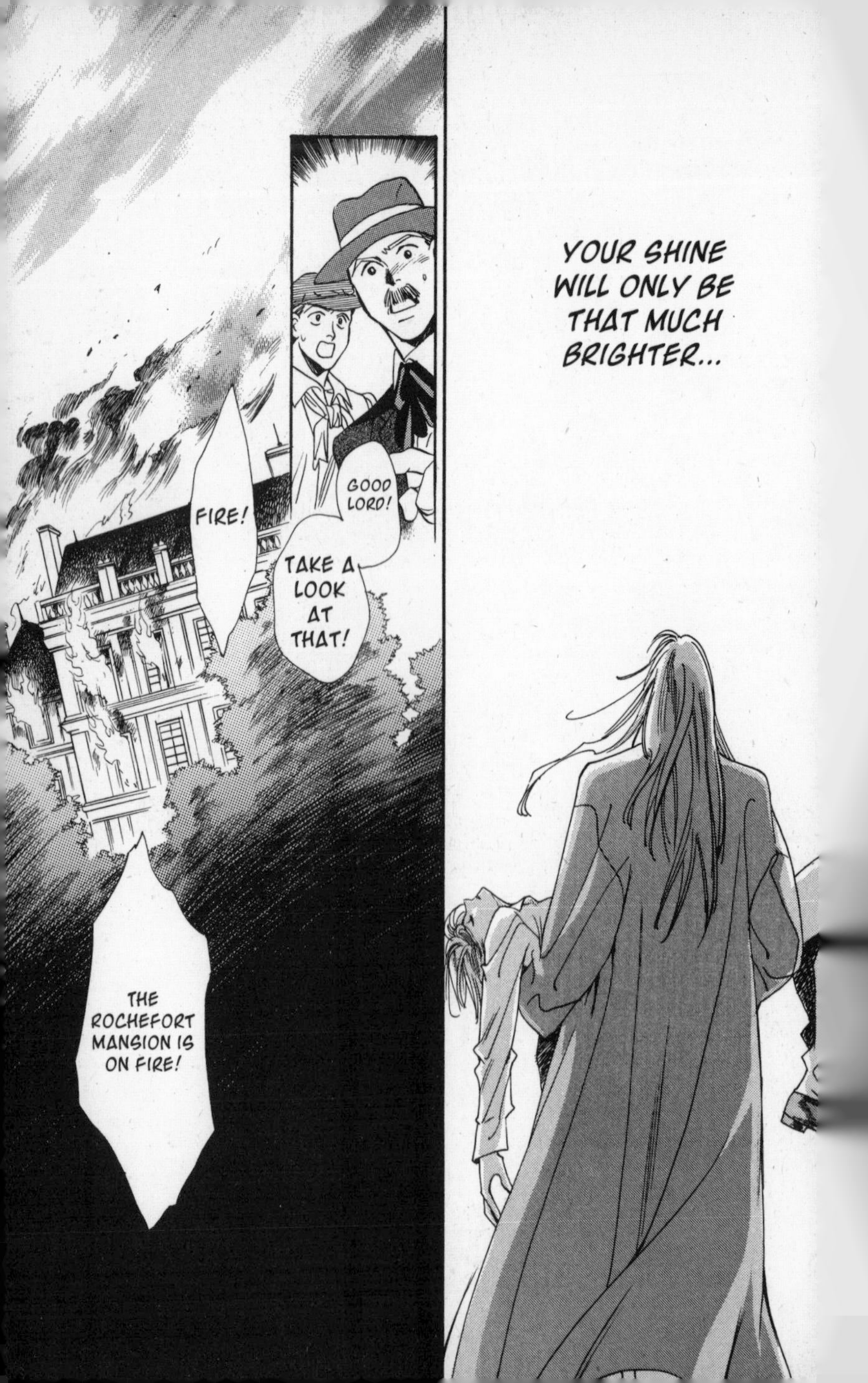
YOUR SHINE WILL ONLY BE THAT MUCH BRIGHTER...
GOOD LORD!
TAKE A LOOK AT THAT!
FIRE!
THE ROCHEFORT MANSION IS ON FIRE!

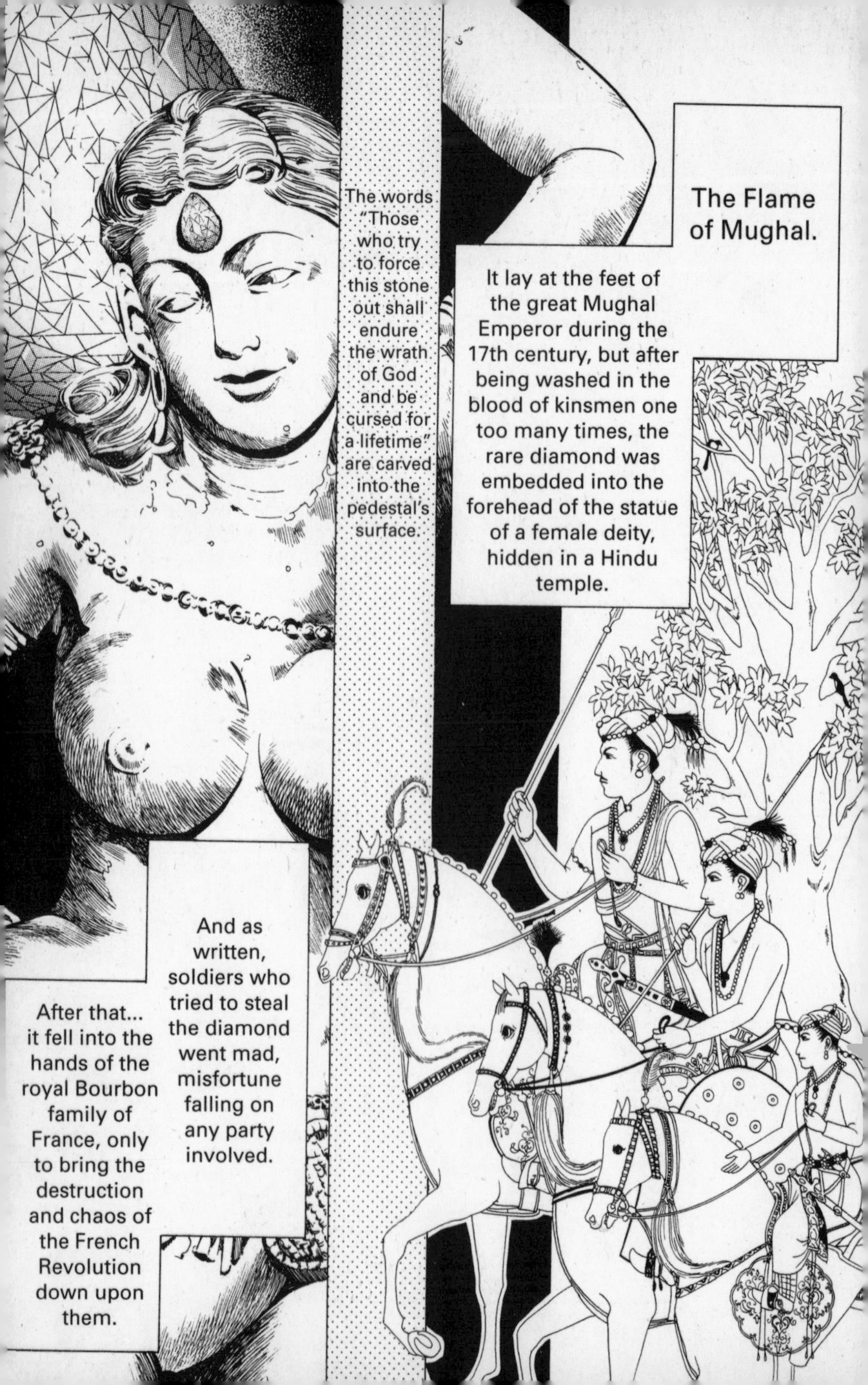
The Flame of Mughal.
It lay at the feet of the great Mughal Emperor during the 17th century, but after being washed in the blood of kinsmen one too many times, the rare diamond was embedded into the forehead of the statue of a female deity, hidden in a Hindu temple.
The words "Those who try to force this stone out shall endure the wrath of God and be cursed for a lifetime" are carved into the pedestal's surface.
And as written, soldiers who tried to steal the diamond went mad, misfortune falling on any party involved.
After that... it fell into the hands of the royal Bourbon family of France, only to bring the destruction and chaos of the French Revolution down upon them.

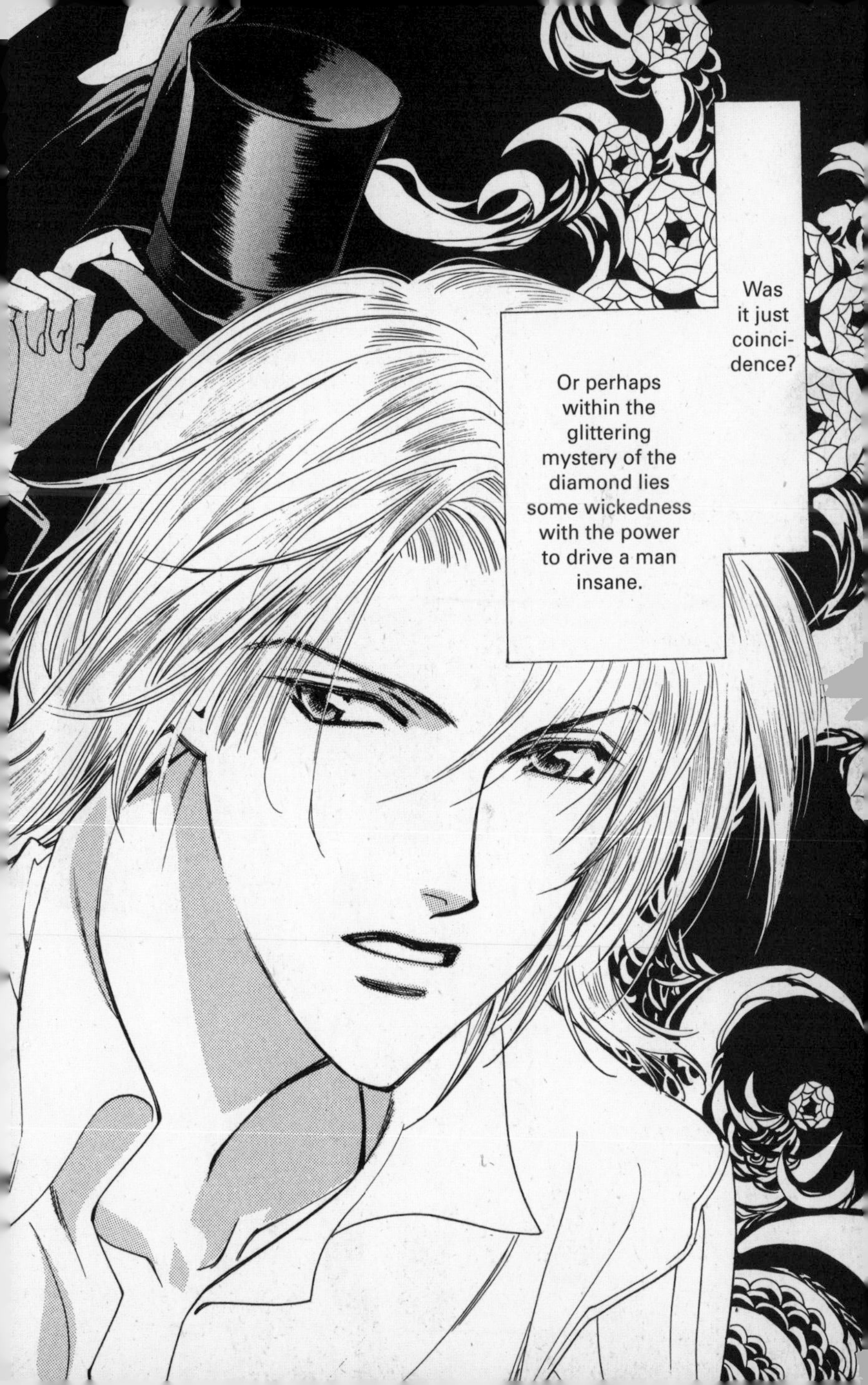
Was it just coinci- dence?
Or perhaps within the glittering mystery of the diamond lies some wickedness with the power to drive a man insane.

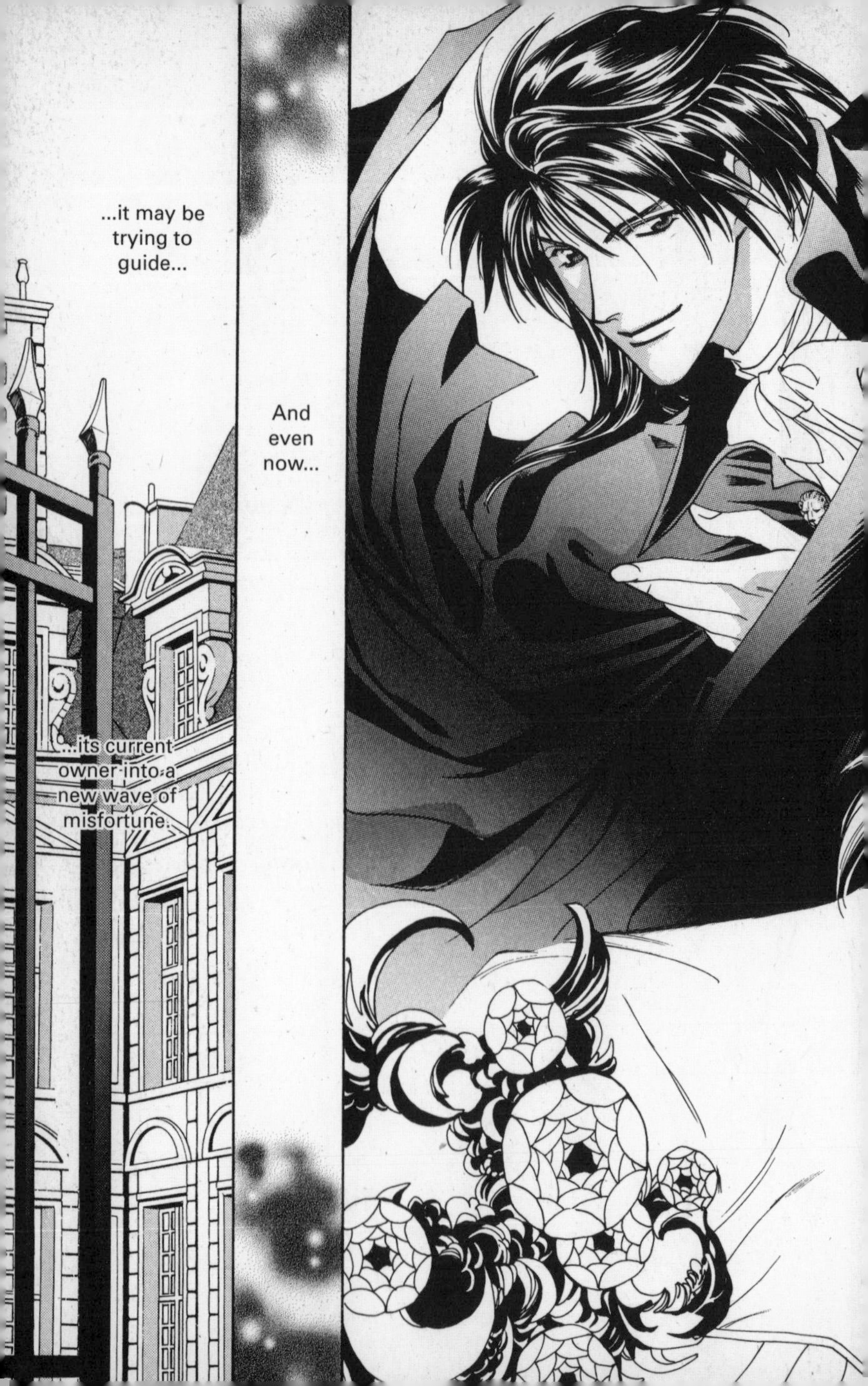
And even now...
...it may be trying to guide...
...its current owner into a new wave of misfortune.

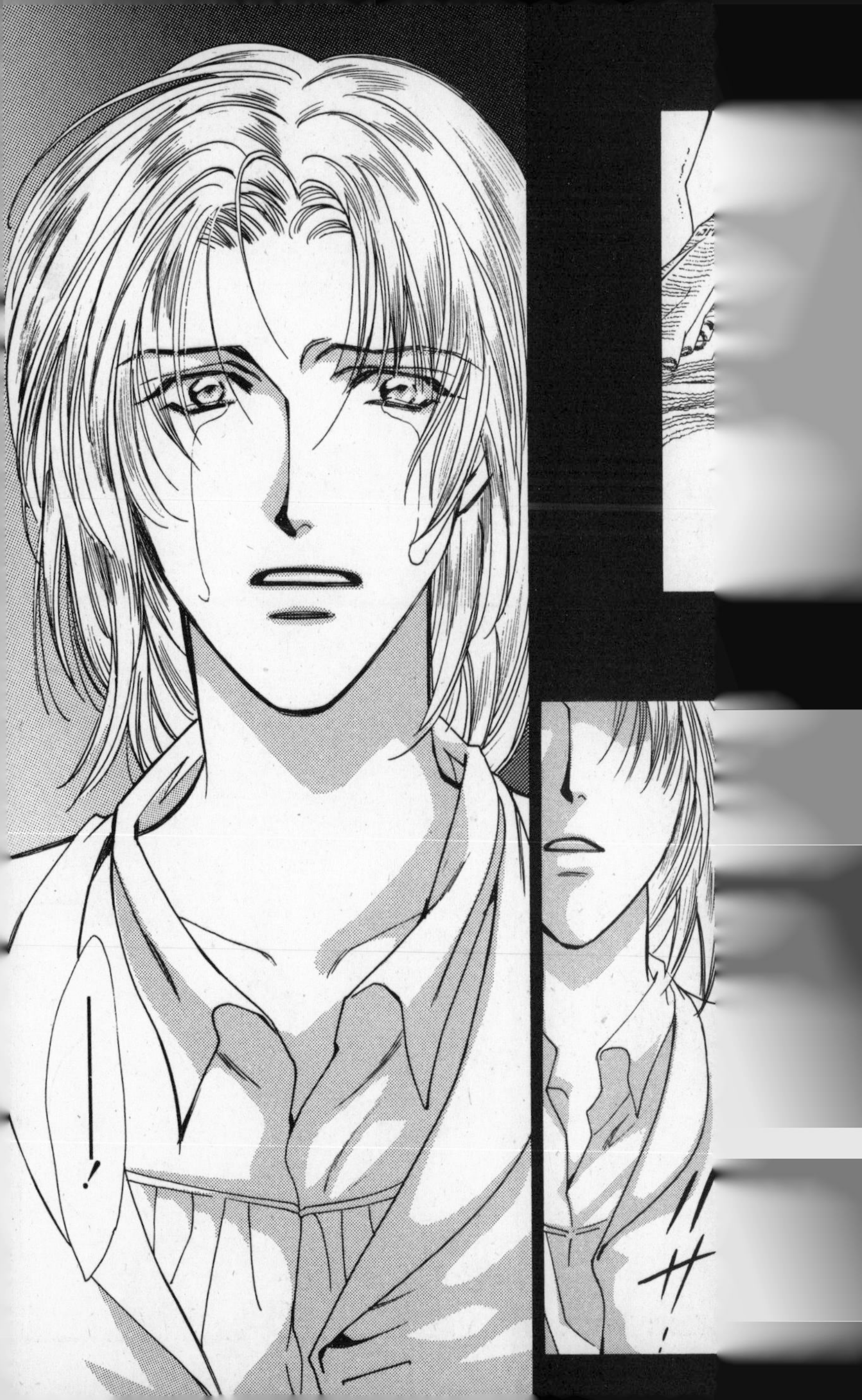

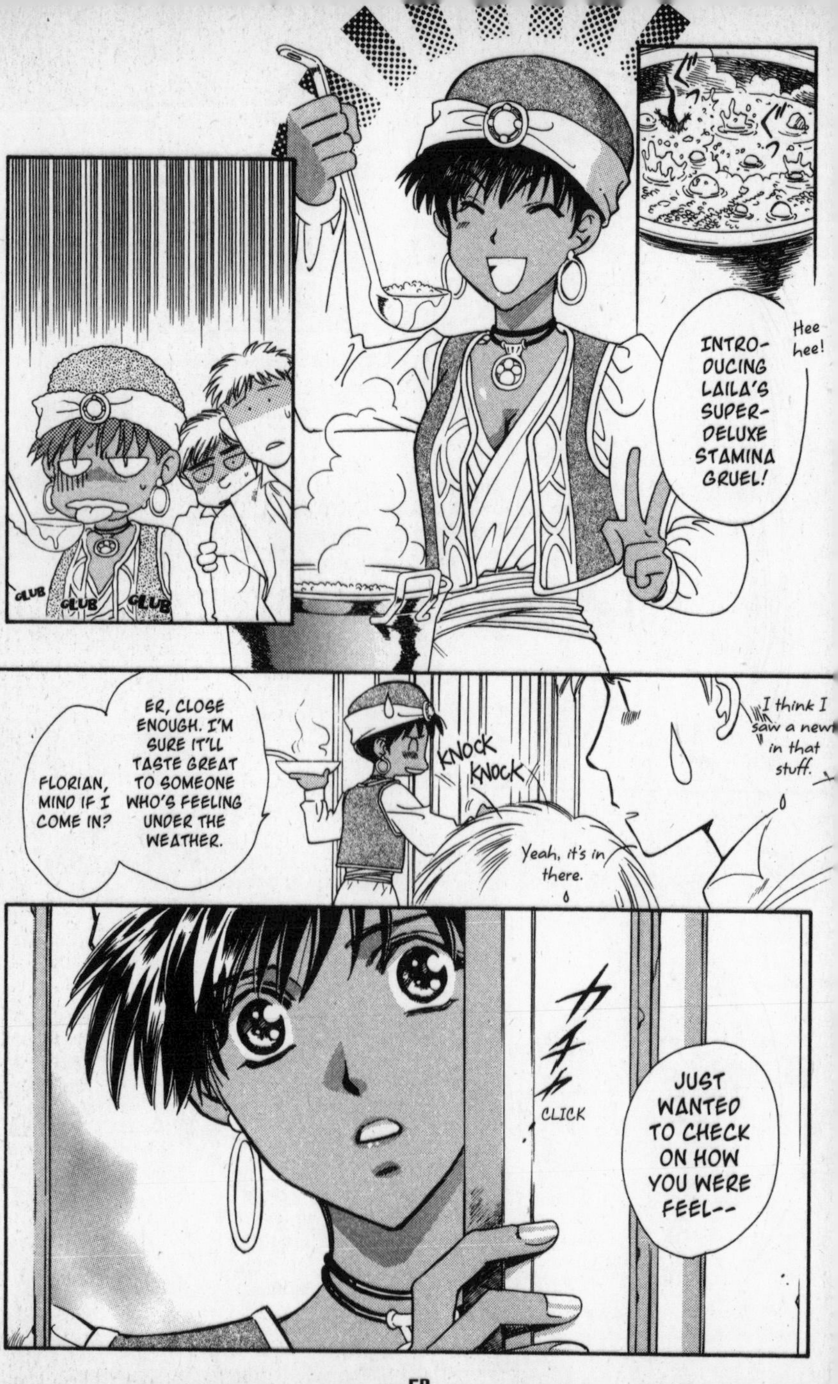
Hee hee!
INTRODUCING LAILA'S SUPER-DELUXE STAMINA GRUEL!
GLUB GLUB GLUB
I think I saw a newt in that stuff.
Yeah, it's in there.
ER, CLOSE ENOUGH. I'M SURE IT'LL TASTE GREAT TO SOMEONE WHO'S FEELING UNDER THE WEATHER.
KNOCK KNOCK
FLORIAN, MIND IF I COME IN?
CLICK
JUST WANTED TO CHECK ON HOW YOU WERE FEEL--

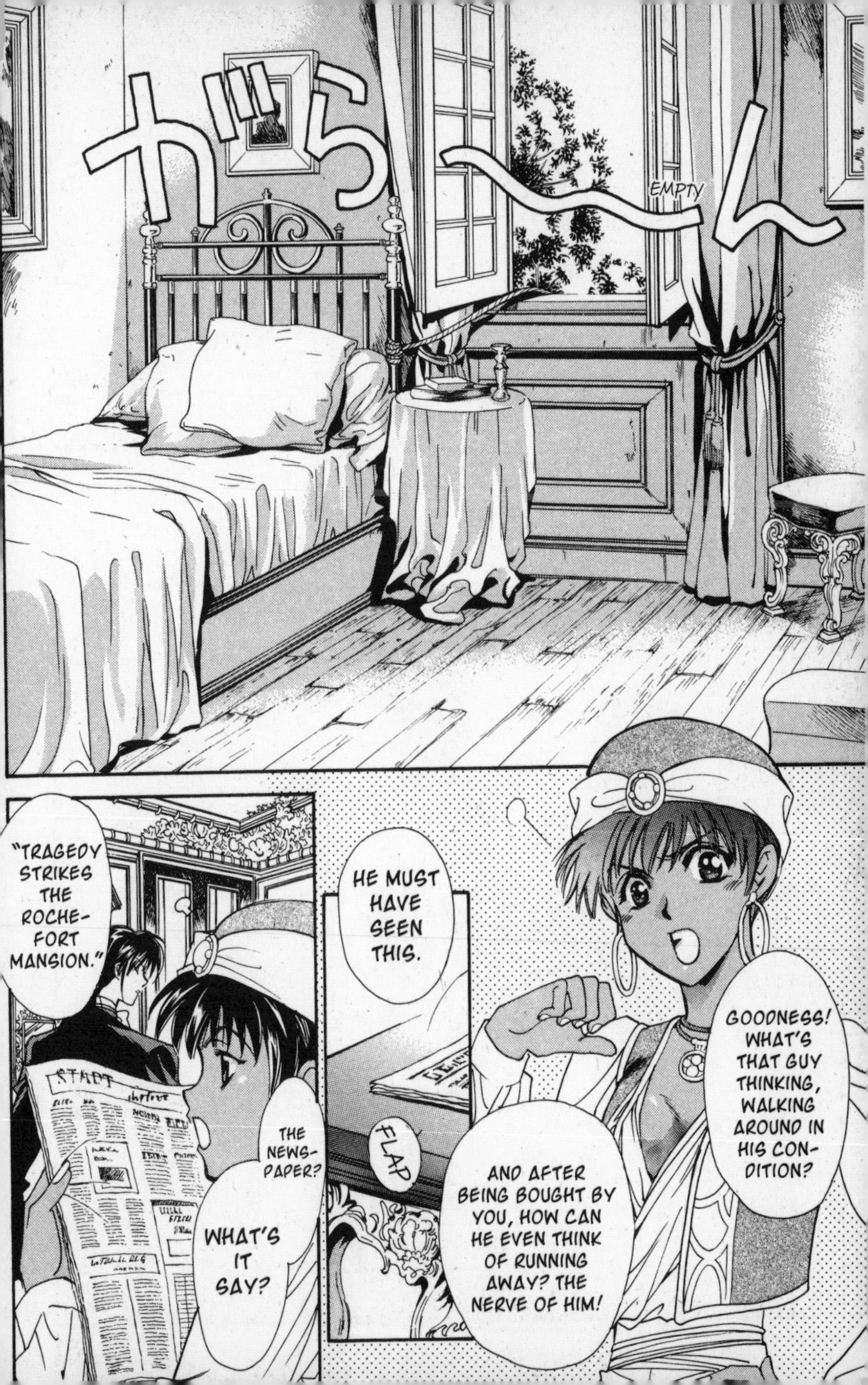
がら〜ん
EMPTY
GOODNESS! WHAT'S THAT GUY THINKING, WALKING AROUND IN HIS CON-DITION?
AND AFTER BEING BOUGHT BY YOU, HOW CAN HE EVEN THINK OF RUNNING AWAY? THE NERVE OF HIM!
HE MUST HAVE SEEN THIS.
FLAP
THE NEWS-PAPER?
WHAT'S IT SAY?
"TRAGEDY STRIKES THE ROCHE-FORT MANSION."

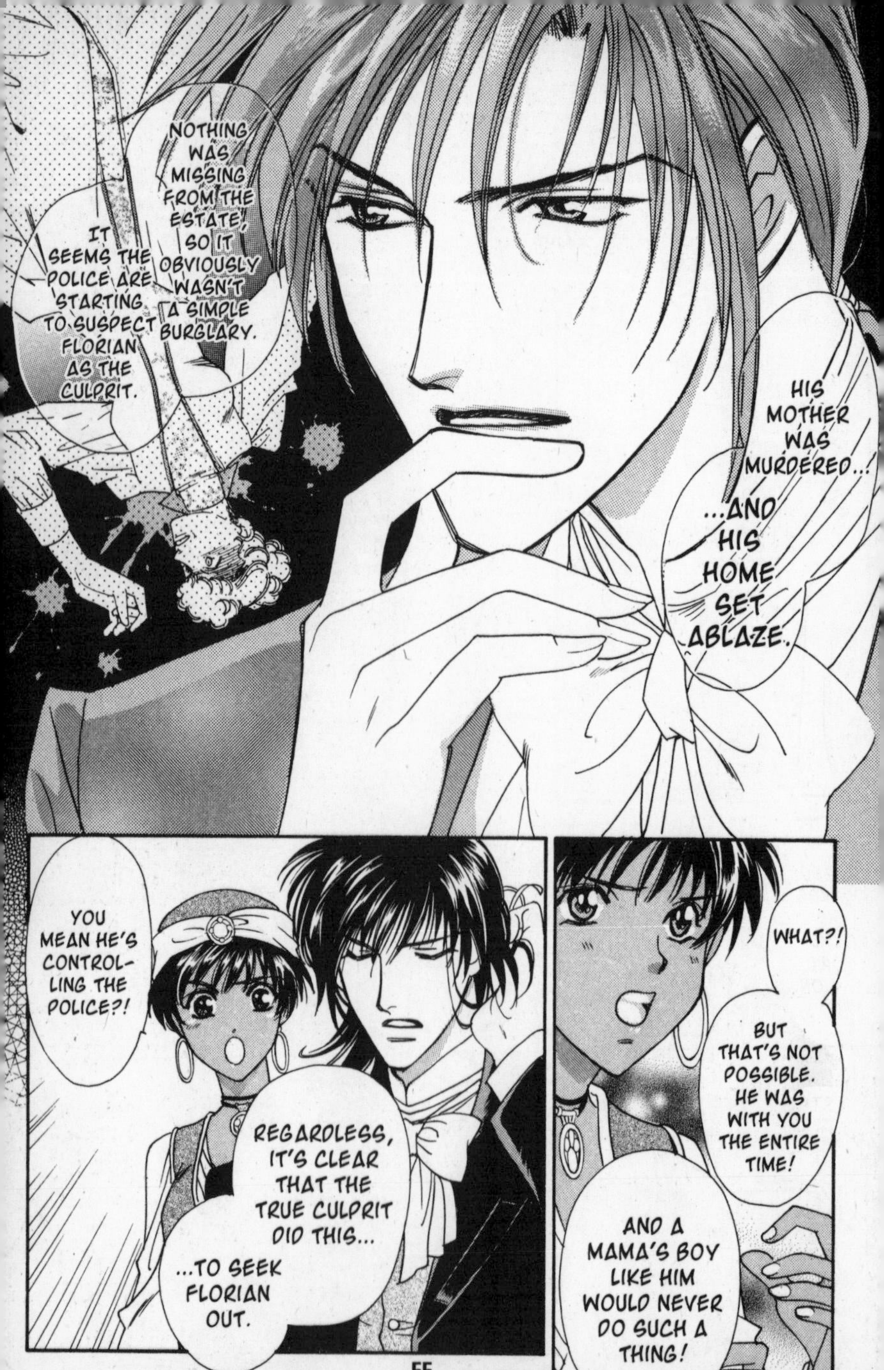
HIS MOTHER WAS MURDERED...
...AND HIS HOME SET ABLAZE.
NOTHING WAS MISSING FROM THE ESTATE, SO IT OBVIOUSLY WASN'T A SIMPLE BURGLARY.
IT SEEMS THE POLICE ARE STARTING TO SUSPECT FLORIAN AS THE CULPRIT.
WHAT?!
BUT THAT'S NOT POSSIBLE. HE WAS WITH YOU THE ENTIRE TIME!
AND A MAMA'S BOY LIKE HIM WOULD NEVER DO SUCH A THING!
YOU MEAN HE'S CONTROL-LING THE POLICE?!
REGARDLESS, IT'S CLEAR THAT THE TRUE CULPRIT DID THIS...
...TO SEEK FLORIAN OUT.

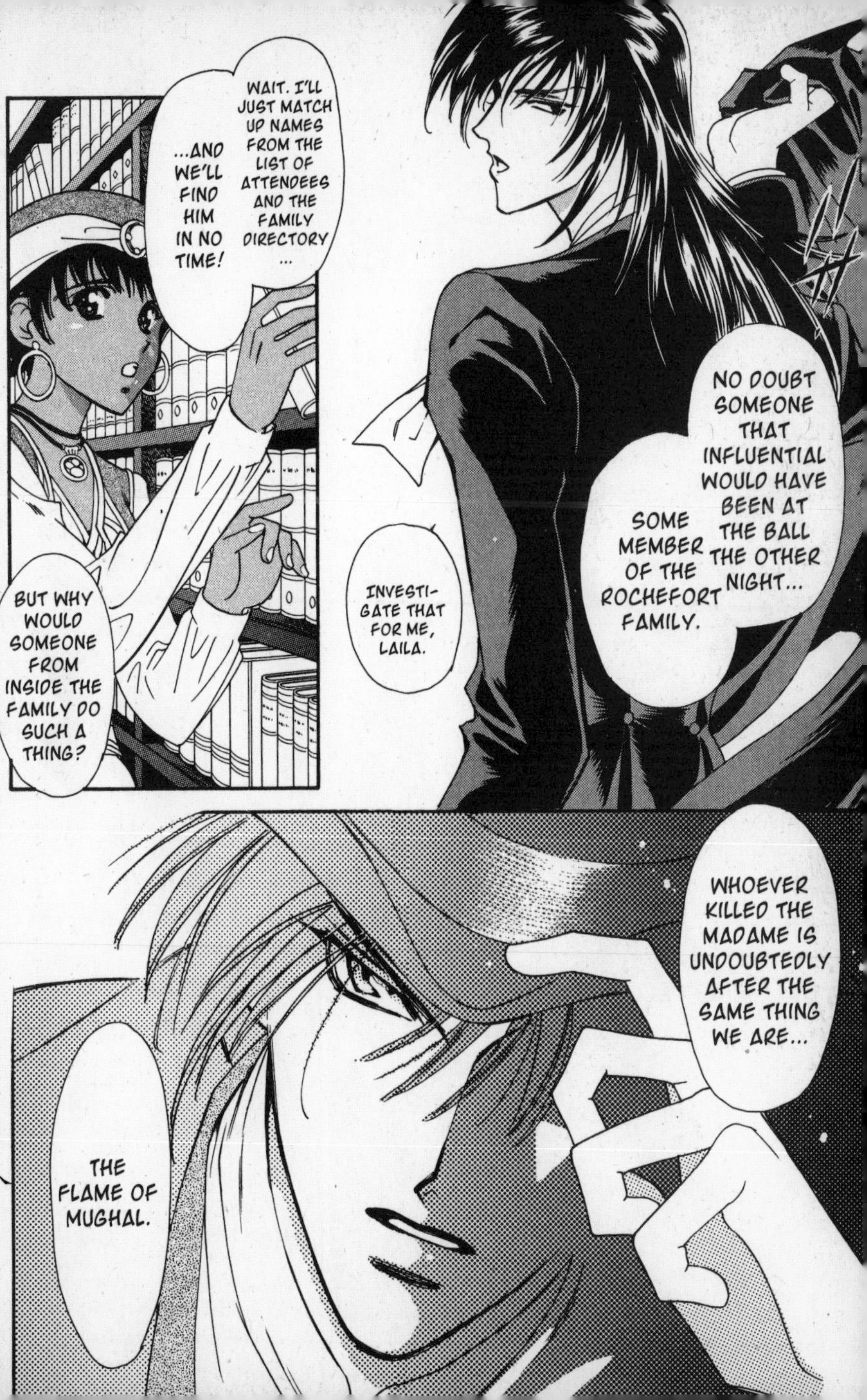
NO DOUBT SOMEONE THAT INFLUENTIAL WOULD HAVE BEEN AT THE BALL THE OTHER NIGHT...
SOME MEMBER OF THE ROCHEFORT FAMILY.
INVESTI-GATE THAT FOR ME, LAILA.
WAIT. I'LL JUST MATCH UP NAMES FROM THE LIST OF ATTENDEES AND THE FAMILY DIRECTORY...
...AND WE'LL FIND HIM IN NO TIME!
BUT WHY WOULD SOMEONE FROM INSIDE THE FAMILY DO SUCH A THING?
WHOEVER KILLED THE MADAME IS UNDOUBTEDLY AFTER THE SAME THING WE ARE...
THE FLAME OF MUGHAL.

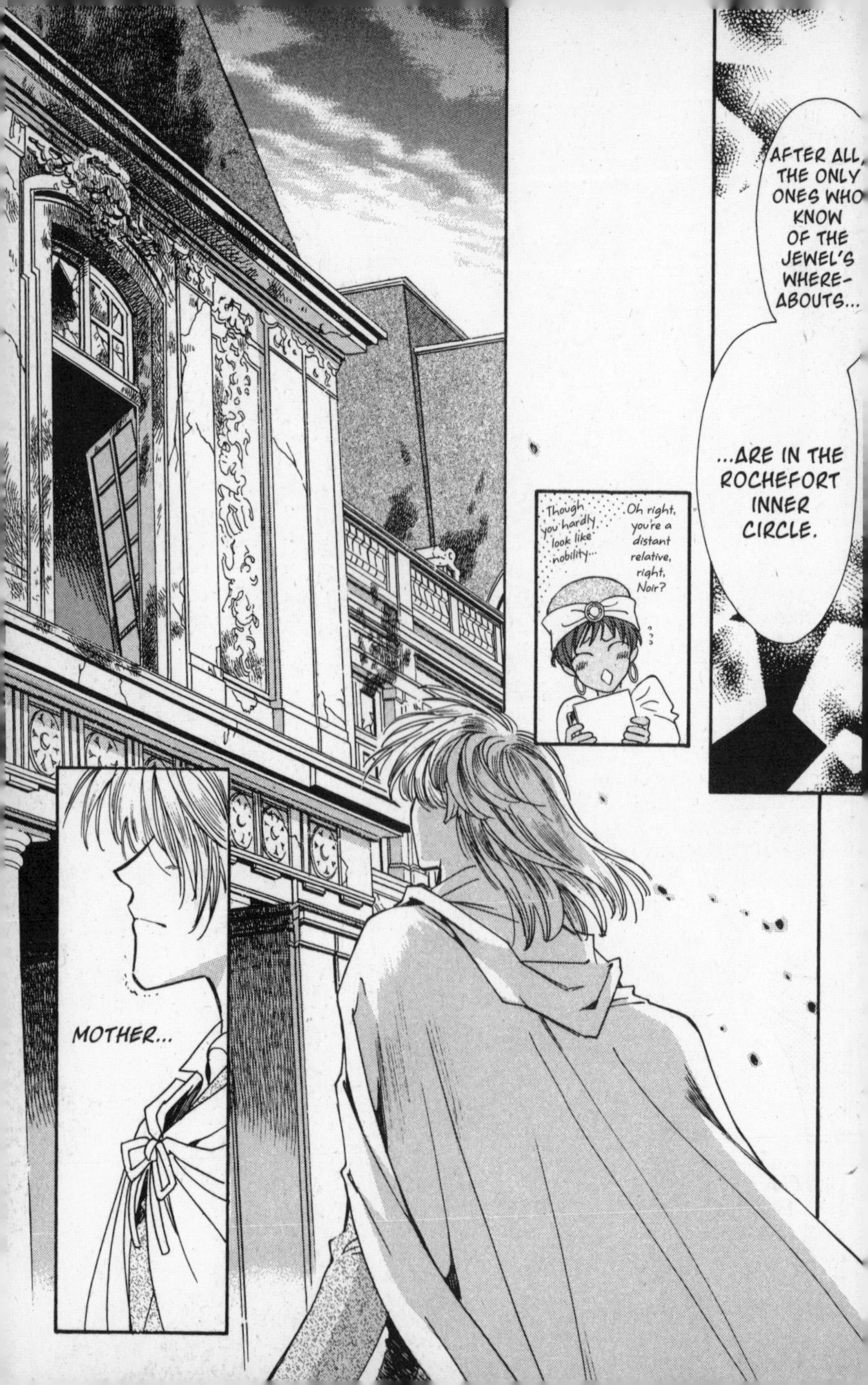
AFTER ALL, THE ONLY ONES WHO KNOW OF THE JEWEL'S WHERE-ABOUTS...
...ARE IN THE ROCHEFORT INNER CIRCLE.
Oh right, you're a distant relative, right, Noir?
Though you hardly look like nobility...
MOTHER...

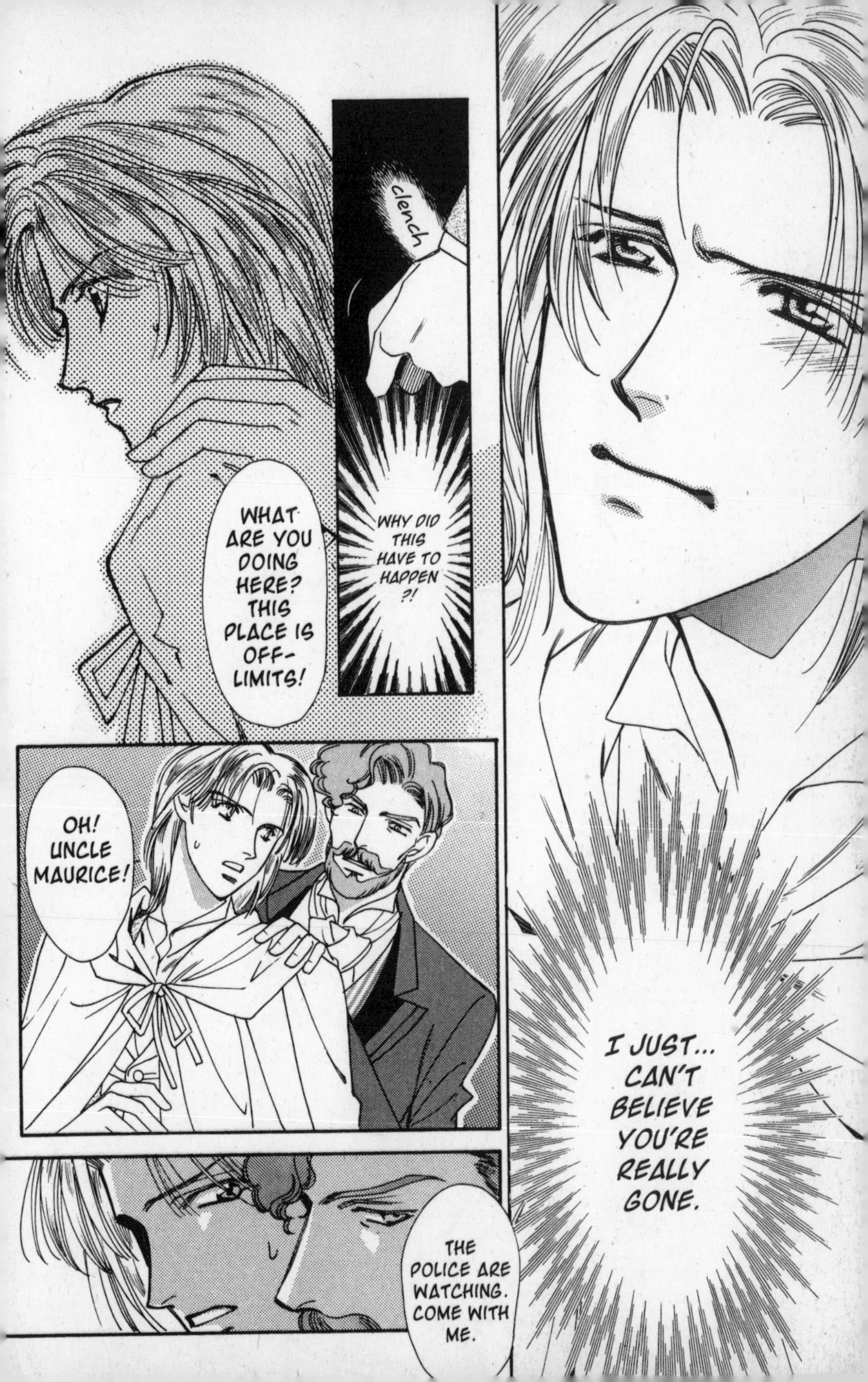
I JUST... CAN'T BELIEVE YOU'RE REALLY GONE.
clench
WHY DID THIS HAVE TO HAPPEN?!
WHAT ARE YOU DOING HERE? THIS PLACE IS OFF-LIMITS!
OH! UNCLE MAURICE!
THE POLICE ARE WATCHING. COME WITH ME.

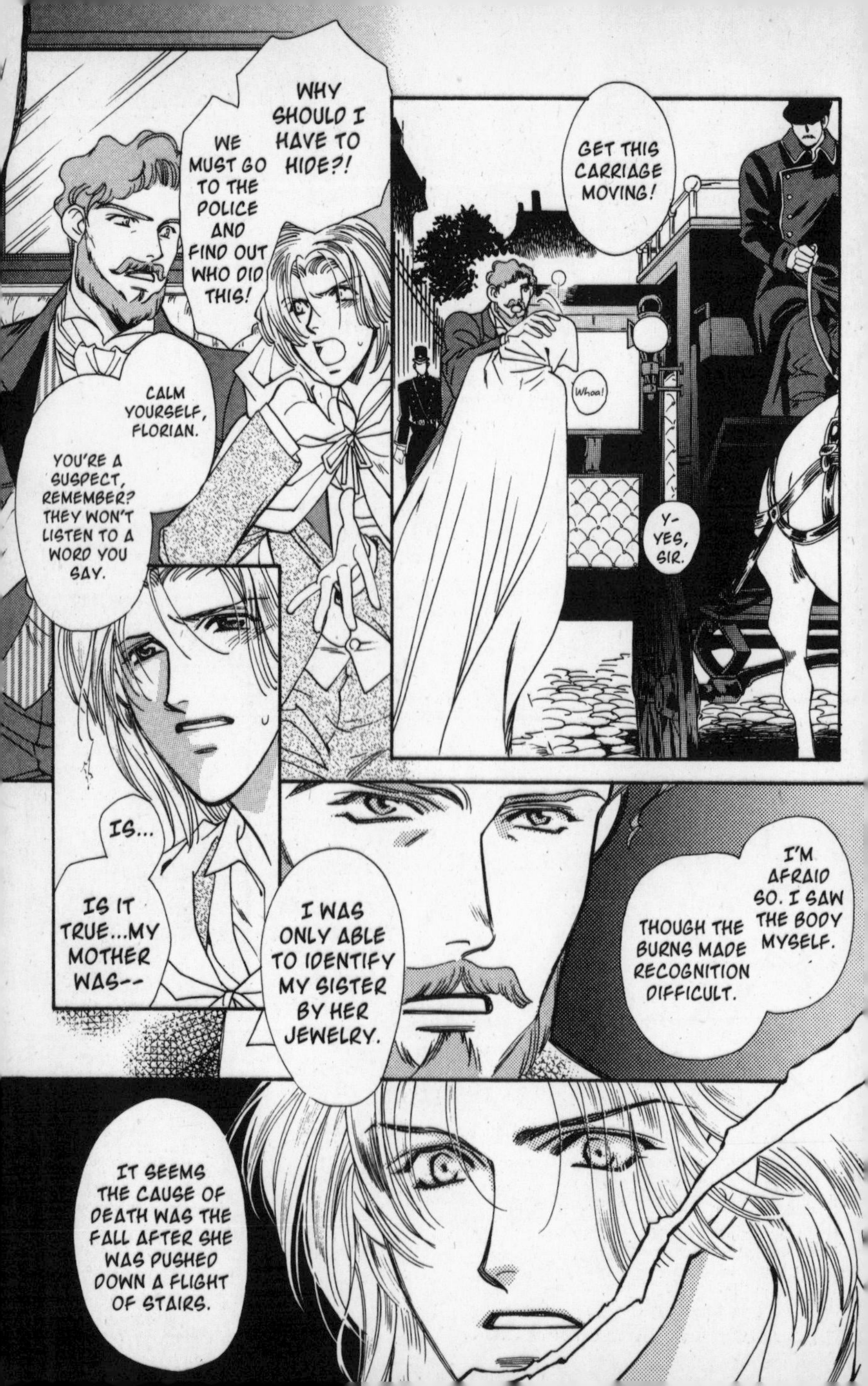
GET THIS CARRIAGE MOVING!
Whoa!
Y-YES, SIR.
WHY SHOULD I HAVE TO HIDE?!
WE MUST GO TO THE POLICE AND FIND OUT WHO DID THIS!
CALM YOURSELF, FLORIAN.
YOU'RE A SUSPECT, REMEMBER? THEY WON'T LISTEN TO A WORD YOU SAY.
IS...
IS IT TRUE...MY MOTHER WAS--
I'M AFRAID SO. I SAW THE BODY MYSELF.
THOUGH THE BURNS MADE RECOGNITION DIFFICULT.
I WAS ONLY ABLE TO IDENTIFY MY SISTER BY HER JEWELRY.
IT SEEMS THE CAUSE OF DEATH WAS THE FALL AFTER SHE WAS PUSHED DOWN A FLIGHT OF STAIRS.

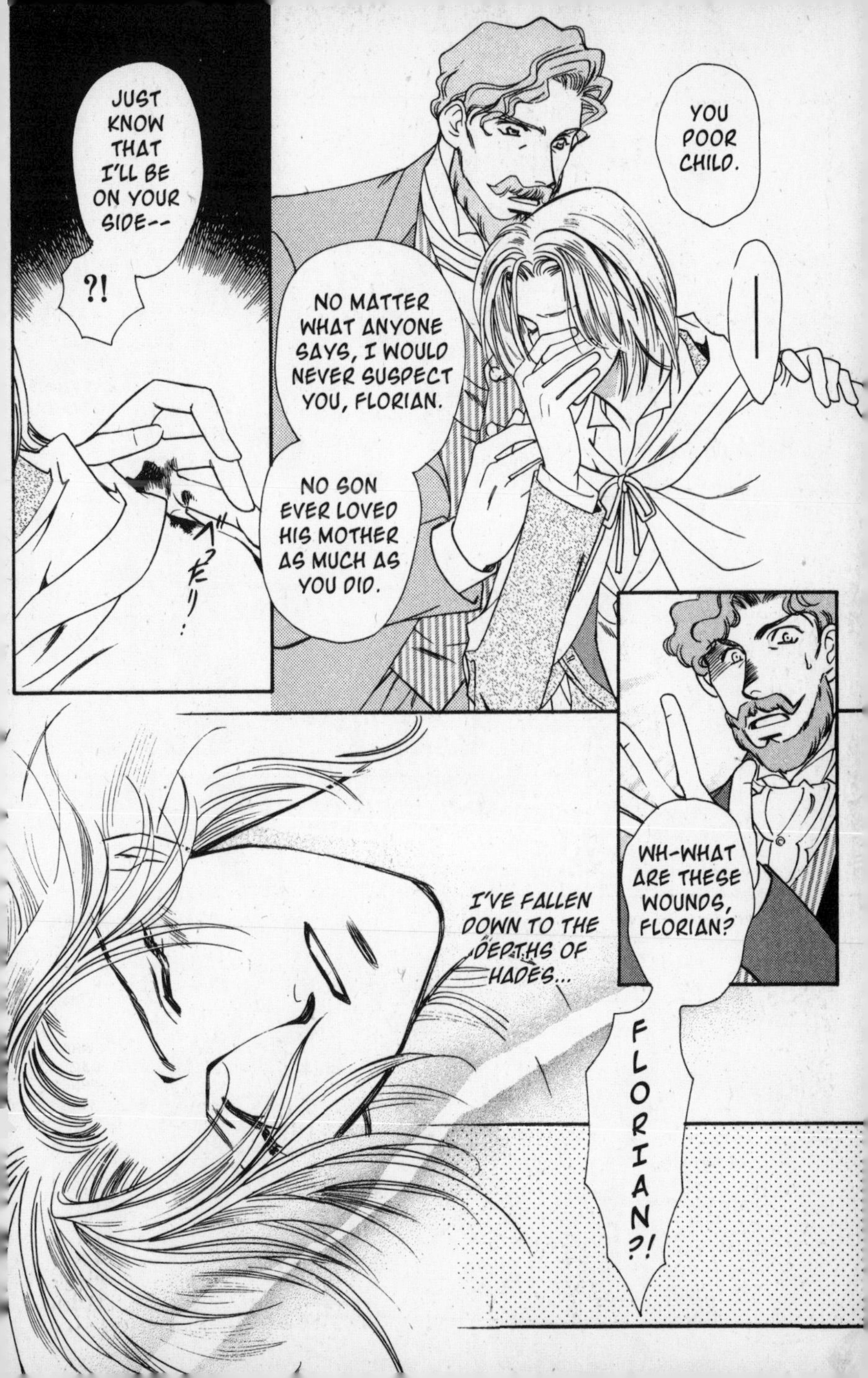
YOU POOR CHILD.
NO MATTER WHAT ANYONE SAYS, I WOULD NEVER SUSPECT YOU, FLORIAN.
NO SON EVER LOVED HIS MOTHER AS MUCH AS YOU DID.
JUST KNOW THAT I'LL BE ON YOUR SIDE--
?!
WH-WHAT ARE THESE WOUNDS, FLORIAN?
FLORIAN?!
I'VE FALLEN DOWN TO THE DEPTHS OF HADES...

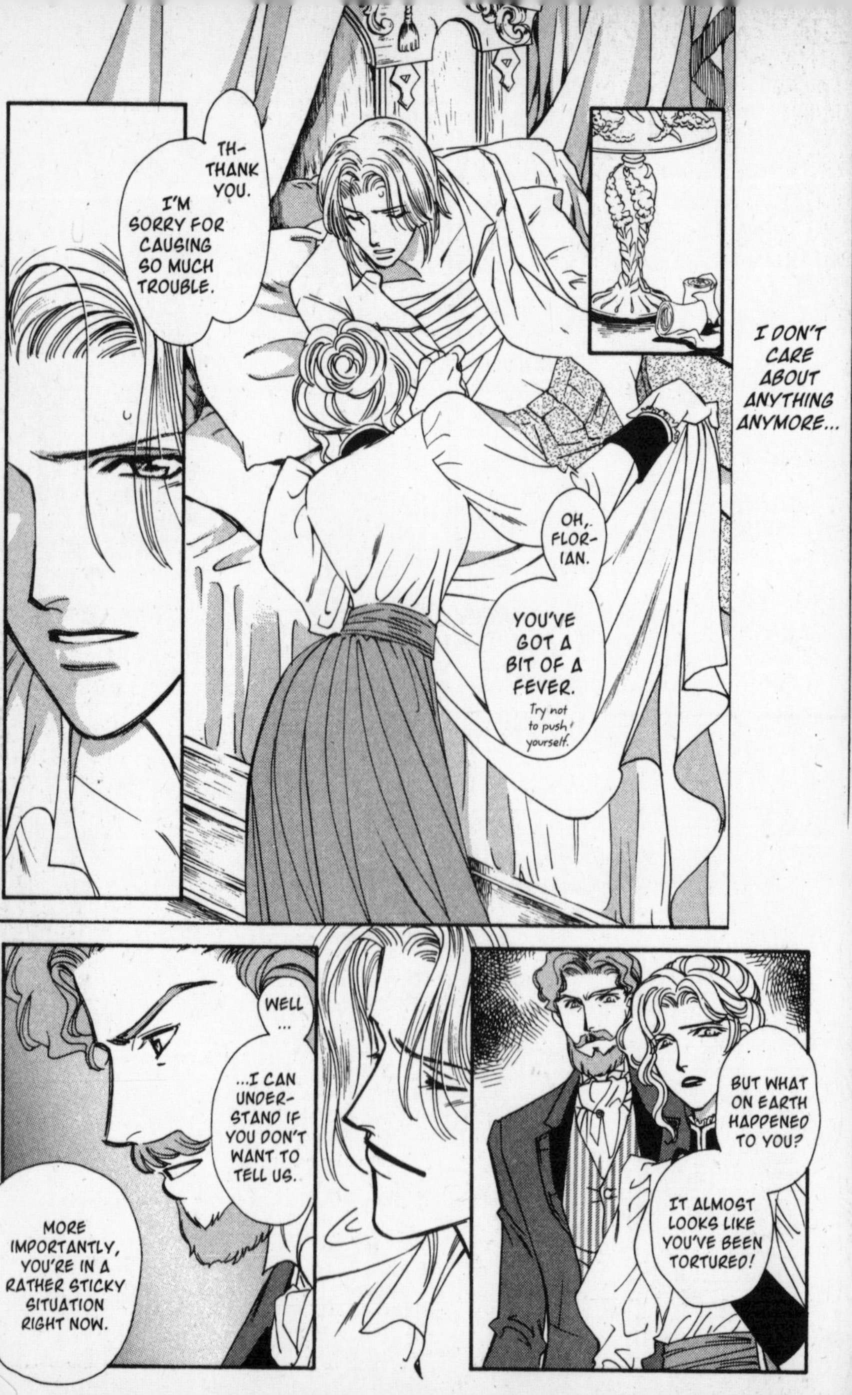
I DON'T CARE ABOUT ANYTHING ANYMORE...
OH, FLORIAN.
YOU'VE GOT A BIT OF A FEVER.
Try not to push yourself.
TH-THANK YOU.
I'M SORRY FOR CAUSING SO MUCH TROUBLE.
BUT WHAT ON EARTH HAPPENED TO YOU?
IT ALMOST LOOKS LIKE YOU'VE BEEN TORTURED!
WELL ...
...I CAN UNDERSTAND IF YOU DON'T WANT TO TELL US.
MORE IMPORTANTLY, YOU'RE IN A RATHER STICKY SITUATION RIGHT NOW.

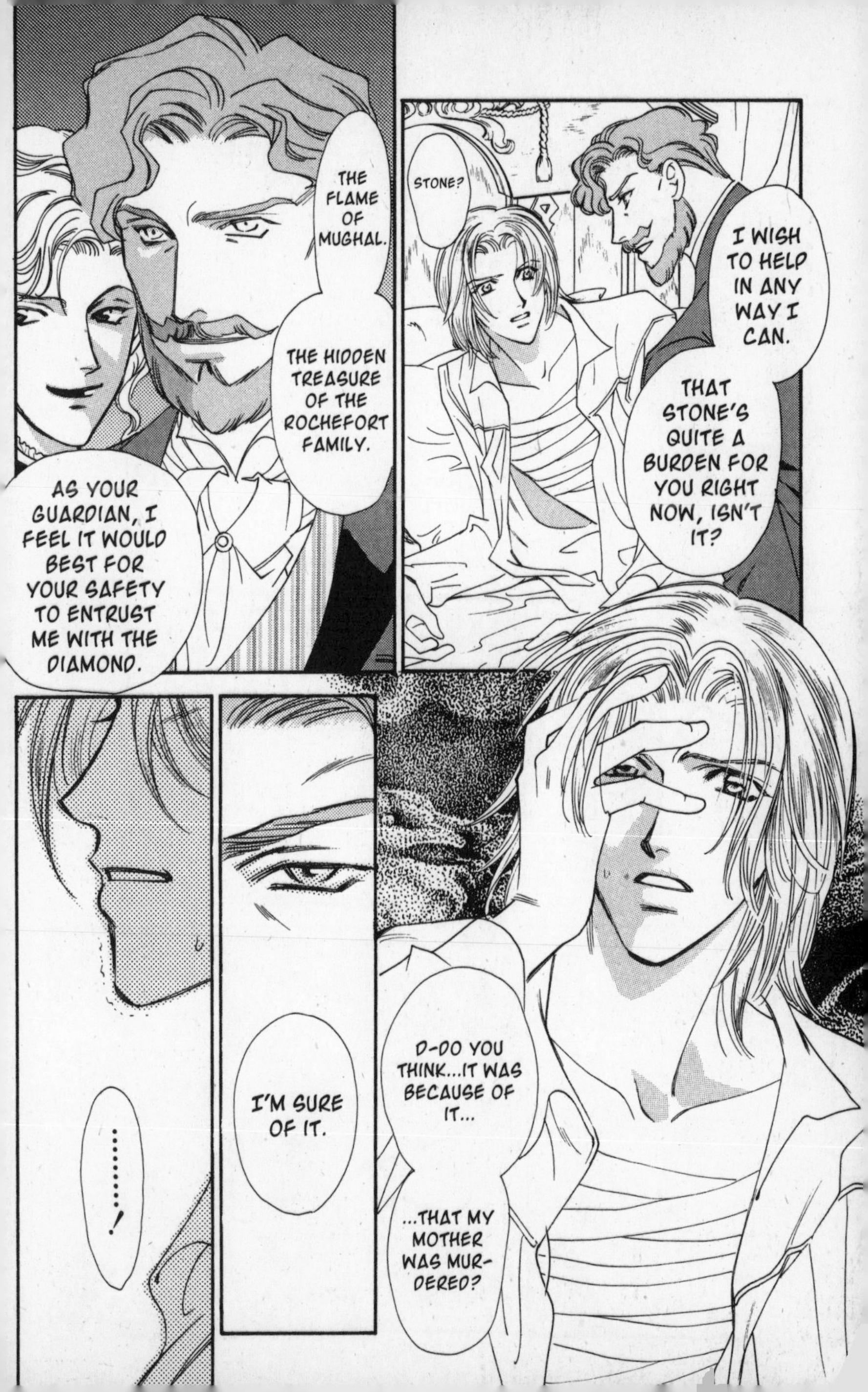
I WISH TO HELP IN ANY WAY I CAN.
THAT STONE'S QUITE A BURDEN FOR YOU RIGHT NOW, ISN'T IT?
STONE?
THE FLAME OF MUGHAL.
THE HIDDEN TREASURE OF THE ROCHEFORT FAMILY.
AS YOUR GUARDIAN, I FEEL IT WOULD BEST FOR YOUR SAFETY TO ENTRUST ME WITH THE DIAMOND.
D-DO YOU THINK...IT WAS BECAUSE OF IT...
...THAT MY MOTHER WAS MURDERED?
I'M SURE OF IT.
......!

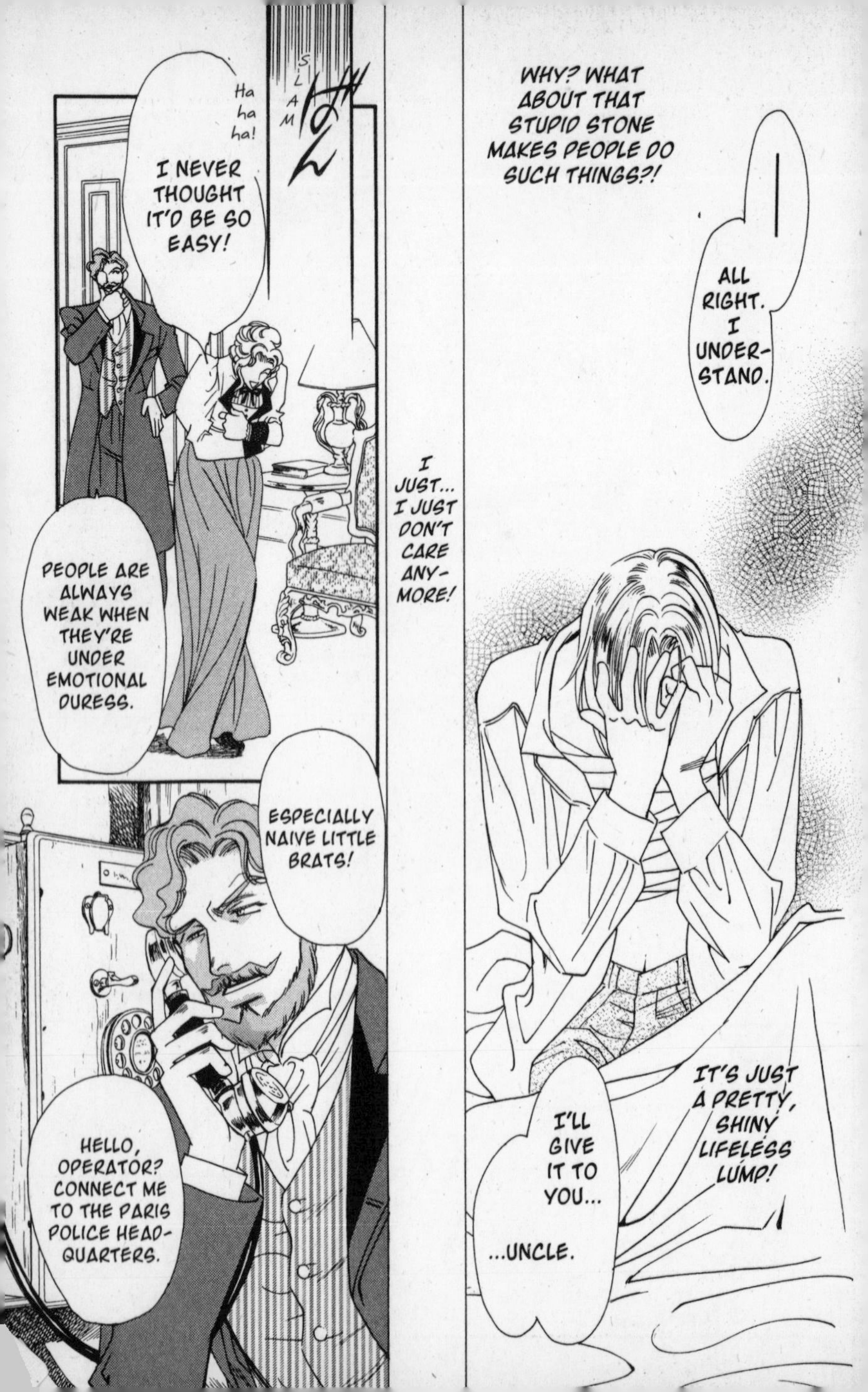

WHY? WHAT ABOUT THAT STUPID STONE MAKES PEOPLE DO SUCH THINGS?!
!
ALL RIGHT. I UNDER-STAND.
IT'S JUST A PRETTY, SHINY LIFELESS LUMP!
I'LL GIVE IT TO YOU...
...UNCLE.
I JUST... I JUST DON'T CARE ANY-MORE!
SLAM
Ha ha ha!
I NEVER THOUGHT IT'D BE SO EASY!
PEOPLE ARE ALWAYS WEAK WHEN THEY'RE UNDER EMOTIONAL DURESS.
ESPECIALLY NAIVE LITTLE BRATS!
HELLO, OPERATOR? CONNECT ME TO THE PARIS POLICE HEAD-QUARTERS.

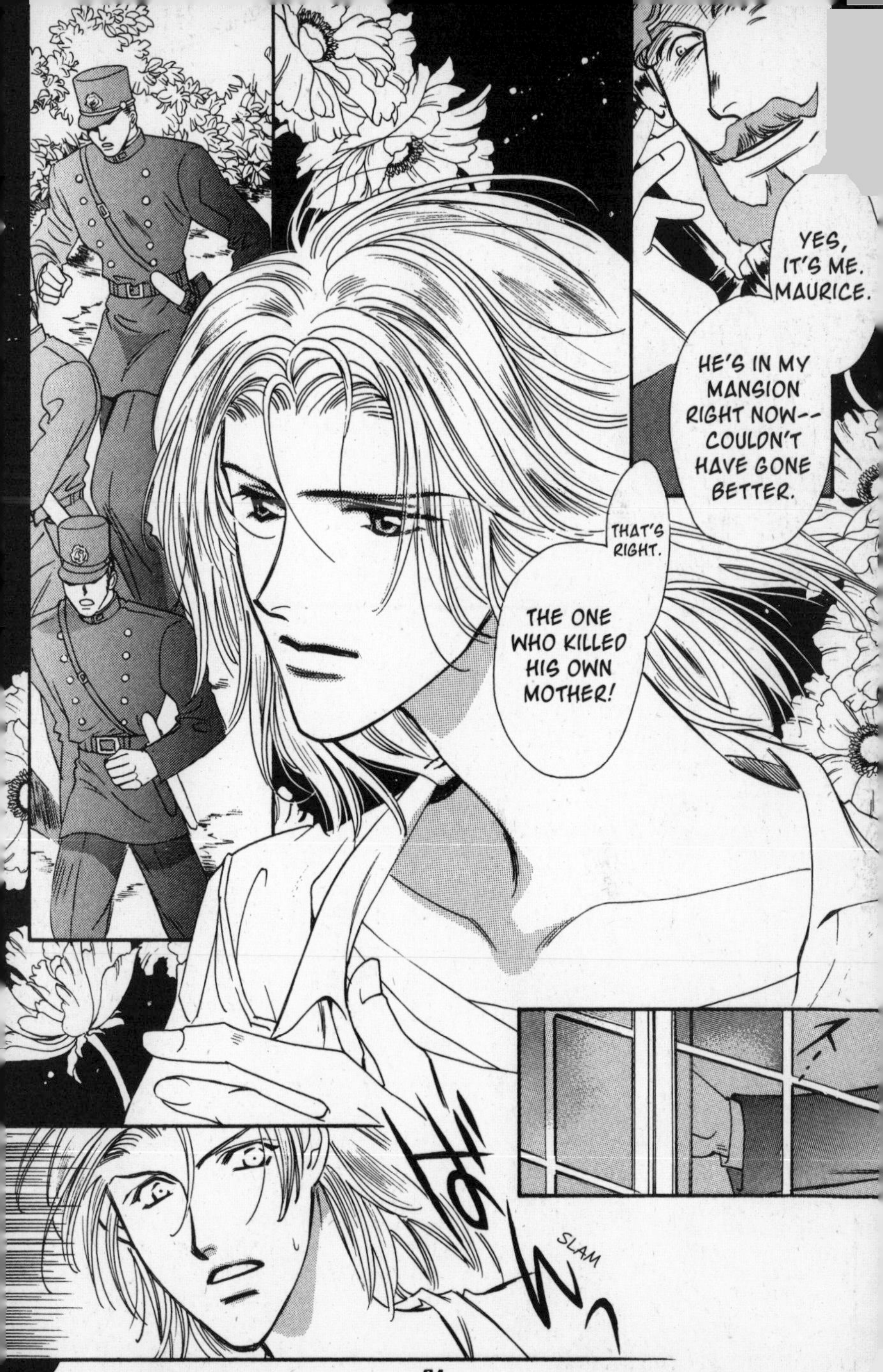
YES, IT'S ME. MAURICE.
HE'S IN MY MANSION RIGHT NOW-- COULDN'T HAVE GONE BETTER.
THAT'S RIGHT.
THE ONE WHO KILLED HIS OWN MOTHER!
SLAM

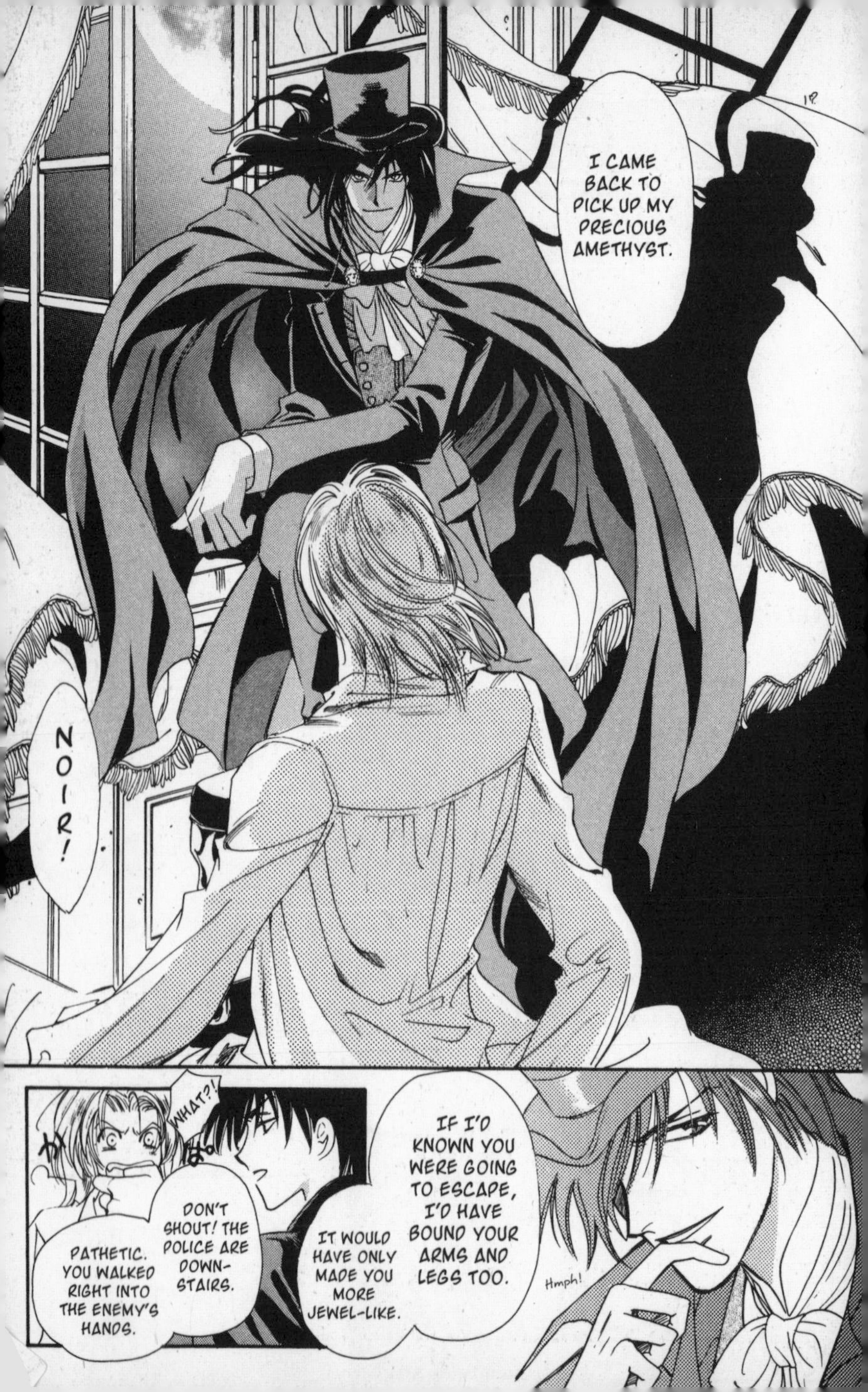
I CAME BACK TO PICK UP MY PRECIOUS AMETHYST.
NOIR!
IF I'D KNOWN YOU WERE GOING TO ESCAPE, I'D HAVE BOUND YOUR ARMS AND LEGS TOO.
Hmph!
IT WOULD HAVE ONLY MADE YOU MORE JEWEL-LIKE.
WHAT?!
DON'T SHOUT! THE POLICE ARE DOWN-STAIRS.
PATHETIC. YOU WALKED RIGHT INTO THE ENEMY'S HANDS.

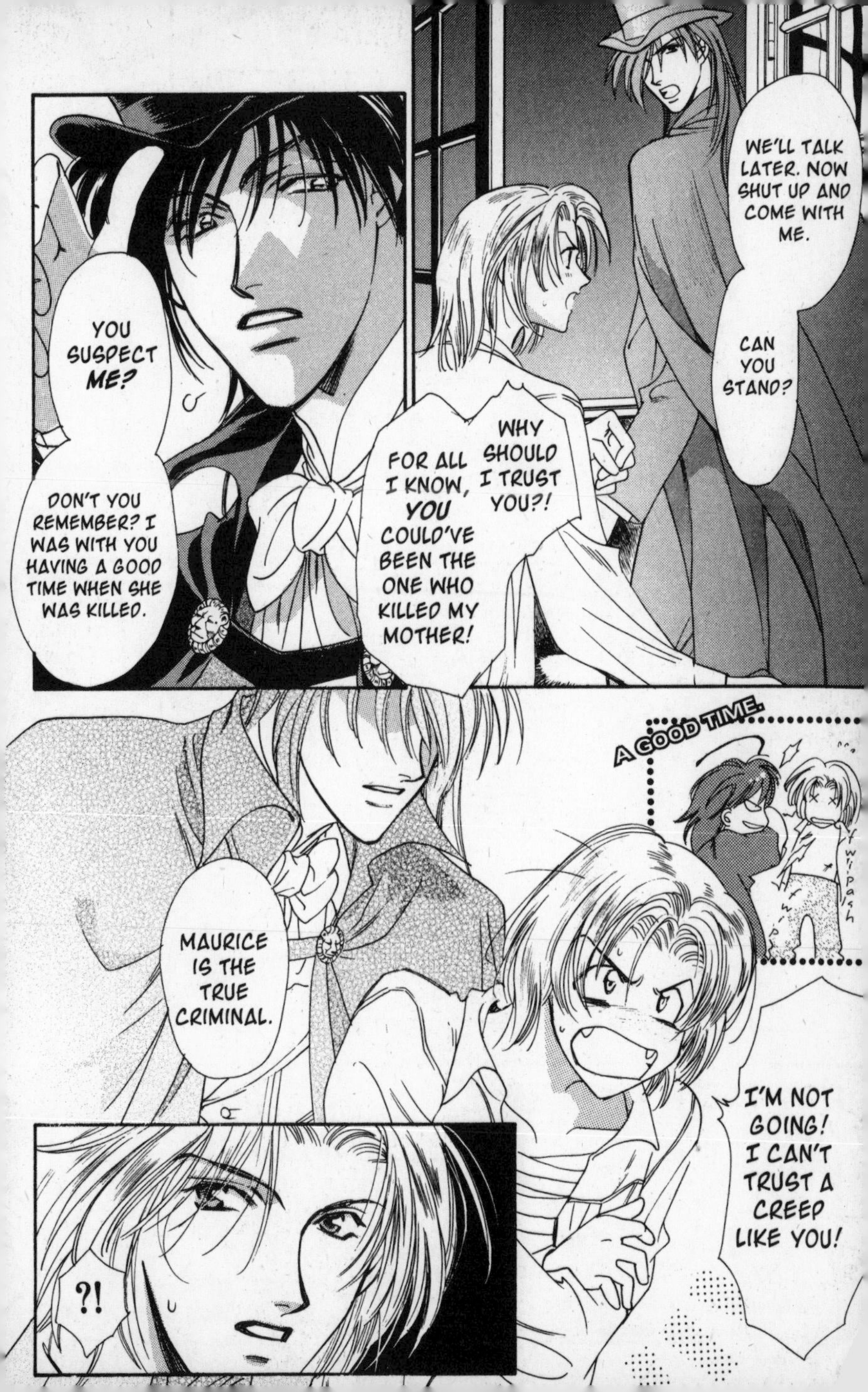
WE'LL TALK LATER. NOW SHUT UP AND COME WITH ME.
CAN YOU STAND?
WHY SHOULD I TRUST YOU?!
FOR ALL I KNOW, YOU COULD'VE BEEN THE ONE WHO KILLED MY MOTHER!
YOU SUSPECT ME?
DON'T YOU REMEMBER? I WAS WITH YOU HAVING A GOOD TIME WHEN SHE WAS KILLED.
A GOOD TIME.
fwipash
I'M NOT GOING! I CAN'T TRUST A CREEP LIKE YOU!
MAURICE IS THE TRUE CRIMINAL.
?!

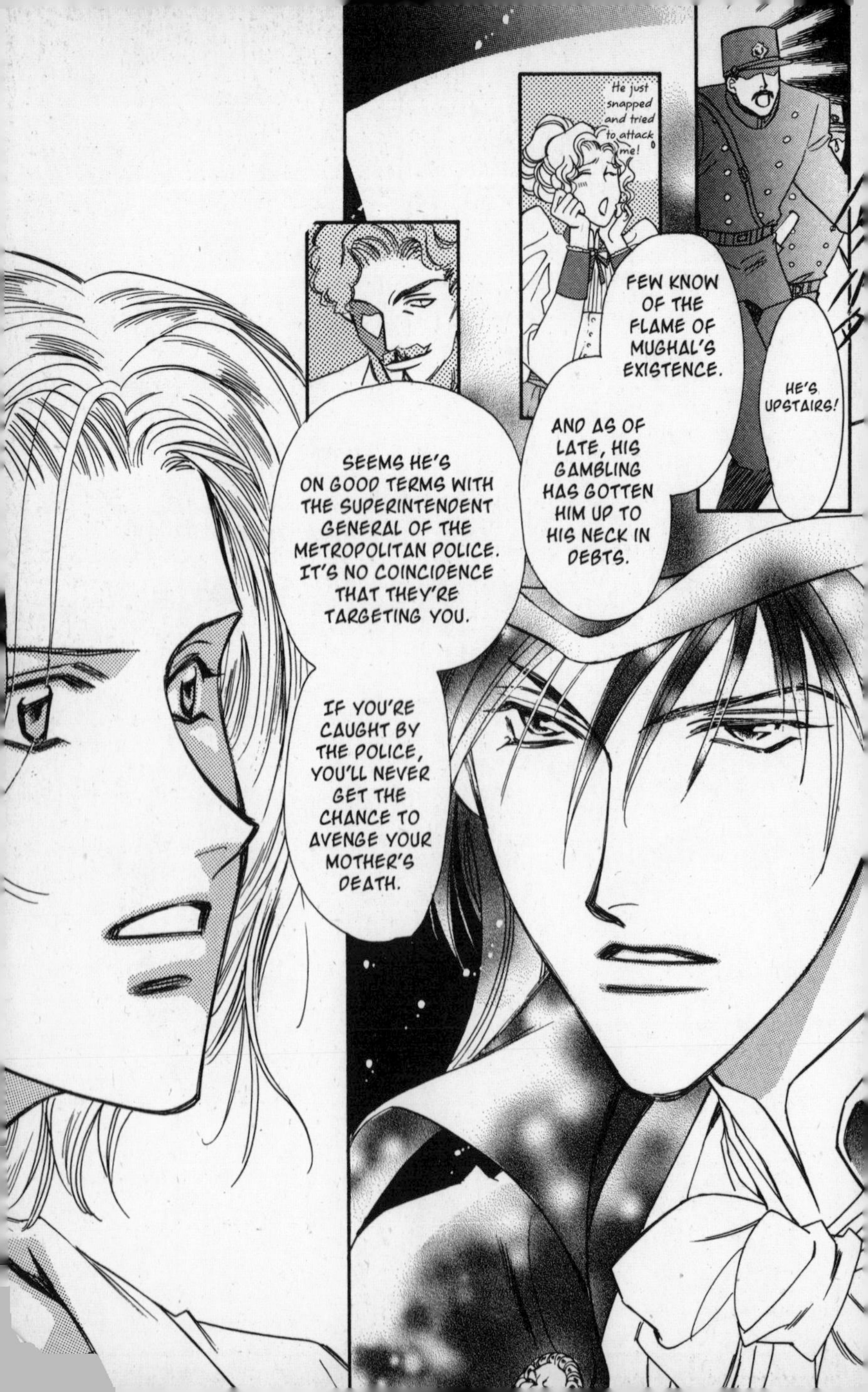
HE'S UPSTAIRS!
He just snapped and tried to attack me!
FEW KNOW OF THE FLAME OF MUGHAL'S EXISTENCE.
AND AS OF LATE, HIS GAMBLING HAS GOTTEN HIM UP TO HIS NECK IN DEBTS.
SEEMS HE'S ON GOOD TERMS WITH THE SUPERINTENDENT GENERAL OF THE METROPOLITAN POLICE. IT'S NO COINCIDENCE THAT THEY'RE TARGETING YOU.
IF YOU'RE CAUGHT BY THE POLICE, YOU'LL NEVER GET THE CHANCE TO AVENGE YOUR MOTHER'S DEATH.

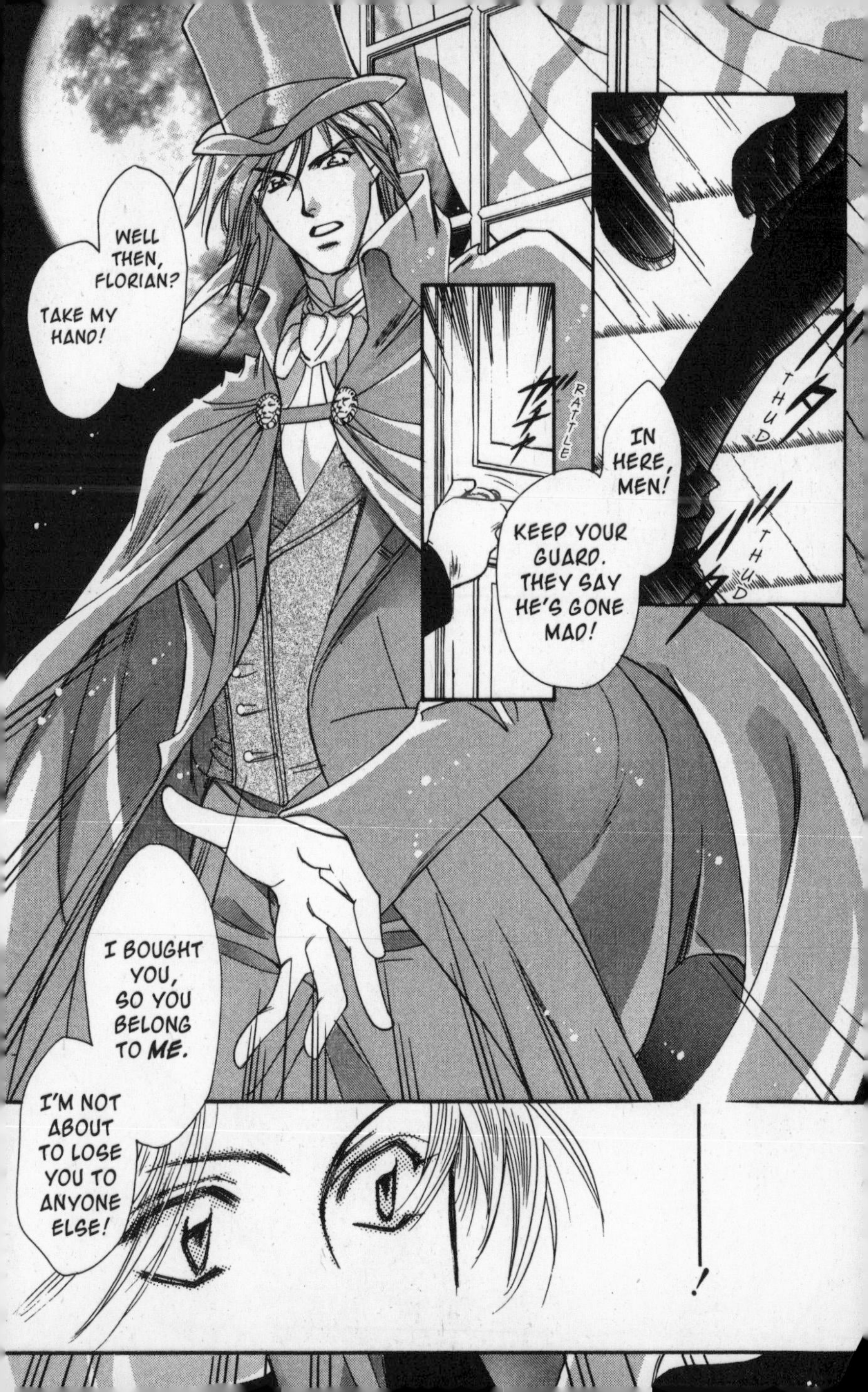
THUD
THUD
RATTLE
IN HERE, MEN!
KEEP YOUR GUARD. THEY SAY HE'S GONE MAD!
WELL THEN, FLORIAN?
TAKE MY HAND!
I BOUGHT YOU, SO YOU BELONG TO *ME*.
I'M NOT ABOUT TO LOSE YOU TO ANYONE ELSE!
!

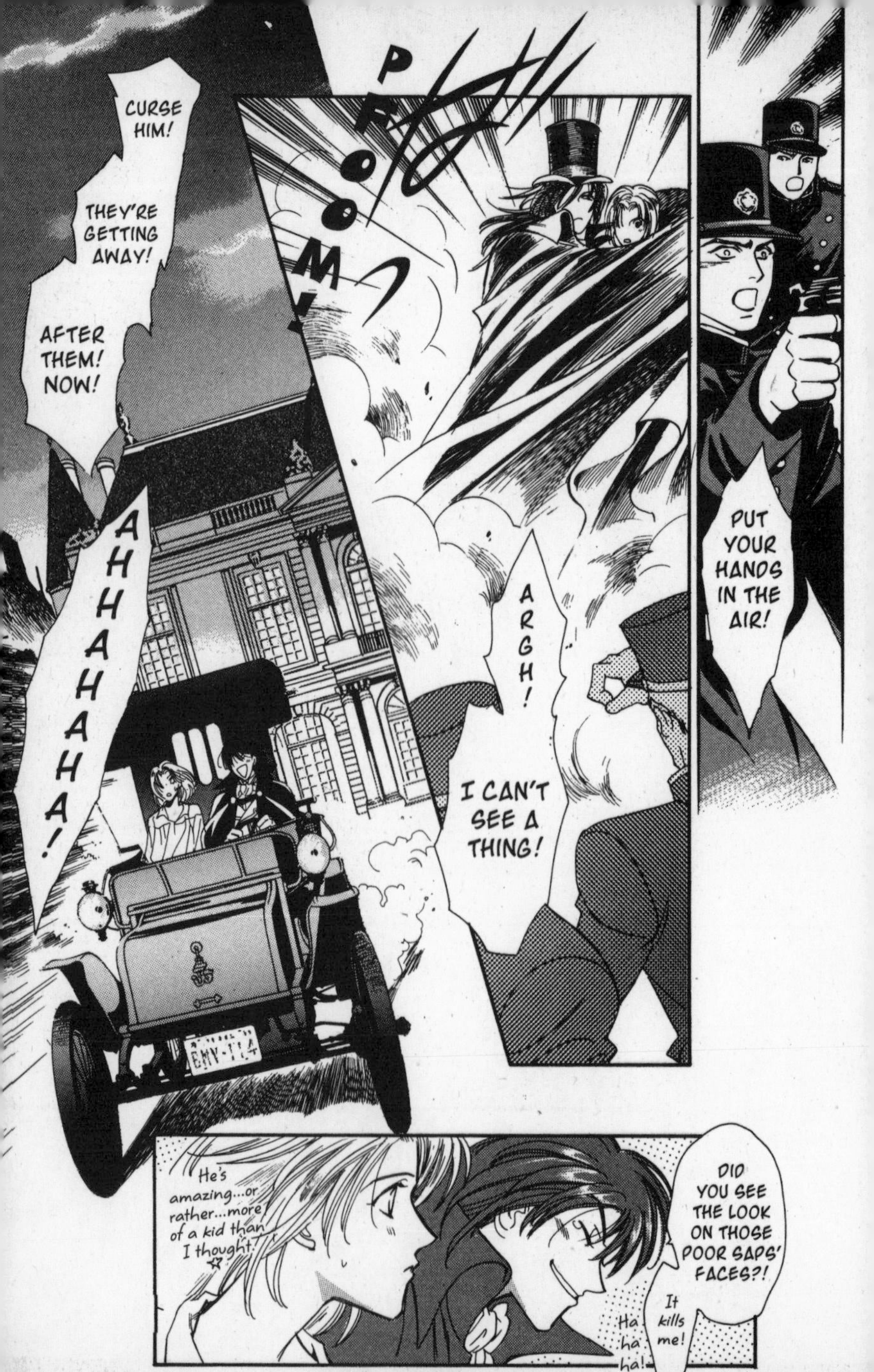
PUT YOUR HANDS IN THE AIR!
PFOOOM!
ARGH!
I CAN'T SEE A THING!
CURSE HIM!
THEY'RE GETTING AWAY!
AFTER THEM! NOW!
AHHAHAHAHA!
DID YOU SEE THE LOOK ON THOSE POOR SAPS' FACES?!
It kills me!
Ha ha ha!
He's amazing...or rather...more of a kid than I thought!

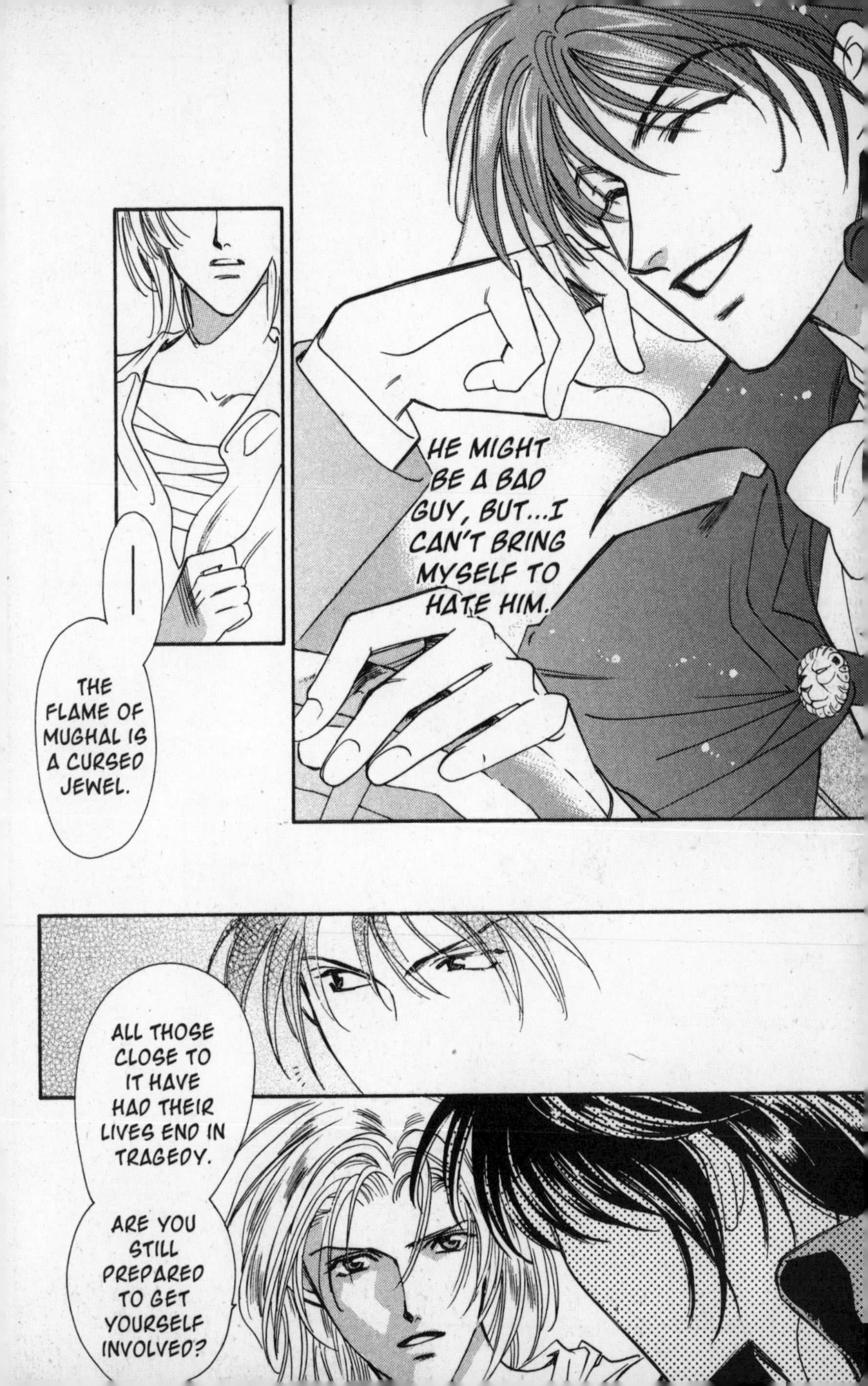
HE MIGHT BE A BAD GUY, BUT...I CAN'T BRING MYSELF TO HATE HIM.
THE FLAME OF MUGHAL IS A CURSED JEWEL.
ALL THOSE CLOSE TO IT HAVE HAD THEIR LIVES END IN TRAGEDY.
ARE YOU STILL PREPARED TO GET YOURSELF INVOLVED?

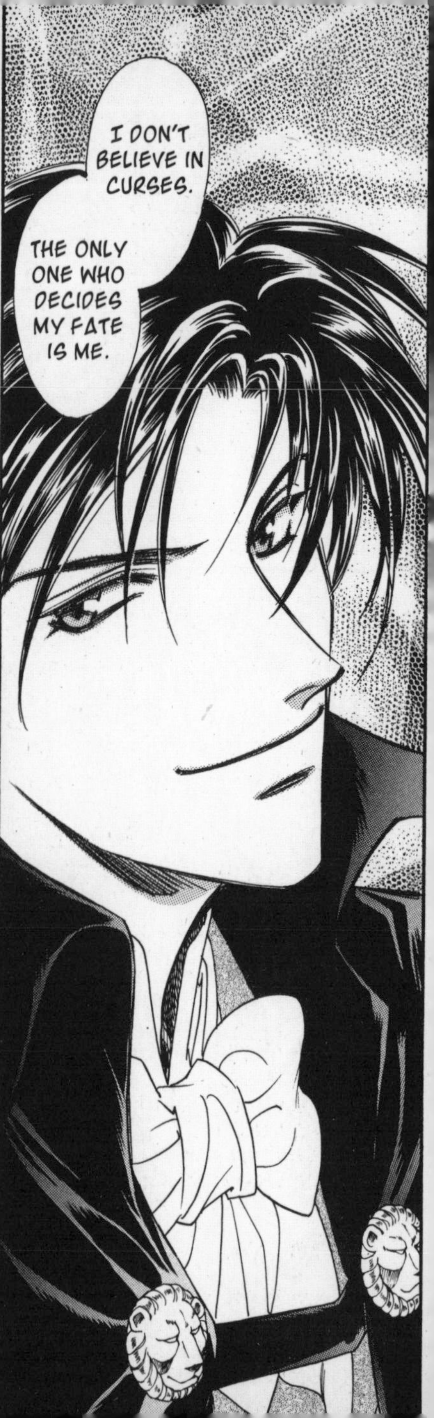
I DON'T BELIEVE IN CURSES.
THE ONLY ONE WHO DECIDES MY FATE IS ME.

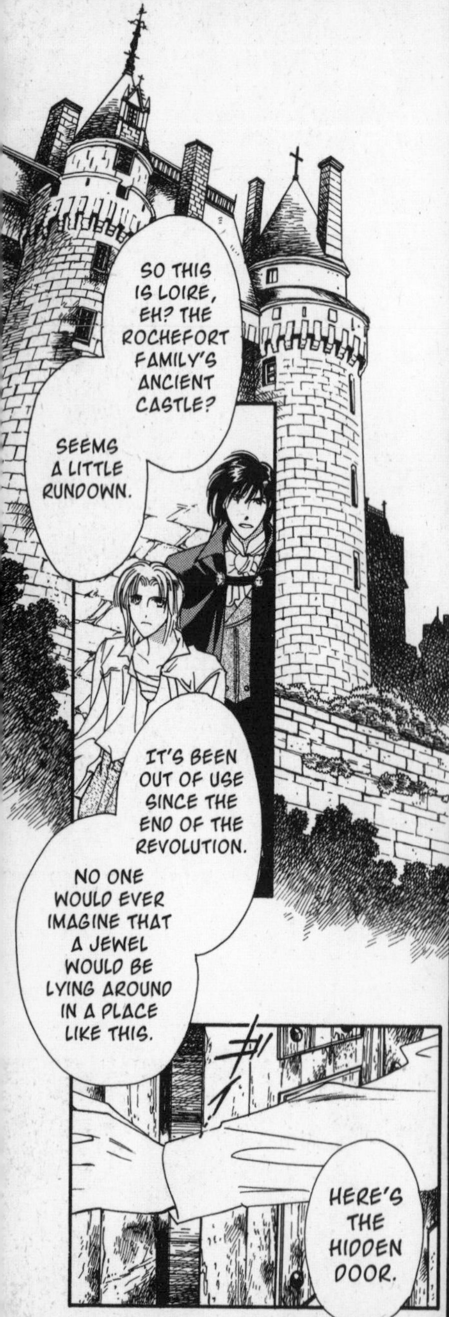
SO THIS IS LOIRE, EH? THE ROCHEFORT FAMILY'S ANCIENT CASTLE?
SEEMS A LITTLE RUNDOWN.
IT'S BEEN OUT OF USE SINCE THE END OF THE REVOLUTION.
NO ONE WOULD EVER IMAGINE THAT A JEWEL WOULD BE LYING AROUND IN A PLACE LIKE THIS.
HERE'S THE HIDDEN DOOR.

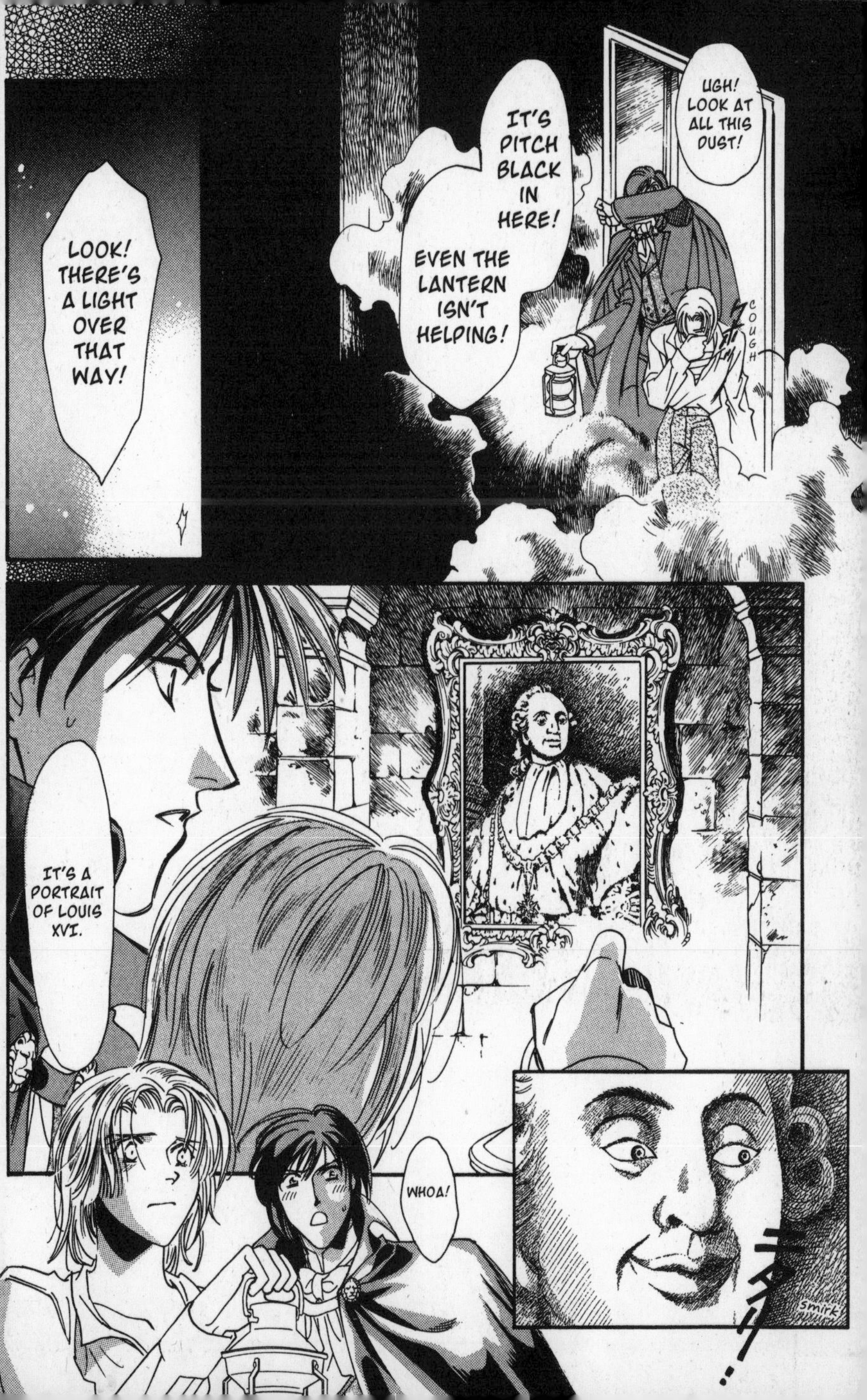
UGH! LOOK AT ALL THIS DUST!
IT'S PITCH BLACK IN HERE!
EVEN THE LANTERN ISN'T HELPING!
COUGH
LOOK! THERE'S A LIGHT OVER THAT WAY!
IT'S A PORTRAIT OF LOUIS XVI.
WHOA!
smirk

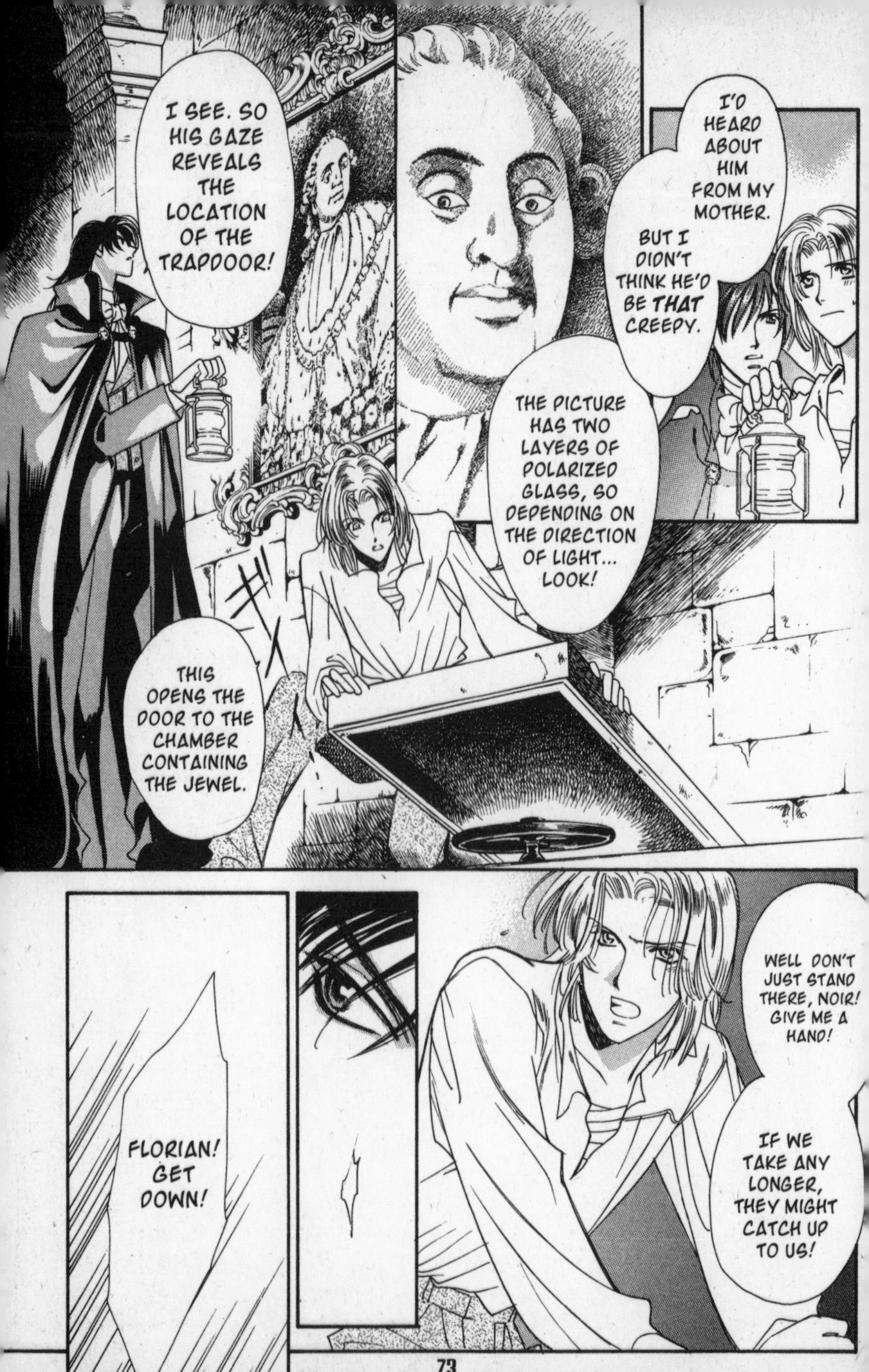
I'D HEARD ABOUT HIM FROM MY MOTHER.
BUT I DIDN'T THINK HE'D BE **THAT** CREEPY.
THE PICTURE HAS TWO LAYERS OF POLARIZED GLASS, SO DEPENDING ON THE DIRECTION OF LIGHT... LOOK!
I SEE. SO HIS GAZE REVEALS THE LOCATION OF THE TRAPDOOR!
THIS OPENS THE DOOR TO THE CHAMBER CONTAINING THE JEWEL.
WELL DON'T JUST STAND THERE, NOIR! GIVE ME A HAND!
IF WE TAKE ANY LONGER, THEY MIGHT CATCH UP TO US!
FLORIAN! GET DOWN!

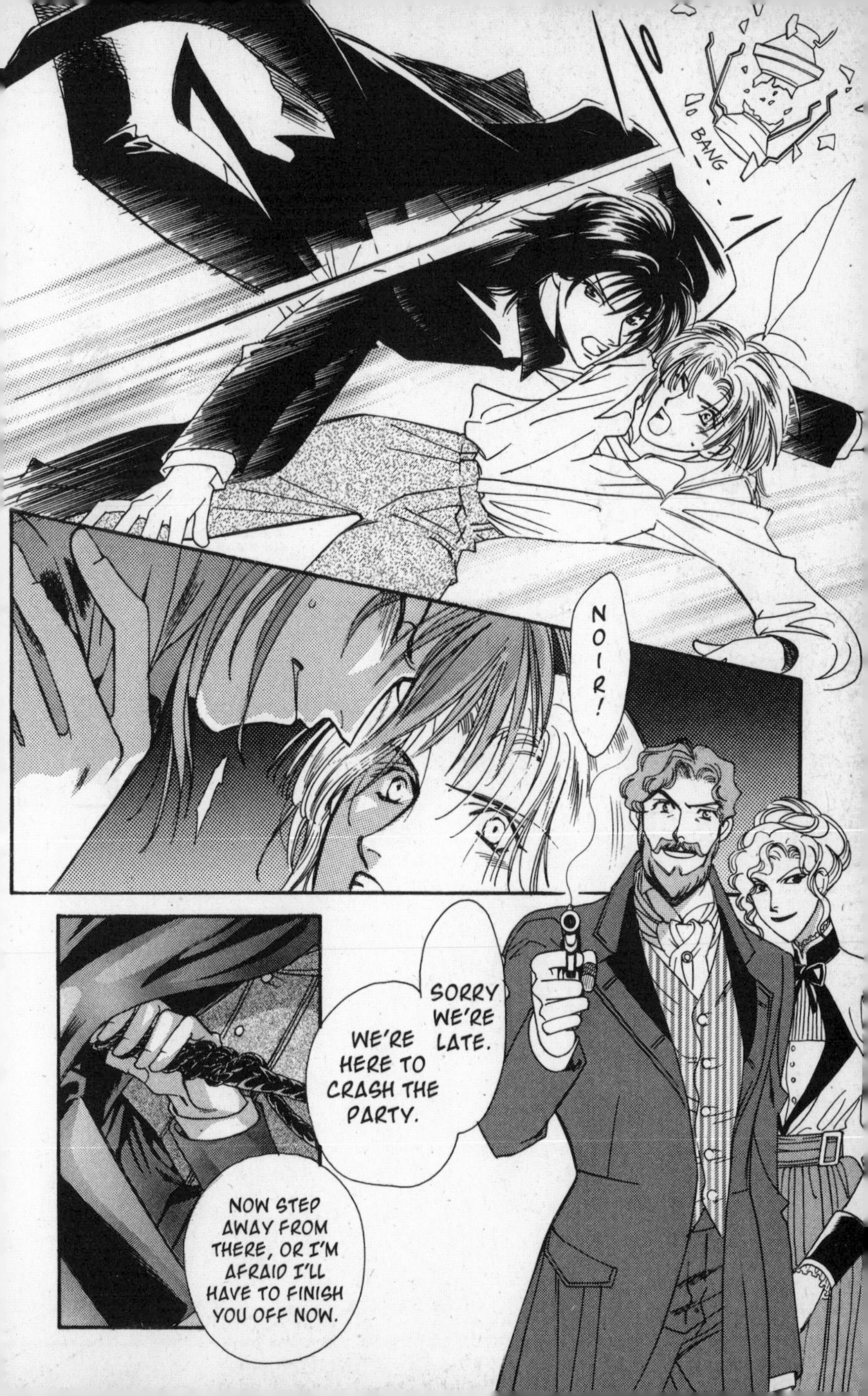
BANG
NOIR!
SORRY WE'RE LATE.
WE'RE HERE TO CRASH THE PARTY.
NOW STEP AWAY FROM THERE, OR I'M AFRAID I'LL HAVE TO FINISH YOU OFF NOW.

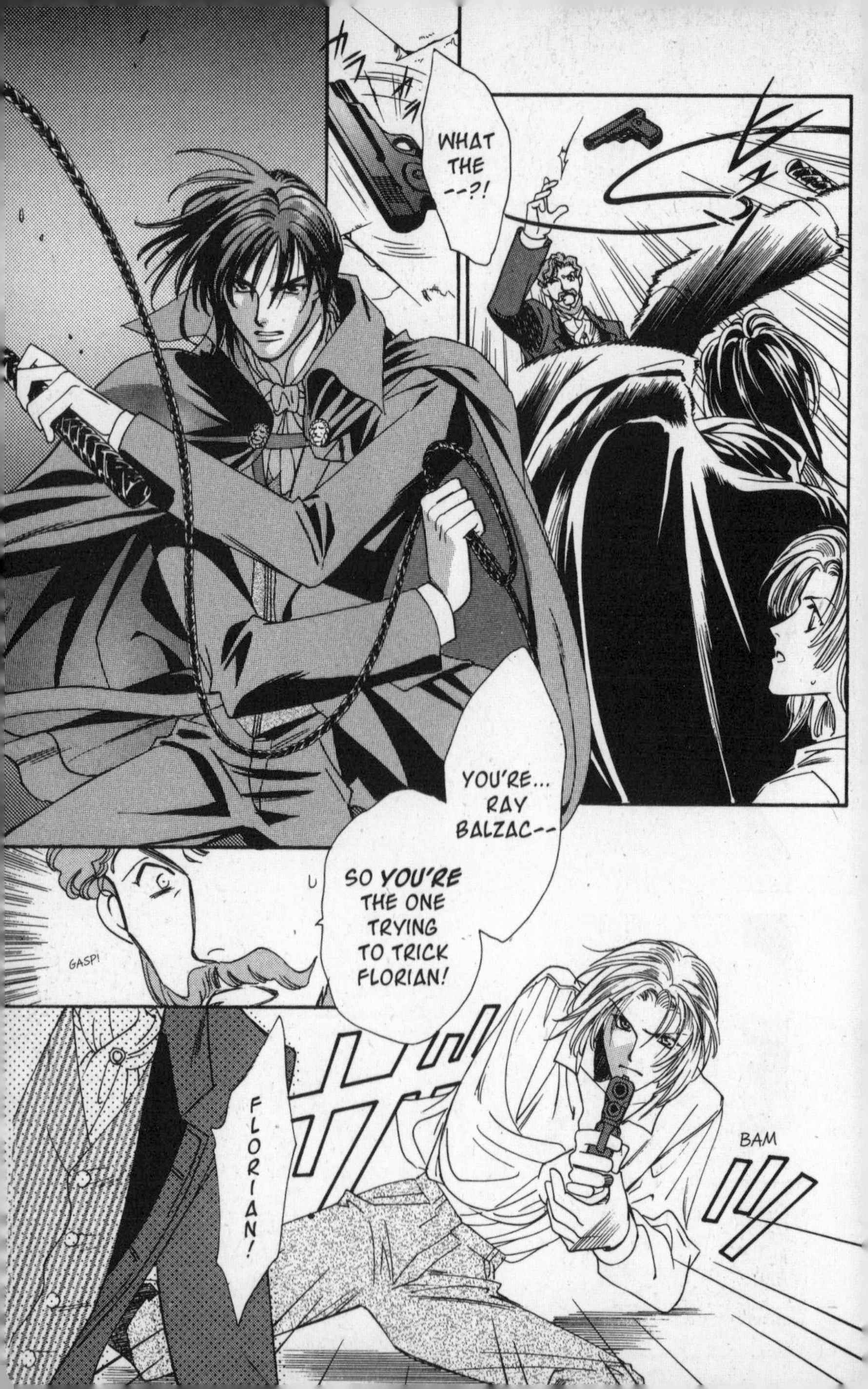
WHAT THE --?!
YOU'RE... RAY BALZAC--
SO *YOU'RE* THE ONE TRYING TO TRICK FLORIAN!
GASP!
BAM
FLORIAN!

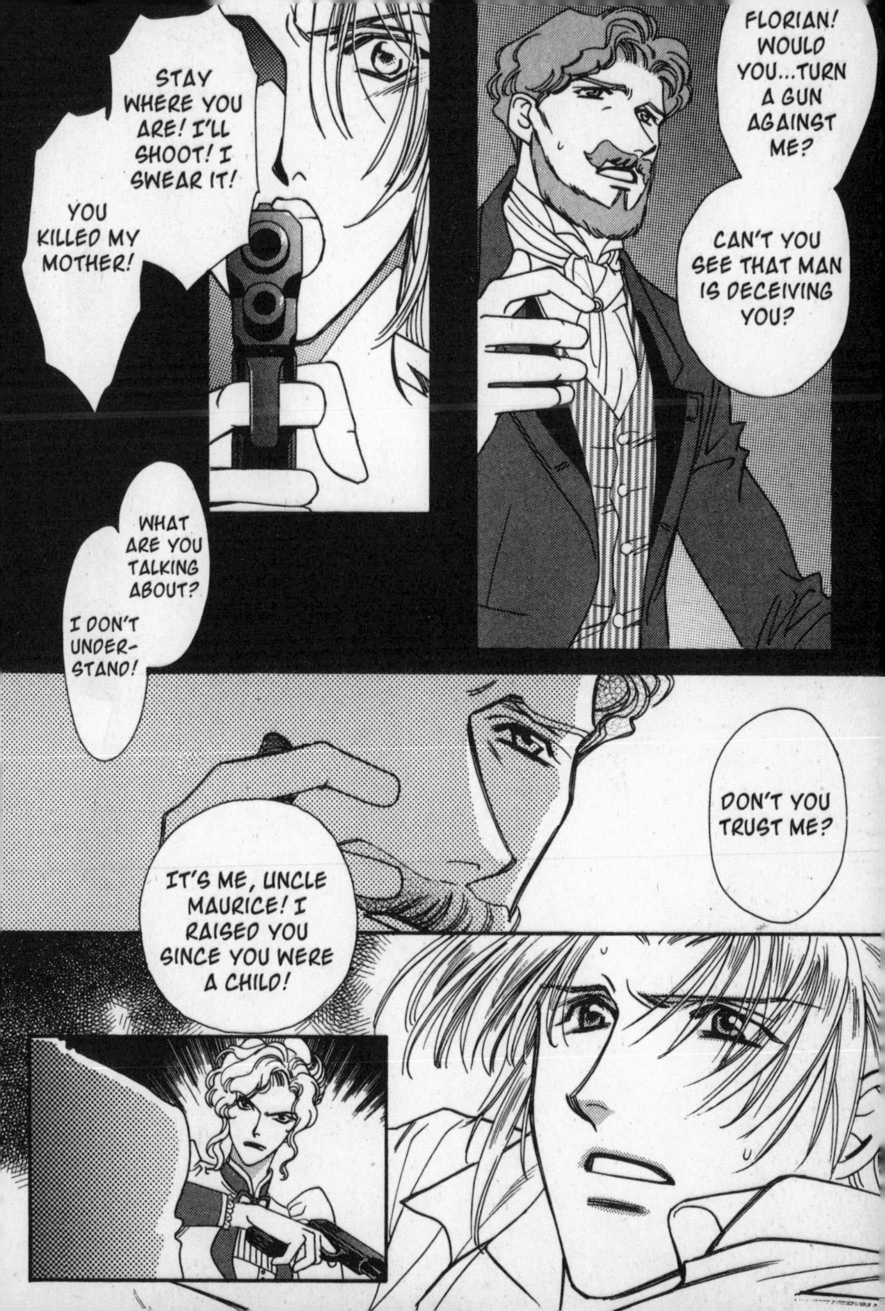
FLORIAN! WOULD YOU...TURN A GUN AGAINST ME?
CAN'T YOU SEE THAT MAN IS DECEIVING YOU?
STAY WHERE YOU ARE! I'LL SHOOT! I SWEAR IT!
YOU KILLED MY MOTHER!
WHAT ARE YOU TALKING ABOUT?
I DON'T UNDER-STAND!
DON'T YOU TRUST ME?
IT'S ME, UNCLE MAURICE! I RAISED YOU SINCE YOU WERE A CHILD!

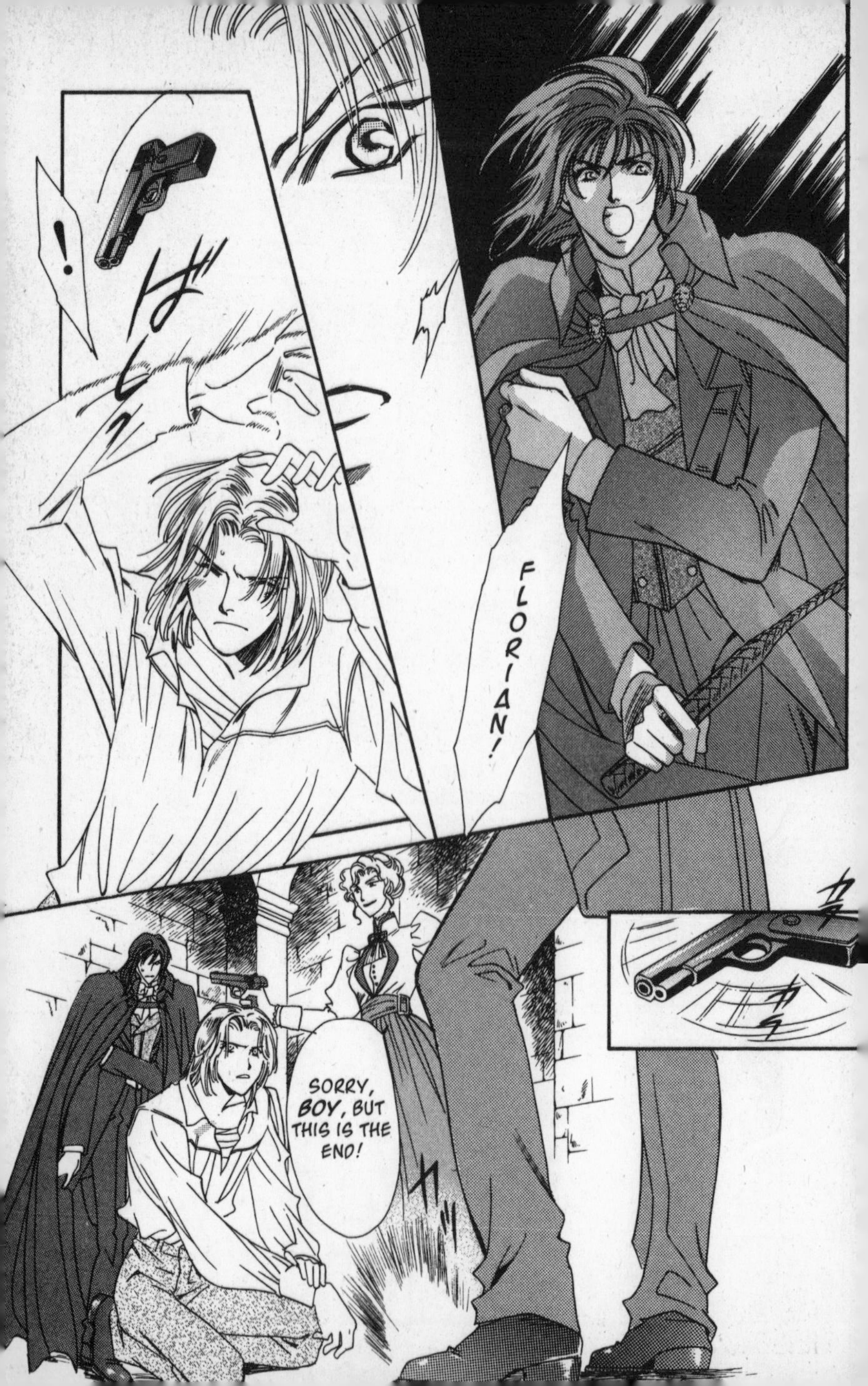
FLORIAN!
!
ばしっ
SORRY, BOY, BUT THIS IS THE END!

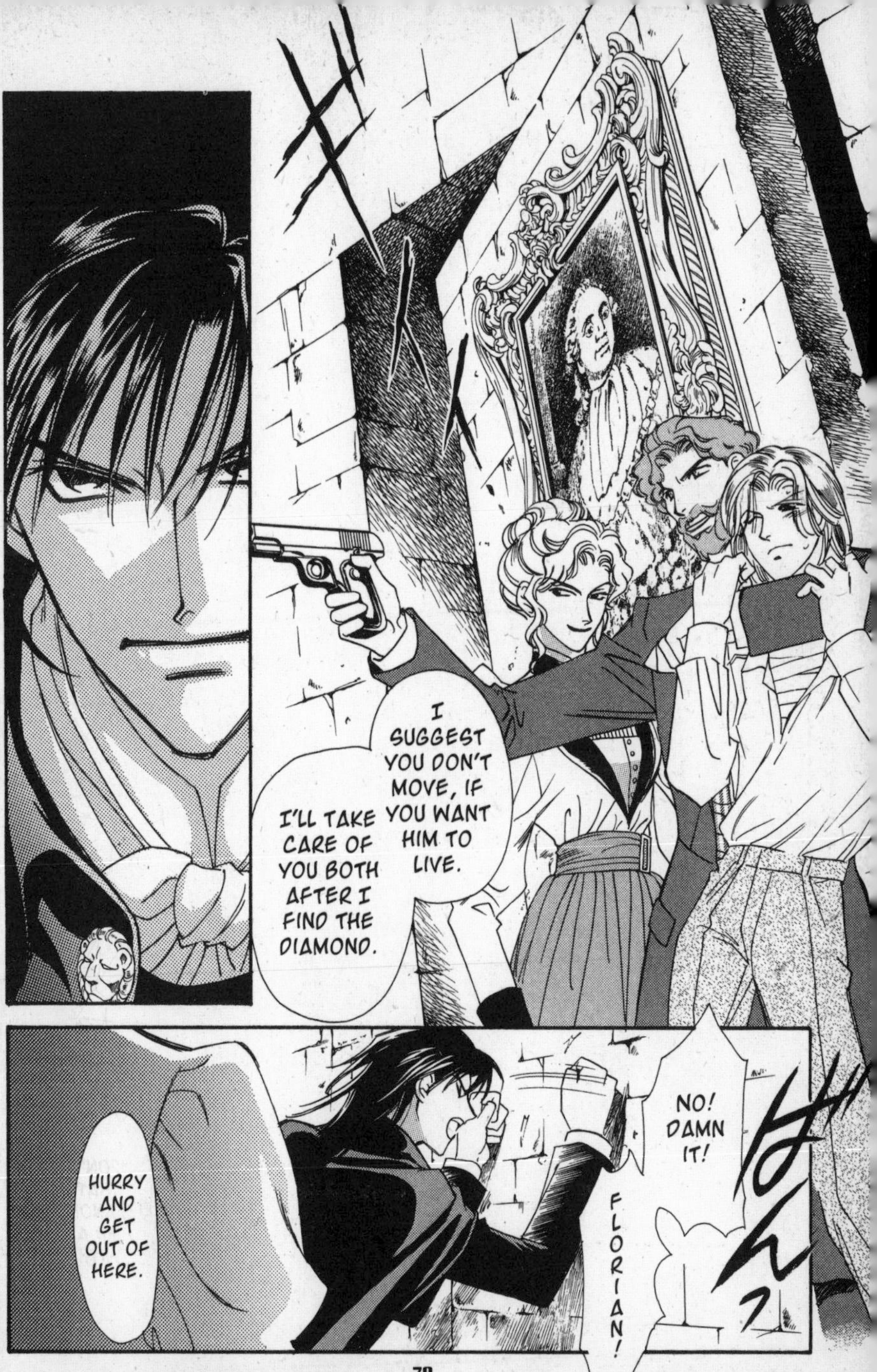
I SUGGEST YOU DON'T MOVE, IF YOU WANT HIM TO LIVE.
I'LL TAKE CARE OF YOU BOTH AFTER I FIND THE DIAMOND.
NO! DAMN IT!
FLORIAN!
HURRY AND GET OUT OF HERE.

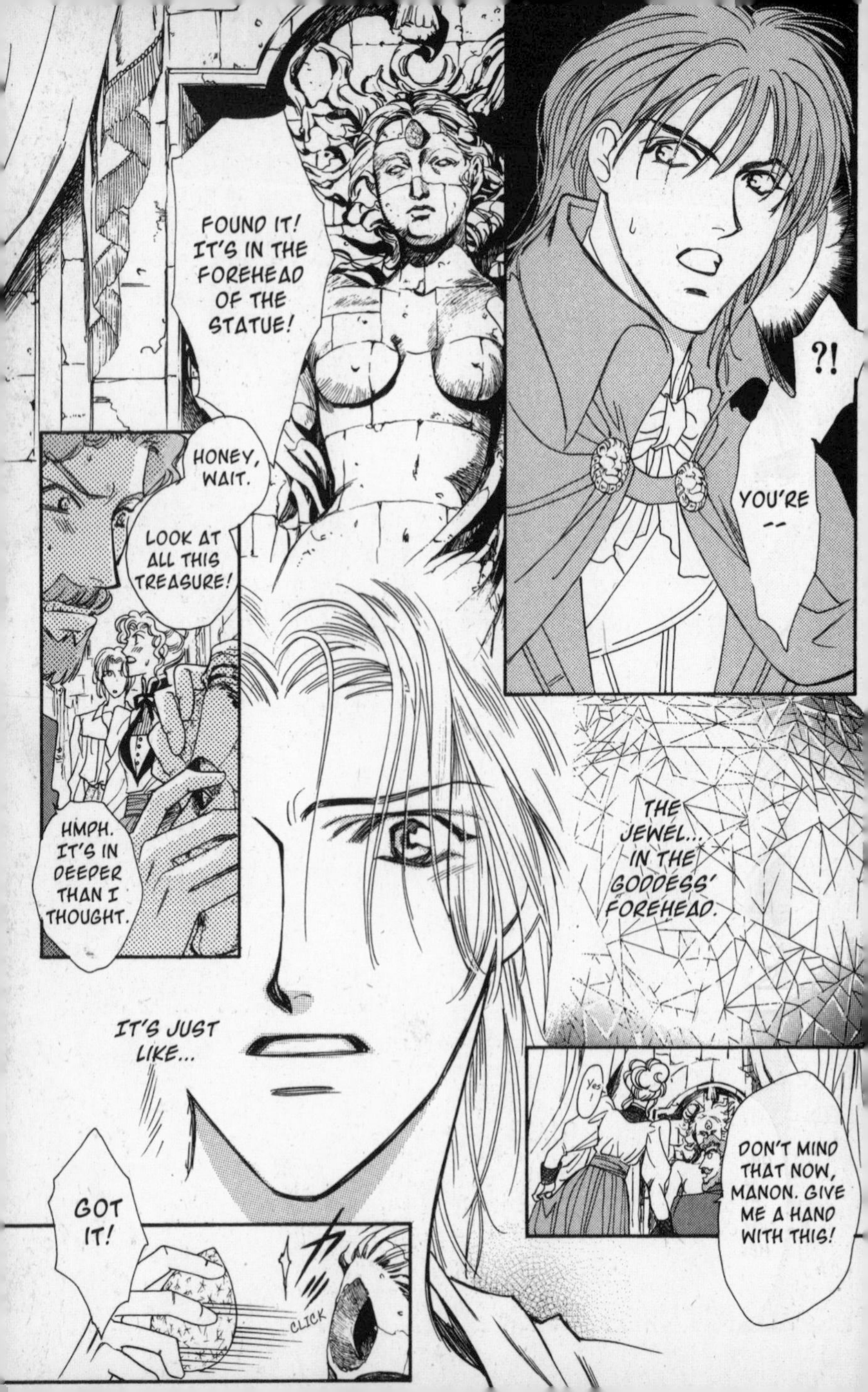
?!
YOU'RE --
FOUND IT! IT'S IN THE FOREHEAD OF THE STATUE!
HONEY, WAIT.
LOOK AT ALL THIS TREASURE!
HMPH. IT'S IN DEEPER THAN I THOUGHT.
THE JEWEL... IN THE GODDESS' FOREHEAD.
IT'S JUST LIKE...
Yes!
DON'T MIND THAT NOW, MANON. GIVE ME A HAND WITH THIS!
GOT IT!
CLICK

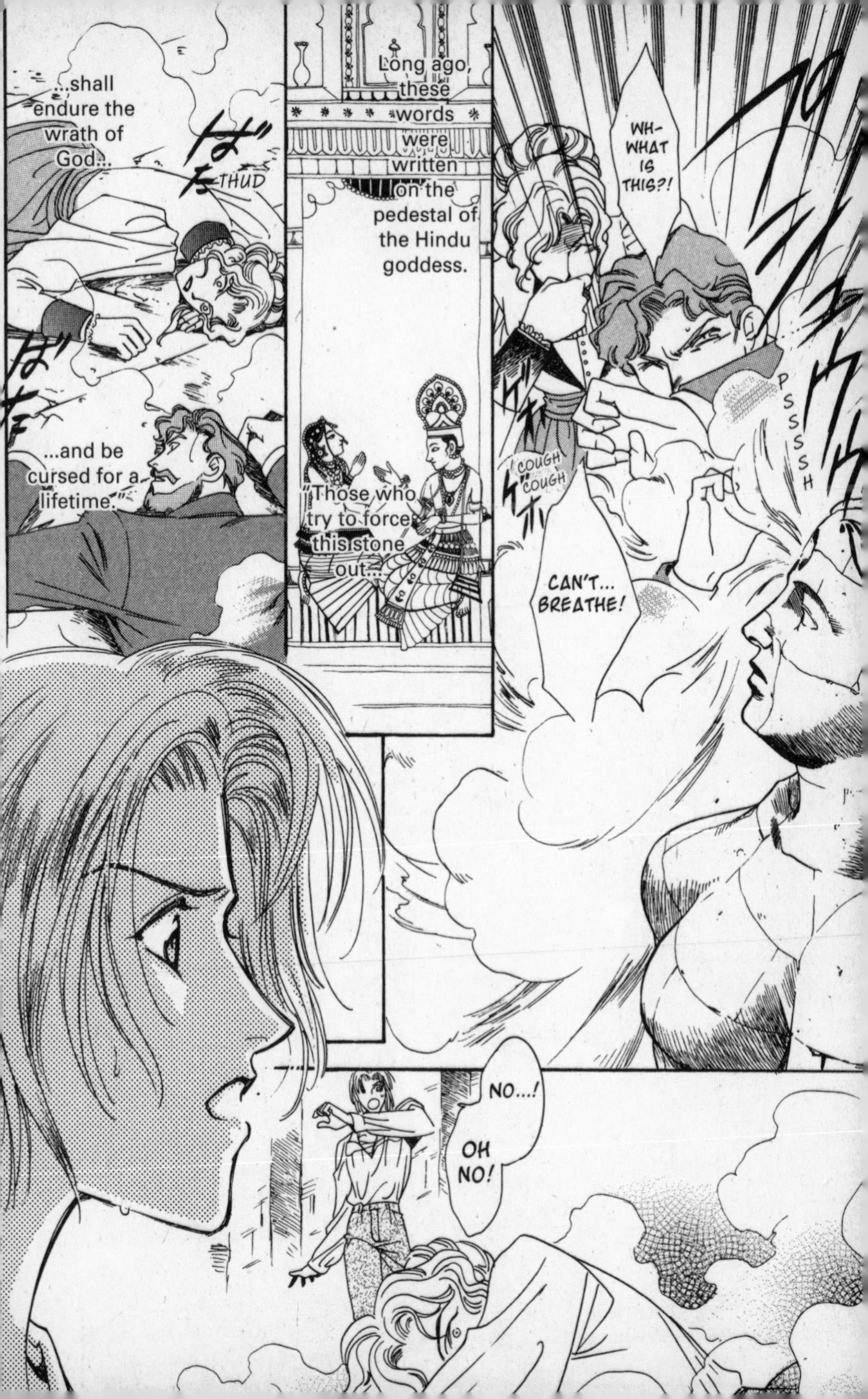
WH-WHAT IS THIS?!
PSSSSH
COUGH COUGH
CAN'T... BREATHE!
Long ago, these words were written on the pedestal of the Hindu goddess.
"Those who try to force this stone out...
THUD
...shall endure the wrath of God...
...and be cursed for a lifetime."
NO...!
OH NO!

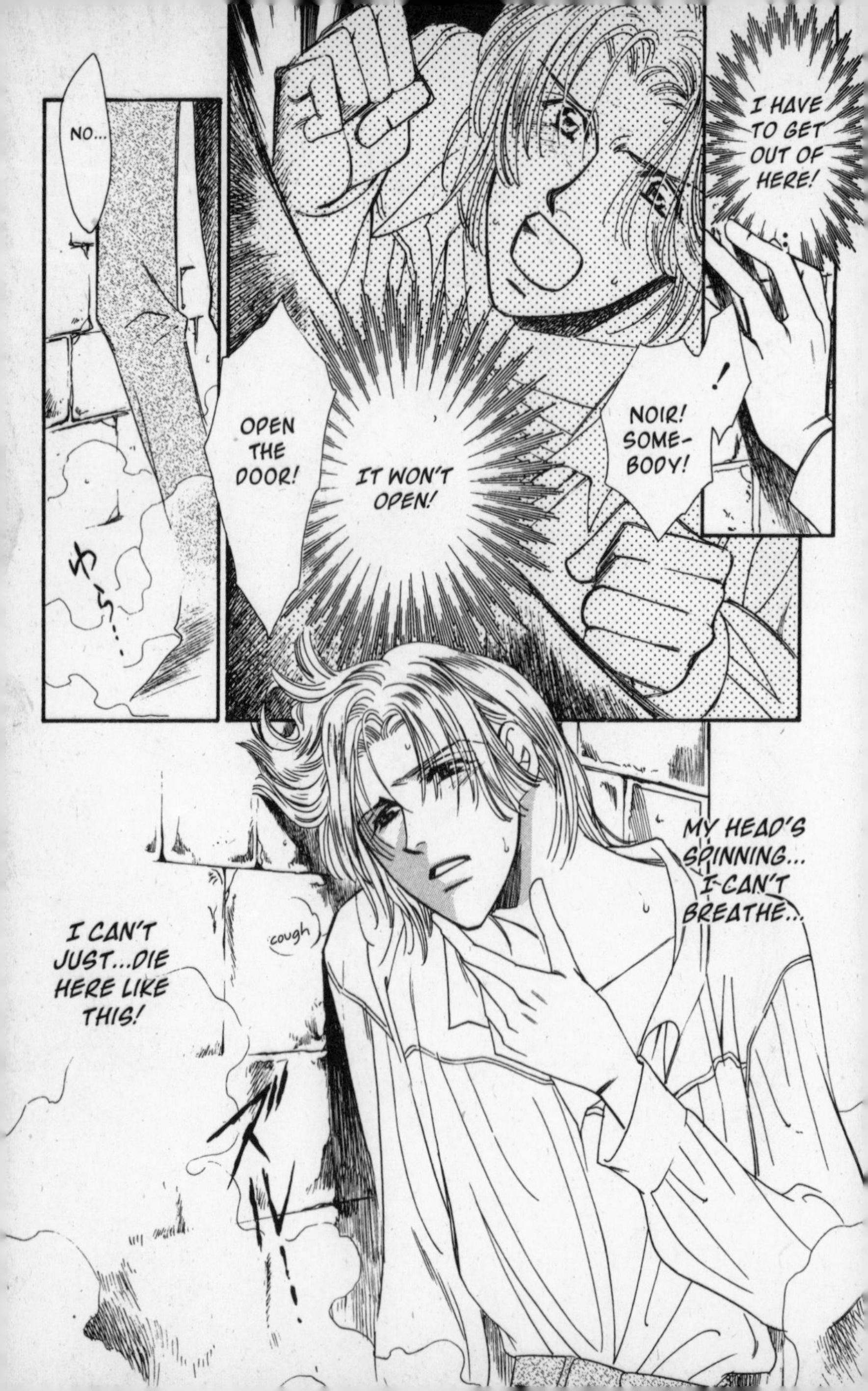
I HAVE TO GET OUT OF HERE!
!
NOIR! SOME-BODY!
IT WON'T OPEN!
OPEN THE DOOR!
NO...
ゆら...
MY HEAD'S SPINNING... I CAN'T BREATHE...
cough
I CAN'T JUST...DIE HERE LIKE THIS!

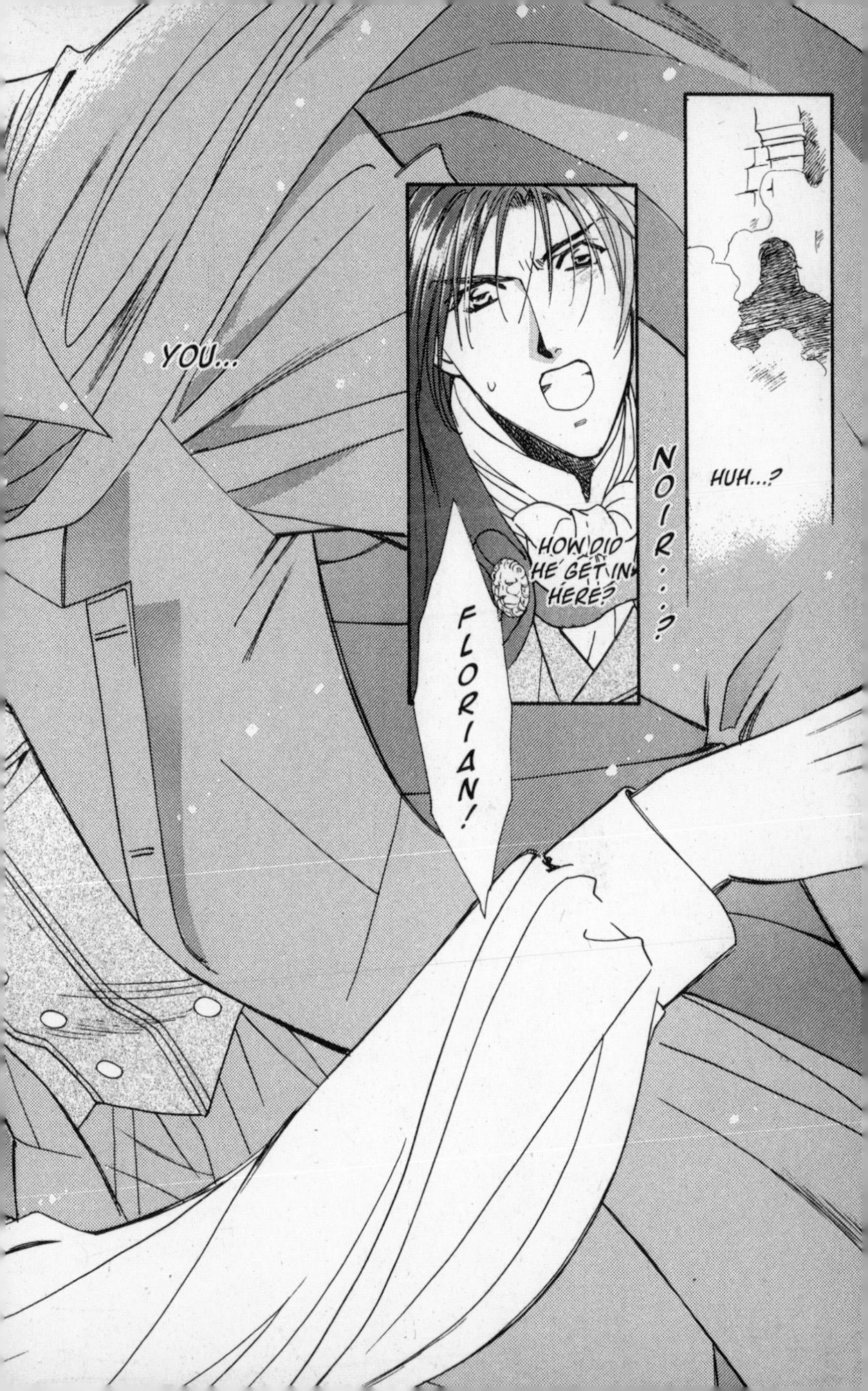
HUH...?
NOIR...?
HOW DID HE GET IN HERE?
FLORIAN!
YOU...

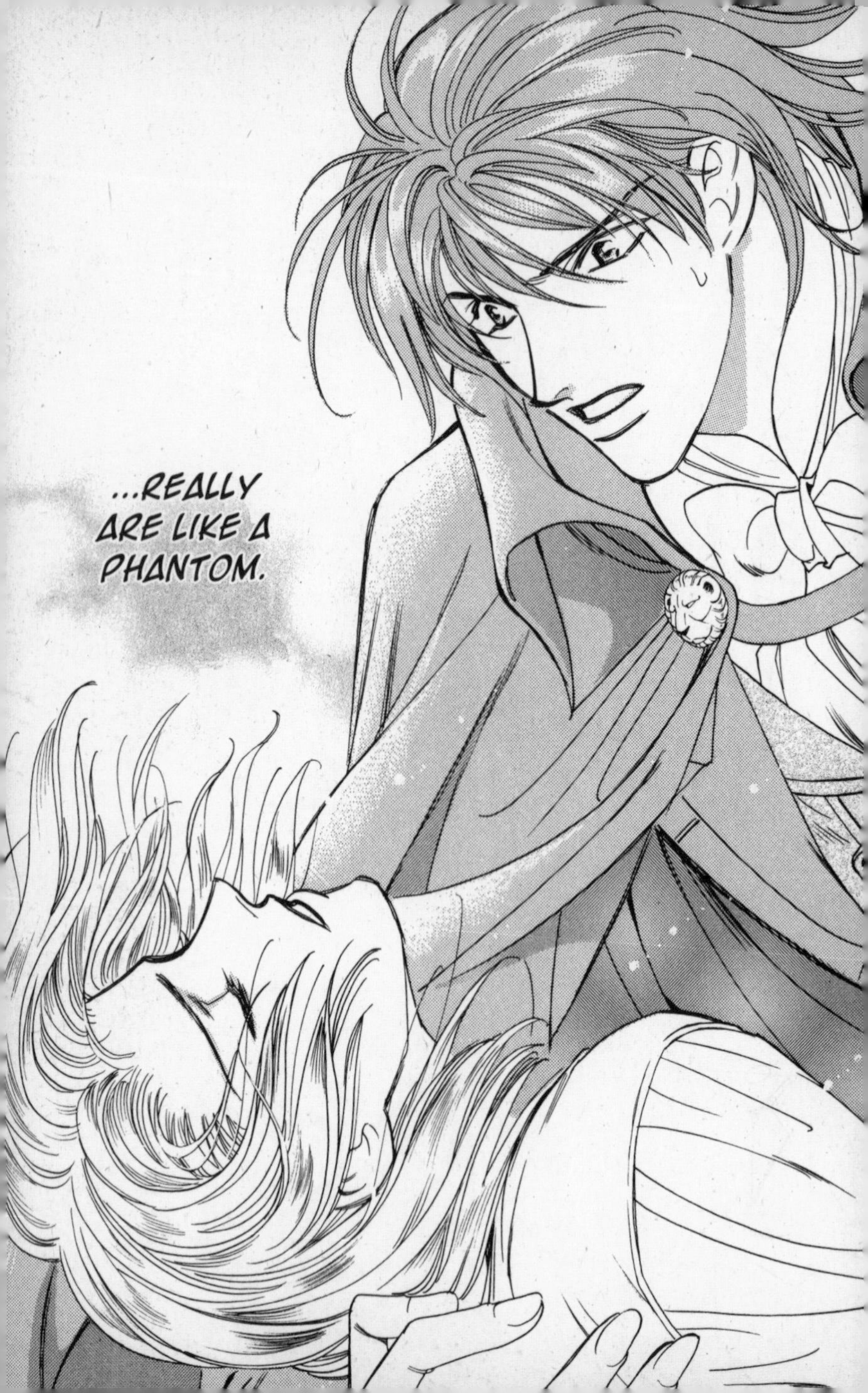
...REALLY ARE LIKE A PHANTOM.

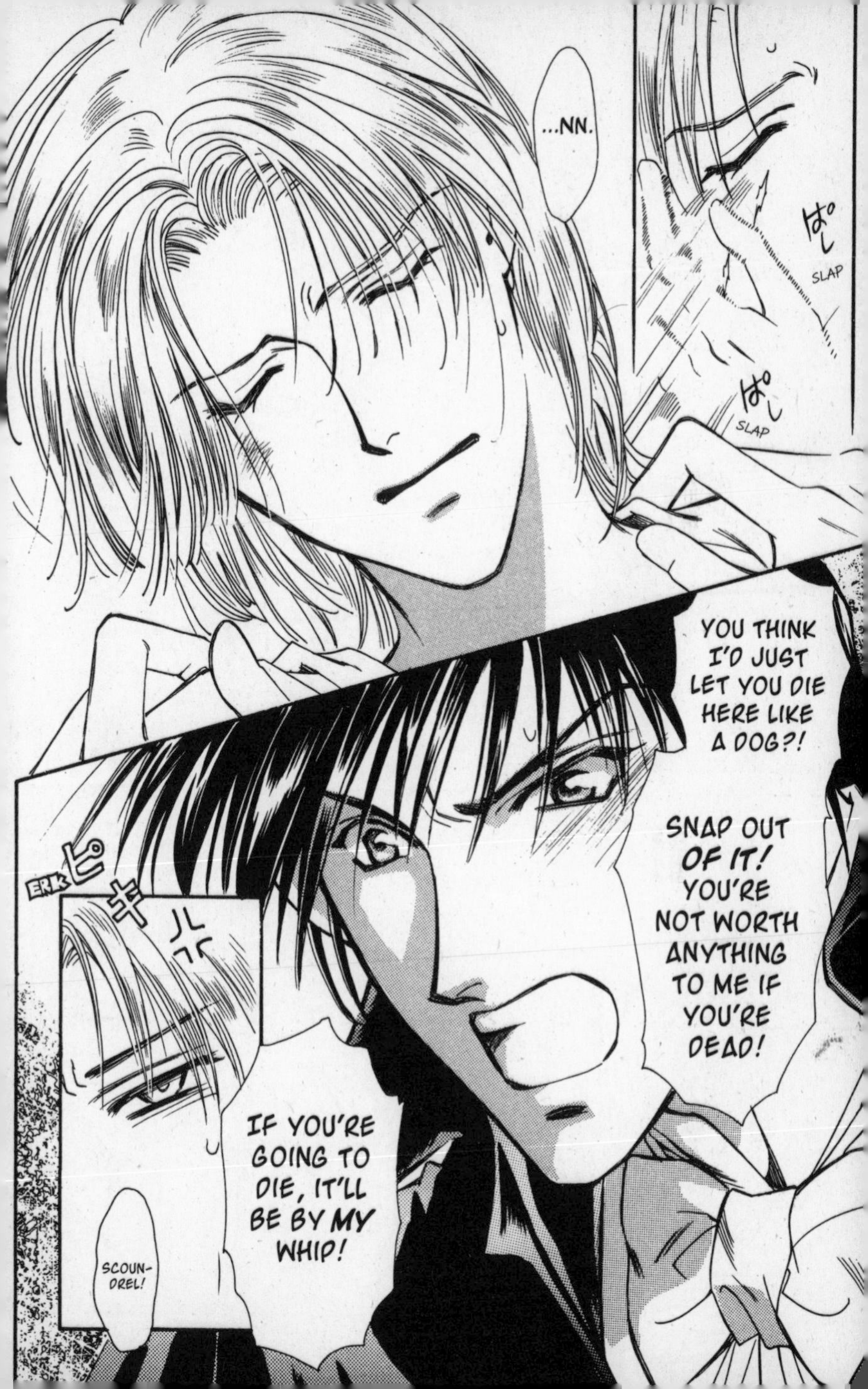
ぱし
SLAP
ぱし
SLAP
...NN.
YOU THINK I'D JUST LET YOU DIE HERE LIKE A DOG?!
SNAP OUT OF IT! YOU'RE NOT WORTH ANYTHING TO ME IF YOU'RE DEAD!
IF YOU'RE GOING TO DIE, IT'LL BE BY MY WHIP!
ピキ
ERK
SCOUN-DREL!

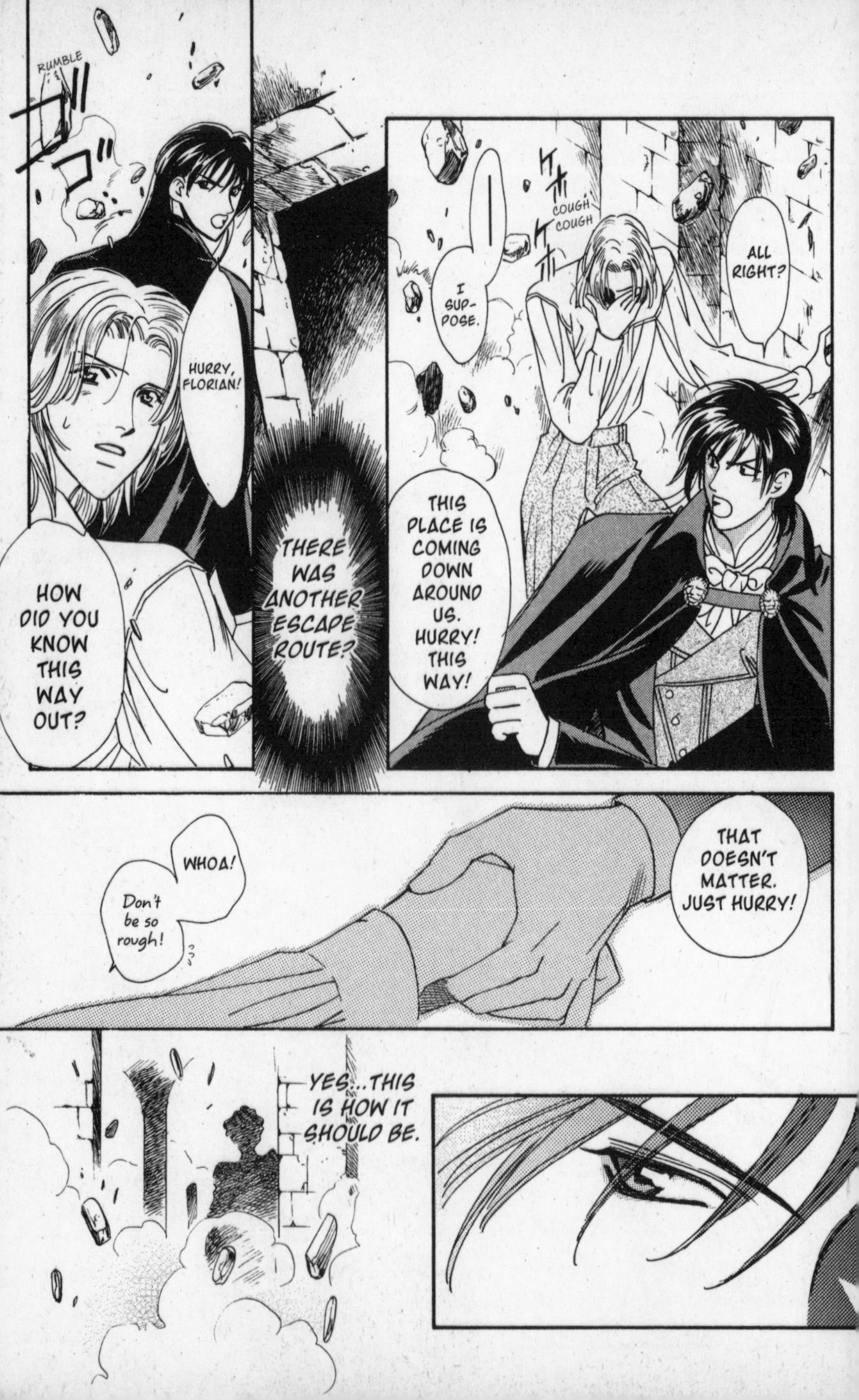
COUGH COUGH
ALL RIGHT?
I SUPPOSE.
THIS PLACE IS COMING DOWN AROUND US. HURRY! THIS WAY!
RUMBLE
HURRY, FLORIAN!
THERE WAS ANOTHER ESCAPE ROUTE?
HOW DID YOU KNOW THIS WAY OUT?
THAT DOESN'T MATTER. JUST HURRY!
WHOA!
Don't be so rough!
YES...THIS IS HOW IT SHOULD BE.

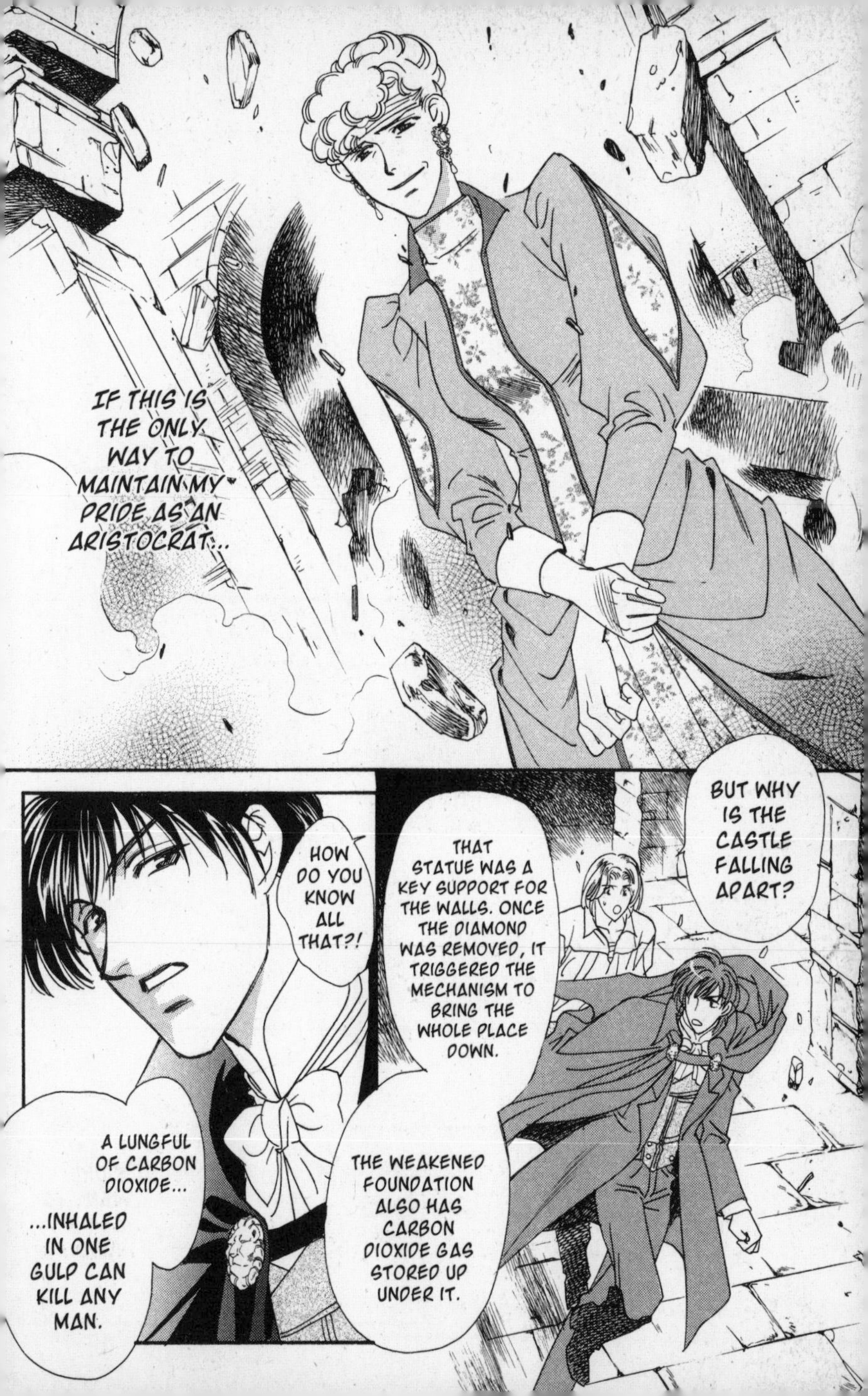
IF THIS IS THE ONLY WAY TO MAINTAIN MY PRIDE AS AN ARISTOCRAT...
BUT WHY IS THE CASTLE FALLING APART?
THAT STATUE WAS A KEY SUPPORT FOR THE WALLS. ONCE THE DIAMOND WAS REMOVED, IT TRIGGERED THE MECHANISM TO BRING THE WHOLE PLACE DOWN.
HOW DO YOU KNOW ALL THAT?!
THE WEAKENED FOUNDATION ALSO HAS CARBON DIOXIDE GAS STORED UP UNDER IT.
A LUNGFUL OF CARBON DIOXIDE...
...INHALED IN ONE GULP CAN KILL ANY MAN.

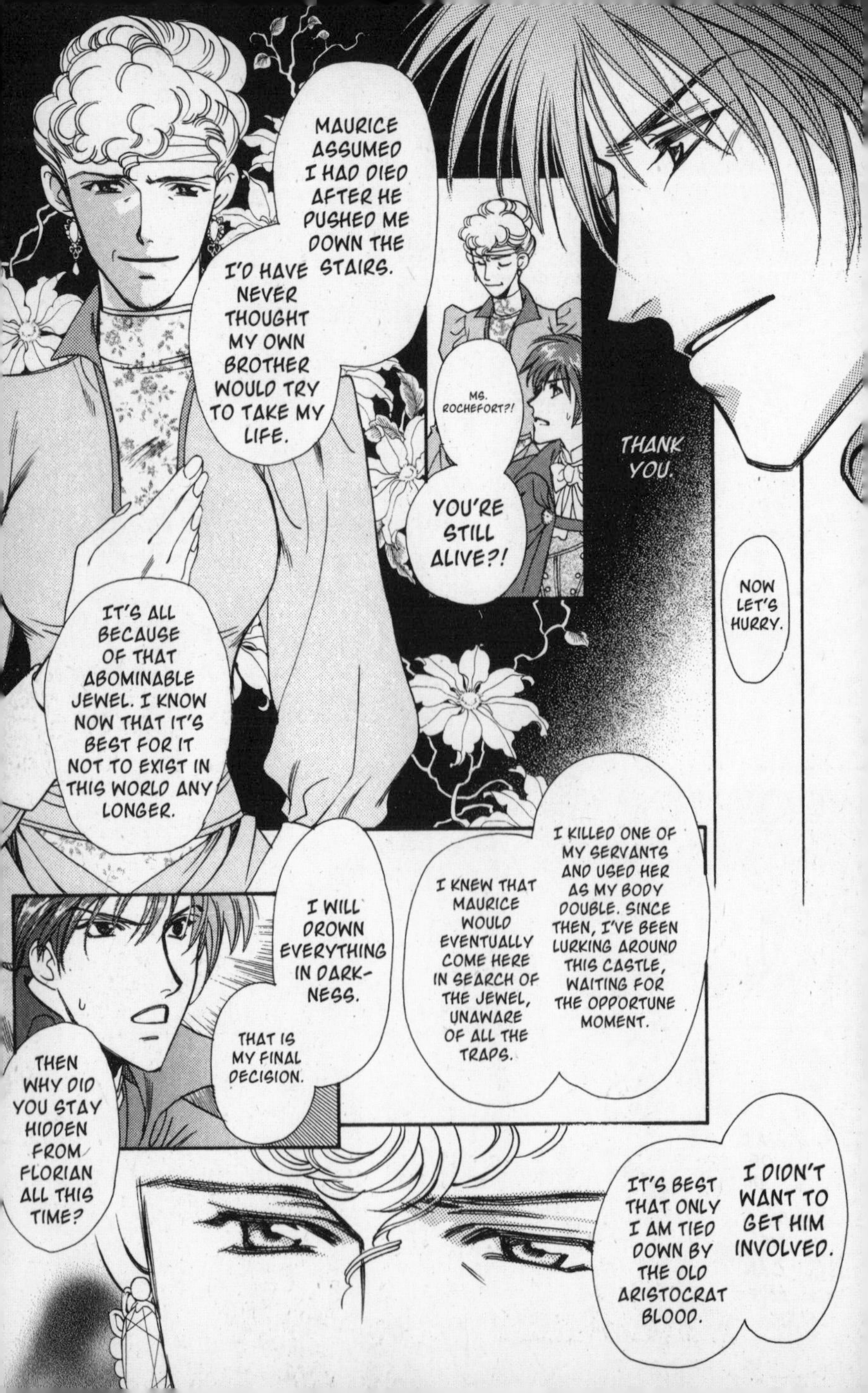
THANK YOU.
NOW LET'S HURRY.
MS. ROCHEFORT?!
YOU'RE STILL ALIVE?!
MAURICE ASSUMED I HAD DIED AFTER HE PUSHED ME DOWN THE STAIRS.
I'D HAVE NEVER THOUGHT MY OWN BROTHER WOULD TRY TO TAKE MY LIFE.
IT'S ALL BECAUSE OF THAT ABOMINABLE JEWEL. I KNOW NOW THAT IT'S BEST FOR IT NOT TO EXIST IN THIS WORLD ANY LONGER.
I KILLED ONE OF MY SERVANTS AND USED HER AS MY BODY DOUBLE. SINCE THEN, I'VE BEEN LURKING AROUND THIS CASTLE, WAITING FOR THE OPPORTUNE MOMENT.
I KNEW THAT MAURICE WOULD EVENTUALLY COME HERE IN SEARCH OF THE JEWEL, UNAWARE OF ALL THE TRAPS.
I WILL DROWN EVERYTHING IN DARK-NESS.
THAT IS MY FINAL DECISION.
THEN WHY DID YOU STAY HIDDEN FROM FLORIAN ALL THIS TIME?
I DIDN'T WANT TO GET HIM INVOLVED.
IT'S BEST THAT ONLY I AM TIED DOWN BY THE OLD ARISTOCRAT BLOOD.

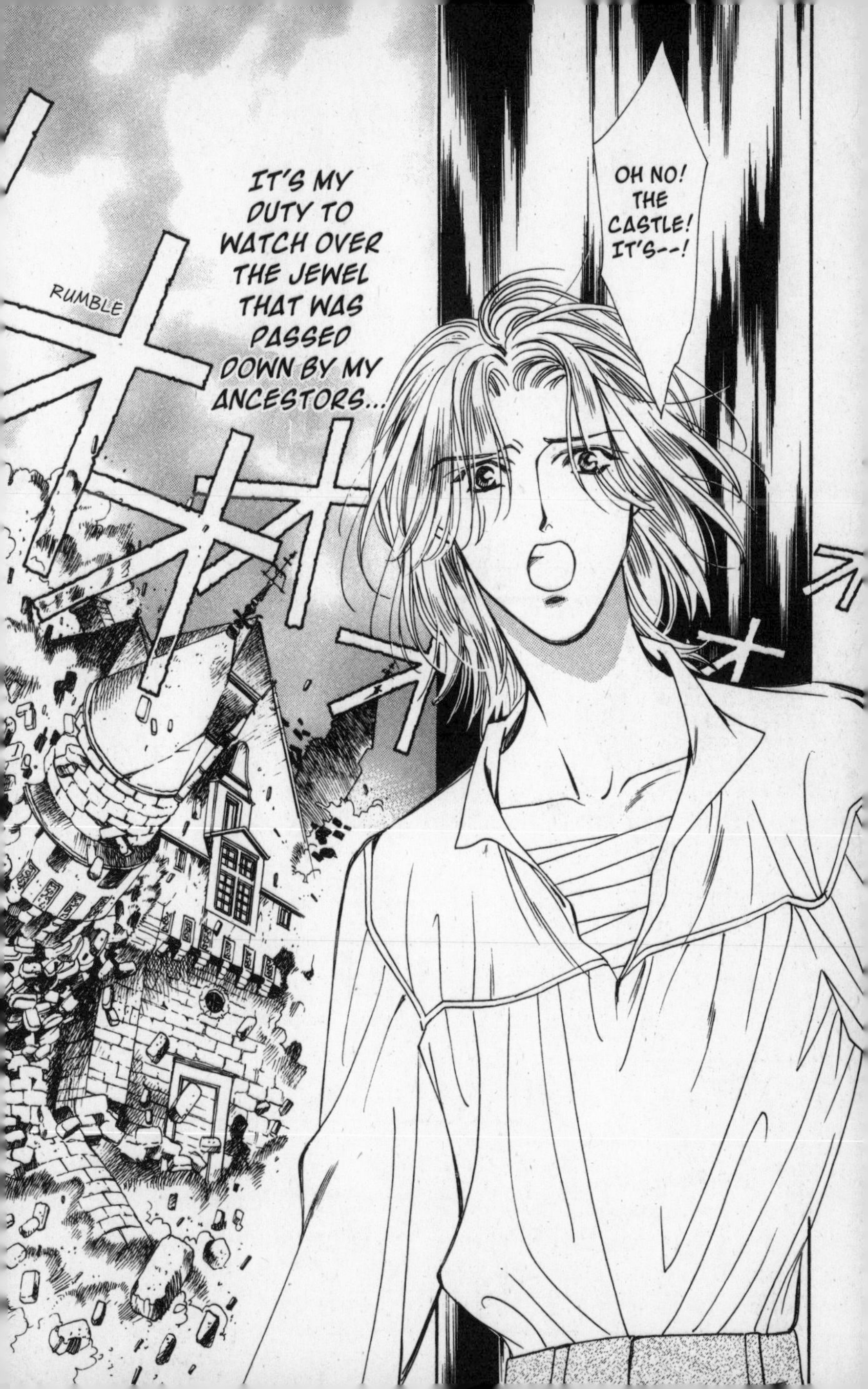
OH NO! THE CASTLE! IT'S--!
IT'S MY DUTY TO WATCH OVER THE JEWEL THAT WAS PASSED DOWN BY MY ANCESTORS...
RUMBLE

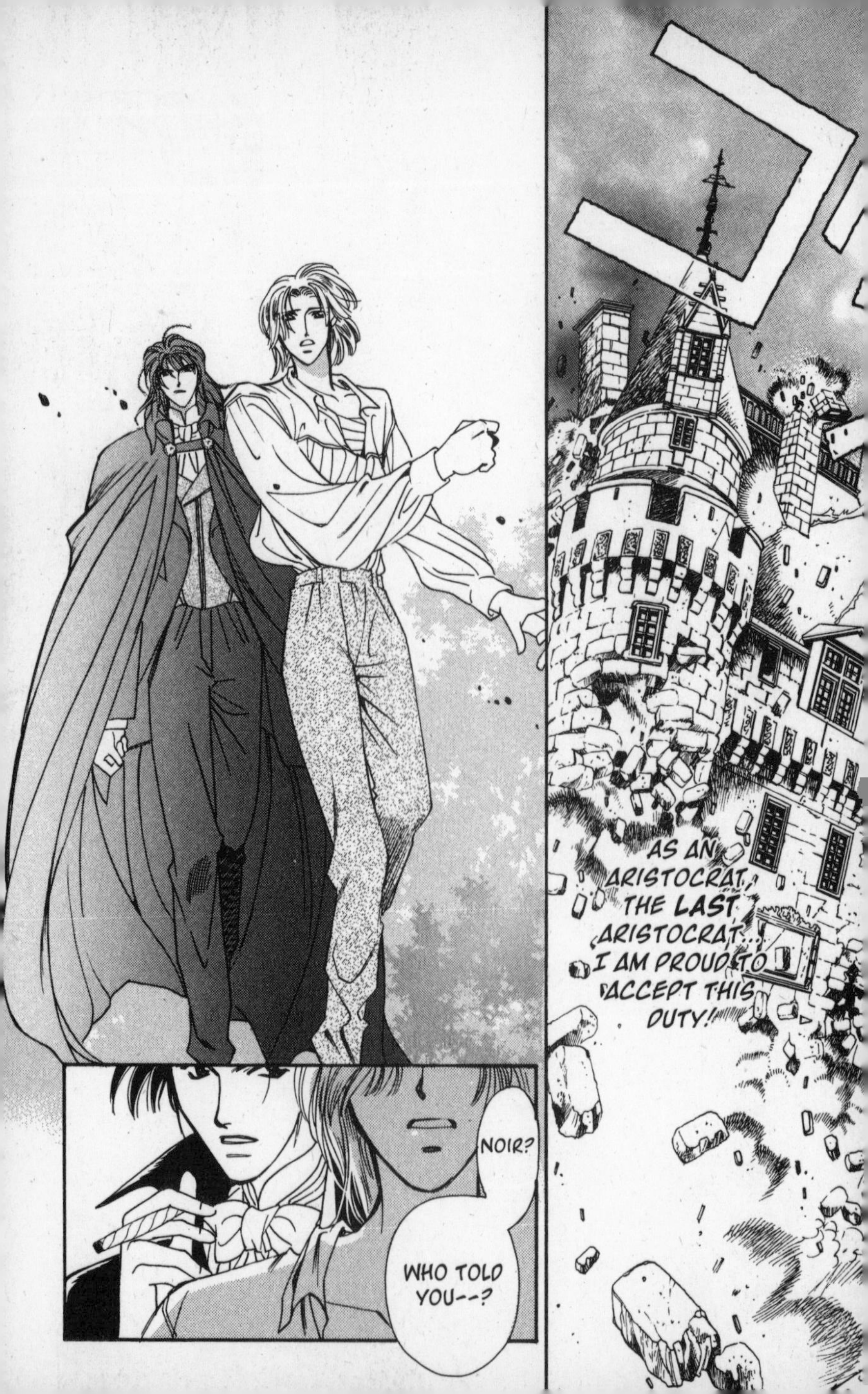
AS AN ARISTOCRAT, THE LAST ARISTOCRAT... I AM PROUD TO ACCEPT THIS DUTY!!
NOIR?
WHO TOLD YOU--?

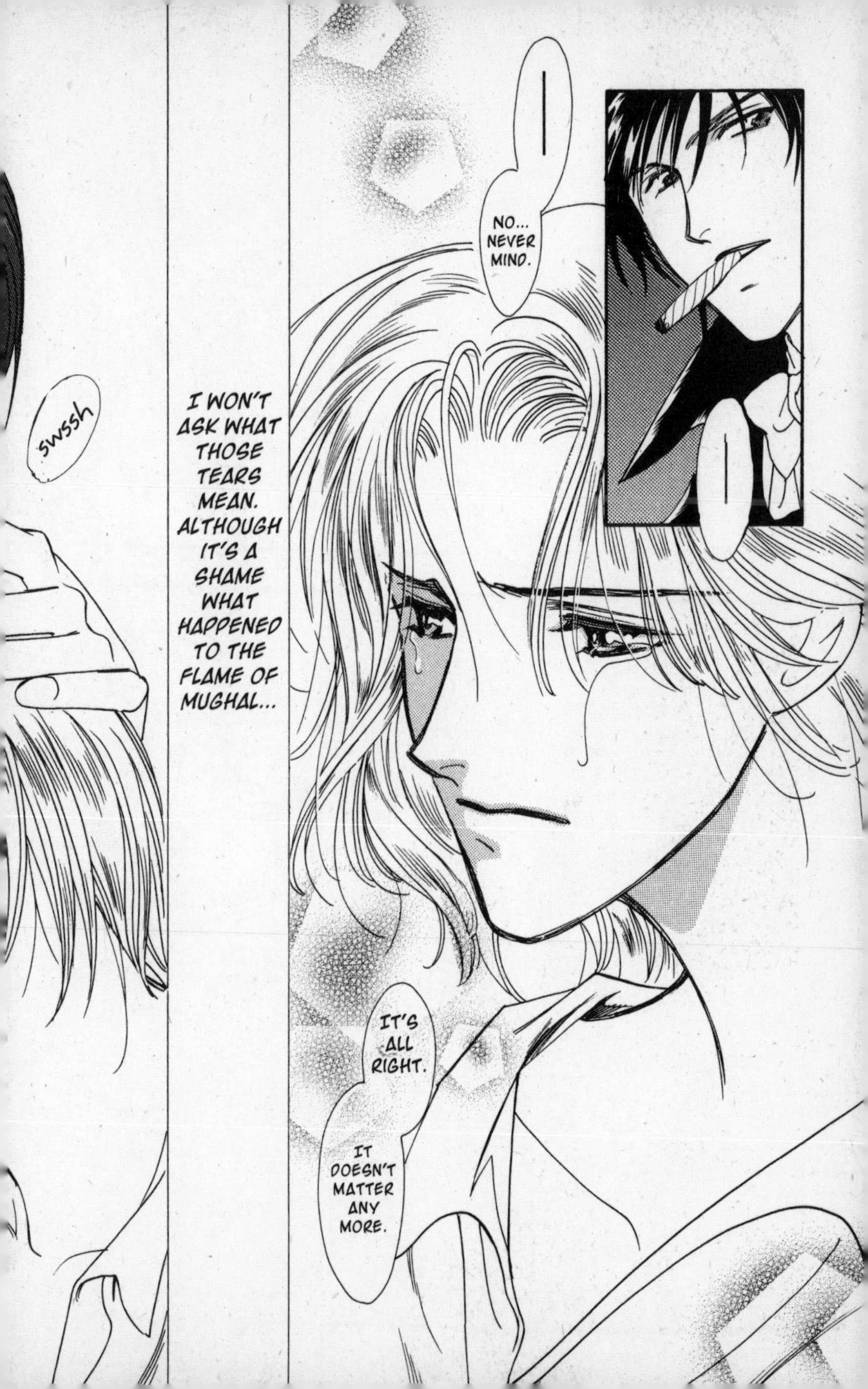
NO... NEVER MIND.
IT'S ALL RIGHT.
IT DOESN'T MATTER ANY MORE.
I WON'T ASK WHAT THOSE TEARS MEAN. ALTHOUGH IT'S A SHAME WHAT HAPPENED TO THE FLAME OF MUGHAL...
swssh

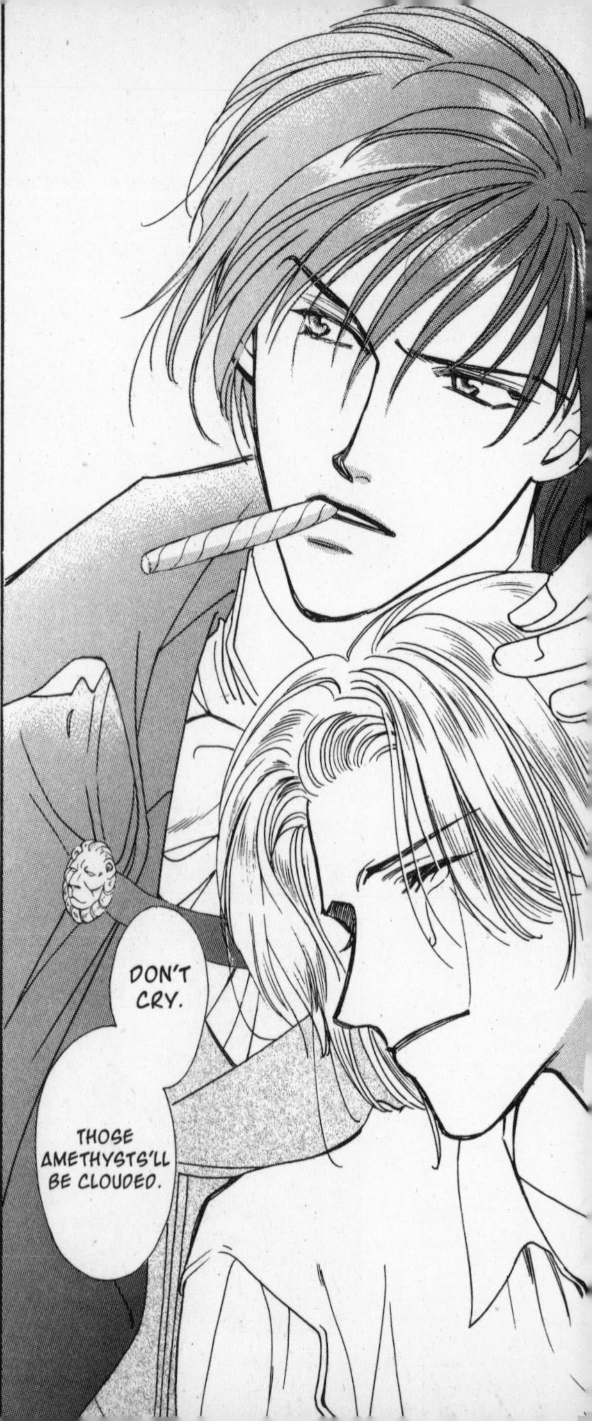
DON'T CRY.
THOSE AMETHYSTS'LL BE CLOUDED.

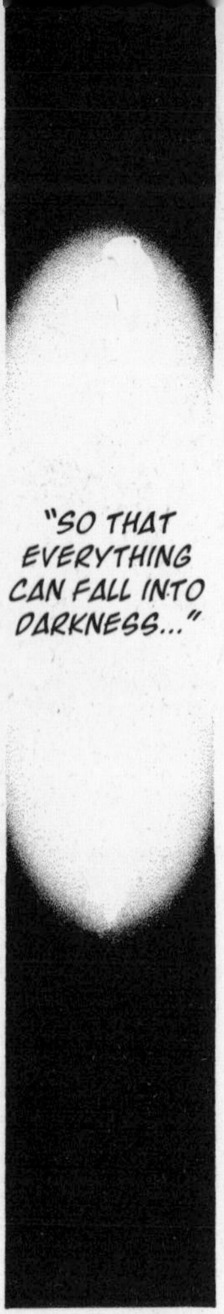
"SO THAT EVERYTHING CAN FALL INTO DARKNESS..."

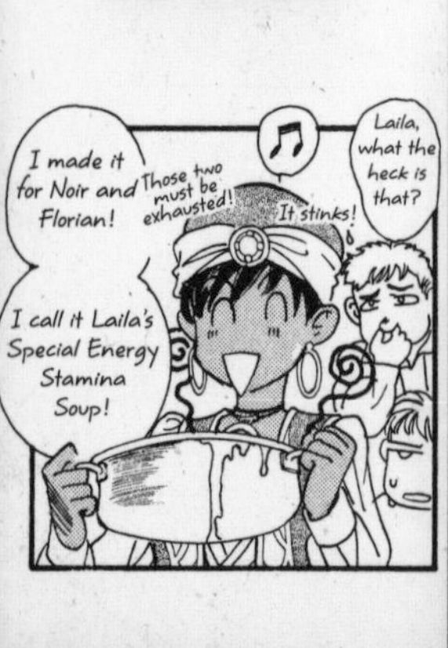
Laila, what the heck is that?
It stinks!
♪
Those two must be exhausted!
I made it for Noir and Florian!
I call it Laila's Special Energy Stamina Soup!

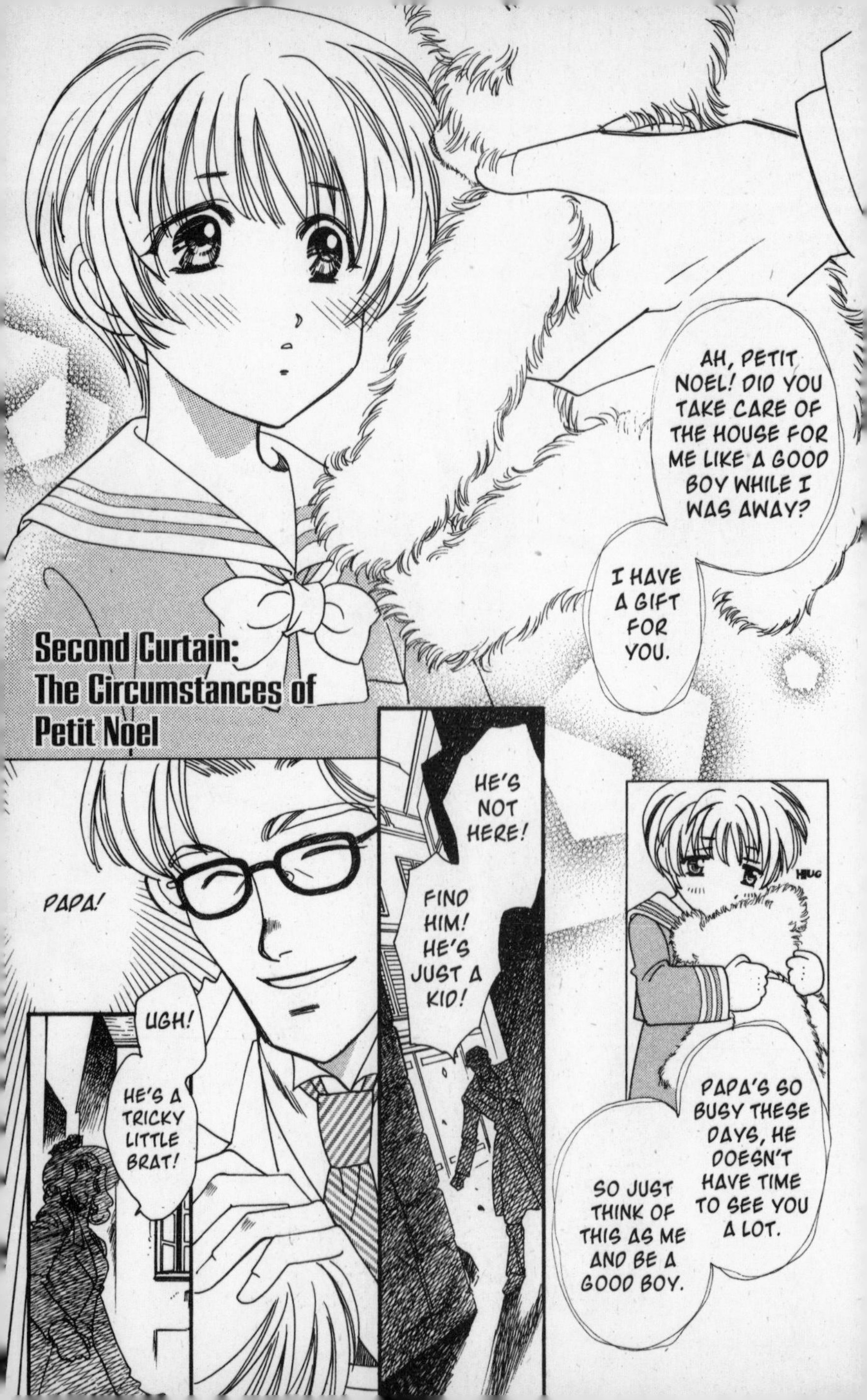
Second Curtain: The Circumstances of Petit Noel
AH, PETIT NOEL! DID YOU TAKE CARE OF THE HOUSE FOR ME LIKE A GOOD BOY WHILE I WAS AWAY?
I HAVE A GIFT FOR YOU.
HUG
PAPA'S SO BUSY THESE DAYS, HE DOESN'T HAVE TIME TO SEE YOU A LOT.
SO JUST THINK OF THIS AS ME AND BE A GOOD BOY.
HE'S NOT HERE!
FIND HIM! HE'S JUST A KID!
PAPA!
UGH!
HE'S A TRICKY LITTLE BRAT!

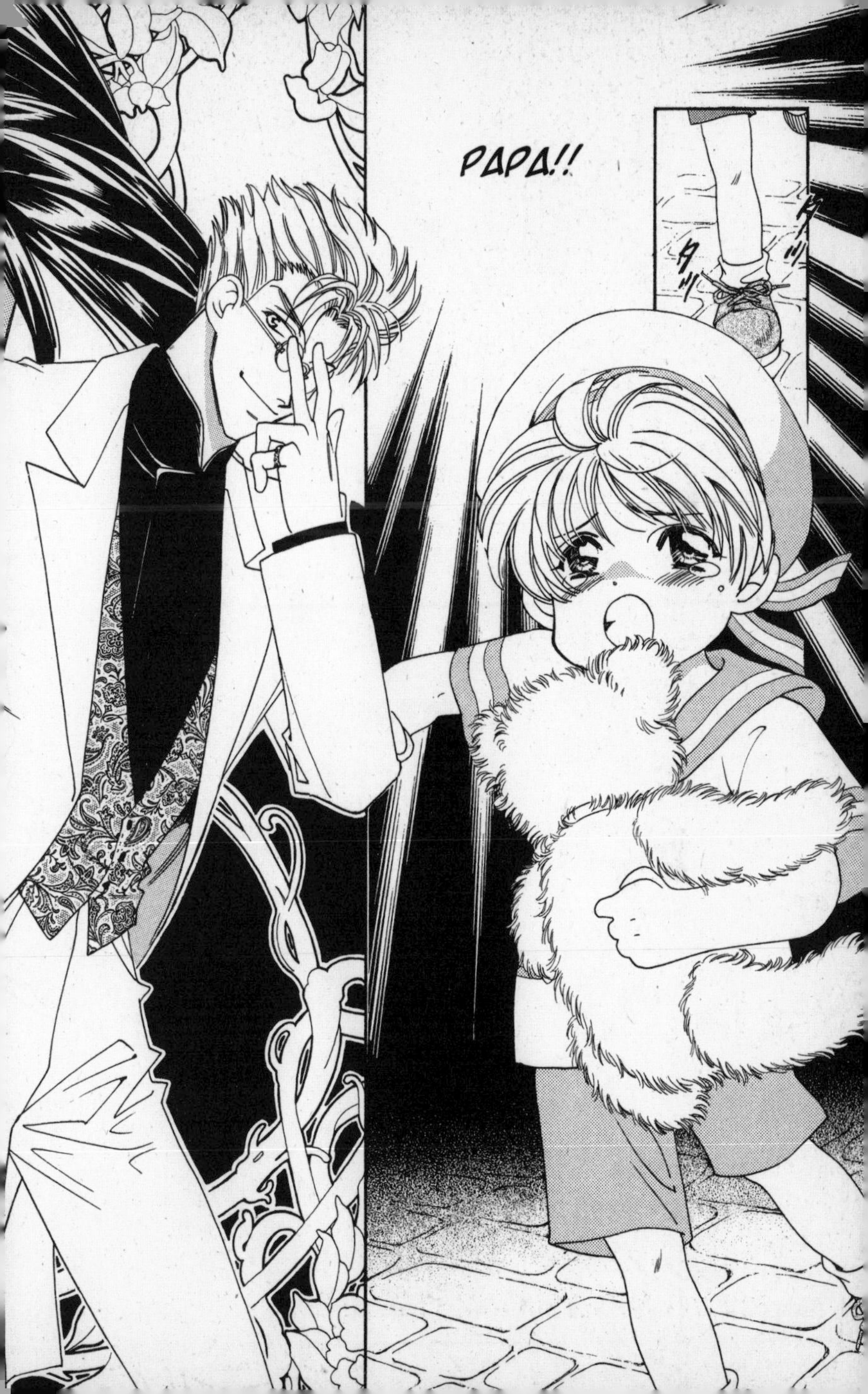
PAPA!!

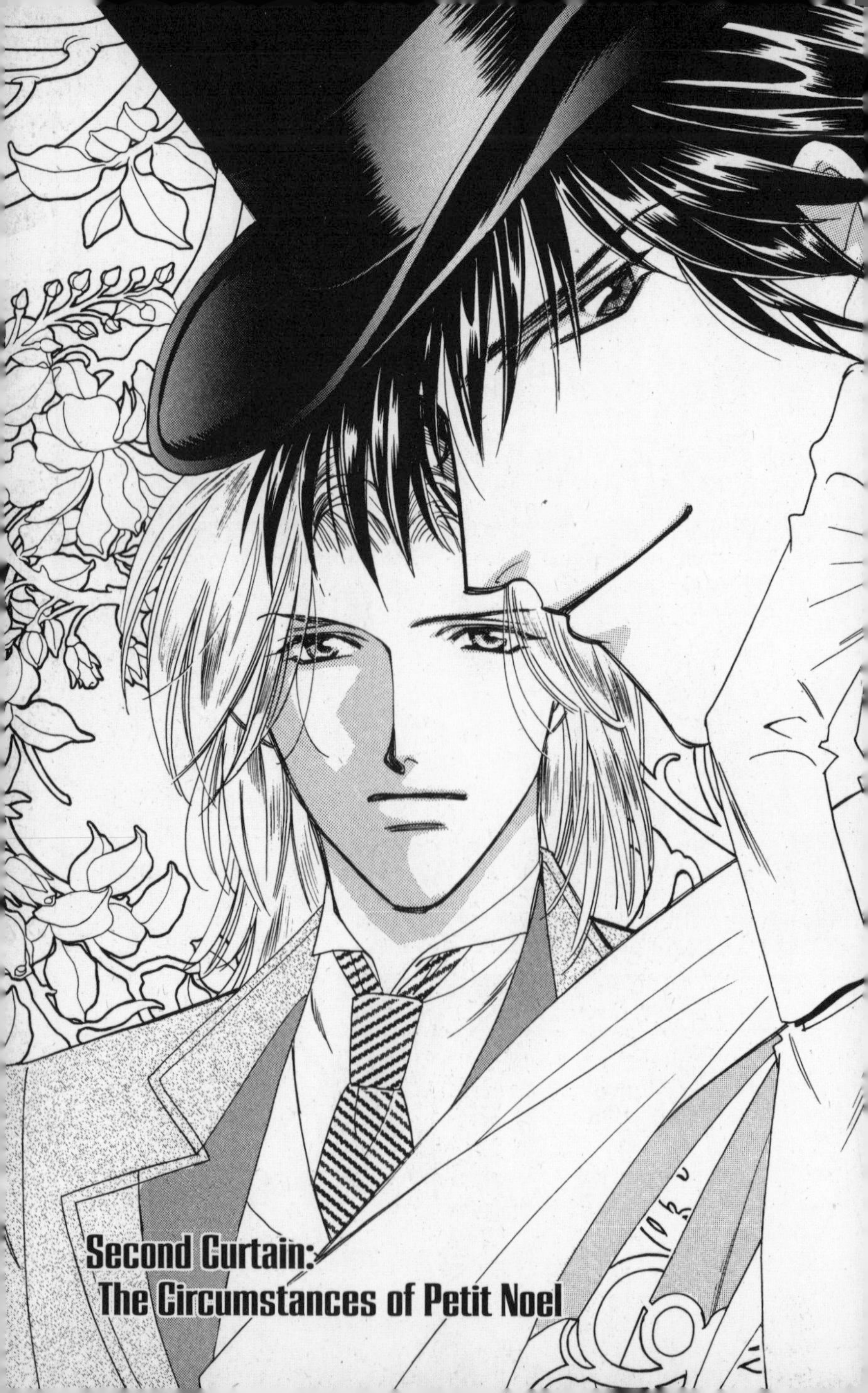
Second Curtain:
The Circumstances of Petit Noel

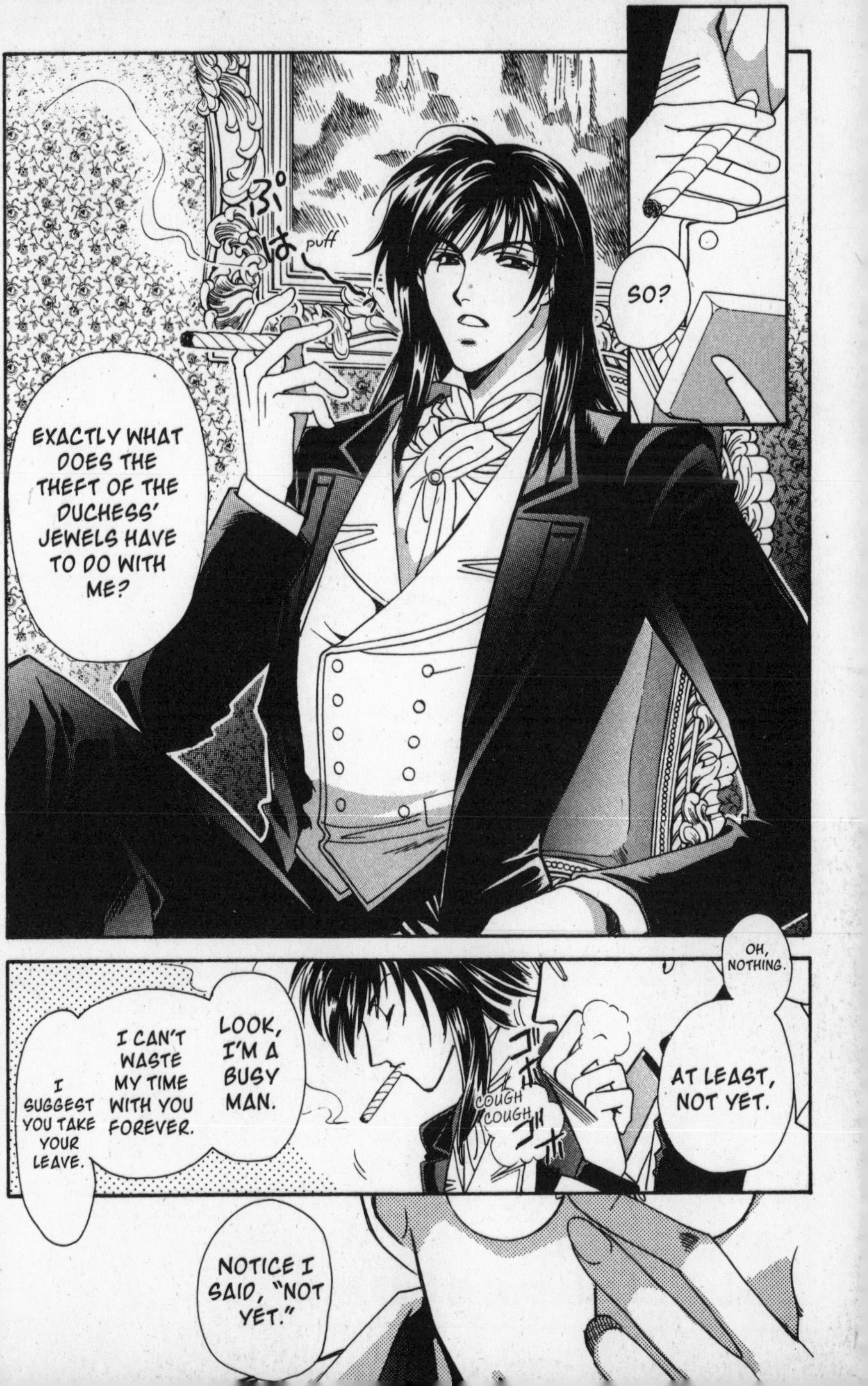
SO?
ぷは
puff
EXACTLY WHAT DOES THE THEFT OF THE DUCHESS' JEWELS HAVE TO DO WITH ME?
OH, NOTHING.
AT LEAST, NOT YET.
COUGH COUGH
LOOK, I'M A BUSY MAN.
I CAN'T WASTE MY TIME WITH YOU FOREVER.
I SUGGEST YOU TAKE YOUR LEAVE.
NOTICE I SAID, "NOT YET."

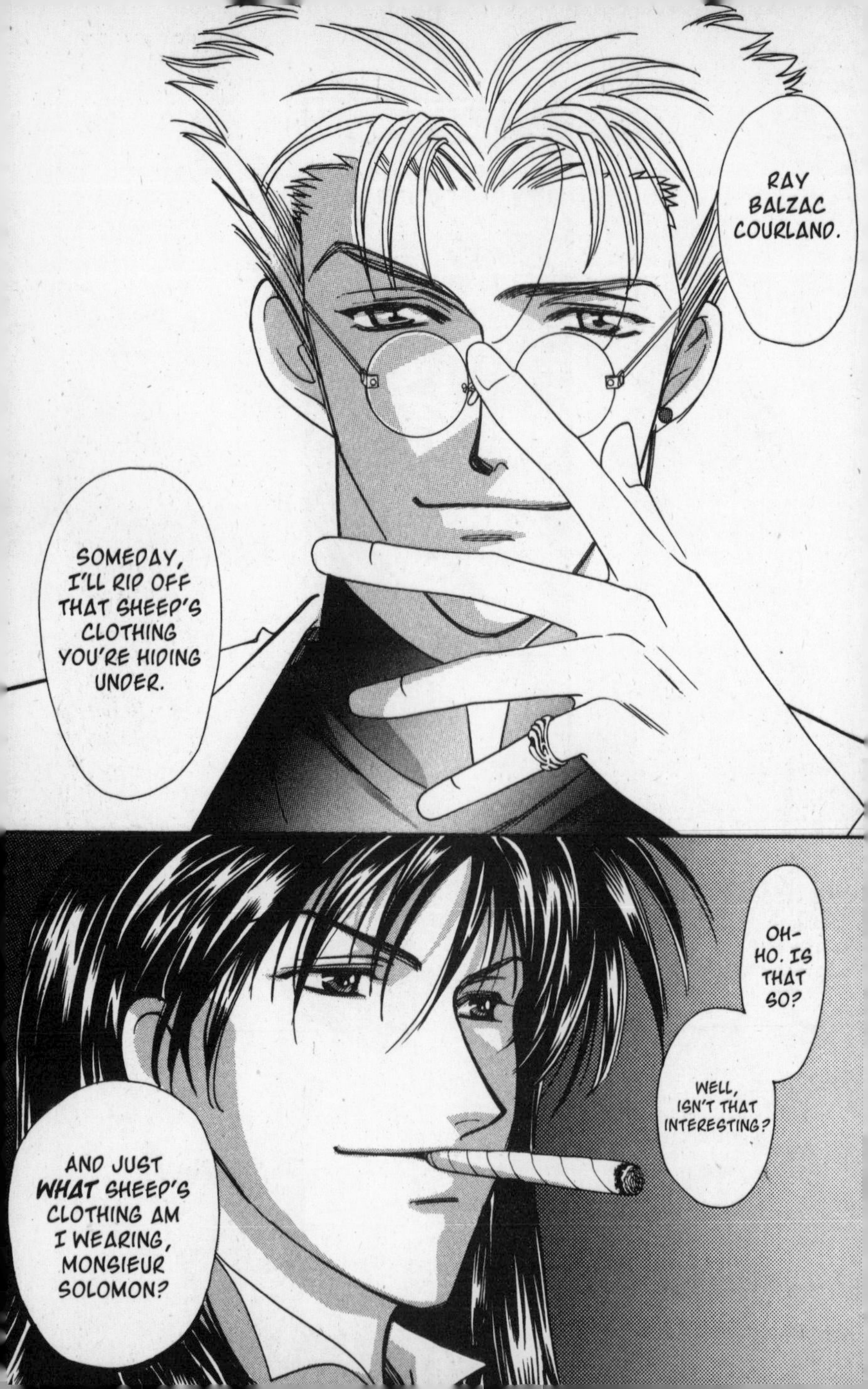
RAY BALZAC COURLAND.
SOMEDAY, I'LL RIP OFF THAT SHEEP'S CLOTHING YOU'RE HIDING UNDER.
OH-HO. IS THAT SO?
WELL, ISN'T THAT INTERESTING?
AND JUST **WHAT** SHEEP'S CLOTHING AM I WEARING, MONSIEUR SOLOMON?

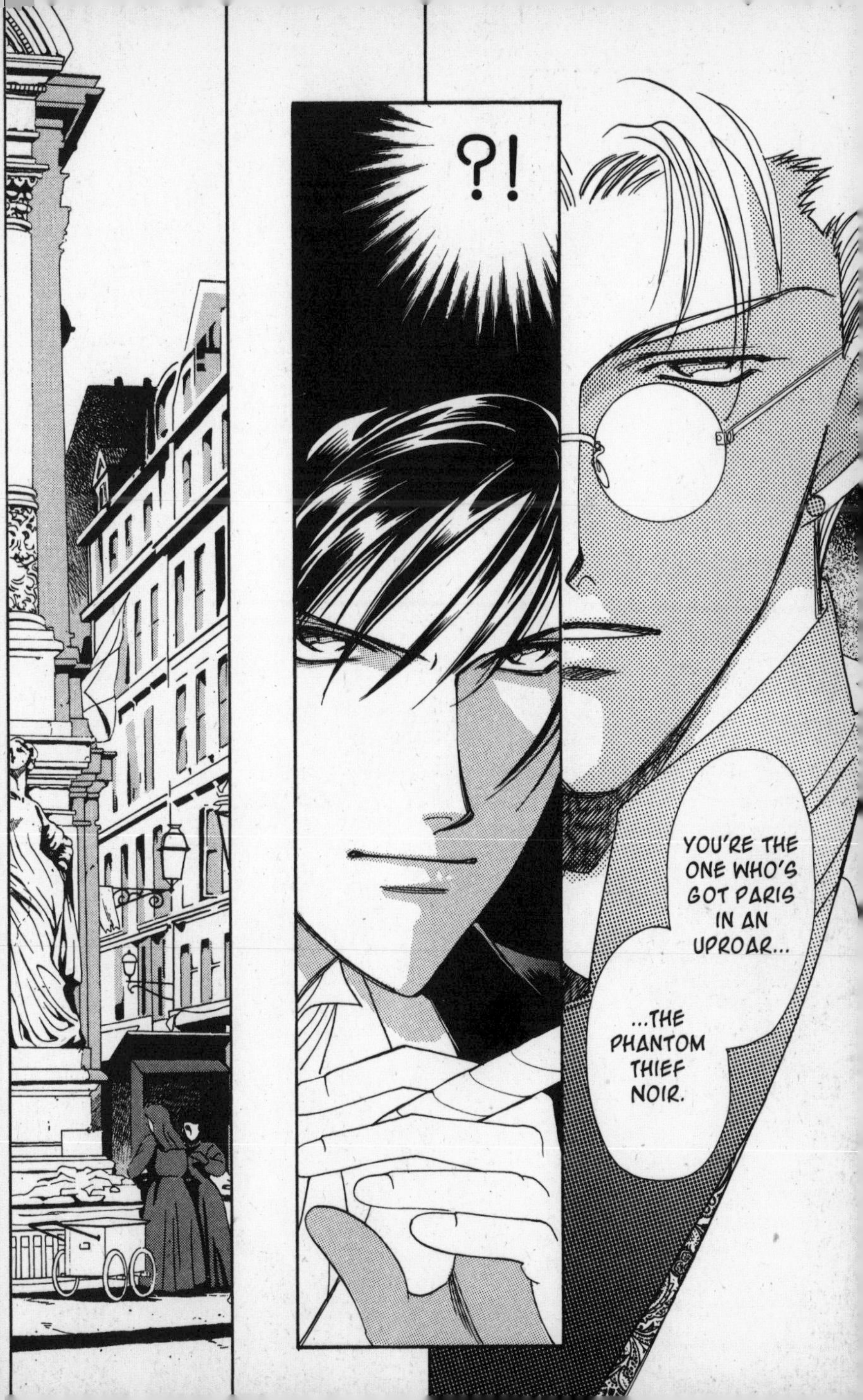
?!
YOU'RE THE ONE WHO'S GOT PARIS IN AN UPROAR...
...THE PHANTOM THIEF NOIR.

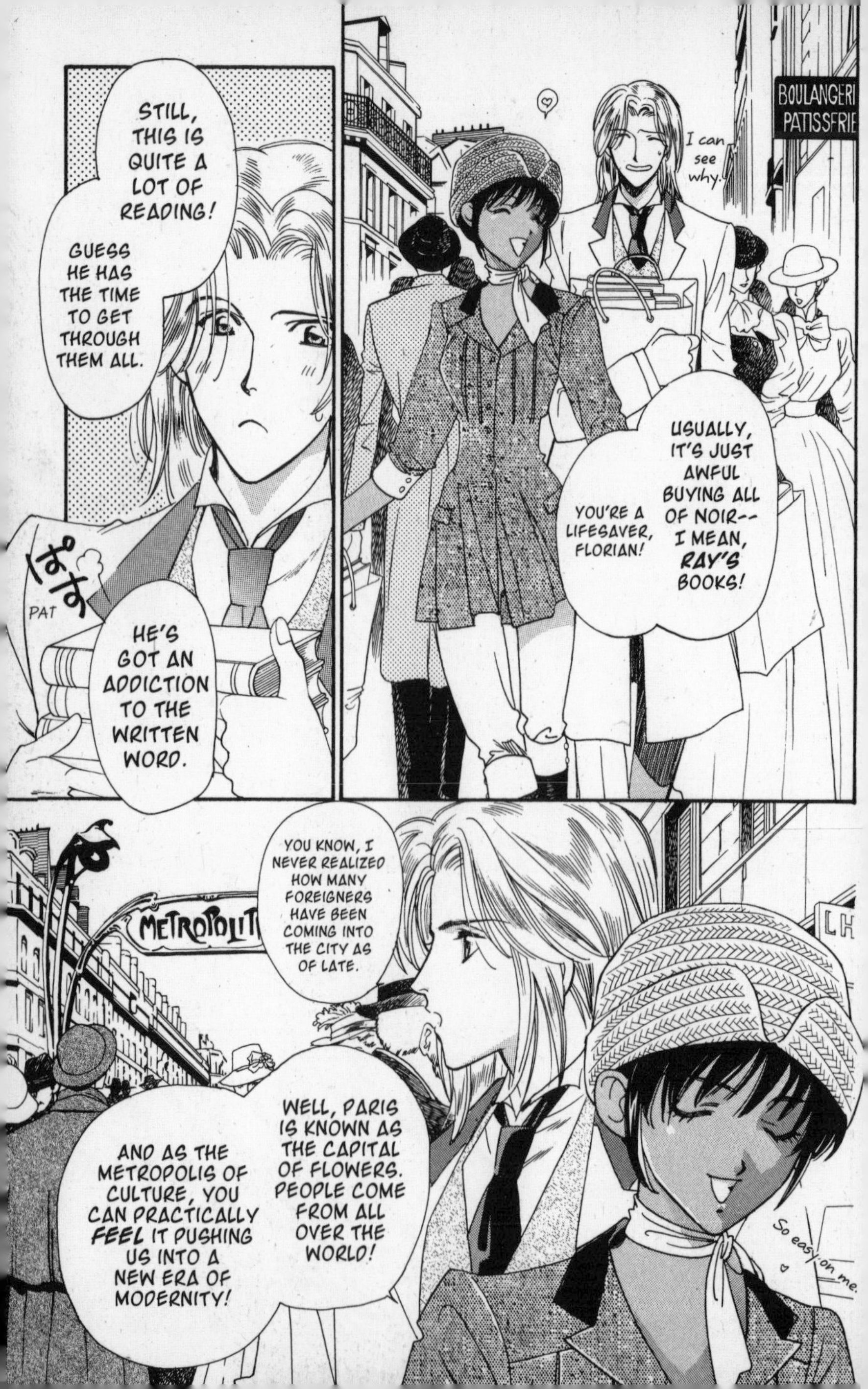
BOULANGERI PATISSFRIE
I can see why.
USUALLY, IT'S JUST AWFUL BUYING ALL OF NOIR-- I MEAN, RAY'S BOOKS!
YOU'RE A LIFESAVER, FLORIAN!
STILL, THIS IS QUITE A LOT OF READING!
GUESS HE HAS THE TIME TO GET THROUGH THEM ALL.
ぱす
PAT
HE'S GOT AN ADDICTION TO THE WRITTEN WORD.
YOU KNOW, I NEVER REALIZED HOW MANY FOREIGNERS HAVE BEEN COMING INTO THE CITY AS OF LATE.
METROPOLIT
So easy on me.
WELL, PARIS IS KNOWN AS THE CAPITAL OF FLOWERS. PEOPLE COME FROM ALL OVER THE WORLD!
AND AS THE METROPOLIS OF CULTURE, YOU CAN PRACTICALLY FEEL IT PUSHING US INTO A NEW ERA OF MODERNITY!

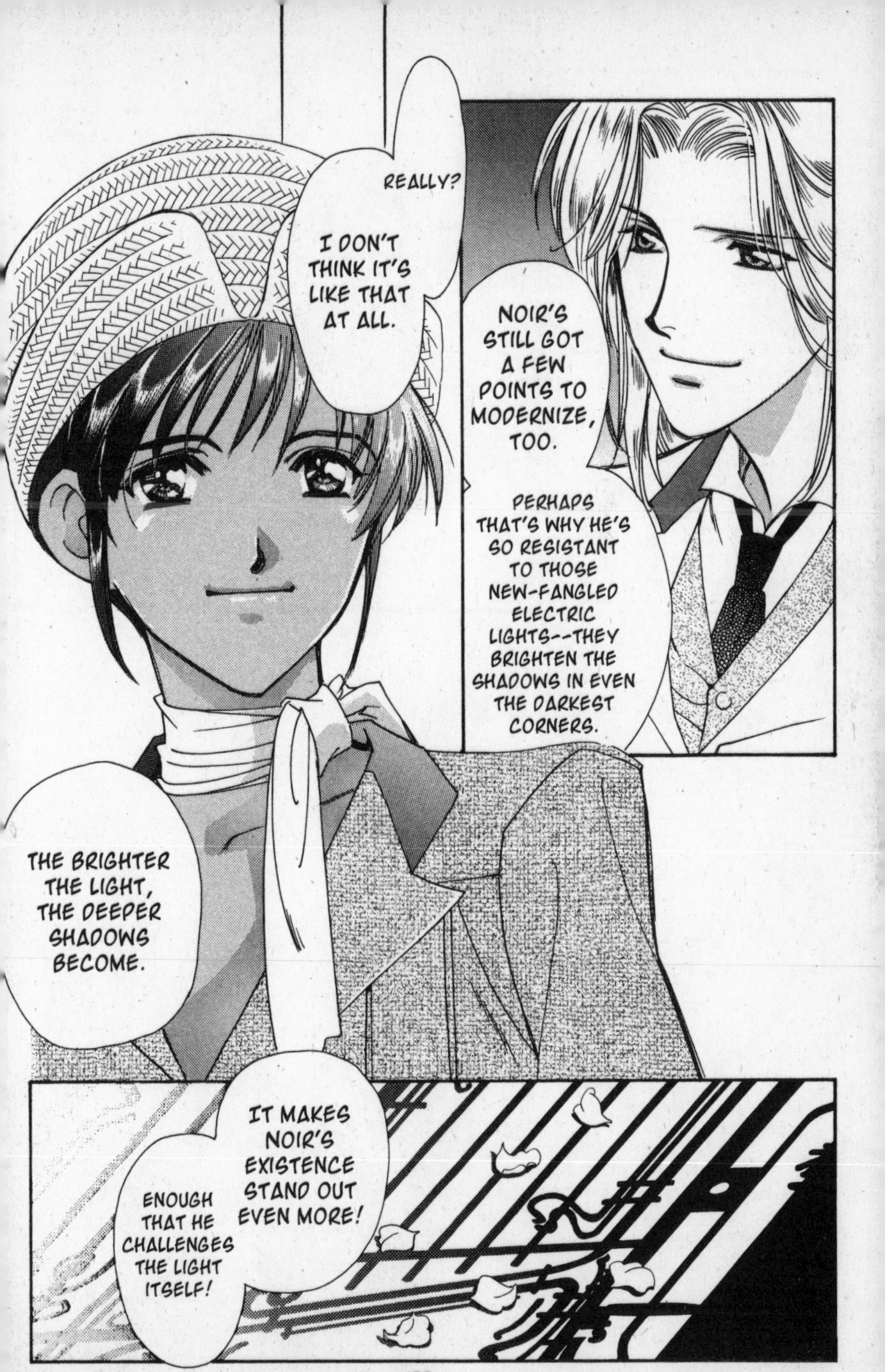
NOIR'S STILL GOT A FEW POINTS TO MODERNIZE, TOO.
PERHAPS THAT'S WHY HE'S SO RESISTANT TO THOSE NEW-FANGLED ELECTRIC LIGHTS--THEY BRIGHTEN THE SHADOWS IN EVEN THE DARKEST CORNERS.
REALLY?
I DON'T THINK IT'S LIKE THAT AT ALL.
THE BRIGHTER THE LIGHT, THE DEEPER SHADOWS BECOME.
IT MAKES NOIR'S EXISTENCE STAND OUT EVEN MORE!
ENOUGH THAT HE CHALLENGES THE LIGHT ITSELF!

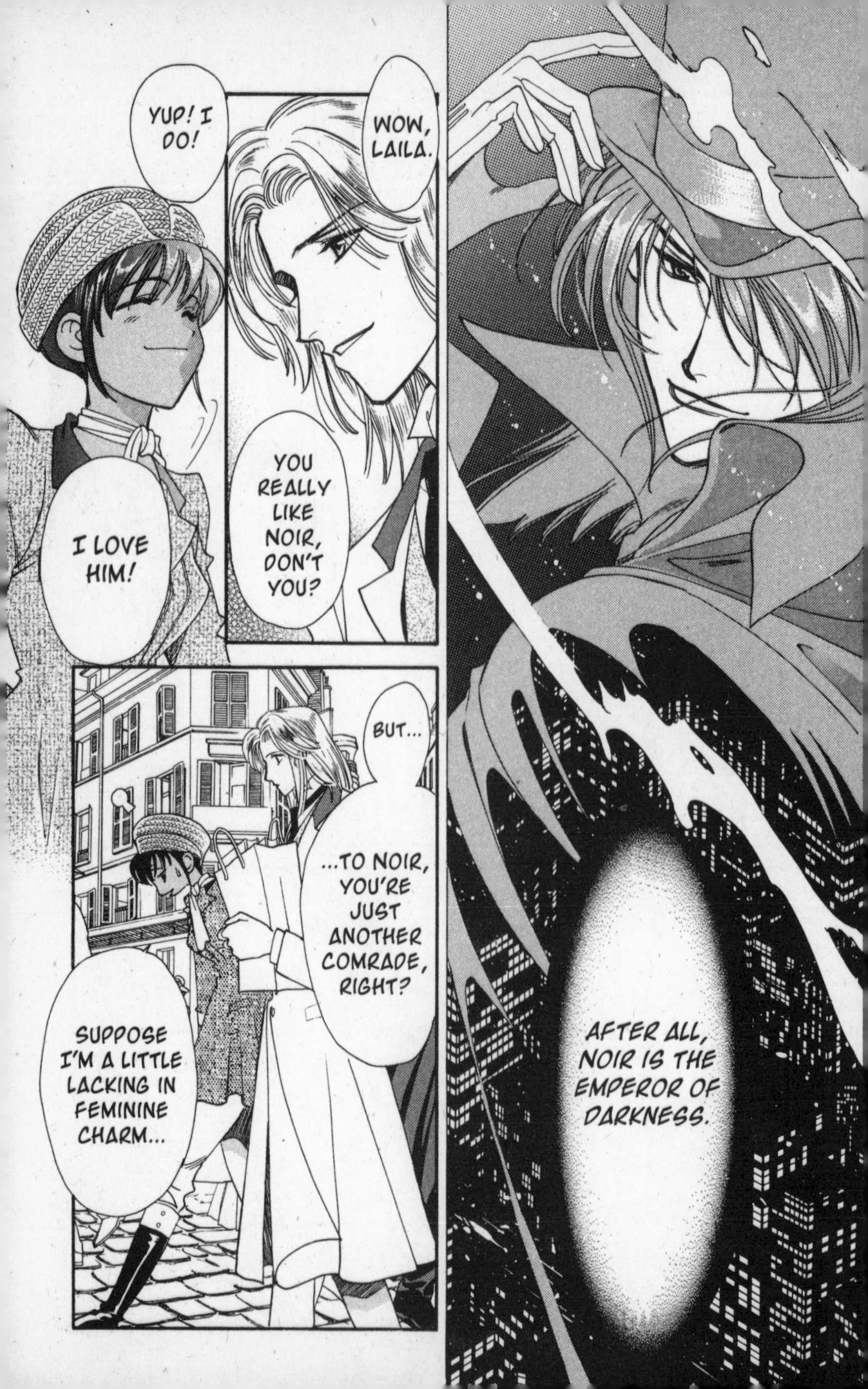
WOW, LAILA.
YOU REALLY LIKE NOIR, DON'T YOU?
YUP! I DO!
I LOVE HIM!
BUT...
...TO NOIR, YOU'RE JUST ANOTHER COMRADE, RIGHT?
SUPPOSE I'M A LITTLE LACKING IN FEMININE CHARM...
AFTER ALL, NOIR IS THE EMPEROR OF DARKNESS.

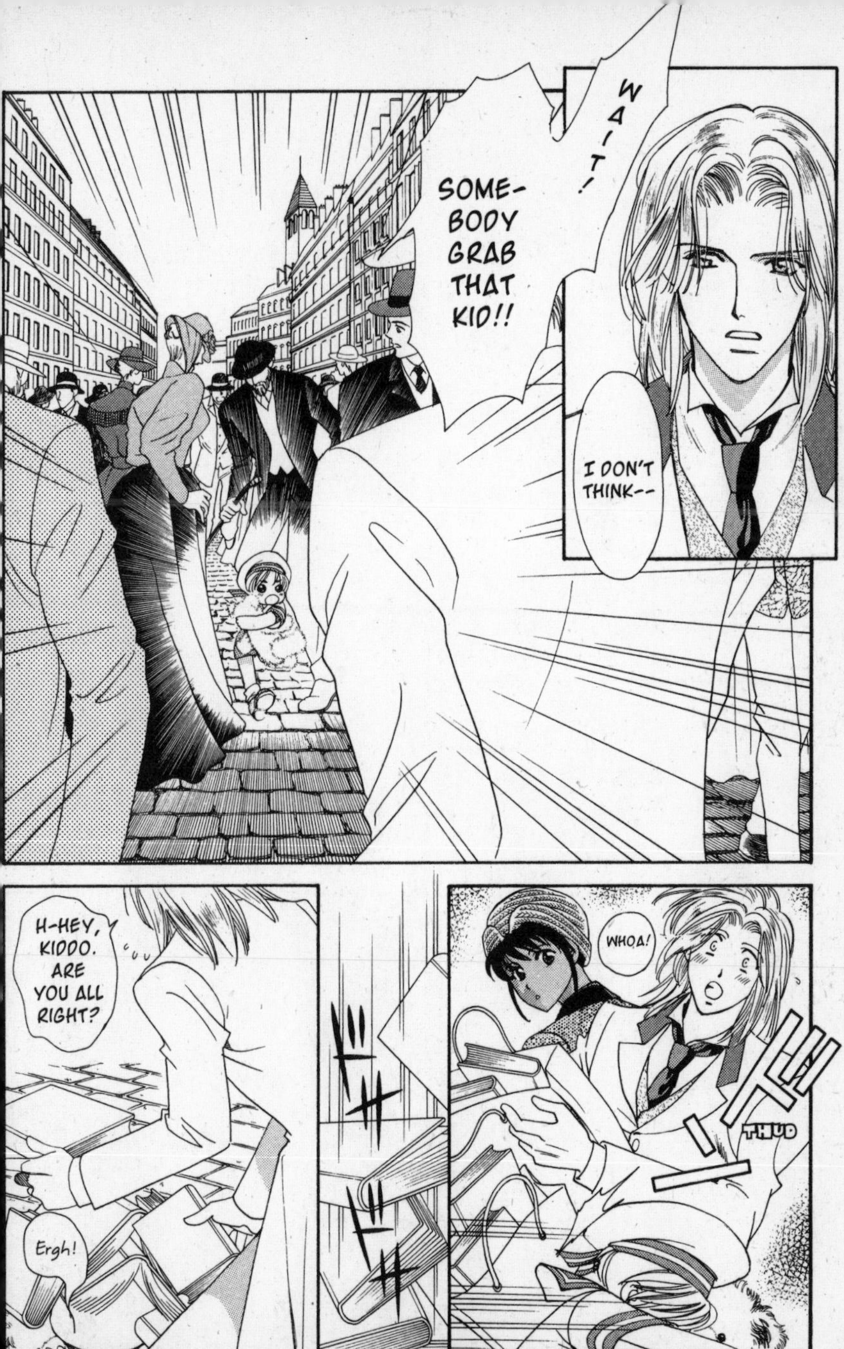
WAIT!
SOME-BODY GRAB THAT KID!!
I DON'T THINK--
WHOA!
THUD
H-HEY, KIDDO. ARE YOU ALL RIGHT?
Ergh!

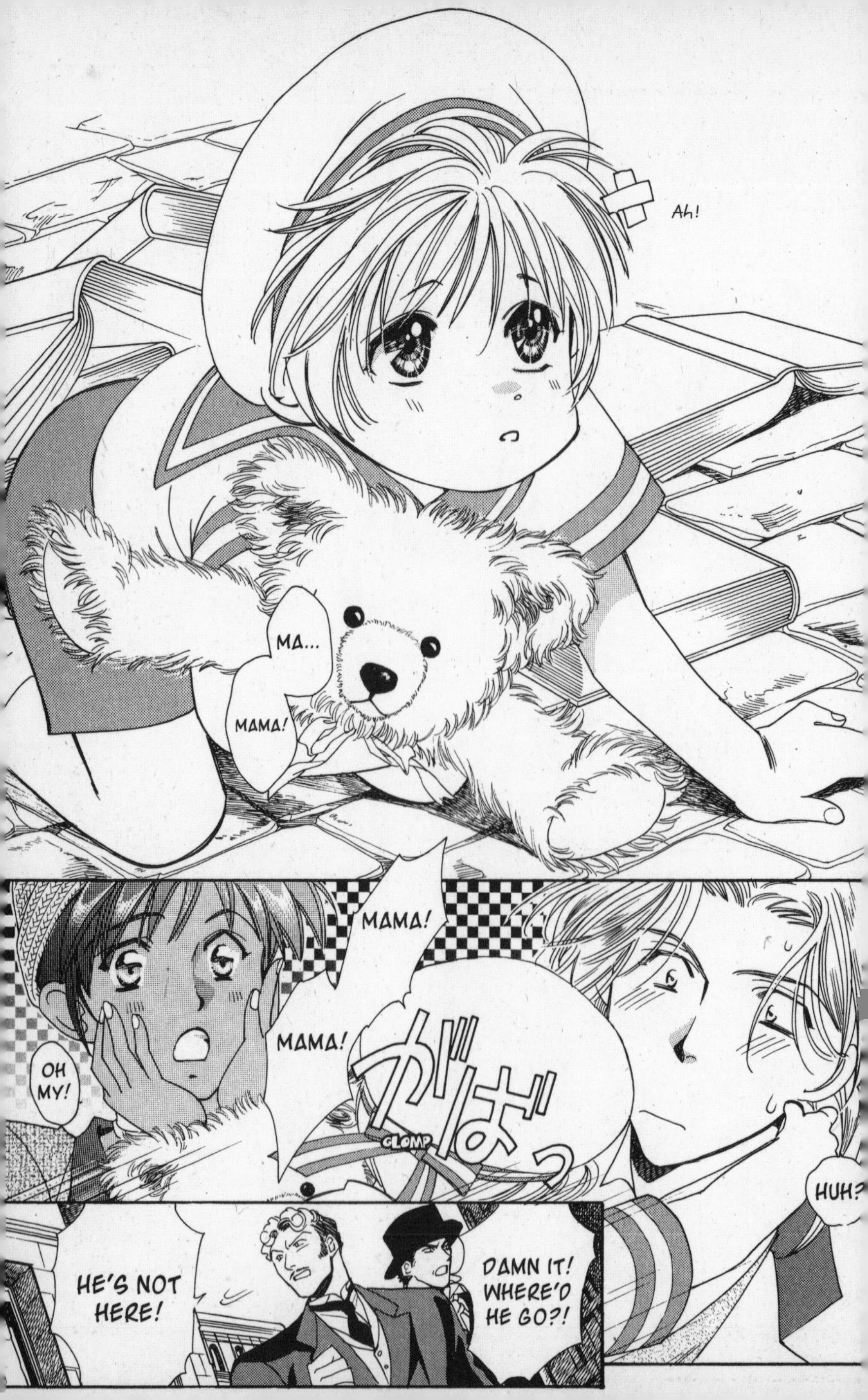
Ah!
MA...
MAMA!
MAMA!
MAMA!
がばっ
GLOMP
HUH?
OH MY!
DAMN IT! WHERE'D HE GO?!
HE'S NOT HERE!

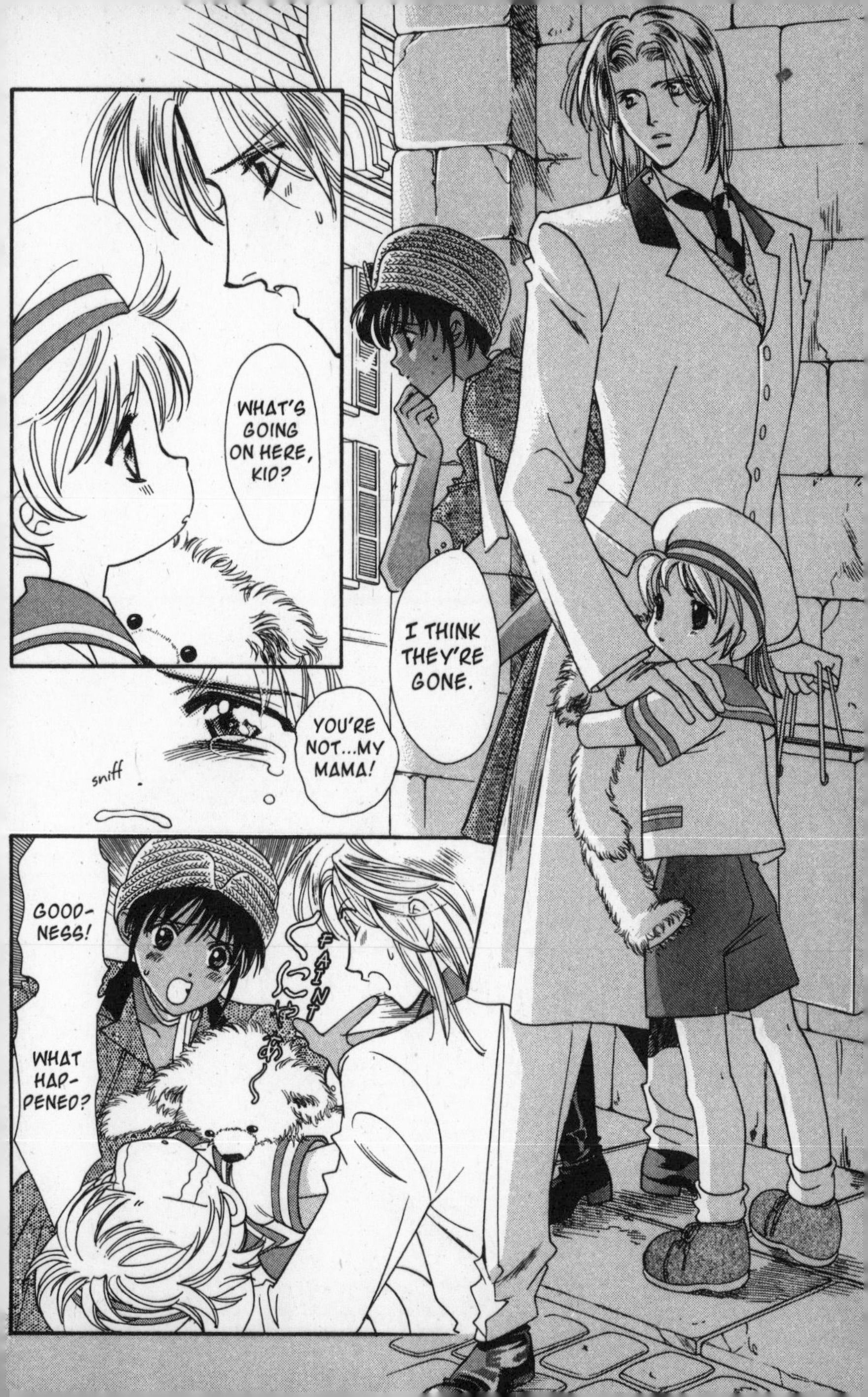

I THINK THEY'RE GONE.
WHAT'S GOING ON HERE, KID?
YOU'RE NOT...MY MAMA!
sniff
FAINT
にゃあ
GOODNESS!
WHAT HAPPENED?

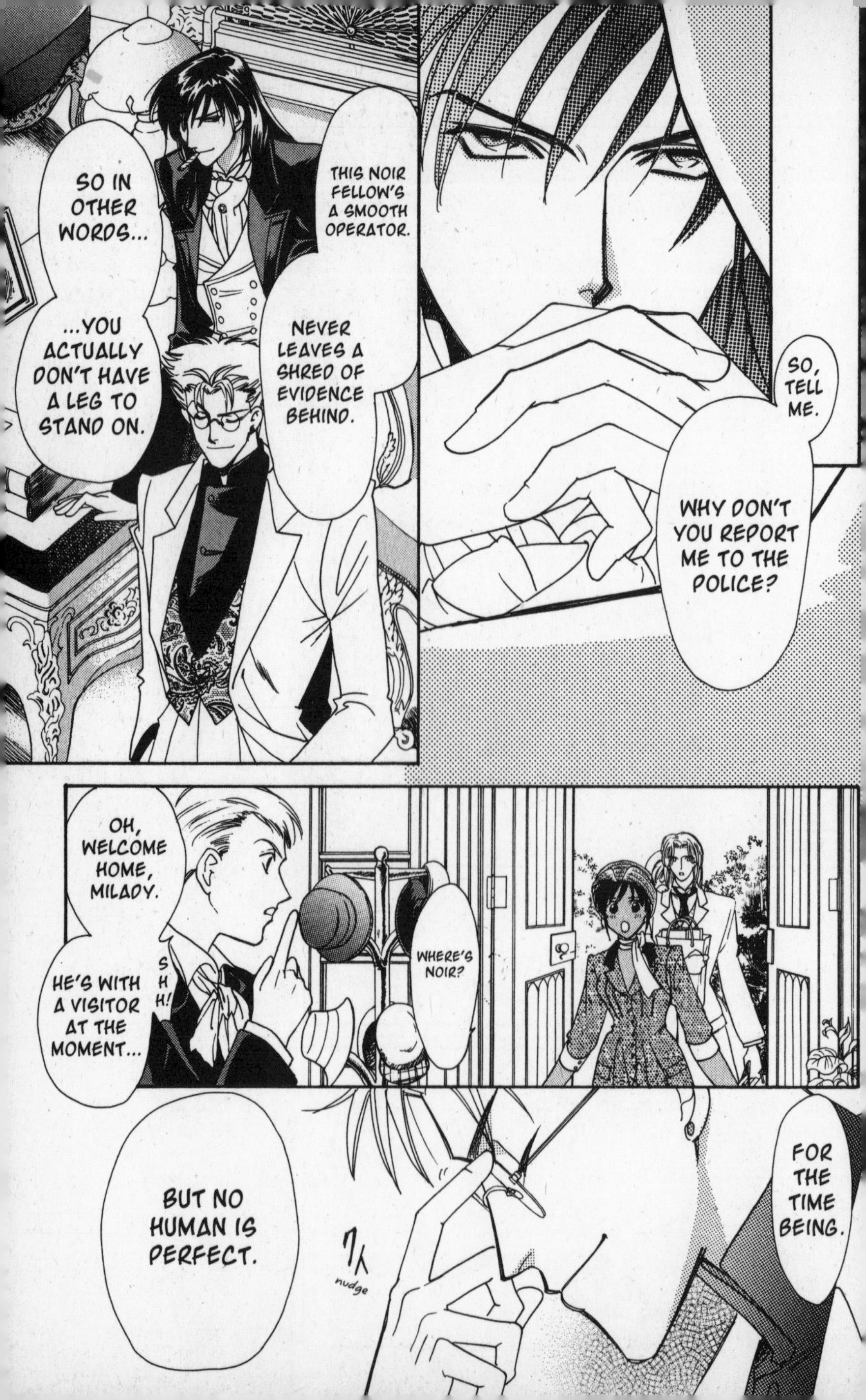
SO, TELL ME.
WHY DON'T YOU REPORT ME TO THE POLICE?
THIS NOIR FELLOW'S A SMOOTH OPERATOR.
NEVER LEAVES A SHRED OF EVIDENCE BEHIND.
SO IN OTHER WORDS...
...YOU ACTUALLY DON'T HAVE A LEG TO STAND ON.
WHERE'S NOIR?
OH, WELCOME HOME, MILADY.
SHH!
HE'S WITH A VISITOR AT THE MOMENT...
FOR THE TIME BEING.
BUT NO HUMAN IS PERFECT.
nudge

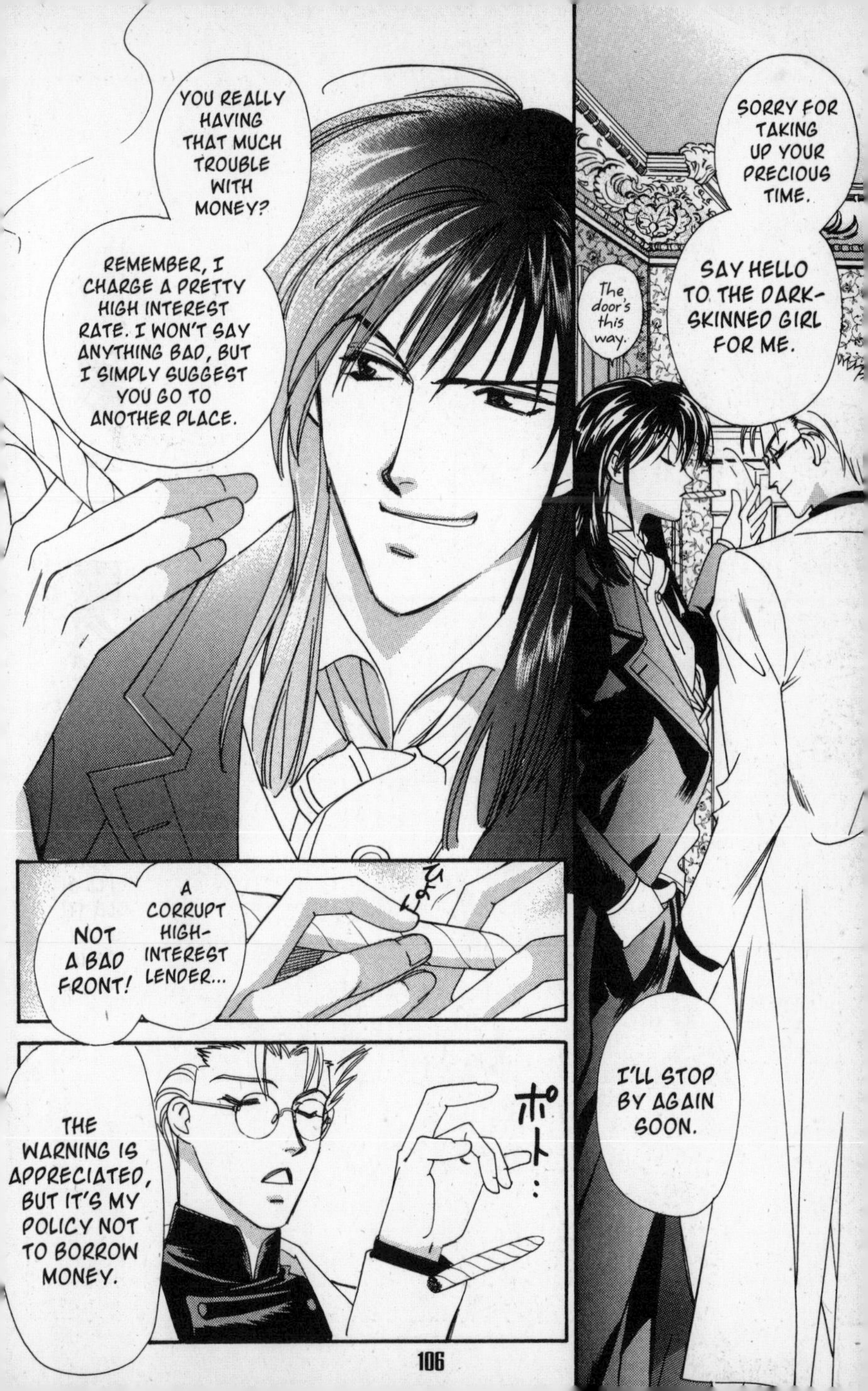
SORRY FOR TAKING UP YOUR PRECIOUS TIME.
SAY HELLO TO THE DARK-SKINNED GIRL FOR ME.
The door's this way.
I'LL STOP BY AGAIN SOON.
YOU REALLY HAVING THAT MUCH TROUBLE WITH MONEY?
REMEMBER, I CHARGE A PRETTY HIGH INTEREST RATE. I WON'T SAY ANYTHING BAD, BUT I SIMPLY SUGGEST YOU GO TO ANOTHER PLACE.
ひょい
A CORRUPT HIGH-INTEREST LENDER...
NOT A BAD FRONT!
ポト‥
THE WARNING IS APPRECIATED, BUT IT'S MY POLICY NOT TO BORROW MONEY.

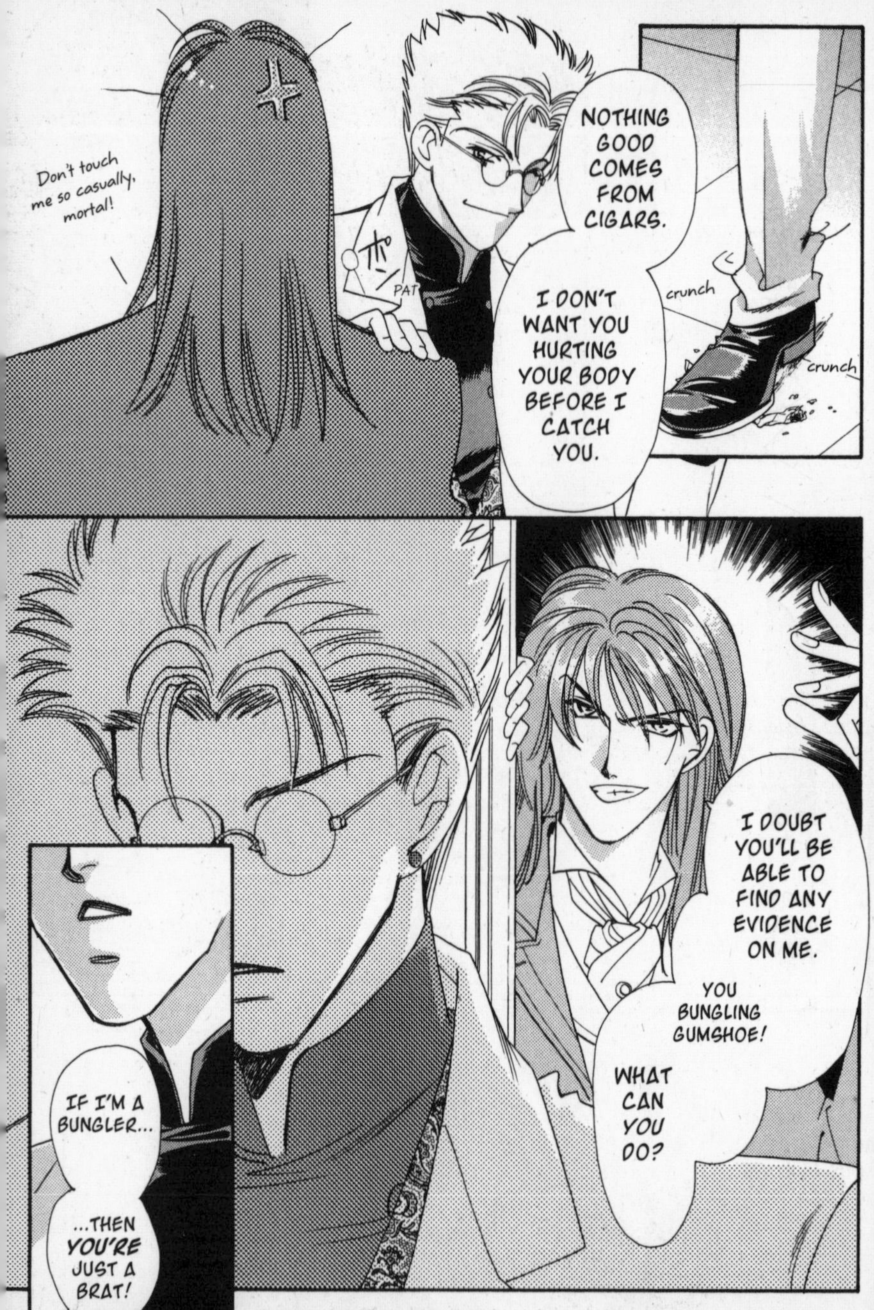
crunch
crunch
NOTHING GOOD COMES FROM CIGARS.
I DON'T WANT YOU HURTING YOUR BODY BEFORE I CATCH YOU.
PAT
Don't touch me so casually, mortal!
I DOUBT YOU'LL BE ABLE TO FIND ANY EVIDENCE ON ME.
YOU BUNGLING GUMSHOE!
WHAT CAN YOU DO?
IF I'M A BUNGLER...
...THEN *YOU'RE* JUST A BRAT!

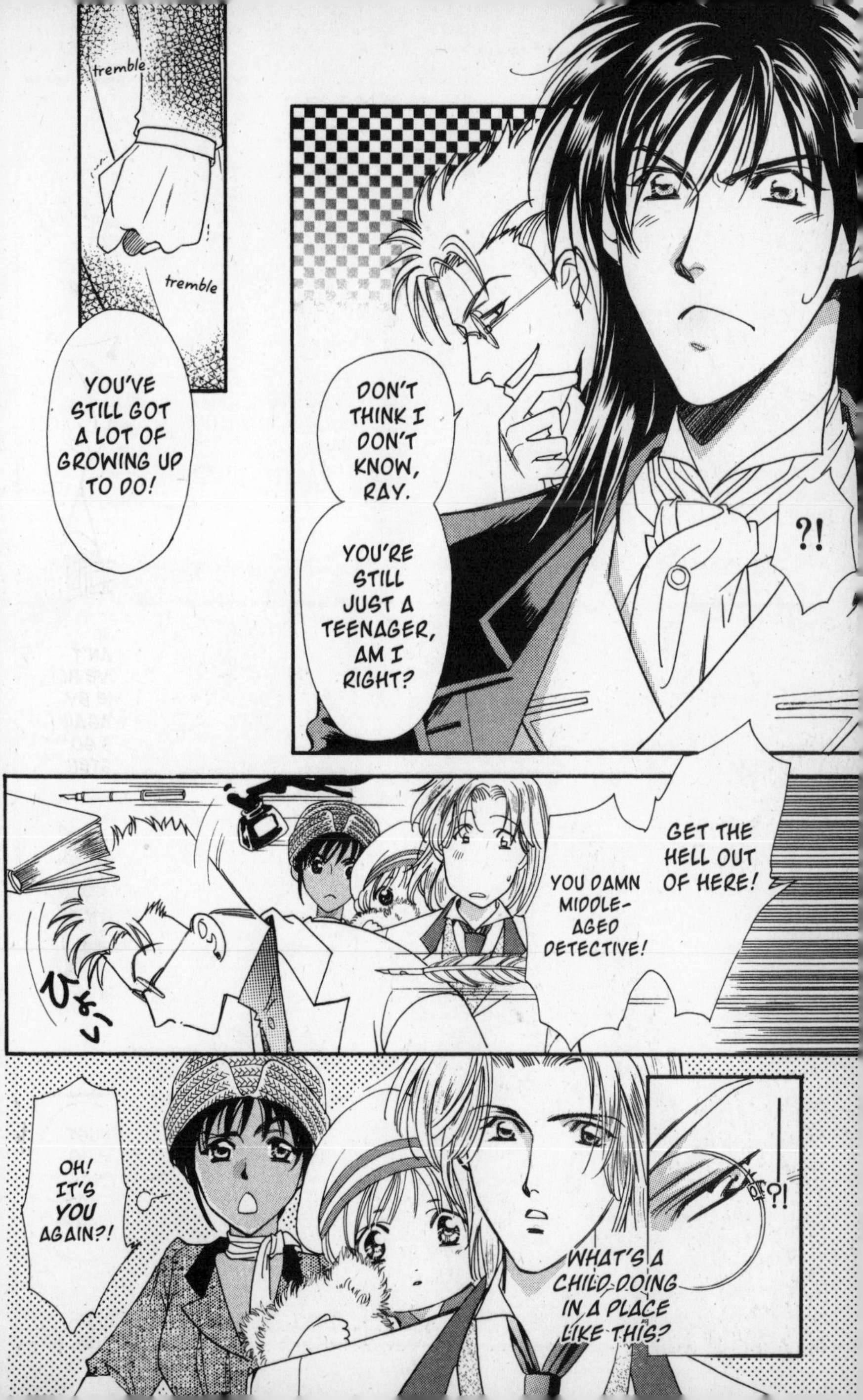
DON'T THINK I DON'T KNOW, RAY.
YOU'RE STILL JUST A TEENAGER, AM I RIGHT?
?!
tremble
tremble
YOU'VE STILL GOT A LOT OF GROWING UP TO DO!
GET THE HELL OUT OF HERE!
YOU DAMN MIDDLE-AGED DETECTIVE!
ひょい
?!
WHAT'S A CHILD DOING IN A PLACE LIKE THIS?
OH! IT'S YOU AGAIN?!

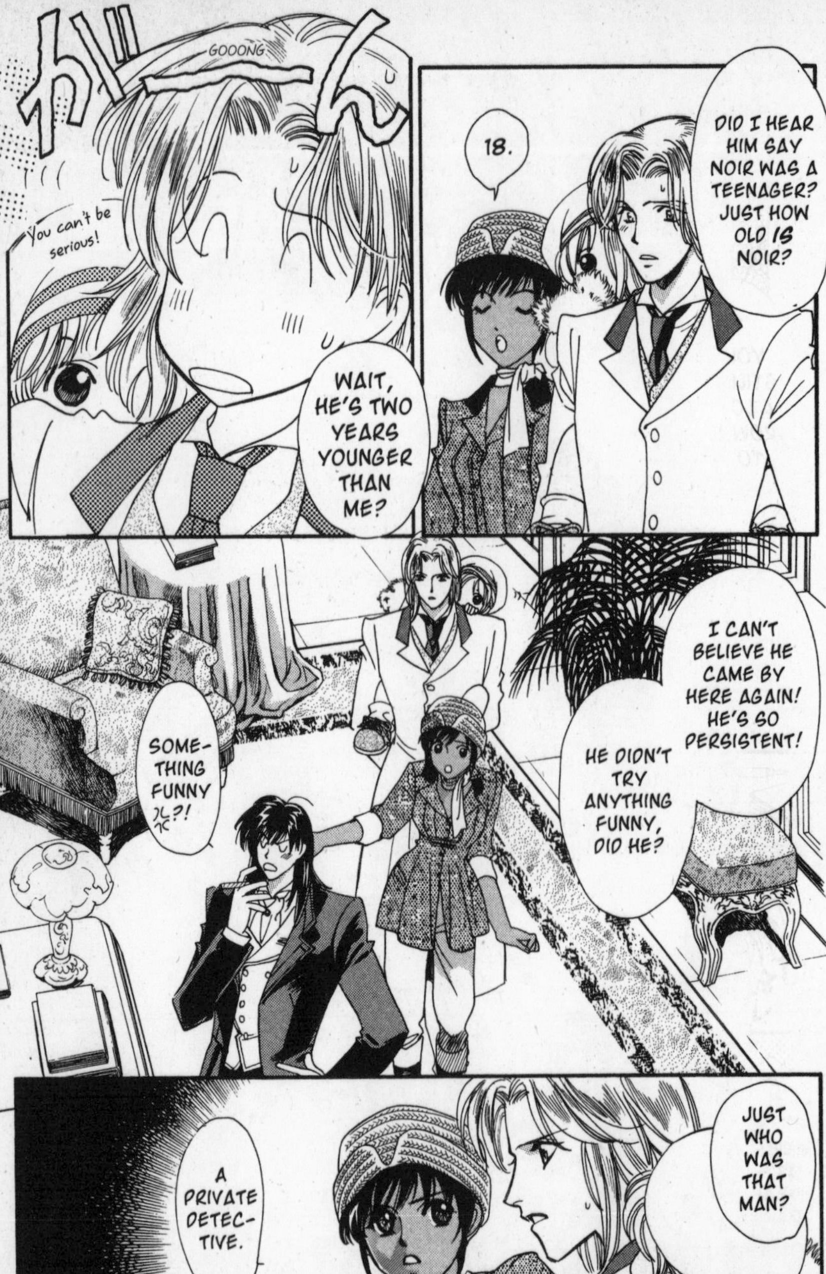
DID I HEAR HIM SAY NOIR WAS A TEENAGER? JUST HOW OLD IS NOIR?
18.
がーん
GOOONG
You can't be serious!
WAIT, HE'S TWO YEARS YOUNGER THAN ME?
I CAN'T BELIEVE HE CAME BY HERE AGAIN! HE'S SO PERSISTENT!
HE DIDN'T TRY ANYTHING FUNNY, DID HE?
SOME-THING FUNNY?!
JUST WHO WAS THAT MAN?
A PRIVATE DETEC-TIVE.

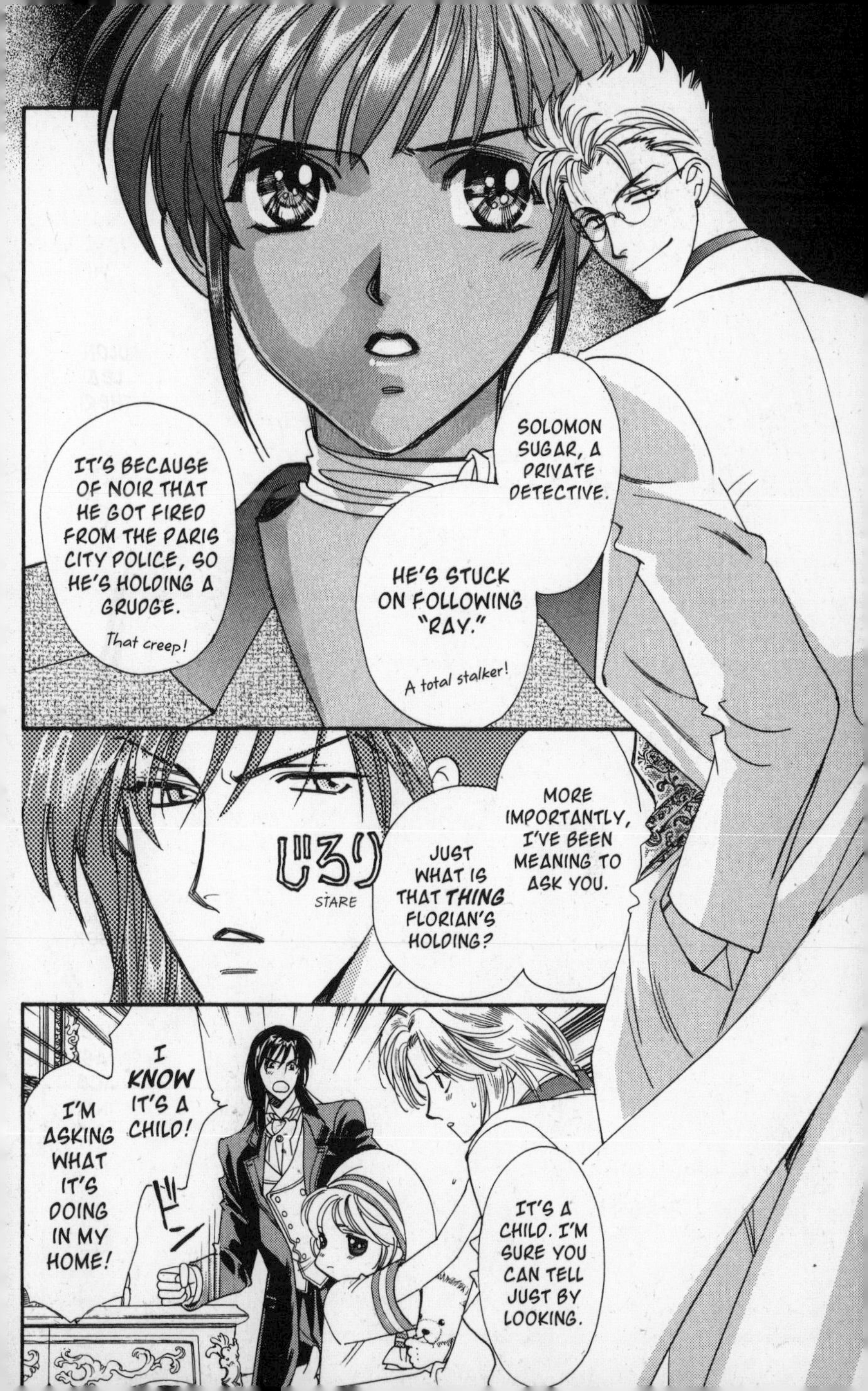
SOLOMON SUGAR, A PRIVATE DETECTIVE.
HE'S STUCK ON FOLLOWING "RAY."
A total stalker!
IT'S BECAUSE OF NOIR THAT HE GOT FIRED FROM THE PARIS CITY POLICE, SO HE'S HOLDING A GRUDGE.
That creep!
MORE IMPORTANTLY, I'VE BEEN MEANING TO ASK YOU.
JUST WHAT IS THAT THING FLORIAN'S HOLDING?
じろり
STARE
IT'S A CHILD. I'M SURE YOU CAN TELL JUST BY LOOKING.
I KNOW IT'S A CHILD!
I'M ASKING WHAT IT'S DOING IN MY HOME!

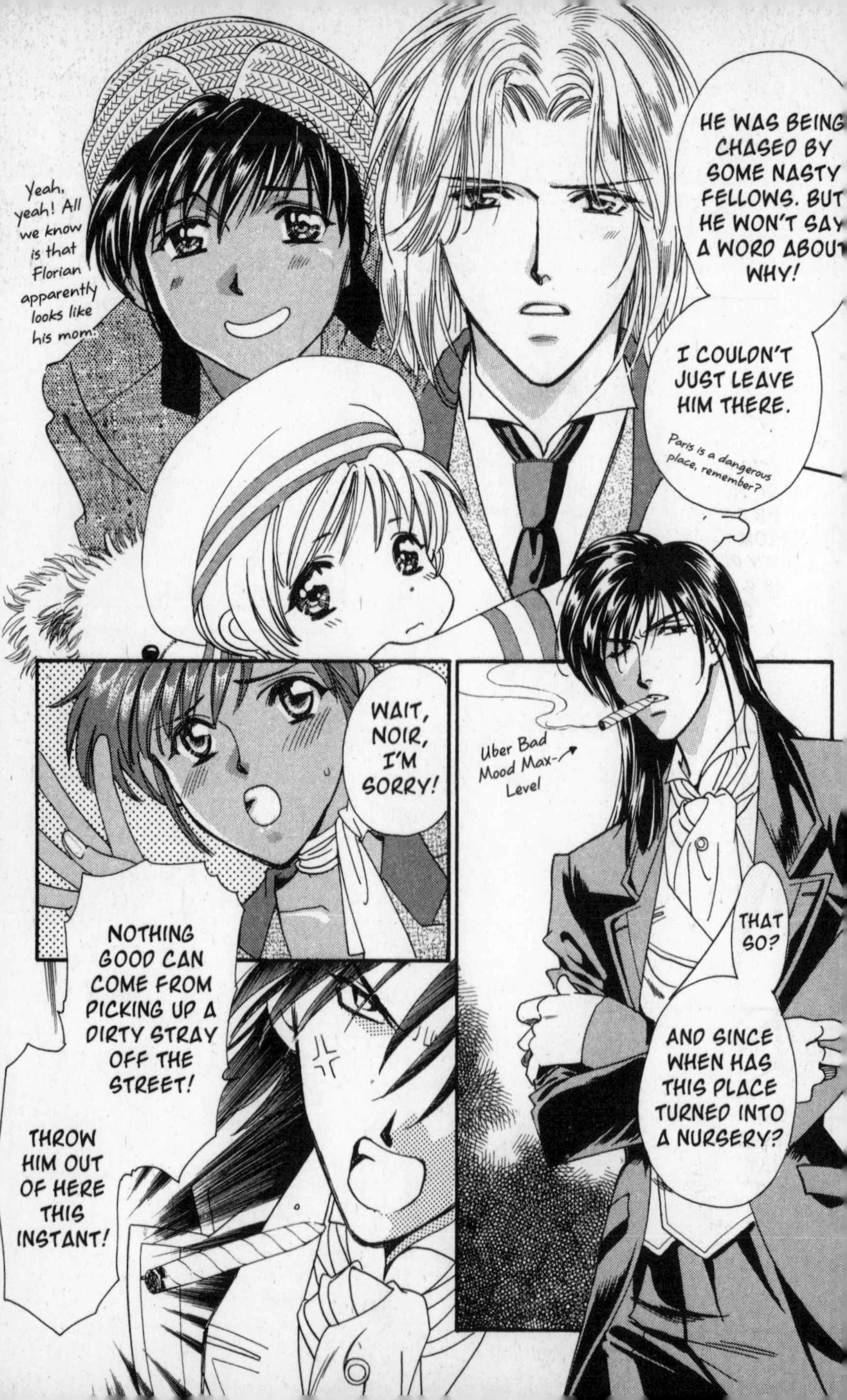
HE WAS BEING CHASED BY SOME NASTY FELLOWS. BUT HE WON'T SAY A WORD ABOUT WHY!
I COULDN'T JUST LEAVE HIM THERE.
Paris is a dangerous place, remember?
Yeah, yeah! All we know is that Florian apparently looks like his mom.
Uber Bad Mood Max-Level
THAT SO?
AND SINCE WHEN HAS THIS PLACE TURNED INTO A NURSERY?
WAIT, NOIR, I'M SORRY!
NOTHING GOOD CAN COME FROM PICKING UP A DIRTY STRAY OFF THE STREET!
THROW HIM OUT OF HERE THIS INSTANT!

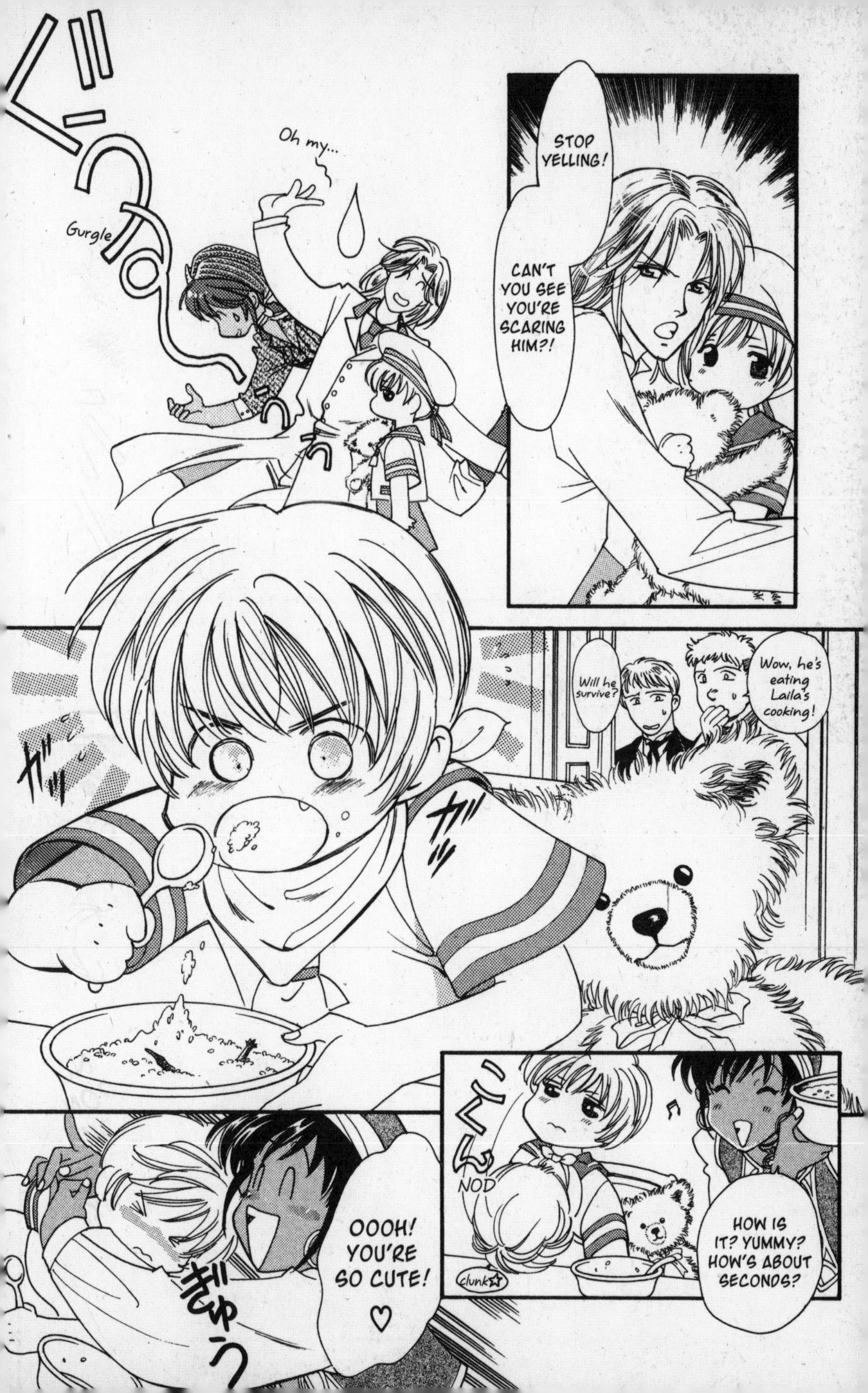
STOP YELLING!
CAN'T YOU SEE YOU'RE SCARING HIM?!
Oh my...
Gurgle
Wow, he's eating Laila's cooking!
Will he survive?
HOW IS IT? YUMMY? HOW'S ABOUT SECONDS?
こくん
NOD
clunk☆
OOOH! YOU'RE SO CUTE! ♡
ぎゅう

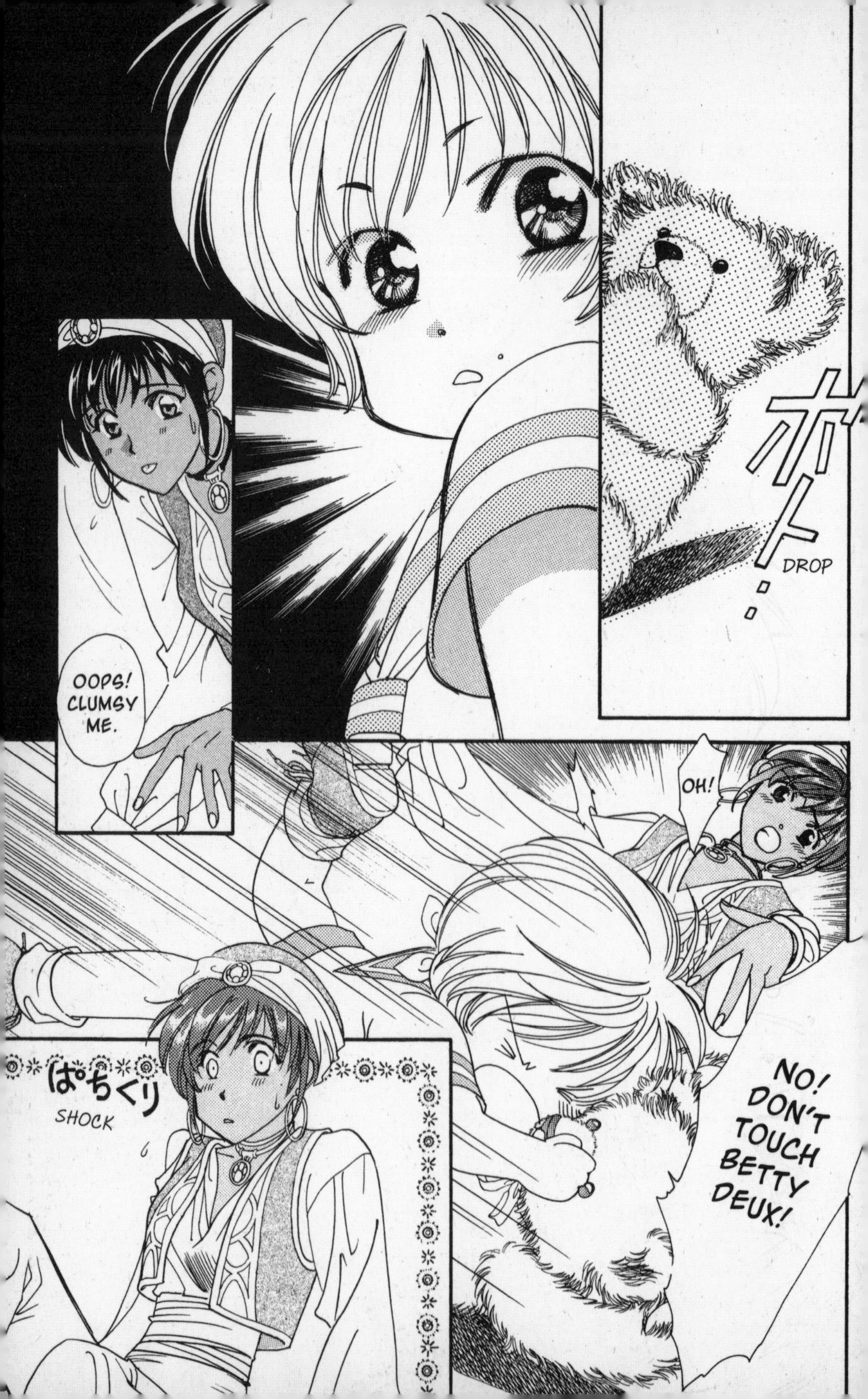
DROP
OOPS! CLUMSY ME.
OH!
NO! DON'T TOUCH BETTY DEUX!
ぱちくり
SHOCK

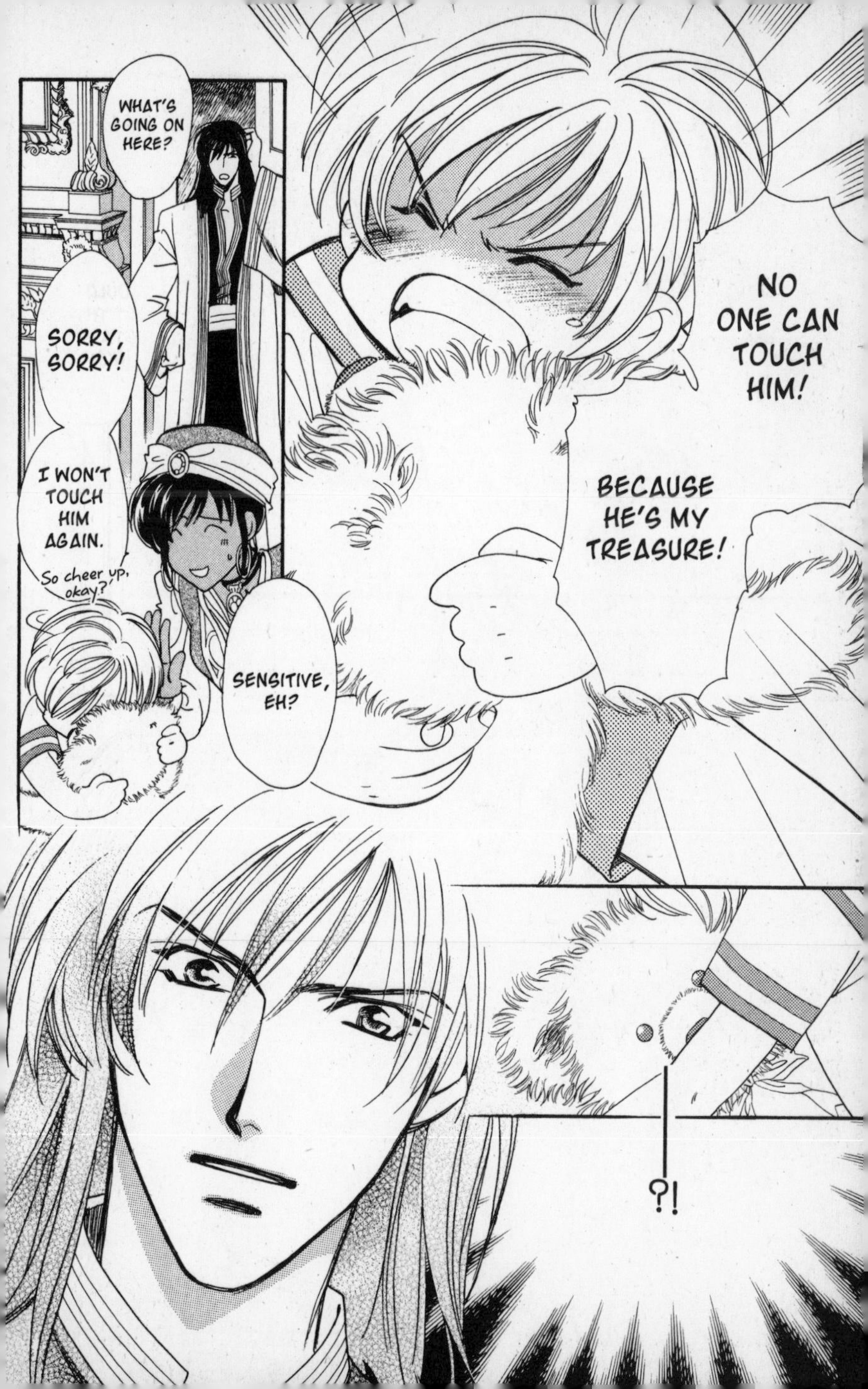
NO ONE CAN TOUCH HIM!
BECAUSE HE'S MY TREASURE!
WHAT'S GOING ON HERE?
SORRY, SORRY!
I WON'T TOUCH HIM AGAIN.
So cheer up, okay?
SENSITIVE, EH?
?!

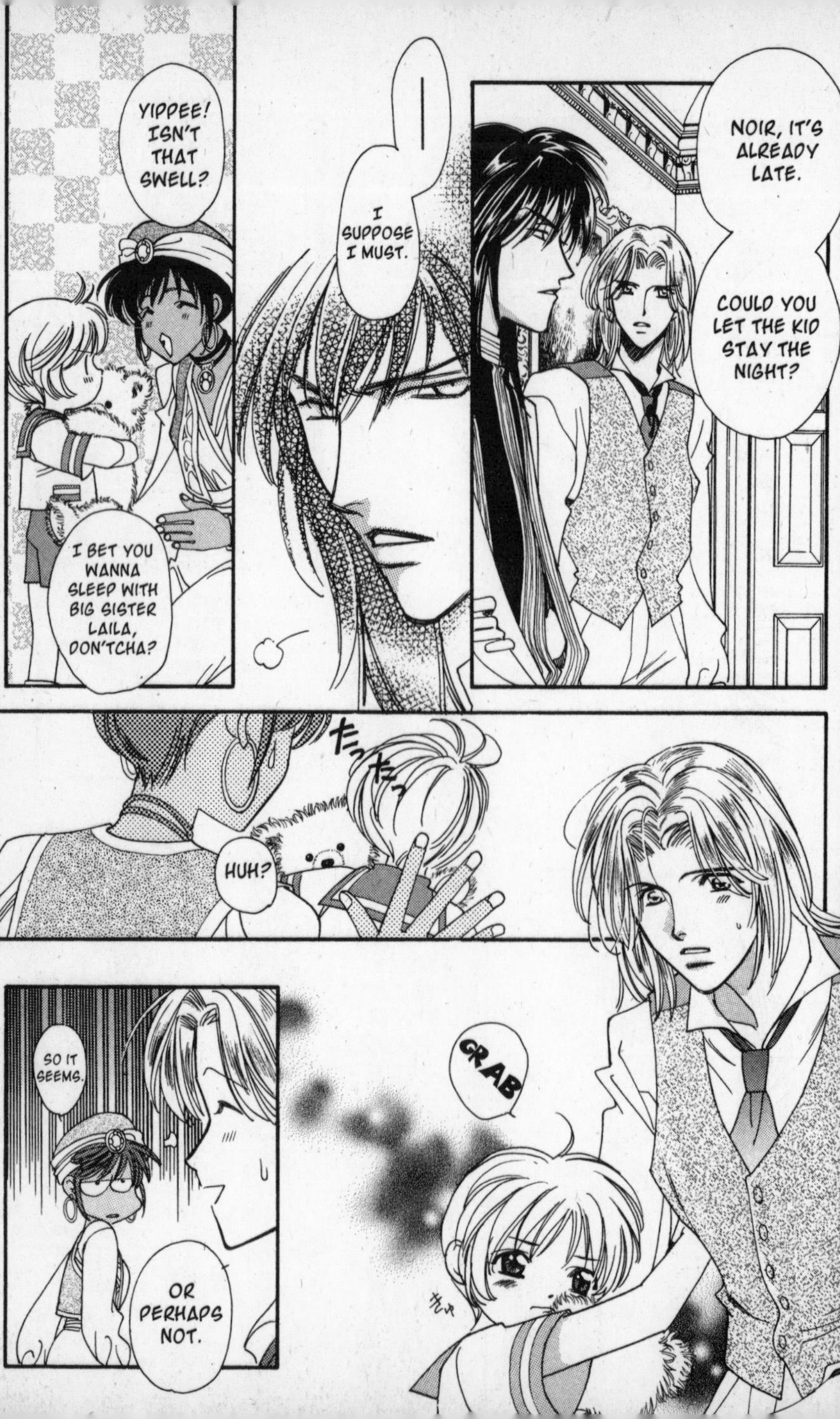
NOIR, IT'S ALREADY LATE.
COULD YOU LET THE KID STAY THE NIGHT?
I SUPPOSE I MUST.
YIPPEE! ISN'T THAT SWELL?
I BET YOU WANNA SLEEP WITH BIG SISTER LAILA, DON'TCHA?
HUH?
GRAB
SO IT SEEMS.
OR PERHAPS NOT.

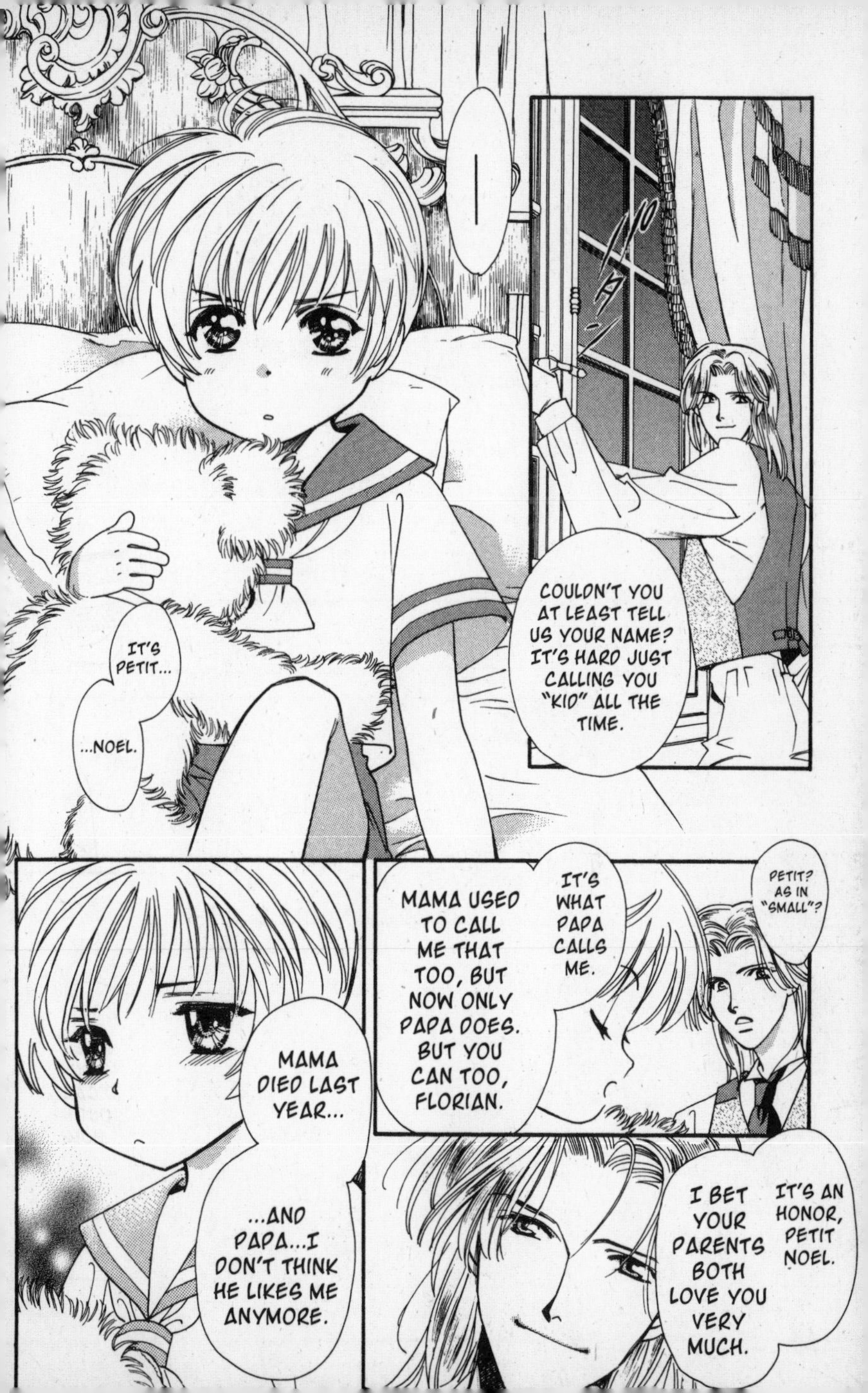
COULDN'T YOU AT LEAST TELL US YOUR NAME? IT'S HARD JUST CALLING YOU "KID" ALL THE TIME.
IT'S PETIT...
...NOEL.
PETIT? AS IN "SMALL"?
IT'S WHAT PAPA CALLS ME.
MAMA USED TO CALL ME THAT TOO, BUT NOW ONLY PAPA DOES. BUT YOU CAN TOO, FLORIAN.
IT'S AN HONOR, PETIT NOEL.
I BET YOUR PARENTS BOTH LOVE YOU VERY MUCH.
MAMA DIED LAST YEAR...
...AND PAPA...I DON'T THINK HE LIKES ME ANYMORE.

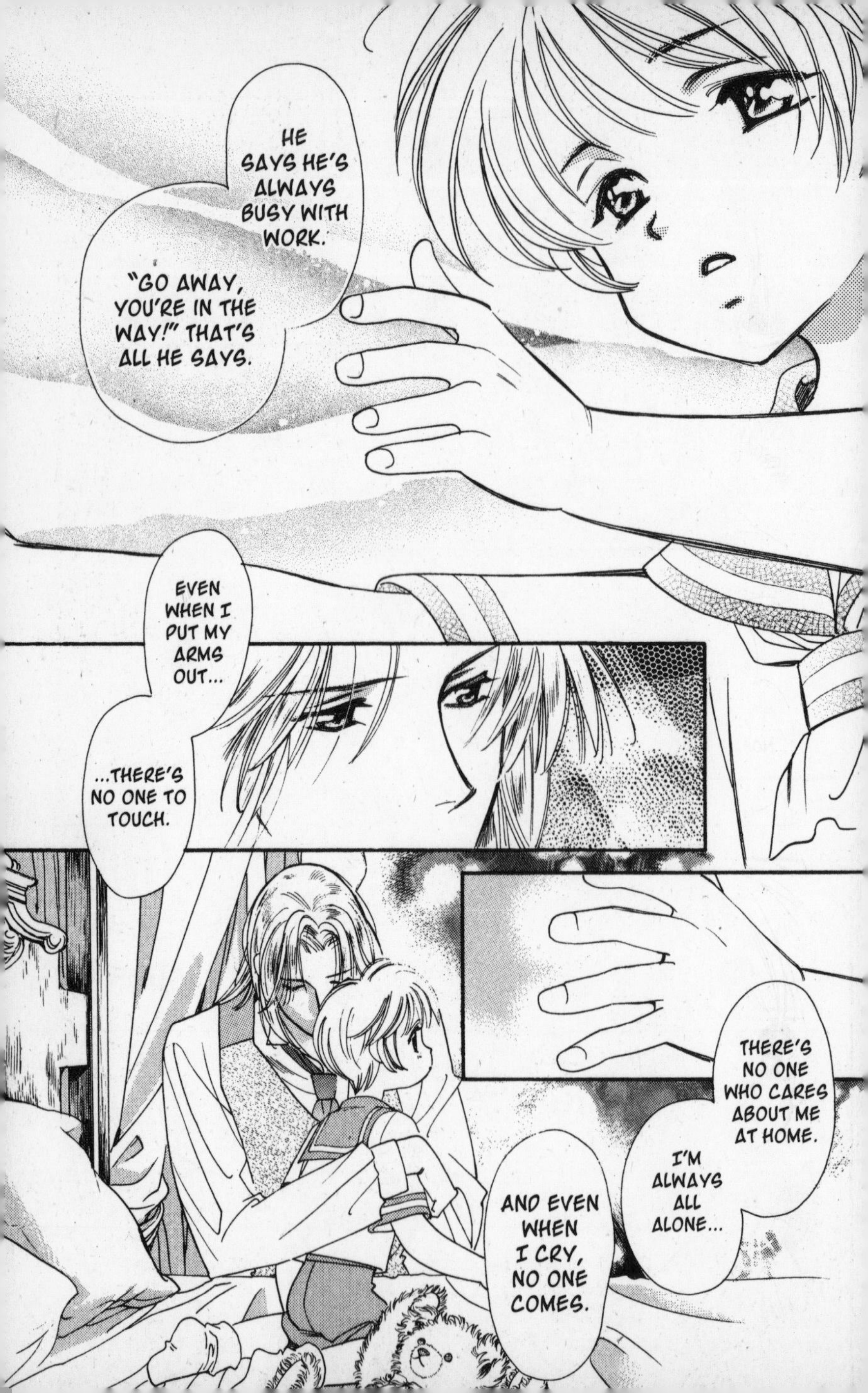
HE SAYS HE'S ALWAYS BUSY WITH WORK.
"GO AWAY, YOU'RE IN THE WAY!" THAT'S ALL HE SAYS.
EVEN WHEN I PUT MY ARMS OUT...
...THERE'S NO ONE TO TOUCH.
THERE'S NO ONE WHO CARES ABOUT ME AT HOME.
I'M ALWAYS ALL ALONE...
AND EVEN WHEN I CRY, NO ONE COMES.

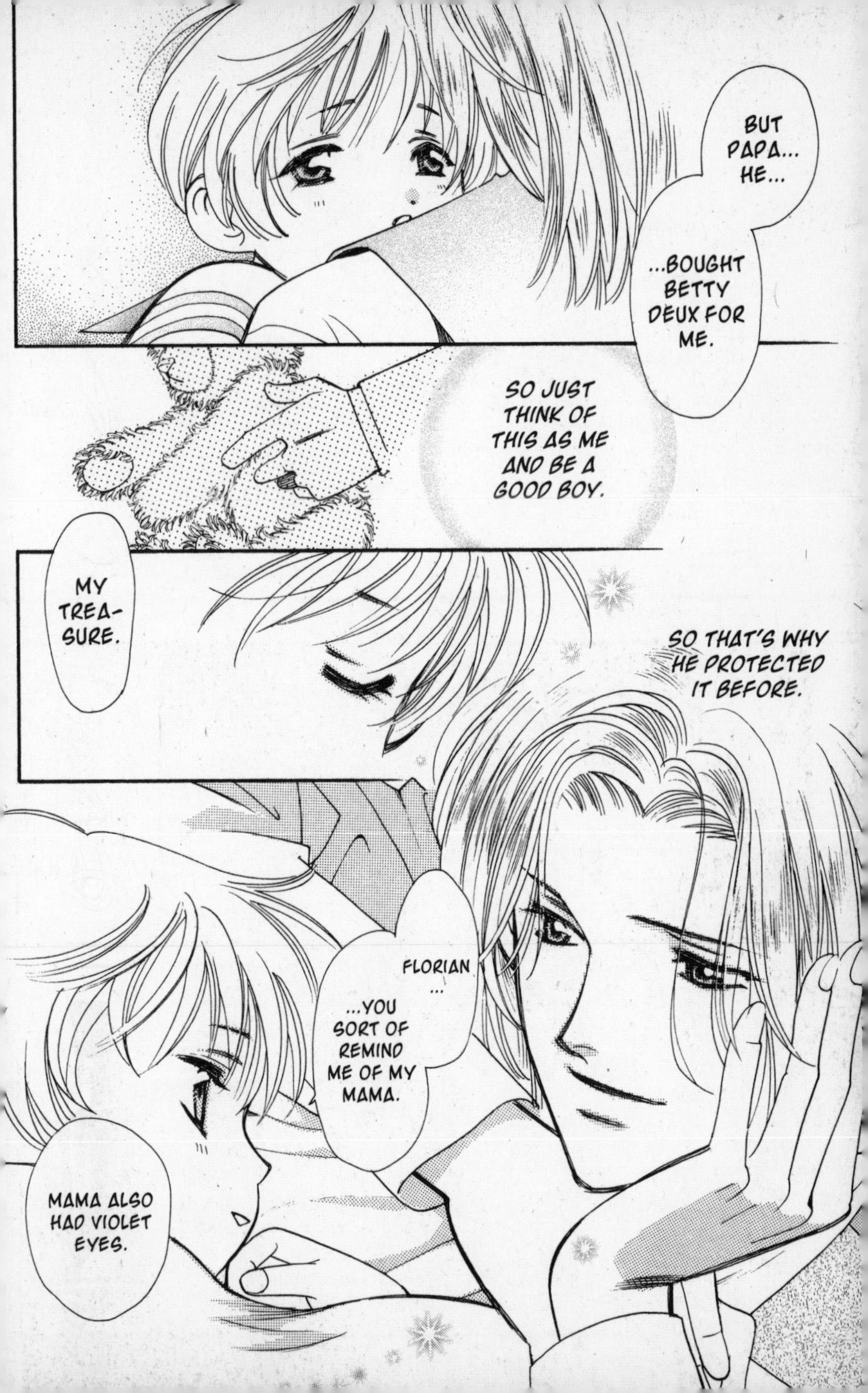
BUT PAPA... HE...
...BOUGHT BETTY DEUX FOR ME.
SO JUST THINK OF THIS AS ME AND BE A GOOD BOY.
MY TREA-SURE.
SO THAT'S WHY HE PROTECTED IT BEFORE.
FLORIAN ... ...YOU SORT OF REMIND ME OF MY MAMA.
MAMA ALSO HAD VIOLET EYES.

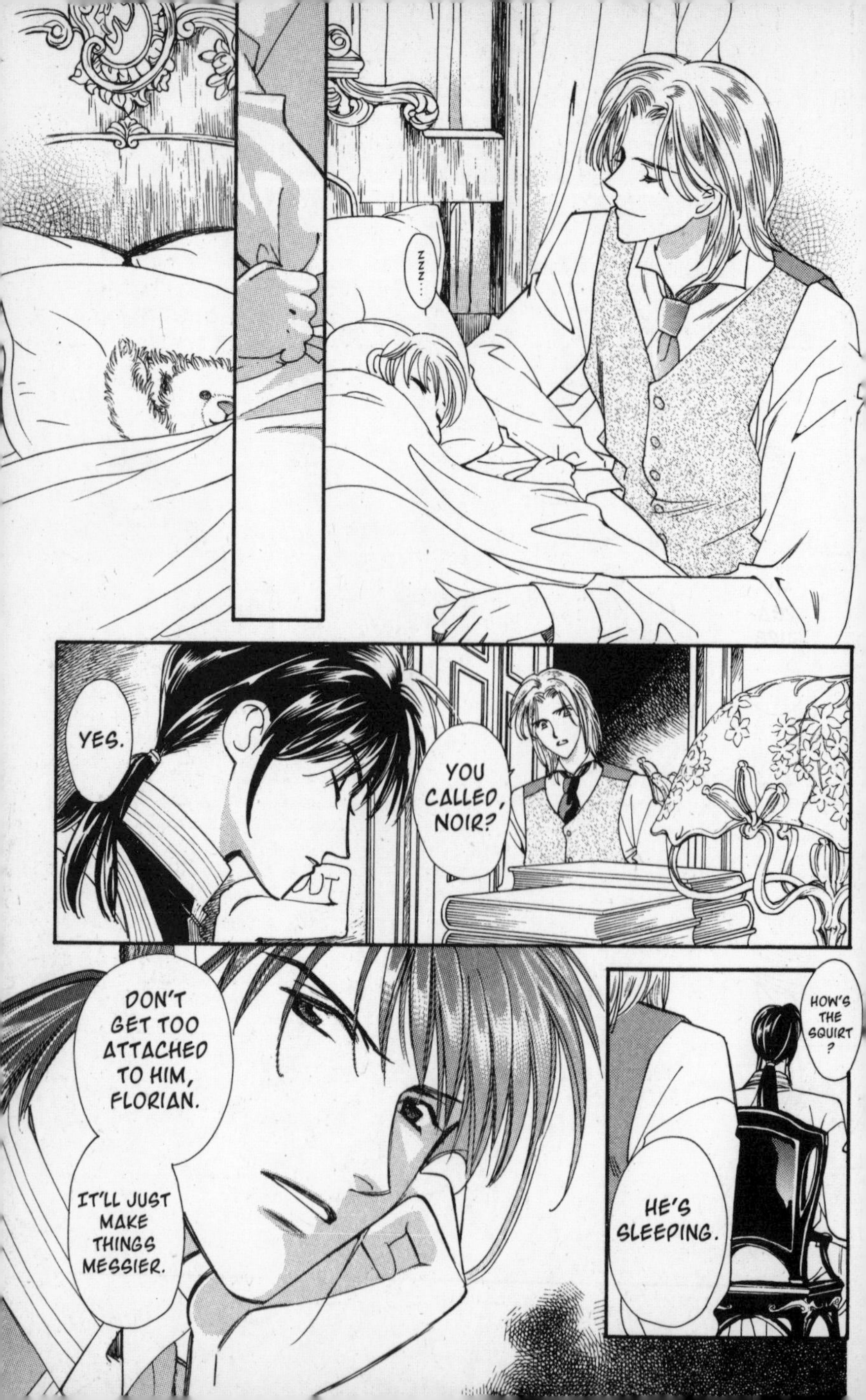
ZZZ...
YOU CALLED, NOIR?
YES.
HOW'S THE SQUIRT?
HE'S SLEEPING.
DON'T GET TOO ATTACHED TO HIM, FLORIAN.
IT'LL JUST MAKE THINGS MESSIER.

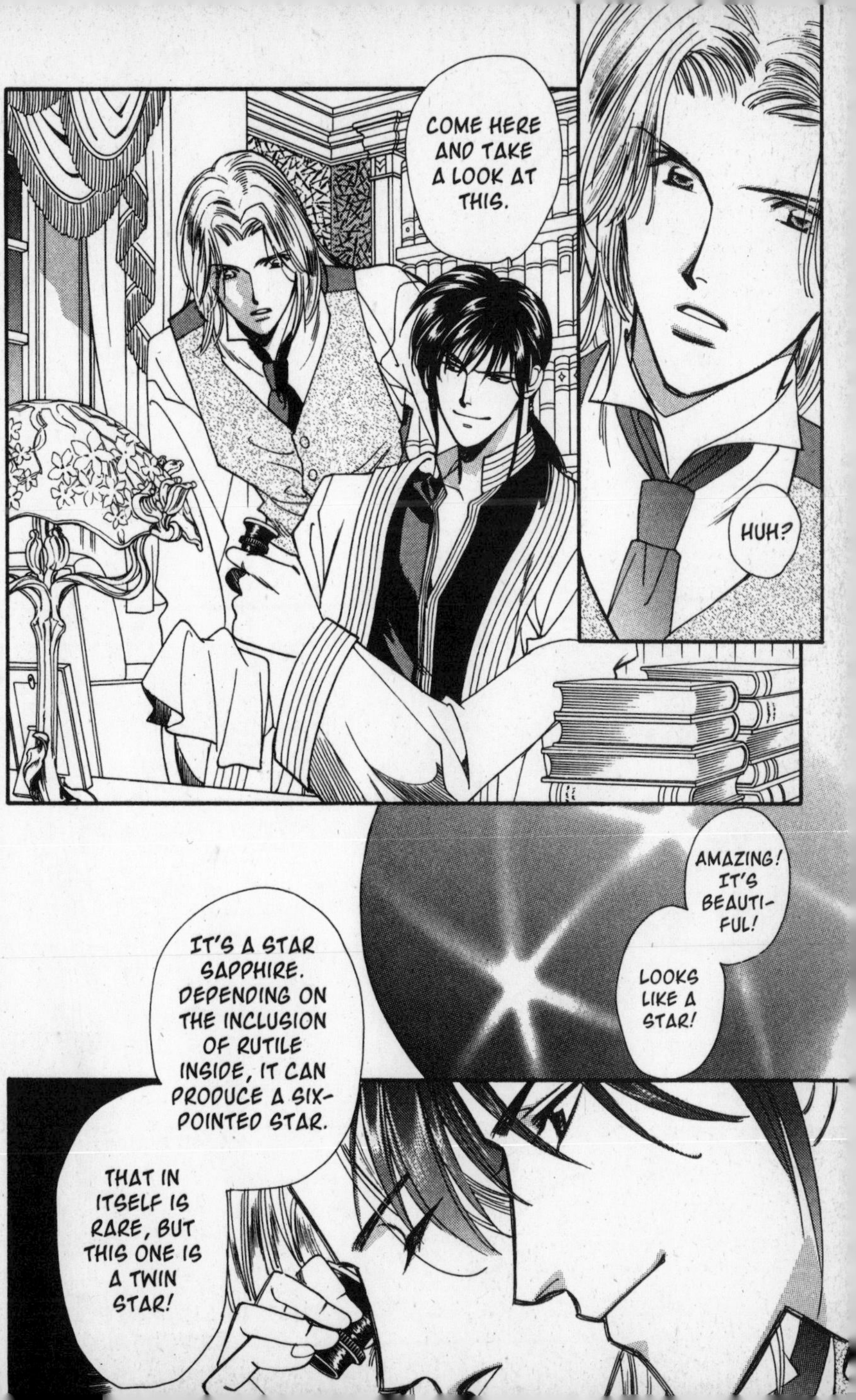
HUH?
COME HERE AND TAKE A LOOK AT THIS.
AMAZING! IT'S BEAUTI-FUL!
LOOKS LIKE A STAR!
IT'S A STAR SAPPHIRE. DEPENDING ON THE INCLUSION OF RUTILE INSIDE, IT CAN PRODUCE A SIX-POINTED STAR.
THAT IN ITSELF IS RARE, BUT THIS ONE IS A TWIN STAR!

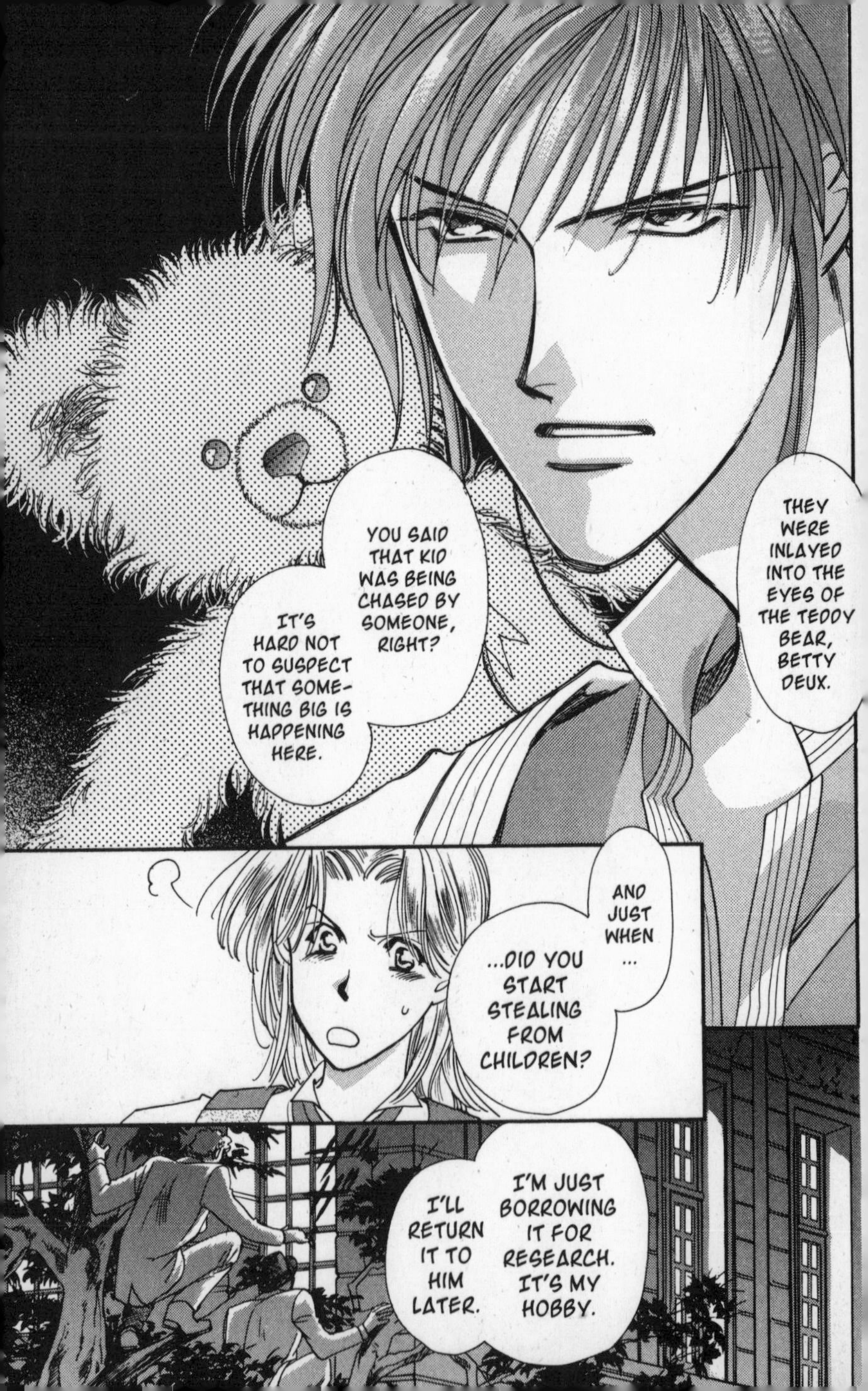
THEY WERE INLAYED INTO THE EYES OF THE TEDDY BEAR, BETTY DEUX.
YOU SAID THAT KID WAS BEING CHASED BY SOMEONE, RIGHT?
IT'S HARD NOT TO SUSPECT THAT SOMETHING BIG IS HAPPENING HERE.
AND JUST WHEN ...
...DID YOU START STEALING FROM CHILDREN?
I'M JUST BORROWING IT FOR RESEARCH. IT'S MY HOBBY.
I'LL RETURN IT TO HIM LATER.

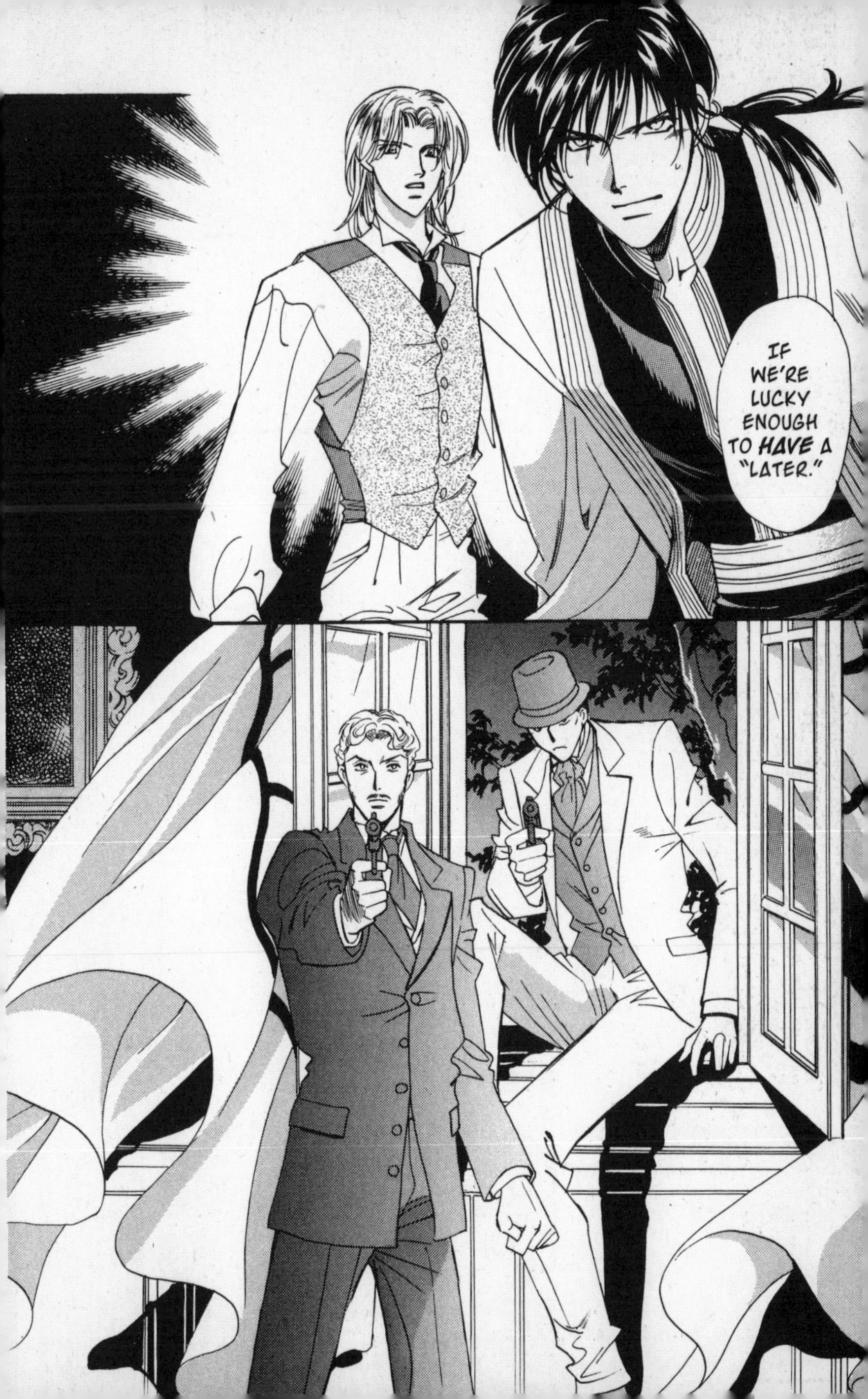
IF WE'RE LUCKY ENOUGH TO *HAVE* A "LATER."

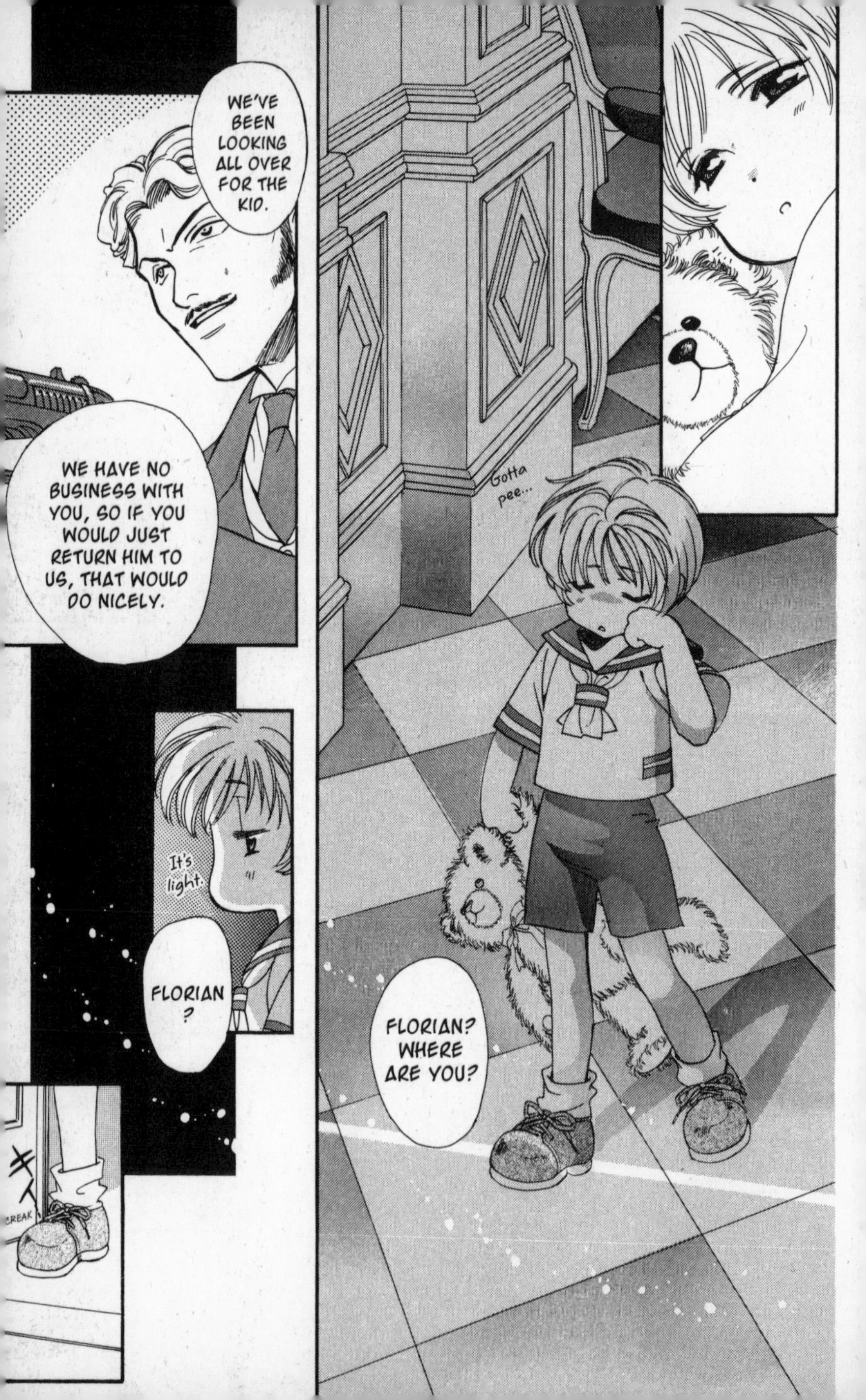
Gotta pee...
FLORIAN? WHERE ARE YOU?
WE'VE BEEN LOOKING ALL OVER FOR THE KID.
WE HAVE NO BUSINESS WITH YOU, SO IF YOU WOULD JUST RETURN HIM TO US, THAT WOULD DO NICELY.
It's light.
FLORIAN?
CREAK

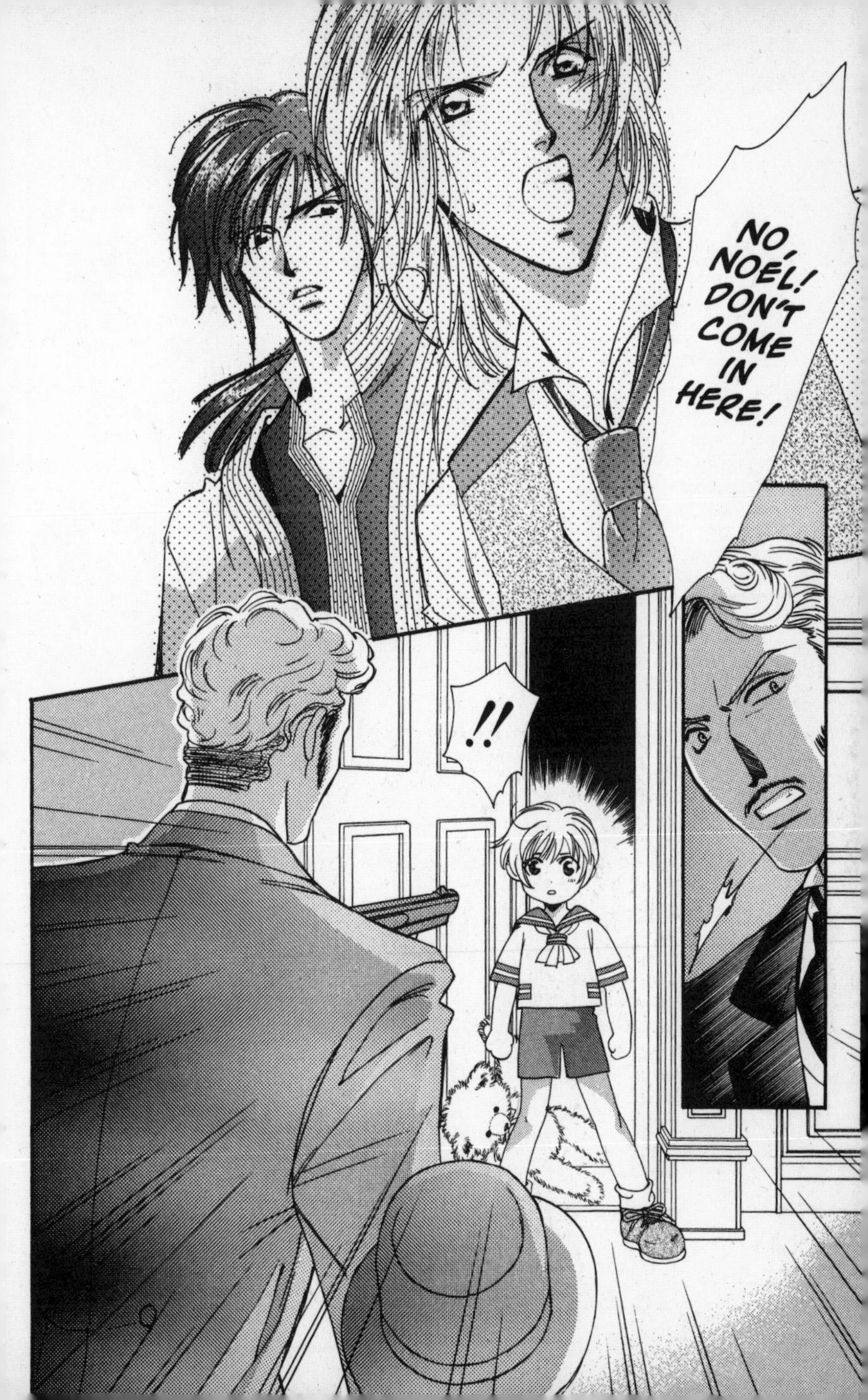
NO, NOEL! DON'T COME IN HERE!
!!

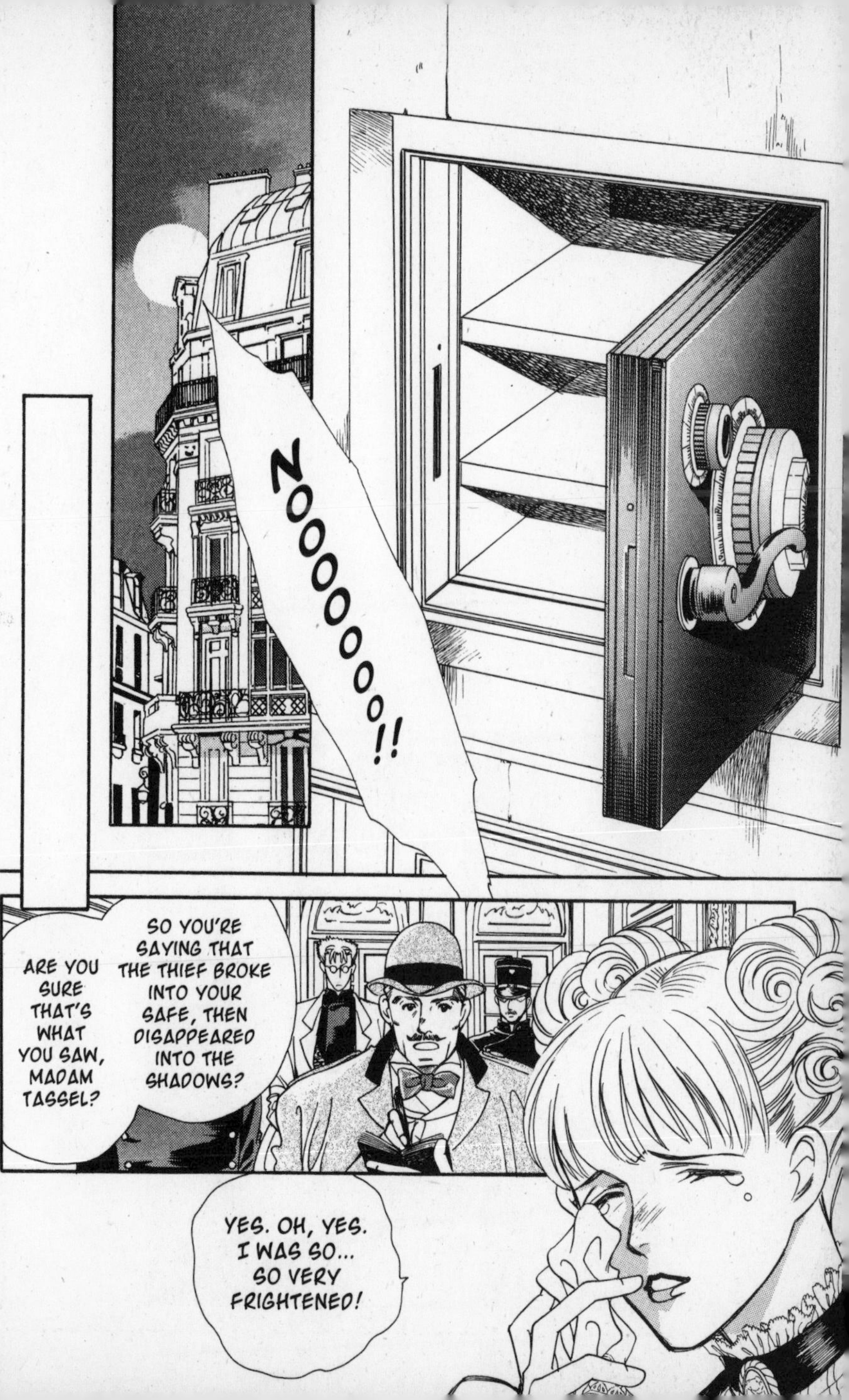
NOOOOOOO!!
SO YOU'RE SAYING THAT THE THIEF BROKE INTO YOUR SAFE, THEN DISAPPEARED INTO THE SHADOWS?
ARE YOU SURE THAT'S WHAT YOU SAW, MADAM TASSEL?
YES. OH, YES. I WAS SO... SO VERY FRIGHTENED!

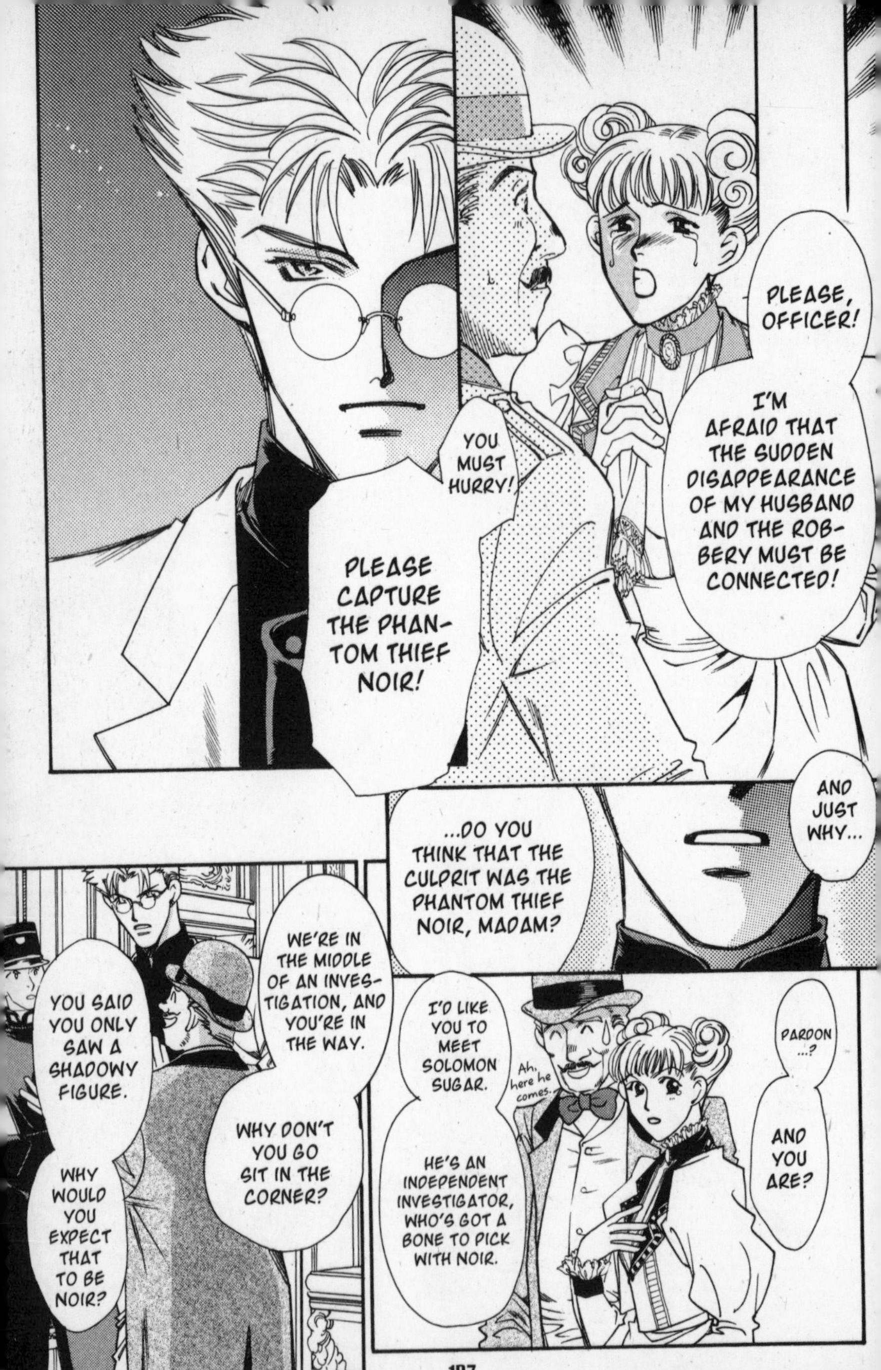
PLEASE, OFFICER!
I'M AFRAID THAT THE SUDDEN DISAPPEARANCE OF MY HUSBAND AND THE ROB-BERY MUST BE CONNECTED!
YOU MUST HURRY!
PLEASE CAPTURE THE PHAN-TOM THIEF NOIR!
AND JUST WHY...
...DO YOU THINK THAT THE CULPRIT WAS THE PHANTOM THIEF NOIR, MADAM?
PARDON ...?
AND YOU ARE?
I'D LIKE YOU TO MEET SOLOMON SUGAR.
Ah, here he comes.
HE'S AN INDEPENDENT INVESTIGATOR, WHO'S GOT A BONE TO PICK WITH NOIR.
WE'RE IN THE MIDDLE OF AN INVES-TIGATION, AND YOU'RE IN THE WAY.
WHY DON'T YOU GO SIT IN THE CORNER?
YOU SAID YOU ONLY SAW A SHADOWY FIGURE.
WHY WOULD YOU EXPECT THAT TO BE NOIR?

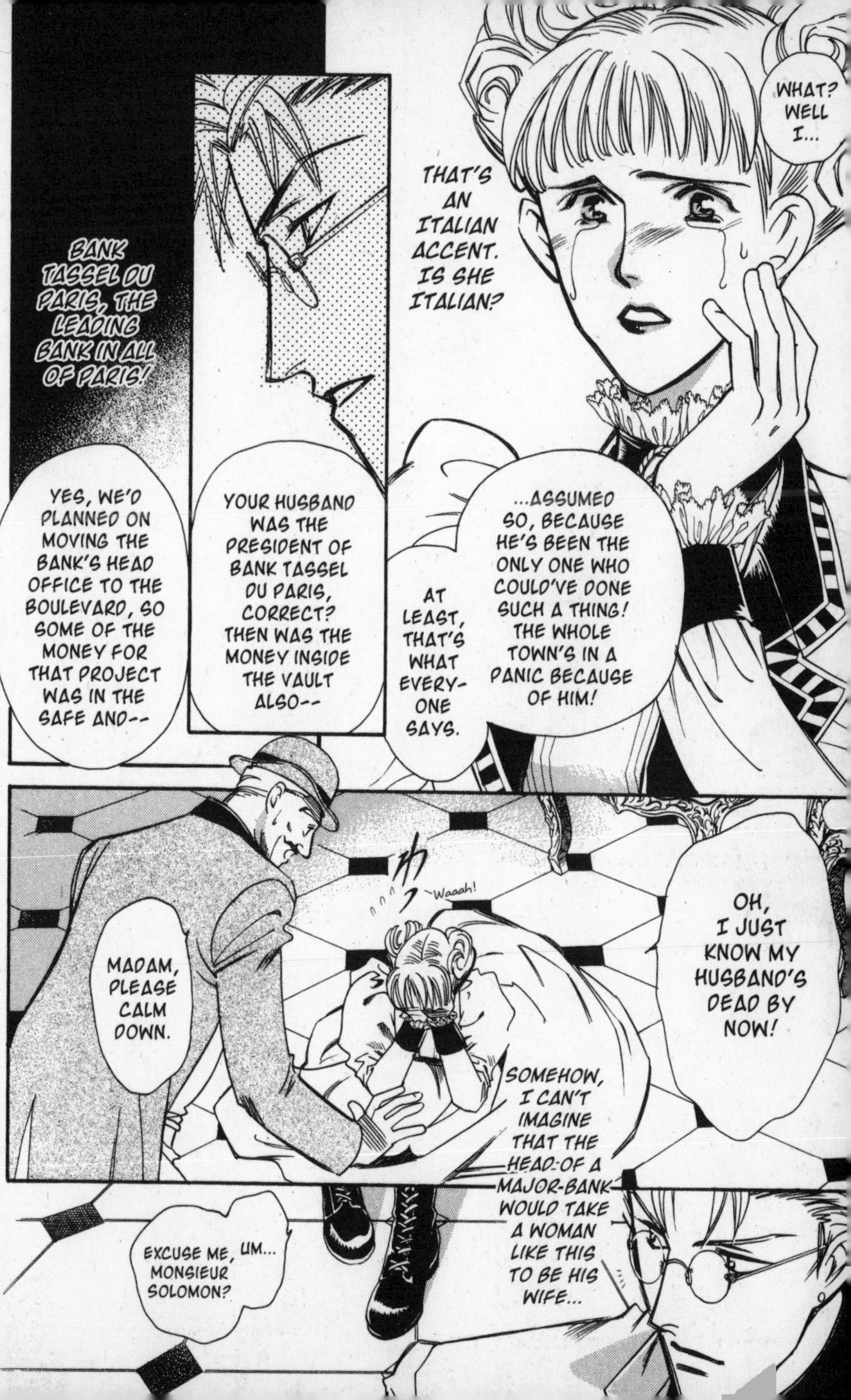
WHAT? WELL I...
THAT'S AN ITALIAN ACCENT. IS SHE ITALIAN?
...ASSUMED SO, BECAUSE HE'S BEEN THE ONLY ONE WHO COULD'VE DONE SUCH A THING! THE WHOLE TOWN'S IN A PANIC BECAUSE OF HIM!
AT LEAST, THAT'S WHAT EVERY-ONE SAYS.
YOUR HUSBAND WAS THE PRESIDENT OF BANK TASSEL DU PARIS, CORRECT? THEN WAS THE MONEY INSIDE THE VAULT ALSO--
BANK TASSEL DU PARIS, THE LEADING BANK IN ALL OF PARIS!
YES, WE'D PLANNED ON MOVING THE BANK'S HEAD OFFICE TO THE BOULEVARD, SO SOME OF THE MONEY FOR THAT PROJECT WAS IN THE SAFE AND--
OH, I JUST KNOW MY HUSBAND'S DEAD BY NOW!
Waaah!
MADAM, PLEASE CALM DOWN.
SOMEHOW, I CAN'T IMAGINE THAT THE HEAD OF A MAJOR BANK WOULD TAKE A WOMAN LIKE THIS TO BE HIS WIFE...
EXCUSE ME, UM... MONSIEUR SOLOMON?

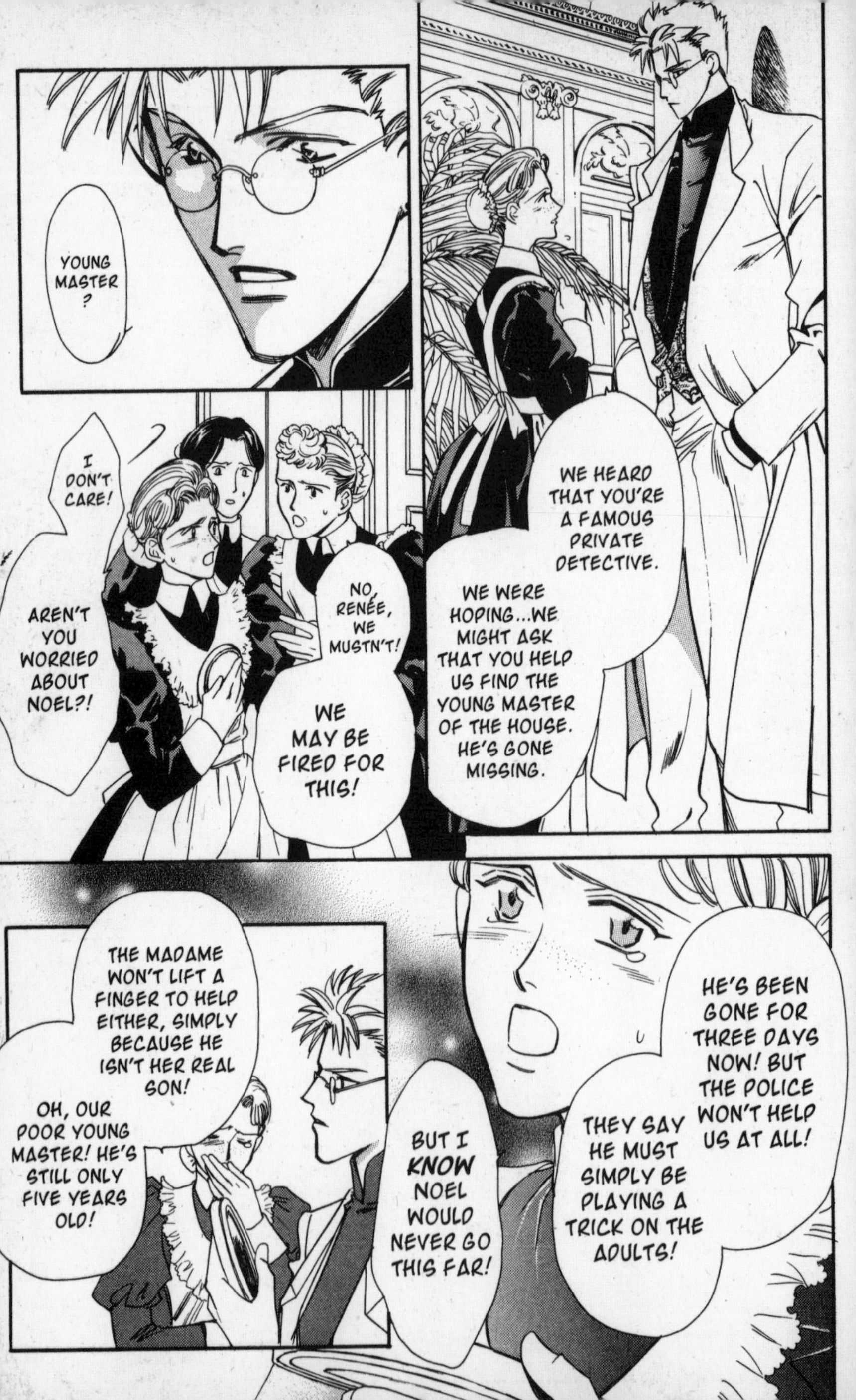
WE HEARD THAT YOU'RE A FAMOUS PRIVATE DETECTIVE.
WE WERE HOPING...WE MIGHT ASK THAT YOU HELP US FIND THE YOUNG MASTER OF THE HOUSE. HE'S GONE MISSING.
YOUNG MASTER?
NO, RENÉE, WE MUSTN'T!
WE MAY BE FIRED FOR THIS!
I DON'T CARE!
AREN'T YOU WORRIED ABOUT NOEL?!
HE'S BEEN GONE FOR THREE DAYS NOW! BUT THE POLICE WON'T HELP US AT ALL!
THEY SAY HE MUST SIMPLY BE PLAYING A TRICK ON THE ADULTS!
BUT I **KNOW** NOEL WOULD NEVER GO THIS FAR!
THE MADAME WON'T LIFT A FINGER TO HELP EITHER, SIMPLY BECAUSE HE ISN'T HER REAL SON!
OH, OUR POOR YOUNG MASTER! HE'S STILL ONLY FIVE YEARS OLD!

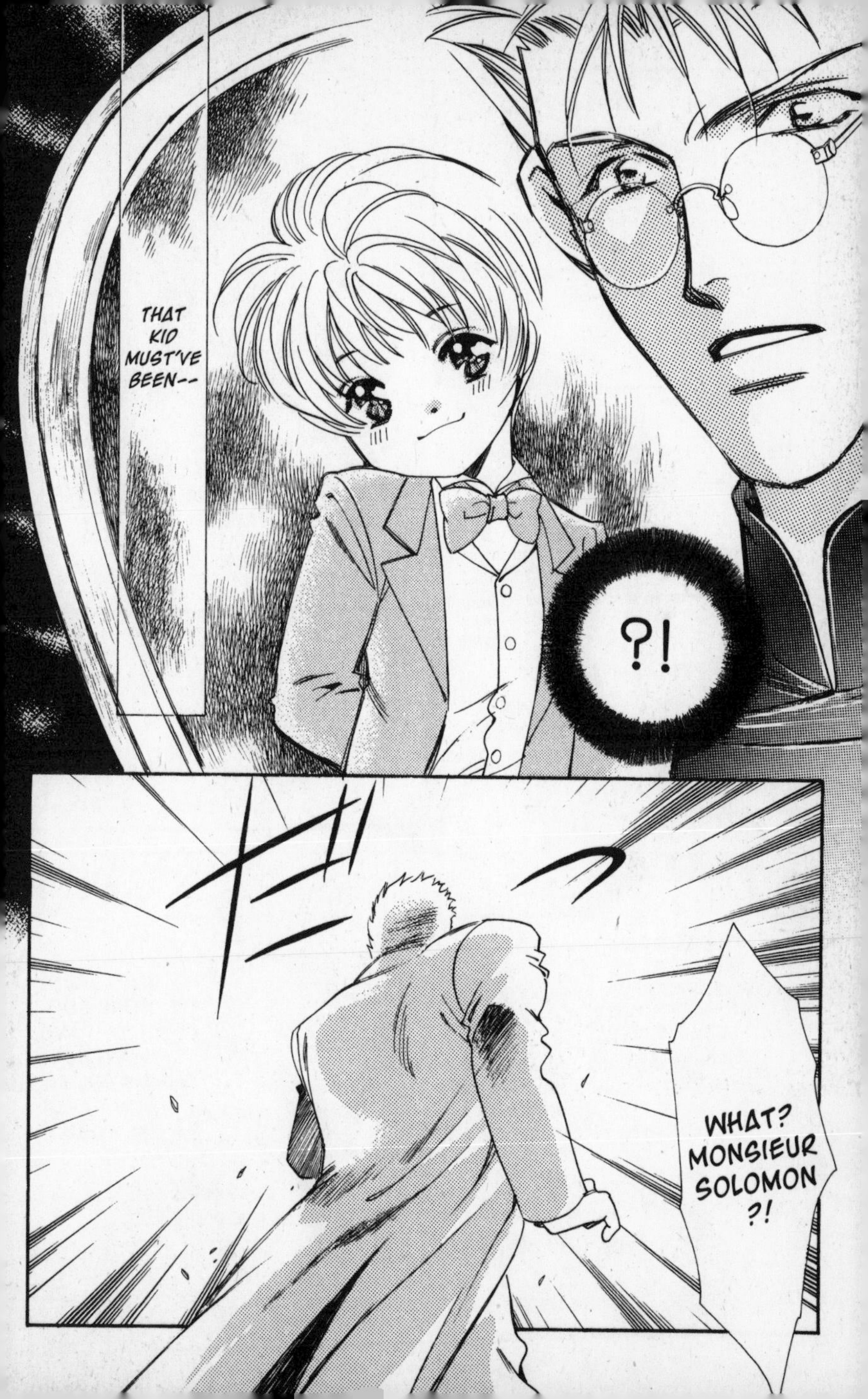
THAT KID MUST'VE BEEN--
?!
WHAT? MONSIEUR SOLOMON ?!

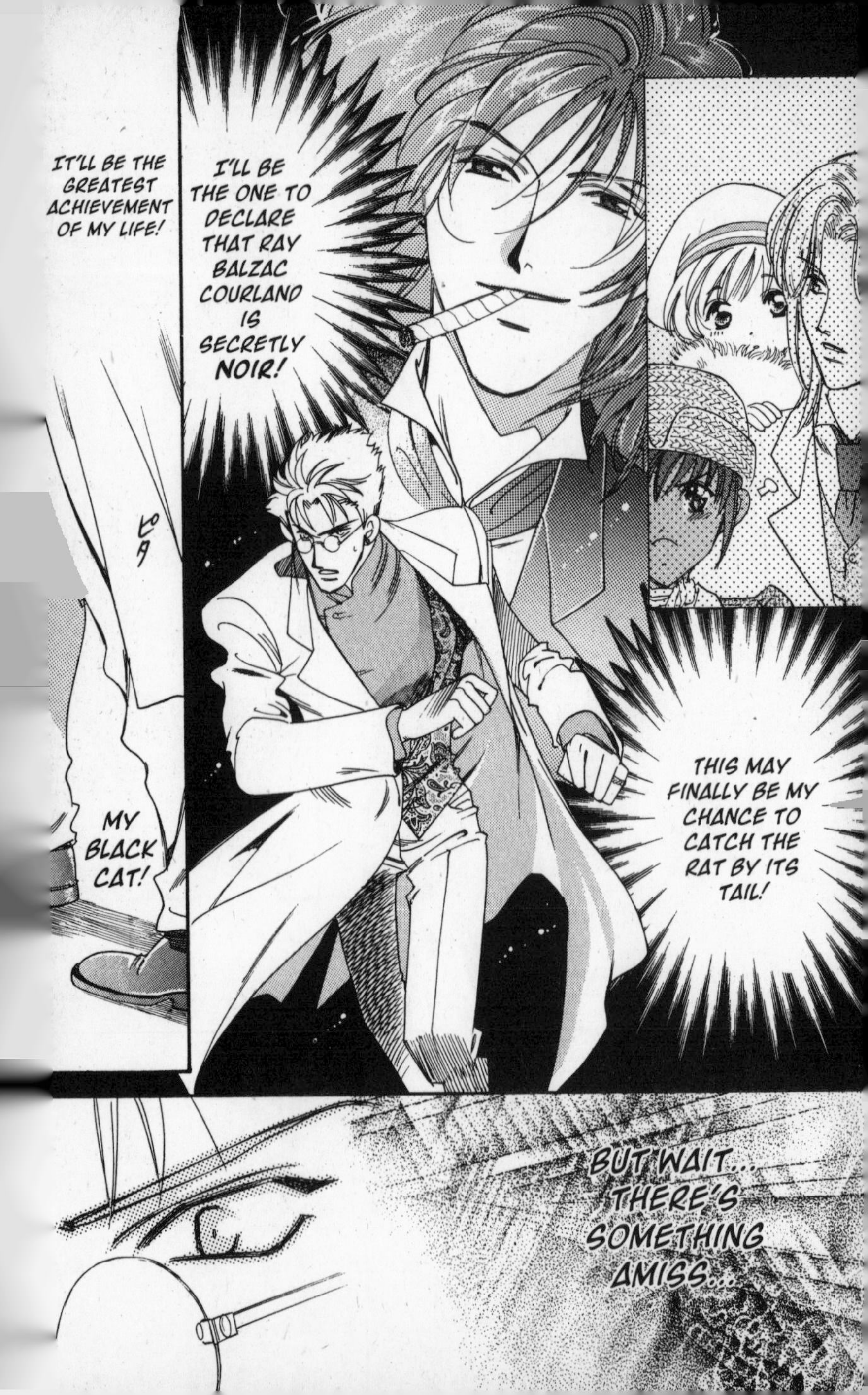

I'LL BE THE ONE TO DECLARE THAT RAY BALZAC COURLAND IS SECRETLY NOIR!
THIS MAY FINALLY BE MY CHANCE TO CATCH THE RAT BY ITS TAIL!
IT'LL BE THE GREATEST ACHIEVEMENT OF MY LIFE!
MY BLACK CAT!
BUT WAIT... THERE'S SOMETHING AMISS...

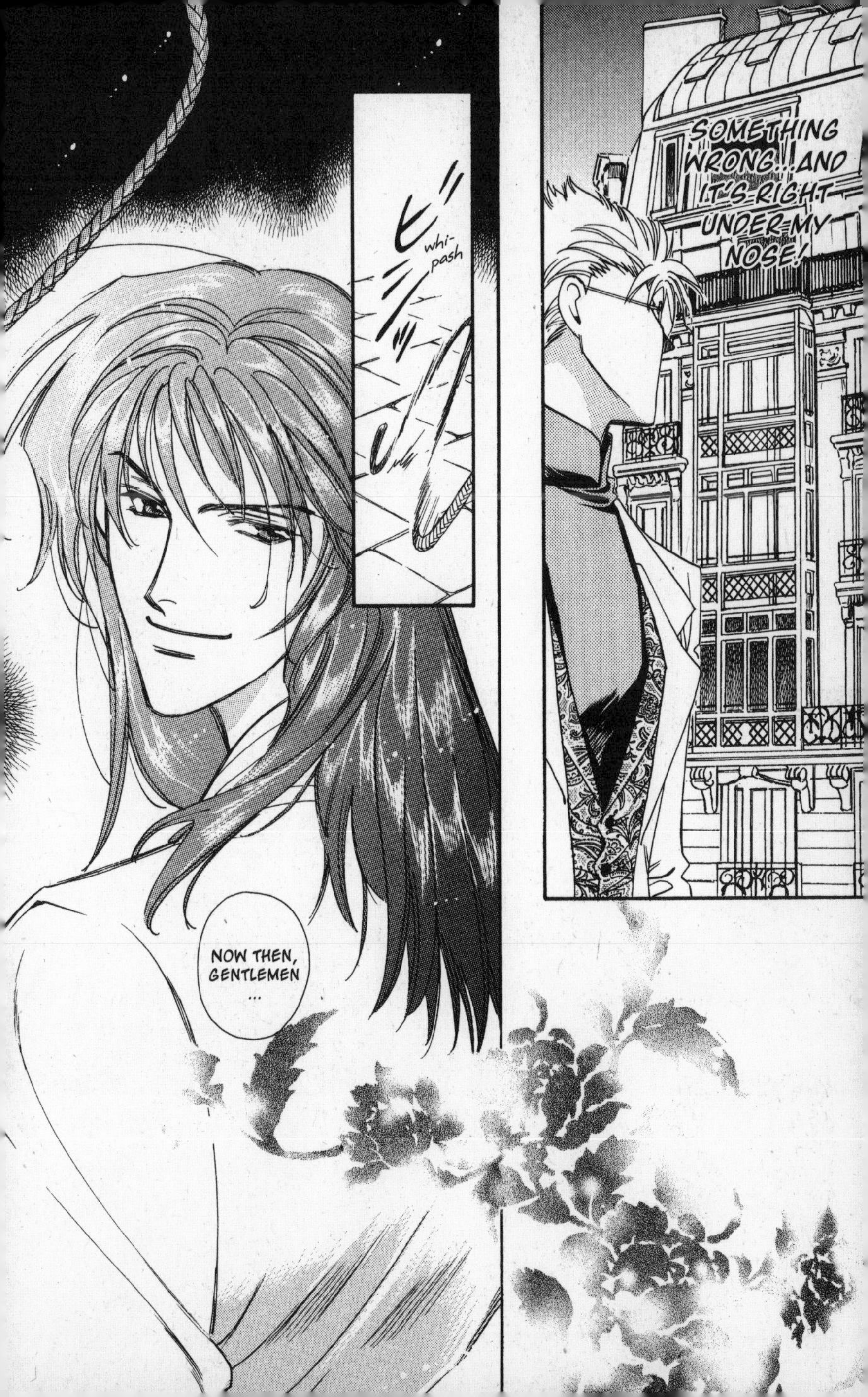
SOMETHING WRONG...AND IT'S RIGHT UNDER MY NOSE!
ヒ
whi-pash
NOW THEN, GENTLEMEN ...

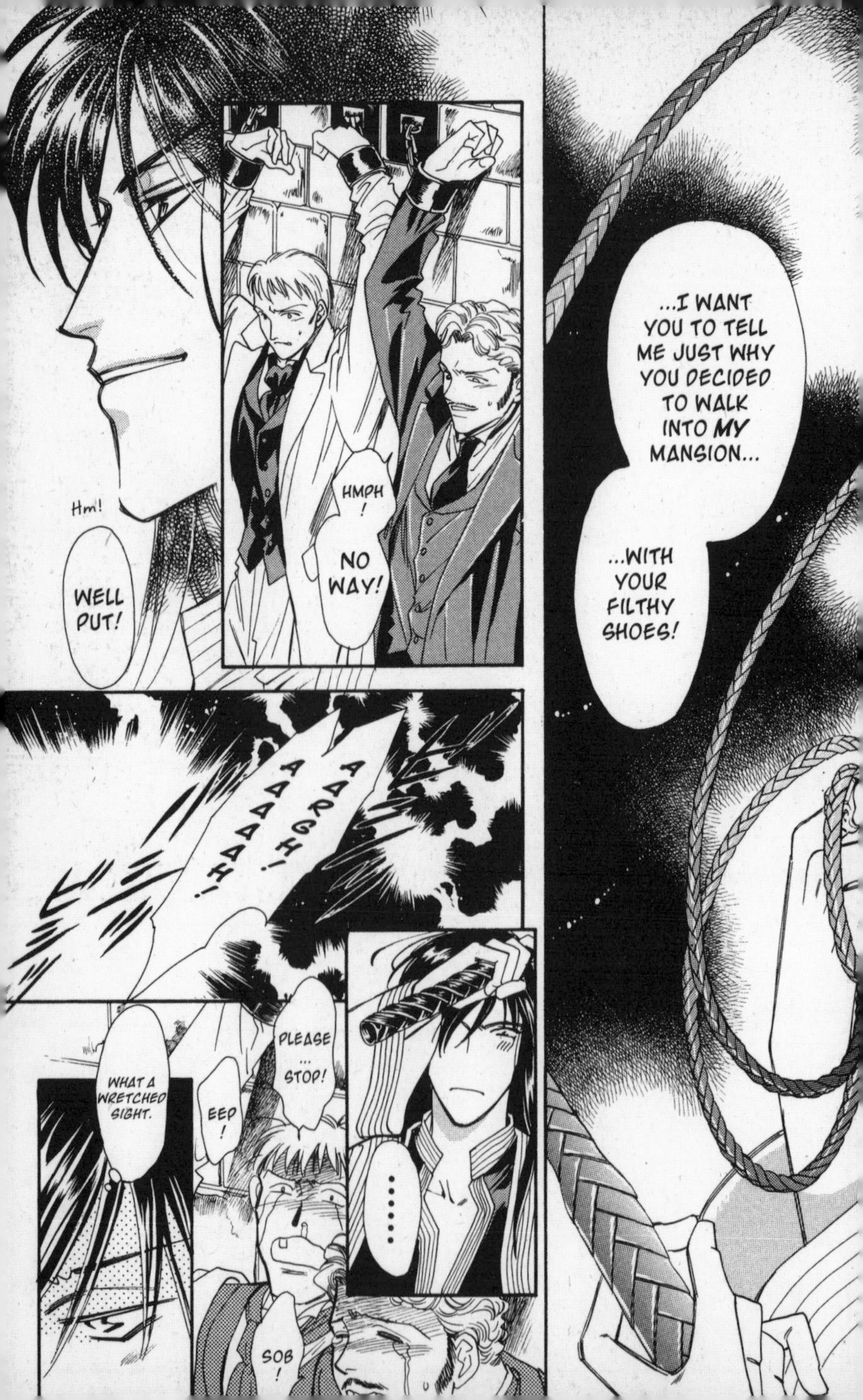

...I WANT YOU TO TELL ME JUST WHY YOU DECIDED TO WALK INTO MY MANSION...
...WITH YOUR FILTHY SHOES!
HMPH!
NO WAY!
Hm!
WELL PUT!
AARGH! AAAAAAH!
......
PLEASE ... STOP!
WHAT A WRETCHED SIGHT.
EEP!
SOB!

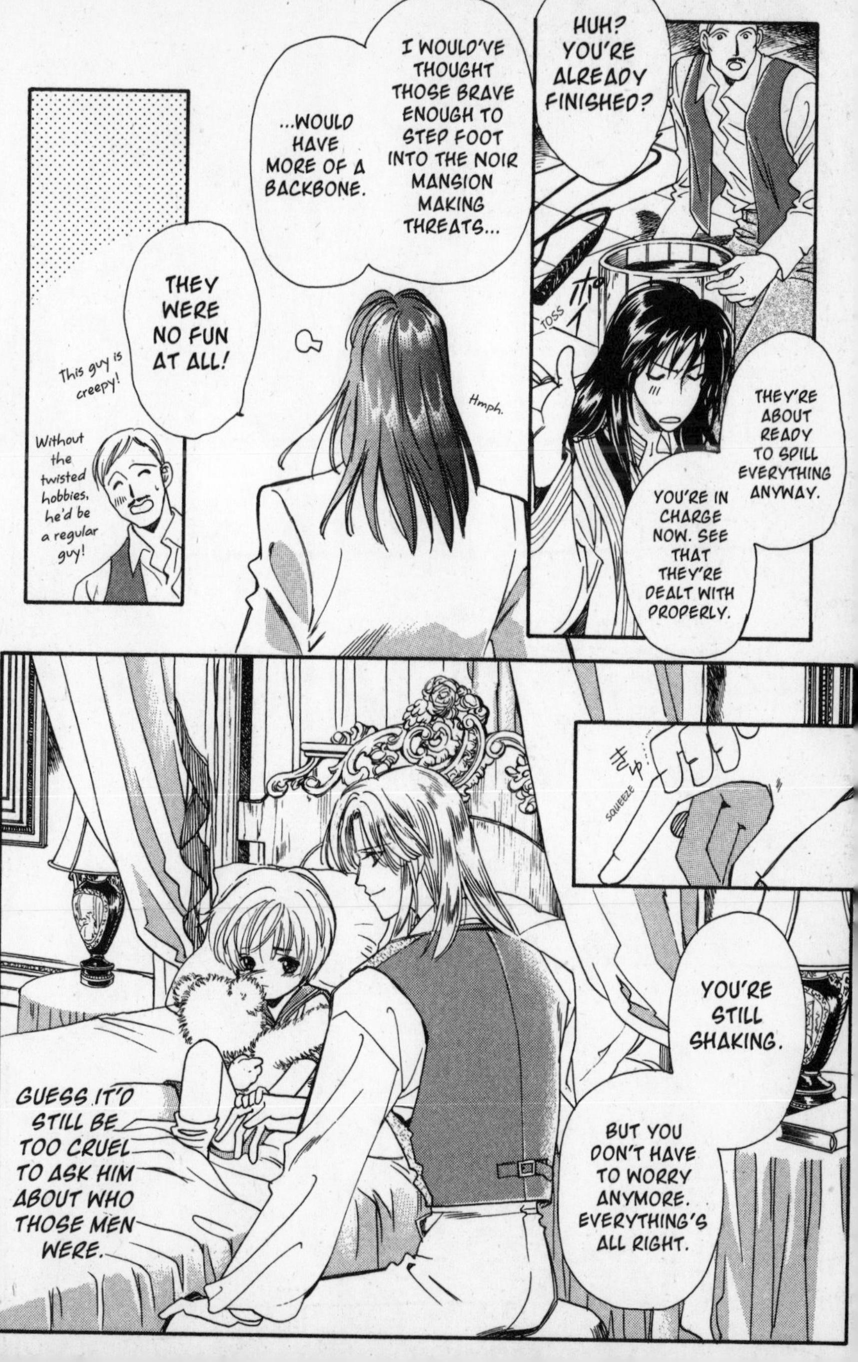
HUH? YOU'RE ALREADY FINISHED?
TOSS
THEY'RE ABOUT READY TO SPILL EVERYTHING ANYWAY.
YOU'RE IN CHARGE NOW. SEE THAT THEY'RE DEALT WITH PROPERLY.
I WOULD'VE THOUGHT THOSE BRAVE ENOUGH TO STEP FOOT INTO THE NOIR MANSION MAKING THREATS...
...WOULD HAVE MORE OF A BACKBONE.
Hmph.
THEY WERE NO FUN AT ALL!
This guy is creepy!
Without the twisted hobbies, he'd be a regular guy!
SQUEEZE
YOU'RE STILL SHAKING.
BUT YOU DON'T HAVE TO WORRY ANYMORE. EVERYTHING'S ALL RIGHT.
GUESS IT'D STILL BE TOO CRUEL TO ASK HIM ABOUT WHO THOSE MEN WERE.

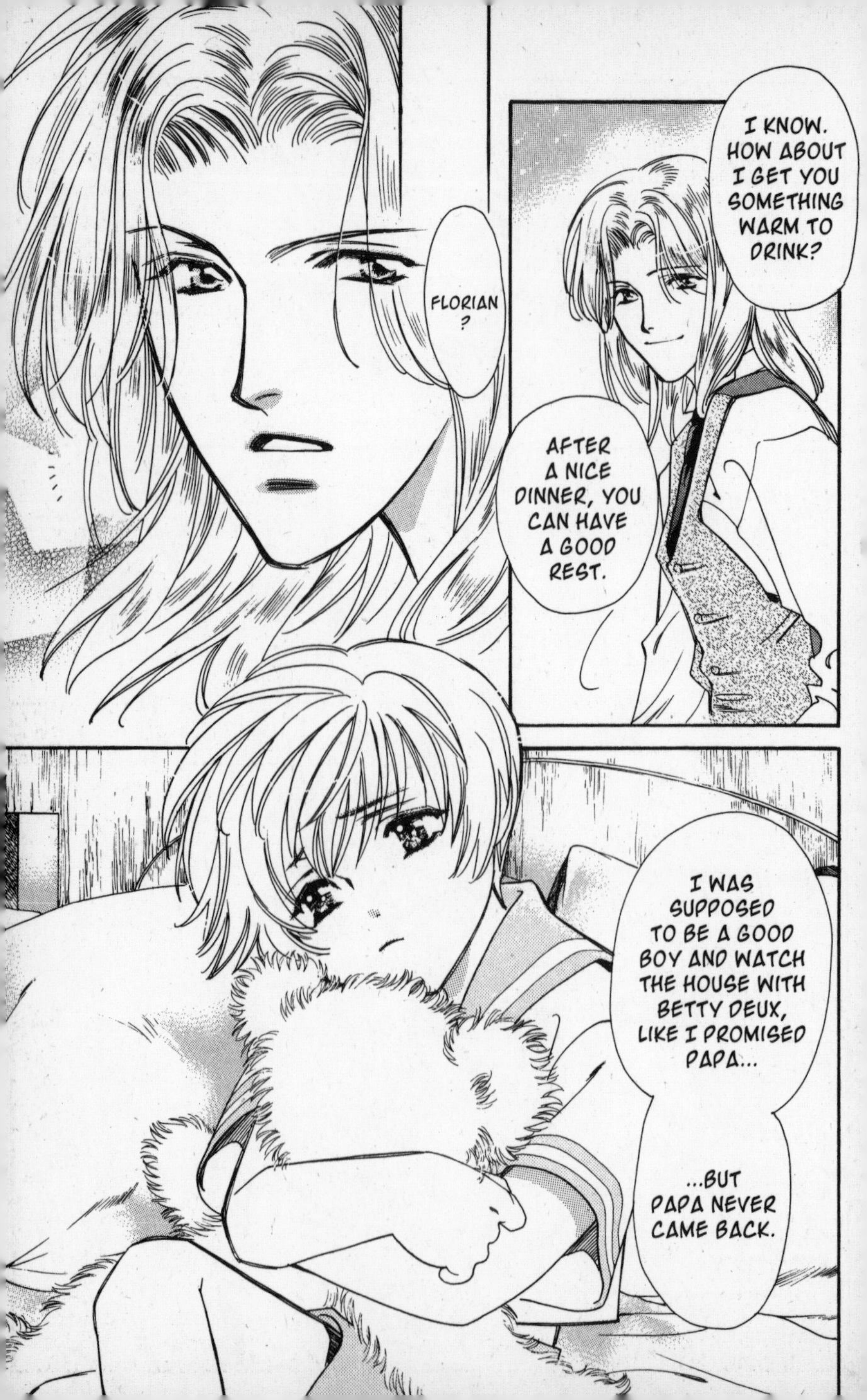
I KNOW. HOW ABOUT I GET YOU SOMETHING WARM TO DRINK?
AFTER A NICE DINNER, YOU CAN HAVE A GOOD REST.
FLORIAN?
I WAS SUPPOSED TO BE A GOOD BOY AND WATCH THE HOUSE WITH BETTY DEUX, LIKE I PROMISED PAPA...
...BUT PAPA NEVER CAME BACK.

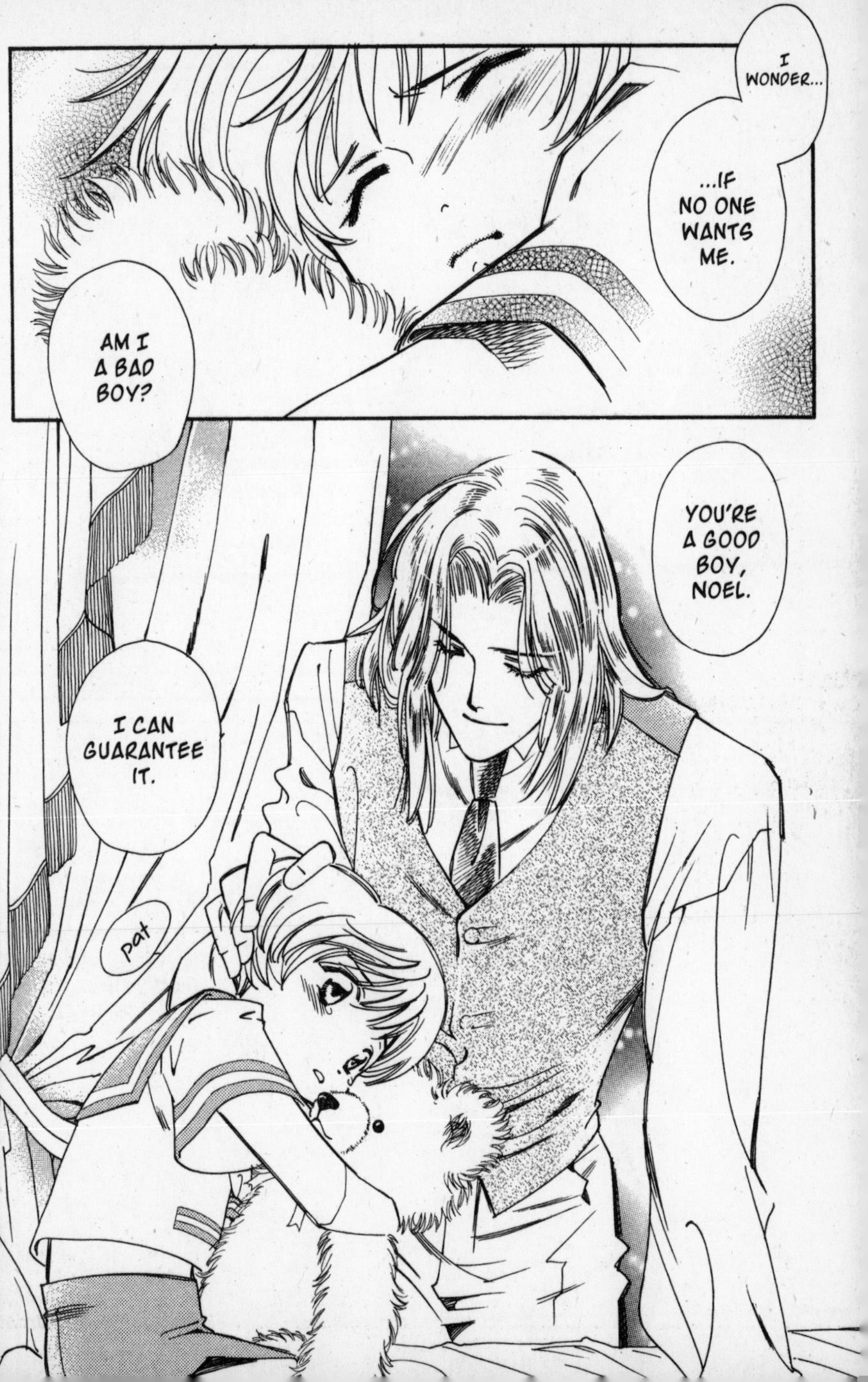
I WONDER...
...IF NO ONE WANTS ME.
AM I A BAD BOY?
YOU'RE A GOOD BOY, NOEL.
I CAN GUARANTEE IT.
pat

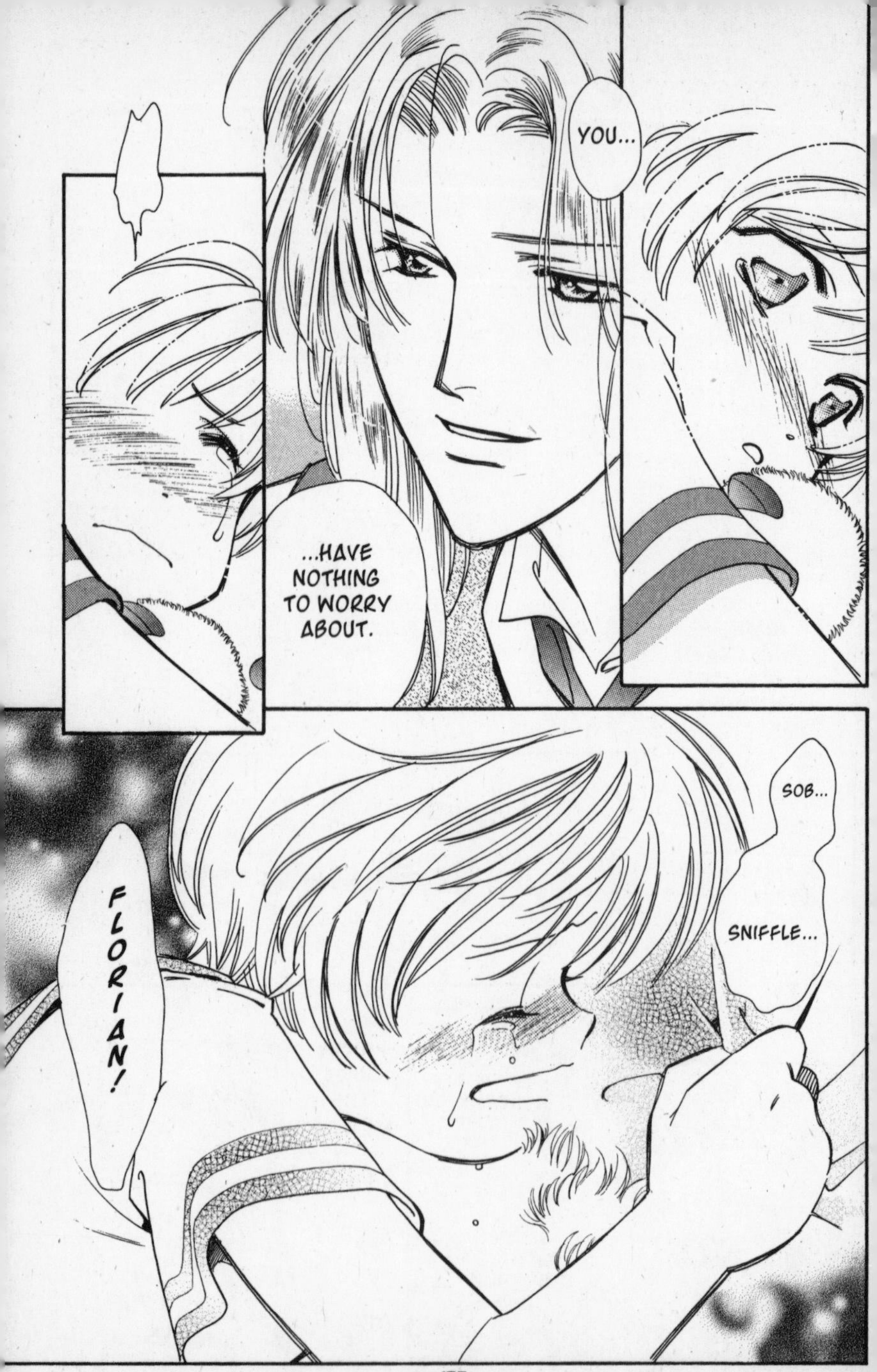
YOU...
...HAVE NOTHING TO WORRY ABOUT.
SOB...
SNIFFLE...
FLORIAN!

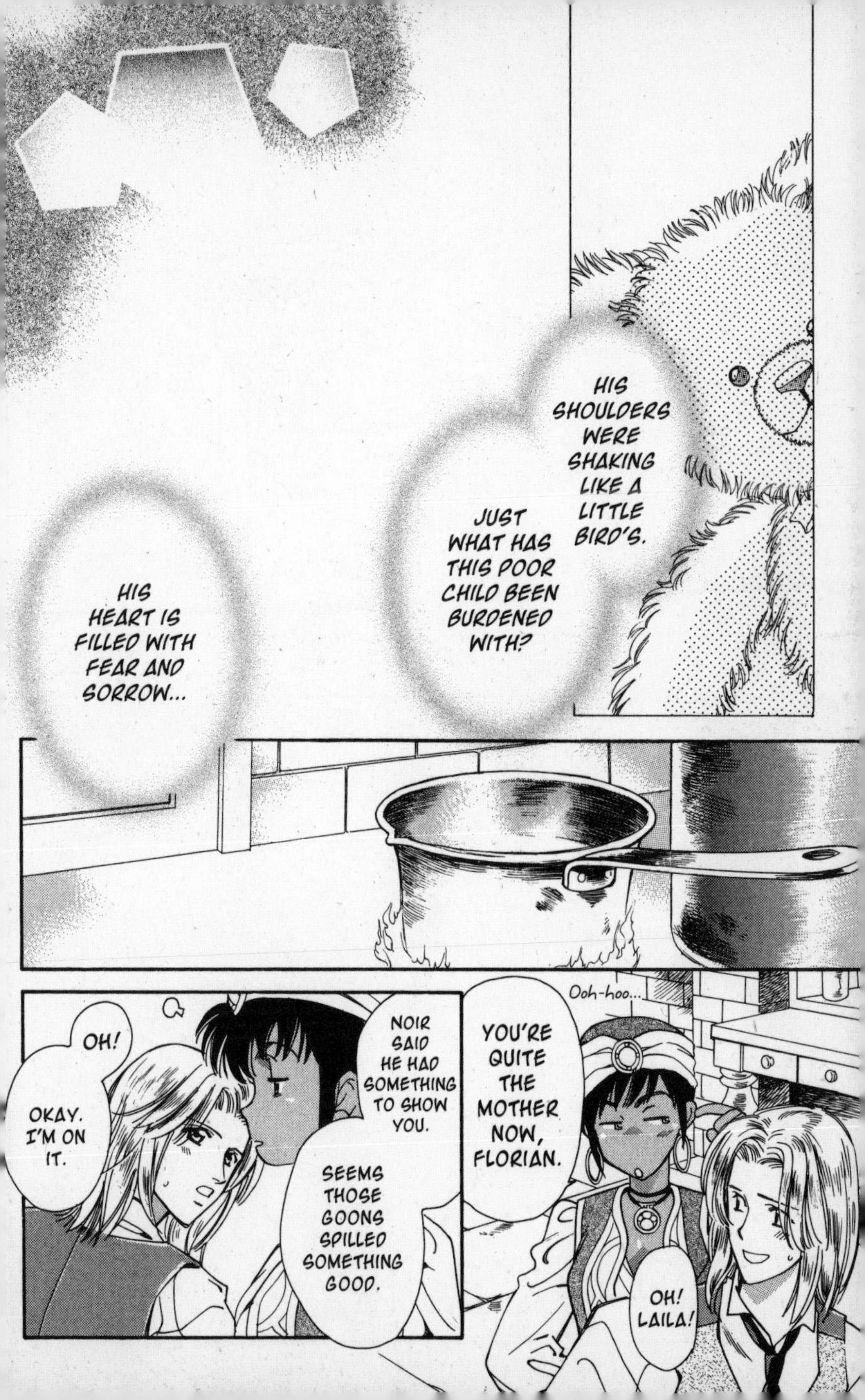
HIS SHOULDERS WERE SHAKING LIKE A LITTLE BIRD'S.
JUST WHAT HAS THIS POOR CHILD BEEN BURDENED WITH?
HIS HEART IS FILLED WITH FEAR AND SORROW...
Ooh-hoo...
YOU'RE QUITE THE MOTHER NOW, FLORIAN.
OH! LAILA!
NOIR SAID HE HAD SOMETHING TO SHOW YOU.
SEEMS THOSE GOONS SPILLED SOMETHING GOOD.
OH!
OKAY. I'M ON IT.

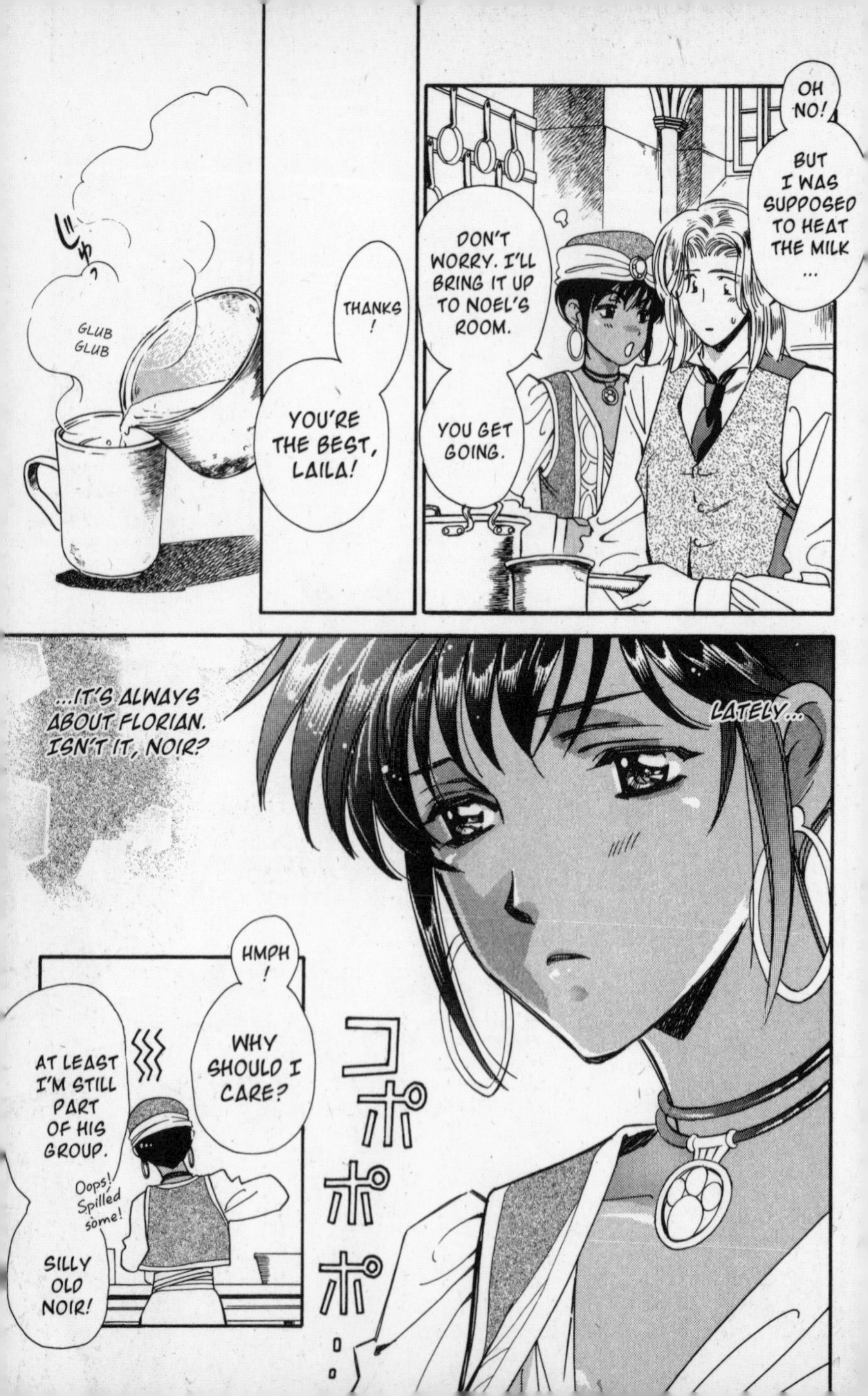

OH NO!
BUT I WAS SUPPOSED TO HEAT THE MILK ...
DON'T WORRY. I'LL BRING IT UP TO NOEL'S ROOM.
YOU GET GOING.
THANKS!
YOU'RE THE BEST, LAILA!
じゅっ
GLUB GLUB
LATELY...
...IT'S ALWAYS ABOUT FLORIAN. ISN'T IT, NOIR?
コポポポ...
HMPH!
WHY SHOULD I CARE?
AT LEAST I'M STILL PART OF HIS GROUP.
Oops! Spilled some!
SILLY OLD NOIR!

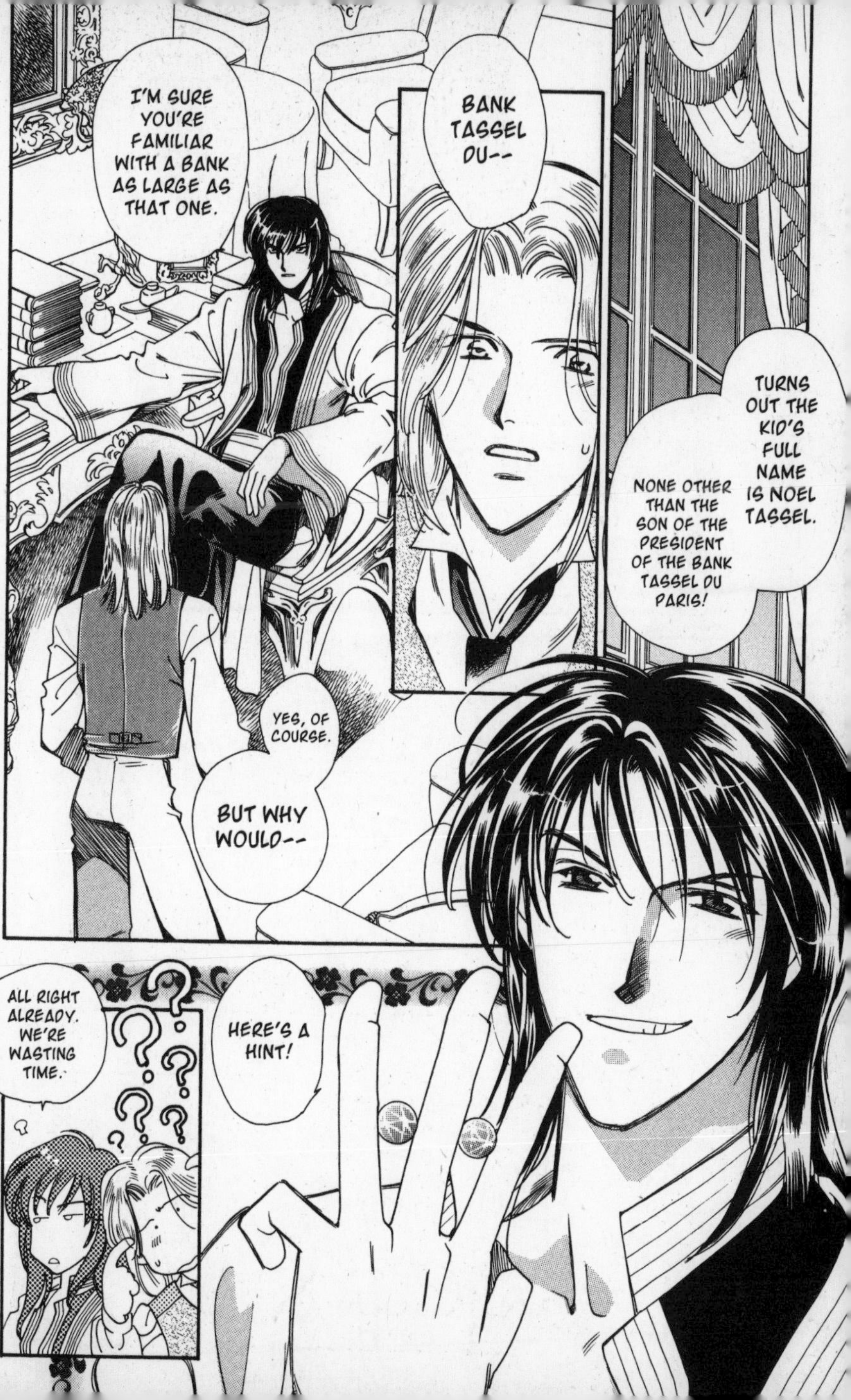
TURNS OUT THE KID'S FULL NAME IS NOEL TASSEL.
NONE OTHER THAN THE SON OF THE PRESIDENT OF THE BANK TASSEL DU PARIS!
BANK TASSEL DU--
I'M SURE YOU'RE FAMILIAR WITH A BANK AS LARGE AS THAT ONE.
YES, OF COURSE.
BUT WHY WOULD--
HERE'S A HINT!
ALL RIGHT ALREADY. WE'RE WASTING TIME.

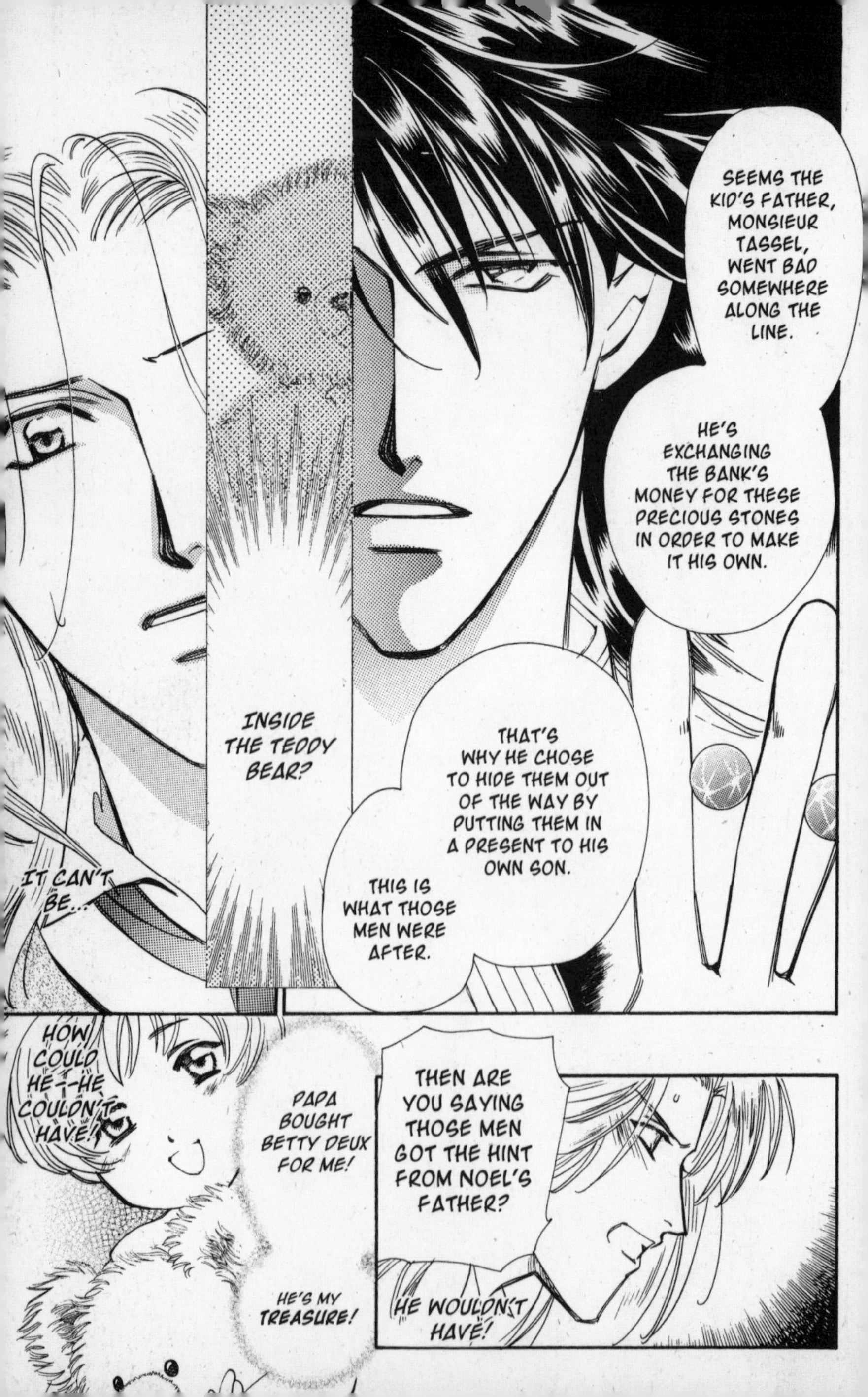
SEEMS THE KID'S FATHER, MONSIEUR TASSEL, WENT BAD SOMEWHERE ALONG THE LINE.
HE'S EXCHANGING THE BANK'S MONEY FOR THESE PRECIOUS STONES IN ORDER TO MAKE IT HIS OWN.
THAT'S WHY HE CHOSE TO HIDE THEM OUT OF THE WAY BY PUTTING THEM IN A PRESENT TO HIS OWN SON.
THIS IS WHAT THOSE MEN WERE AFTER.
INSIDE THE TEDDY BEAR?
IT CAN'T BE...
THEN ARE YOU SAYING THOSE MEN GOT THE HINT FROM NOEL'S FATHER?
HE WOULDN'T HAVE!
PAPA BOUGHT BETTY DEUX FOR ME!
HE'S MY TREASURE!
HOW COULD HE--HE COULDN'T HAVE!

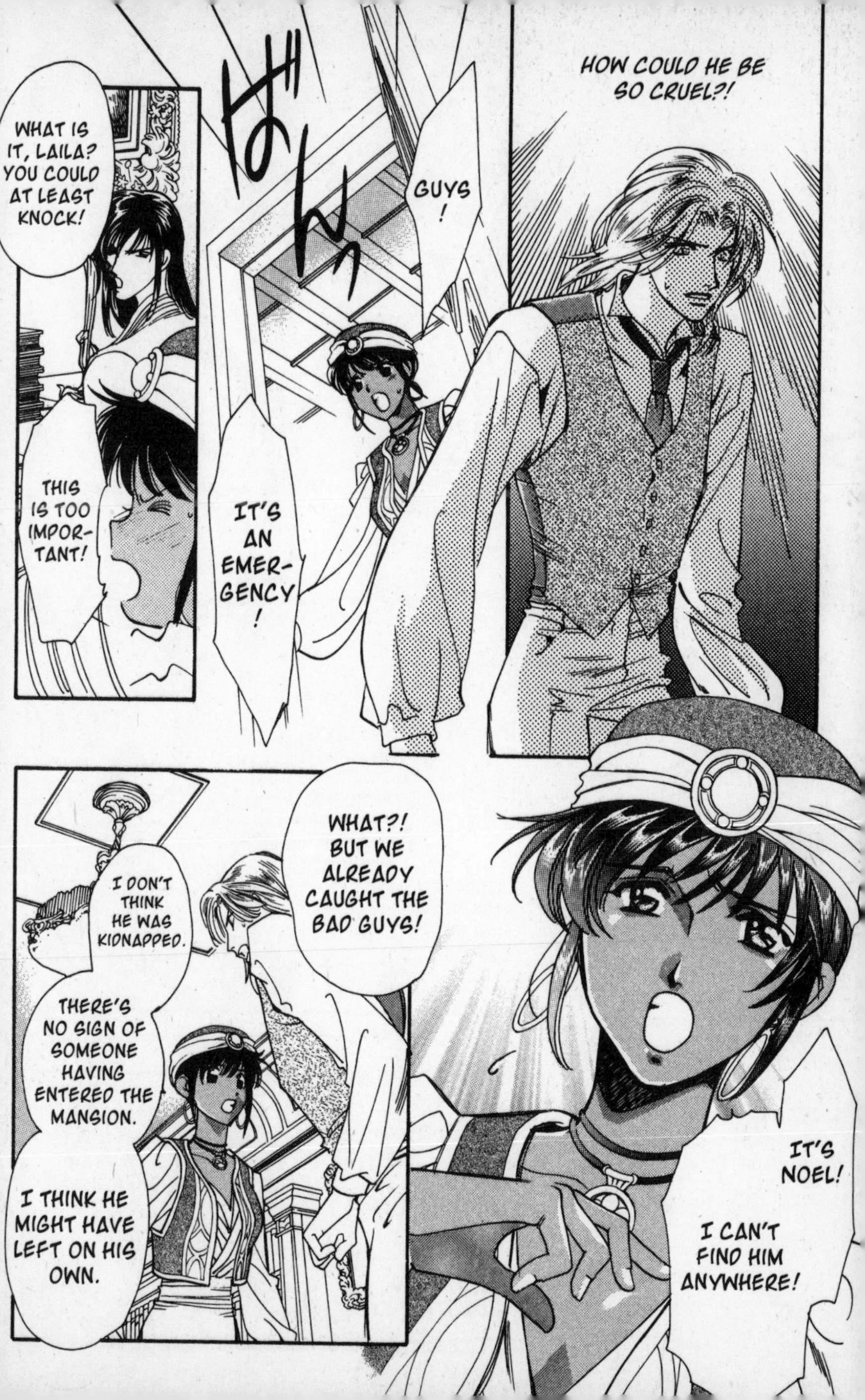
HOW COULD HE BE SO CRUEL?!
ばん
GUYS!
IT'S AN EMERGENCY!
WHAT IS IT, LAILA? YOU COULD AT LEAST KNOCK!
THIS IS TOO IMPORTANT!
IT'S NOEL!
I CAN'T FIND HIM ANYWHERE!
WHAT?! BUT WE ALREADY CAUGHT THE BAD GUYS!
I DON'T THINK HE WAS KIDNAPPED.
THERE'S NO SIGN OF SOMEONE HAVING ENTERED THE MANSION.
I THINK HE MIGHT HAVE LEFT ON HIS OWN.

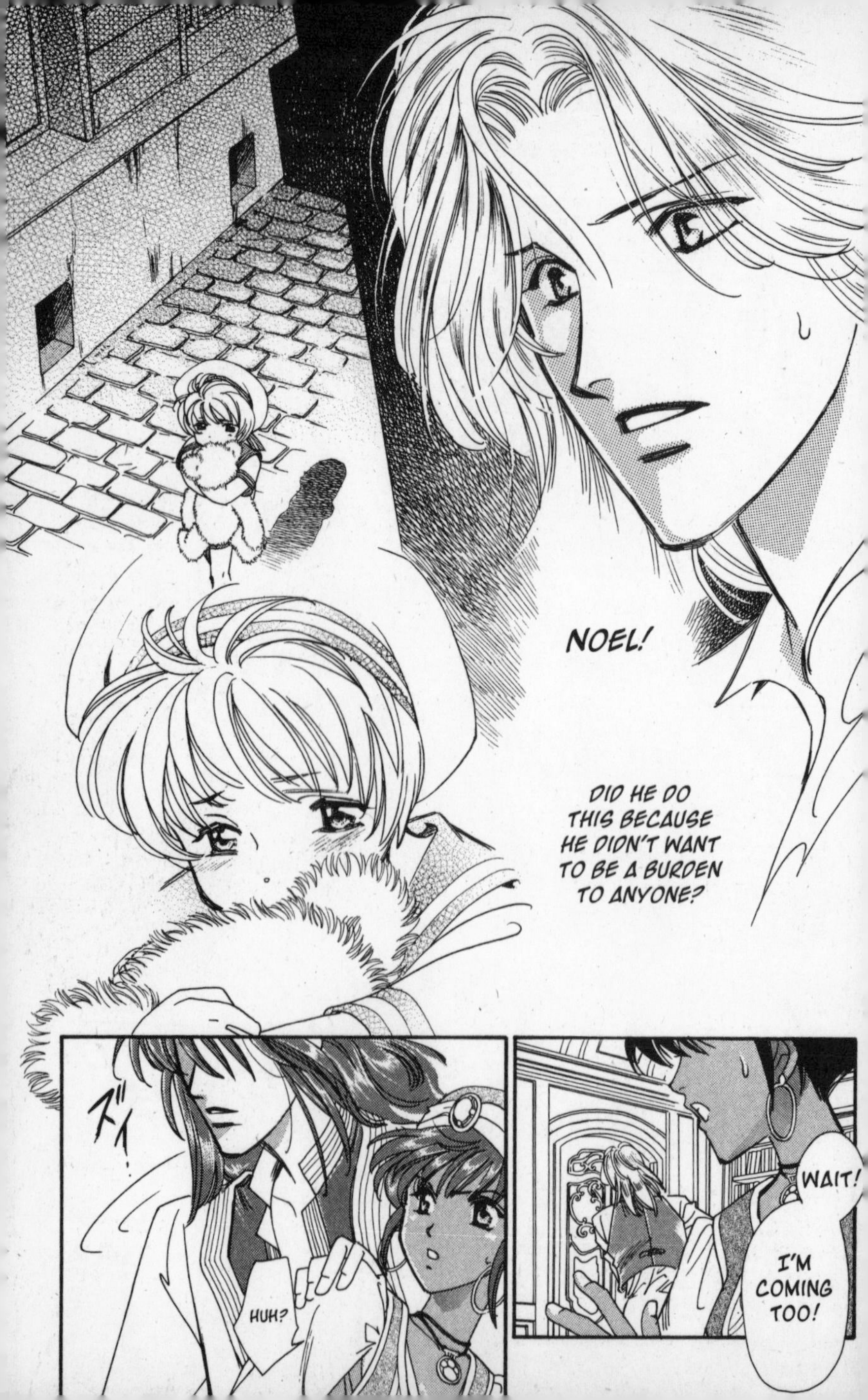
NOEL!
DID HE DO THIS BECAUSE HE DIDN'T WANT TO BE A BURDEN TO ANYONE?
WAIT!
I'M COMING TOO!
ズイ
HUH?

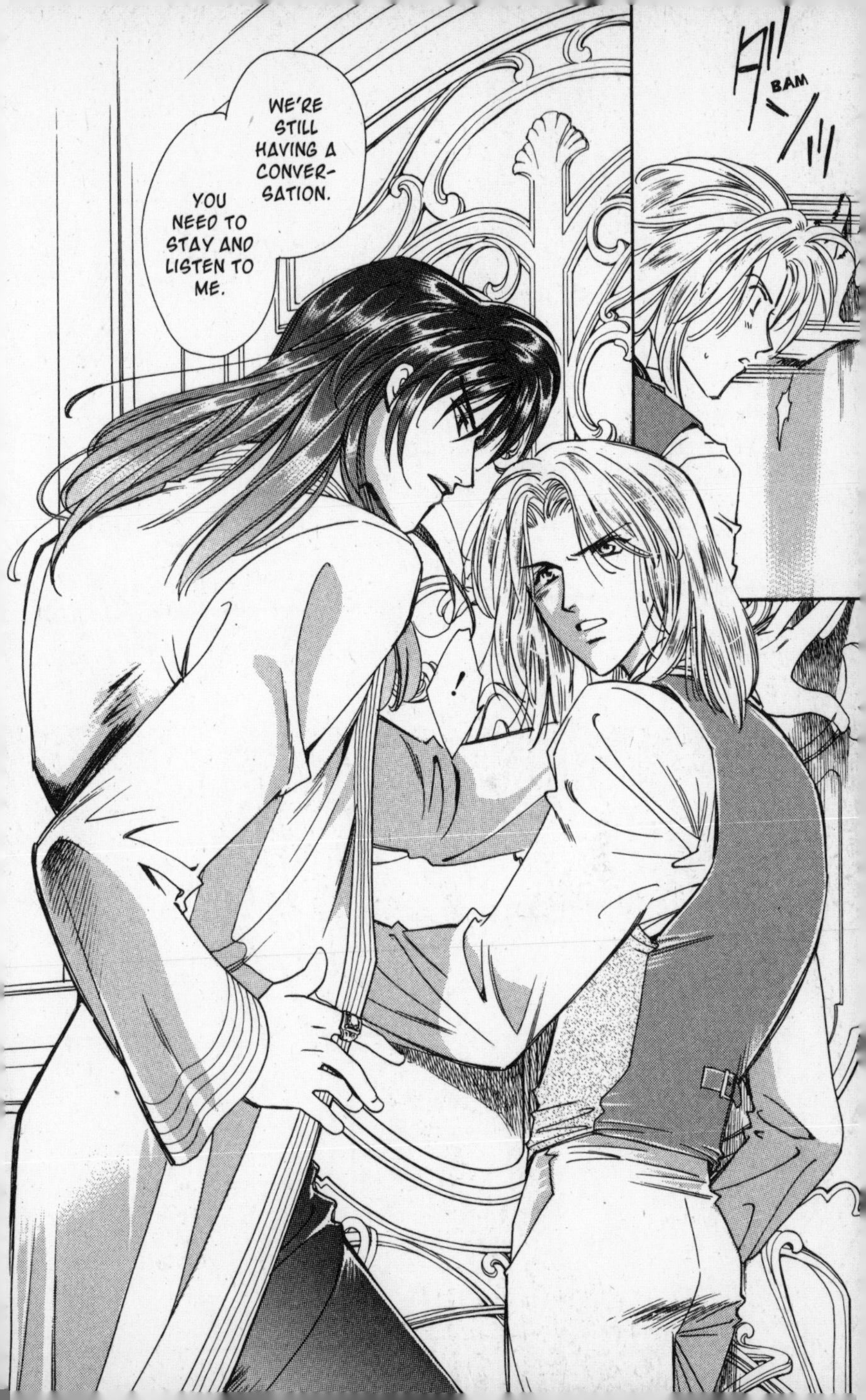
BAM
WE'RE STILL HAVING A CONVERSATION.
YOU NEED TO STAY AND LISTEN TO ME.
!

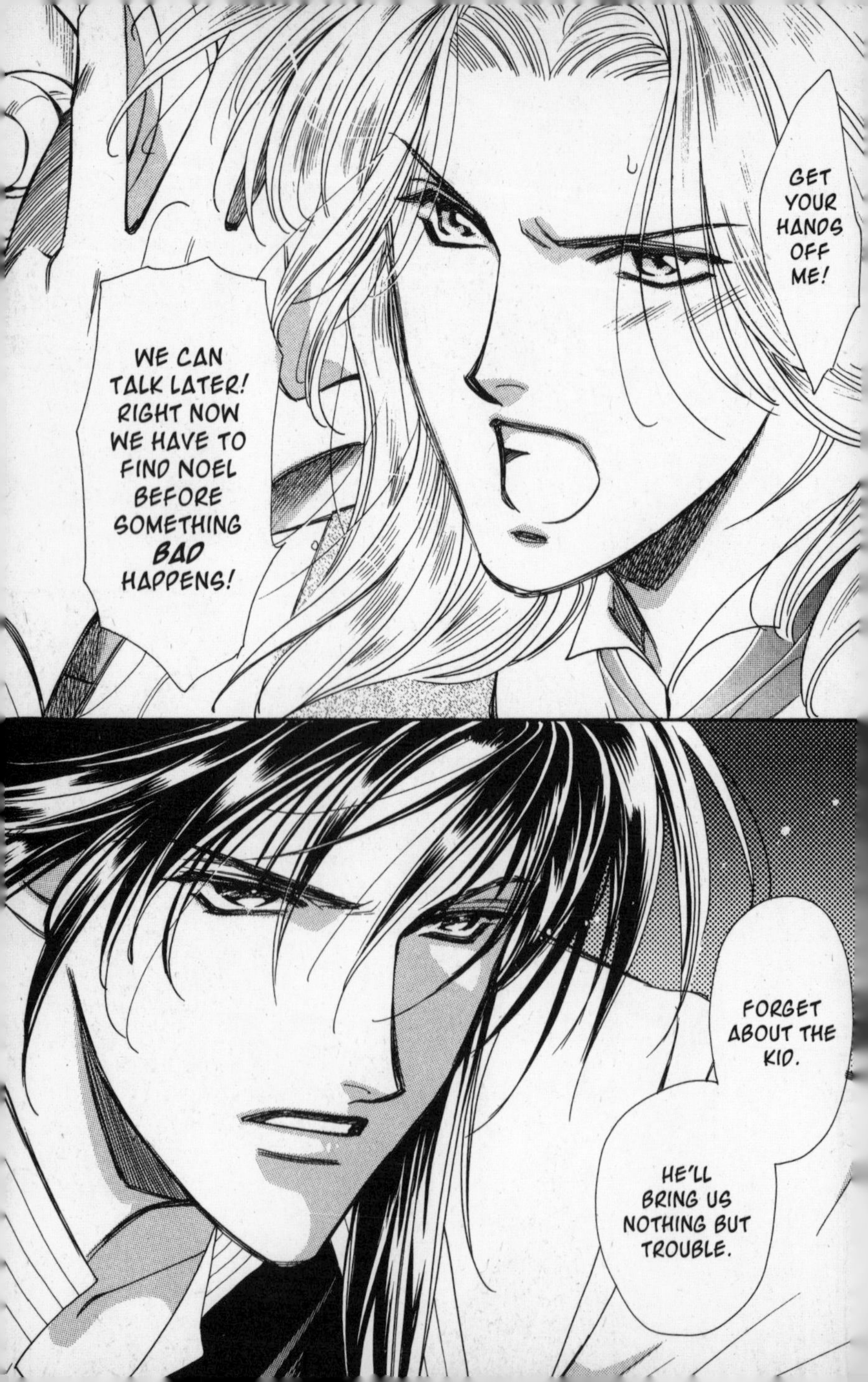
GET YOUR HANDS OFF ME!
WE CAN TALK LATER! RIGHT NOW WE HAVE TO FIND NOEL BEFORE SOMETHING BAD HAPPENS!
FORGET ABOUT THE KID.
HE'LL BRING US NOTHING BUT TROUBLE.

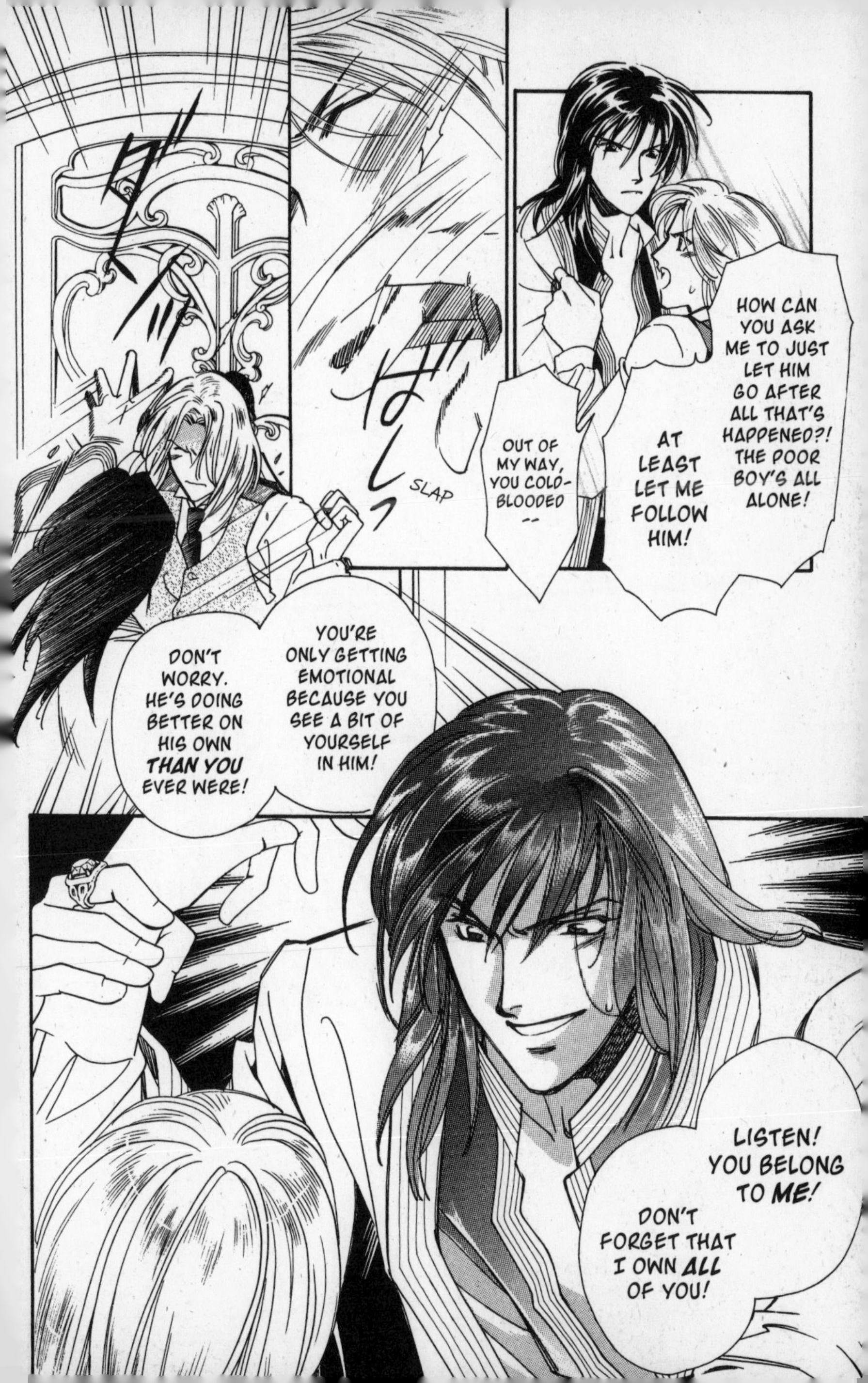
HOW CAN YOU ASK ME TO JUST LET HIM GO AFTER ALL THAT'S HAPPENED?! THE POOR BOY'S ALL ALONE!
AT LEAST LET ME FOLLOW HIM!
OUT OF MY WAY, YOU COLD-BLOODED --
SLAP
YOU'RE ONLY GETTING EMOTIONAL BECAUSE YOU SEE A BIT OF YOURSELF IN HIM!
DON'T WORRY. HE'S DOING BETTER ON HIS OWN THAN YOU EVER WERE!
LISTEN! YOU BELONG TO ME!
DON'T FORGET THAT I OWN ALL OF YOU!

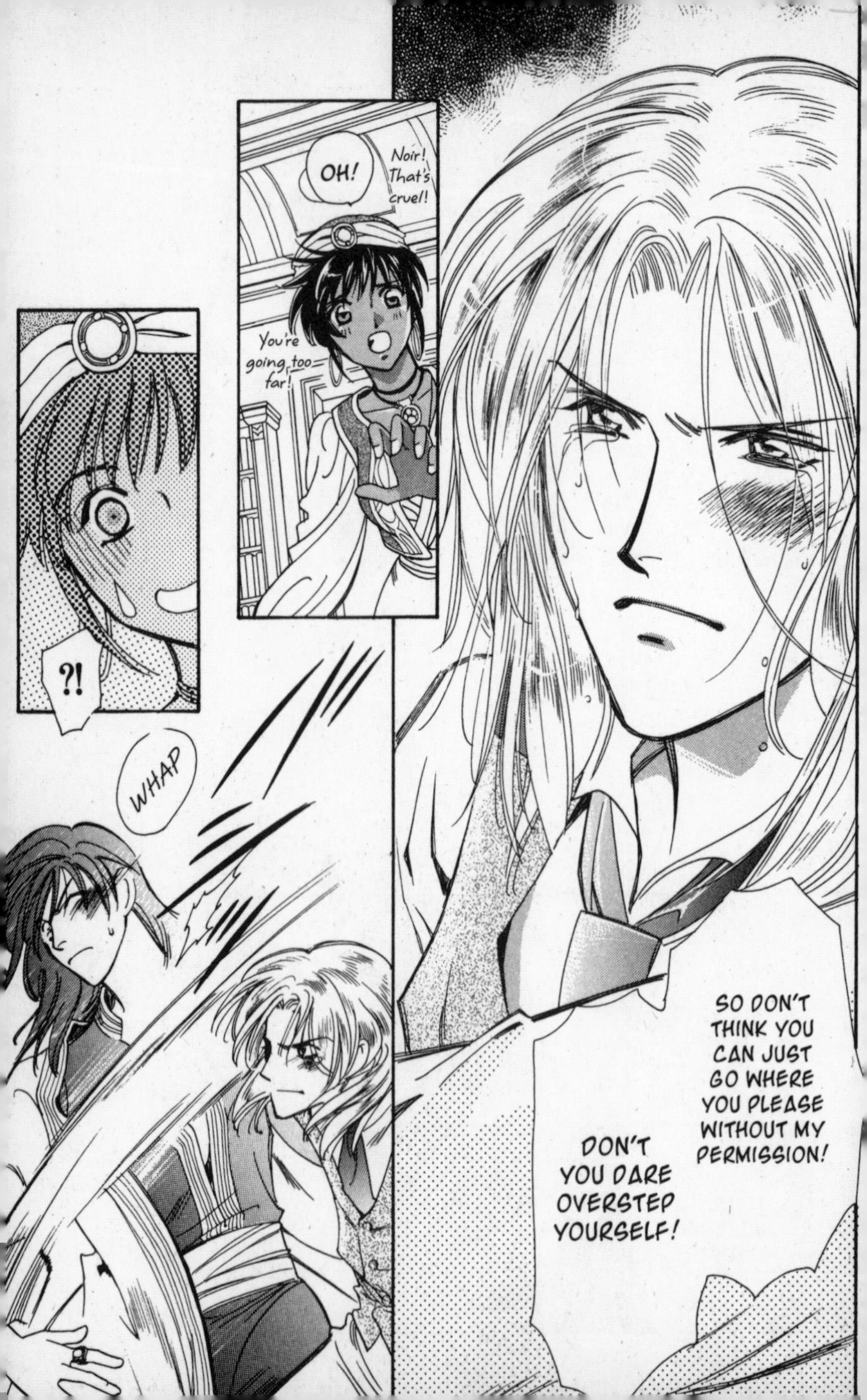
SO DON'T THINK YOU CAN JUST GO WHERE YOU PLEASE WITHOUT MY PERMISSION!
DON'T YOU DARE OVERSTEP YOURSELF!
Noir! That's cruel!
OH!
You're going too far!
?!
WHAP

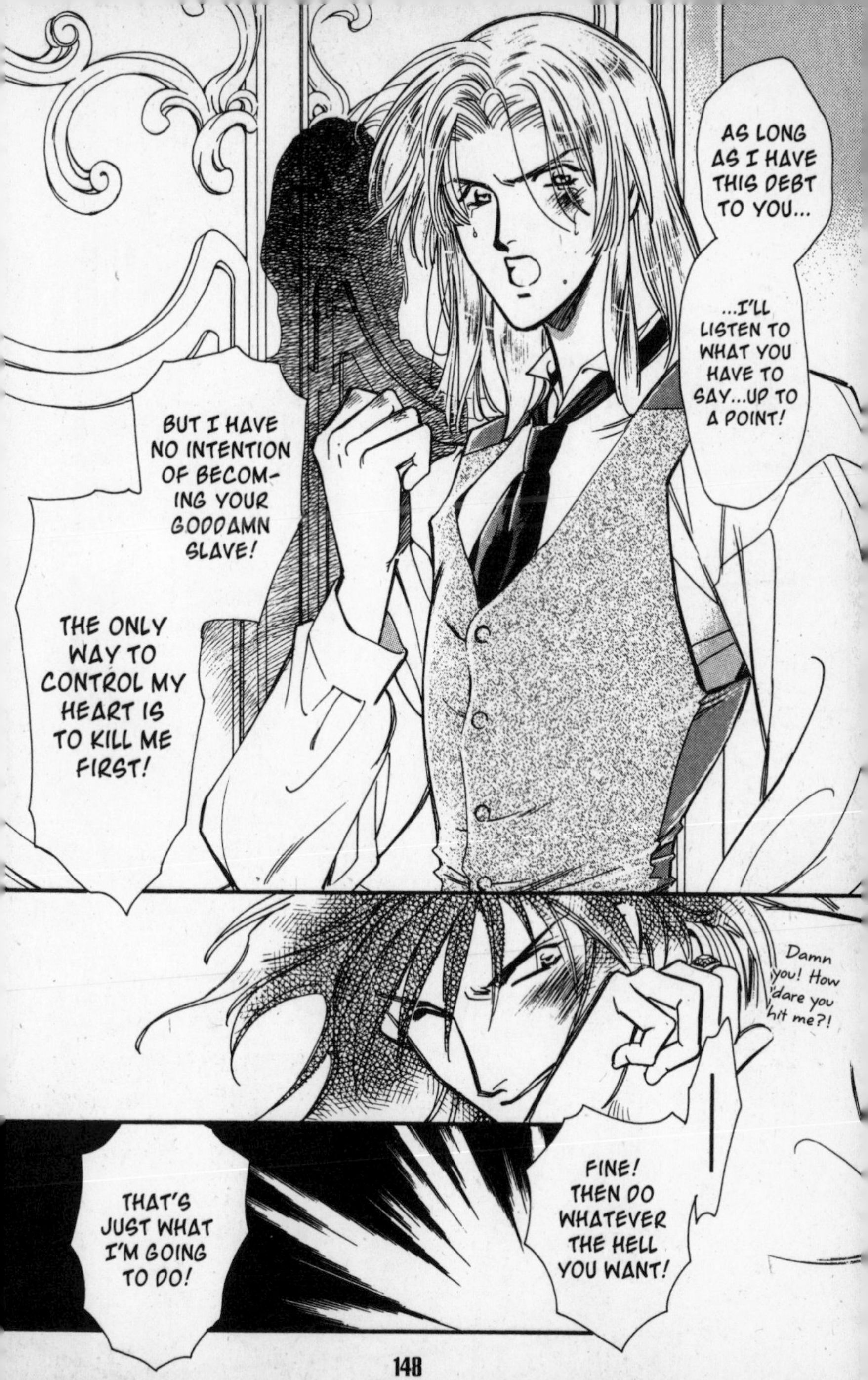
AS LONG AS I HAVE THIS DEBT TO YOU...
...I'LL LISTEN TO WHAT YOU HAVE TO SAY...UP TO A POINT!
BUT I HAVE NO INTENTION OF BECOMING YOUR GODDAMN SLAVE!
THE ONLY WAY TO CONTROL MY HEART IS TO KILL ME FIRST!
Damn you! How dare you hit me?!
FINE! THEN DO WHATEVER THE HELL YOU WANT!
THAT'S JUST WHAT I'M GOING TO DO!

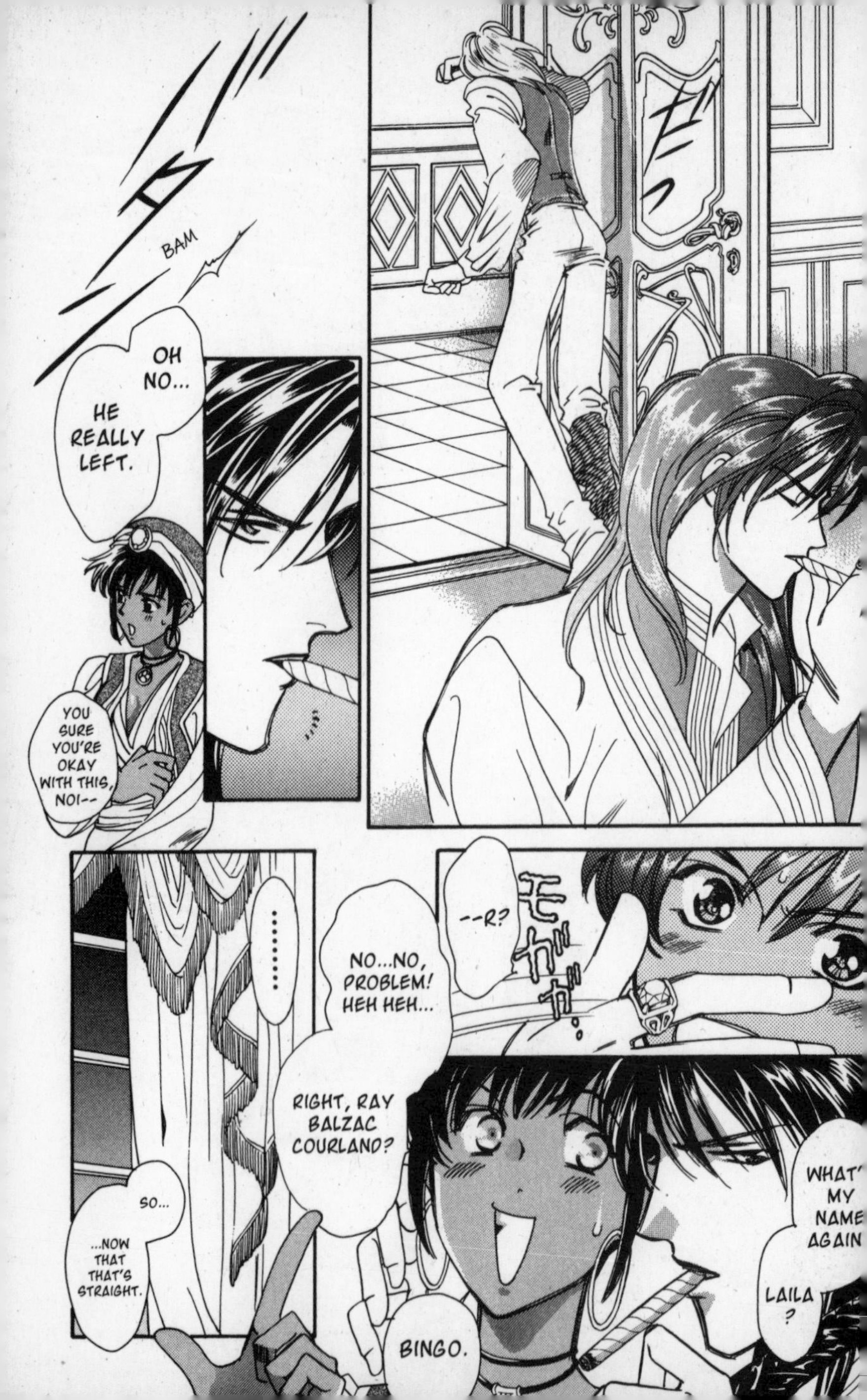
BAM
OH NO... HE REALLY LEFT.
YOU SURE YOU'RE OKAY WITH THIS, NOI--
--R?
NO...NO, PROBLEM! HEH HEH...
WHAT' MY NAME AGAIN
LAILA?
RIGHT, RAY BALZAC COURLAND?
BINGO.
....
SO...
...NOW THAT THAT'S STRAIGHT.

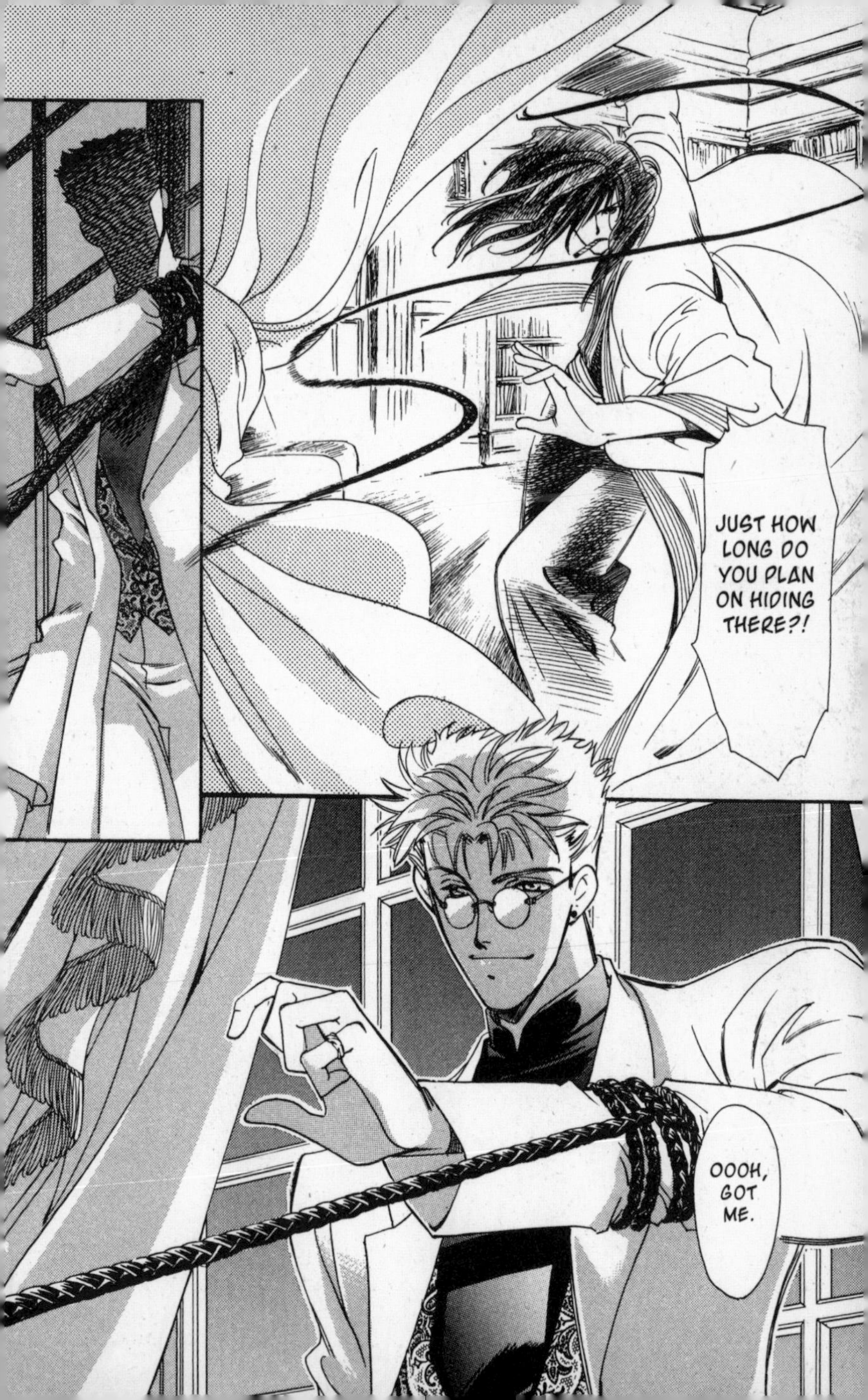
JUST HOW LONG DO YOU PLAN ON HIDING THERE?!
OOOH, GOT ME.

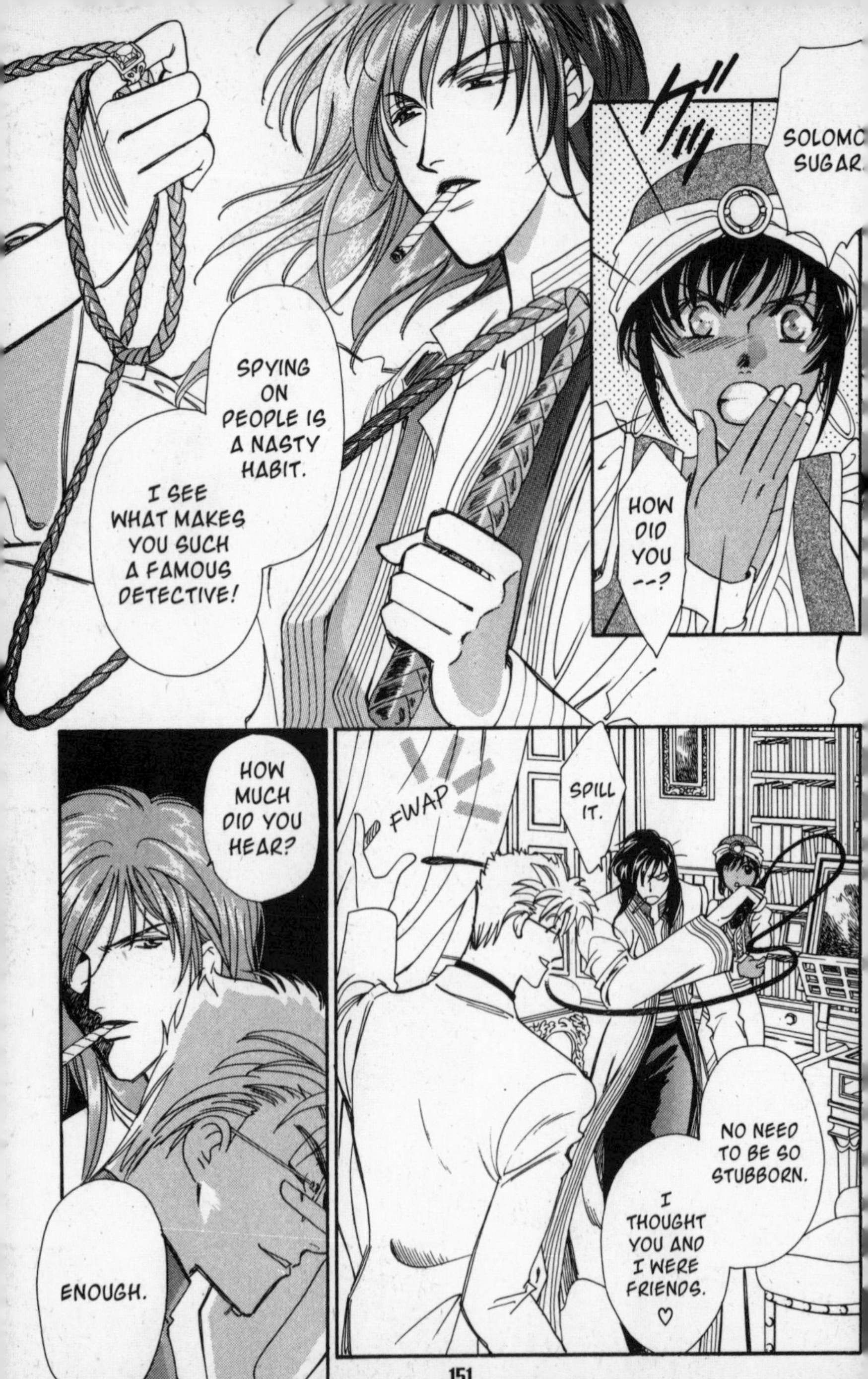
SOLOMO SUGAR.
HOW DID YOU --?
SPYING ON PEOPLE IS A NASTY HABIT.
I SEE WHAT MAKES YOU SUCH A FAMOUS DETECTIVE!
FWAP
SPILL IT.
NO NEED TO BE SO STUBBORN.
I THOUGHT YOU AND I WERE FRIENDS. ♡
HOW MUCH DID YOU HEAR?
ENOUGH.

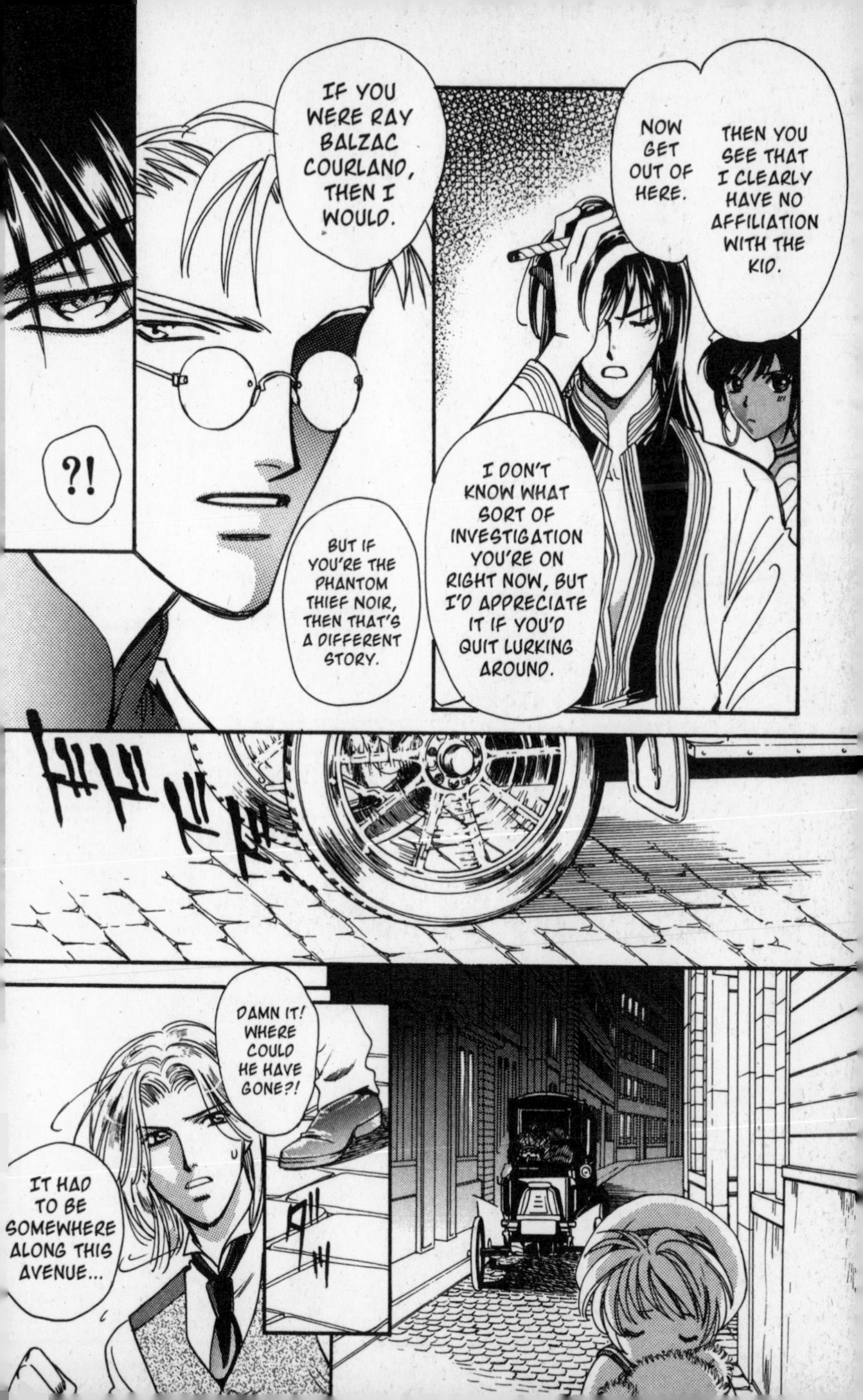
THEN YOU SEE THAT I CLEARLY HAVE NO AFFILIATION WITH THE KID.
NOW GET OUT OF HERE.
I DON'T KNOW WHAT SORT OF INVESTIGATION YOU'RE ON RIGHT NOW, BUT I'D APPRECIATE IT IF YOU'D QUIT LURKING AROUND.
IF YOU WERE RAY BALZAC COURLAND, THEN I WOULD.
?!
BUT IF YOU'RE THE PHANTOM THIEF NOIR, THEN THAT'S A DIFFERENT STORY.
DAMN IT! WHERE COULD HE HAVE GONE?!
IT HAD TO BE SOMEWHERE ALONG THIS AVENUE...

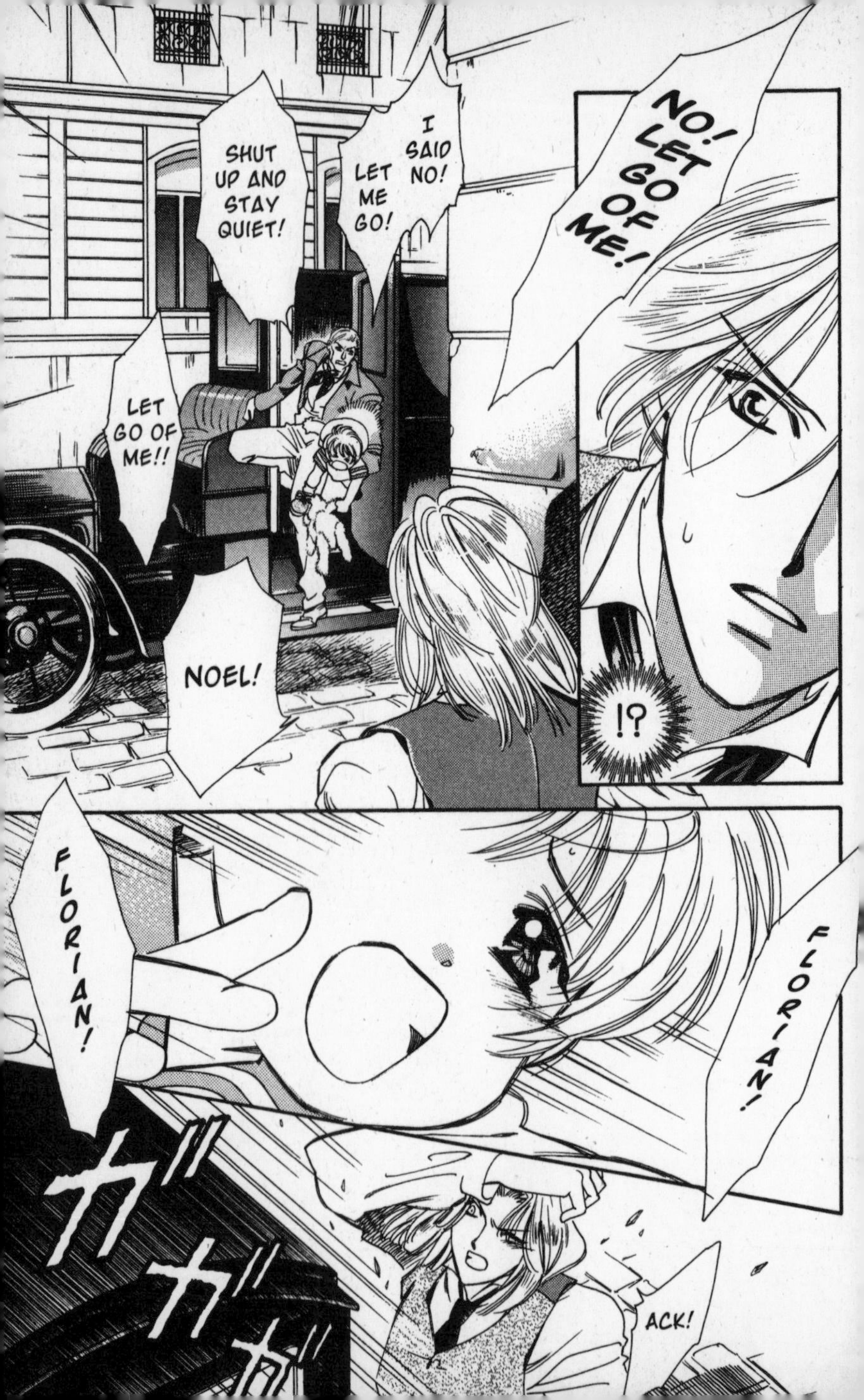

NO! LET GO OF ME!
!?
I SAID NO! LET ME GO!
SHUT UP AND STAY QUIET!
LET GO OF ME!!
NOEL!
FLORIAN!
FLORIAN!
ガガガ
ACK!

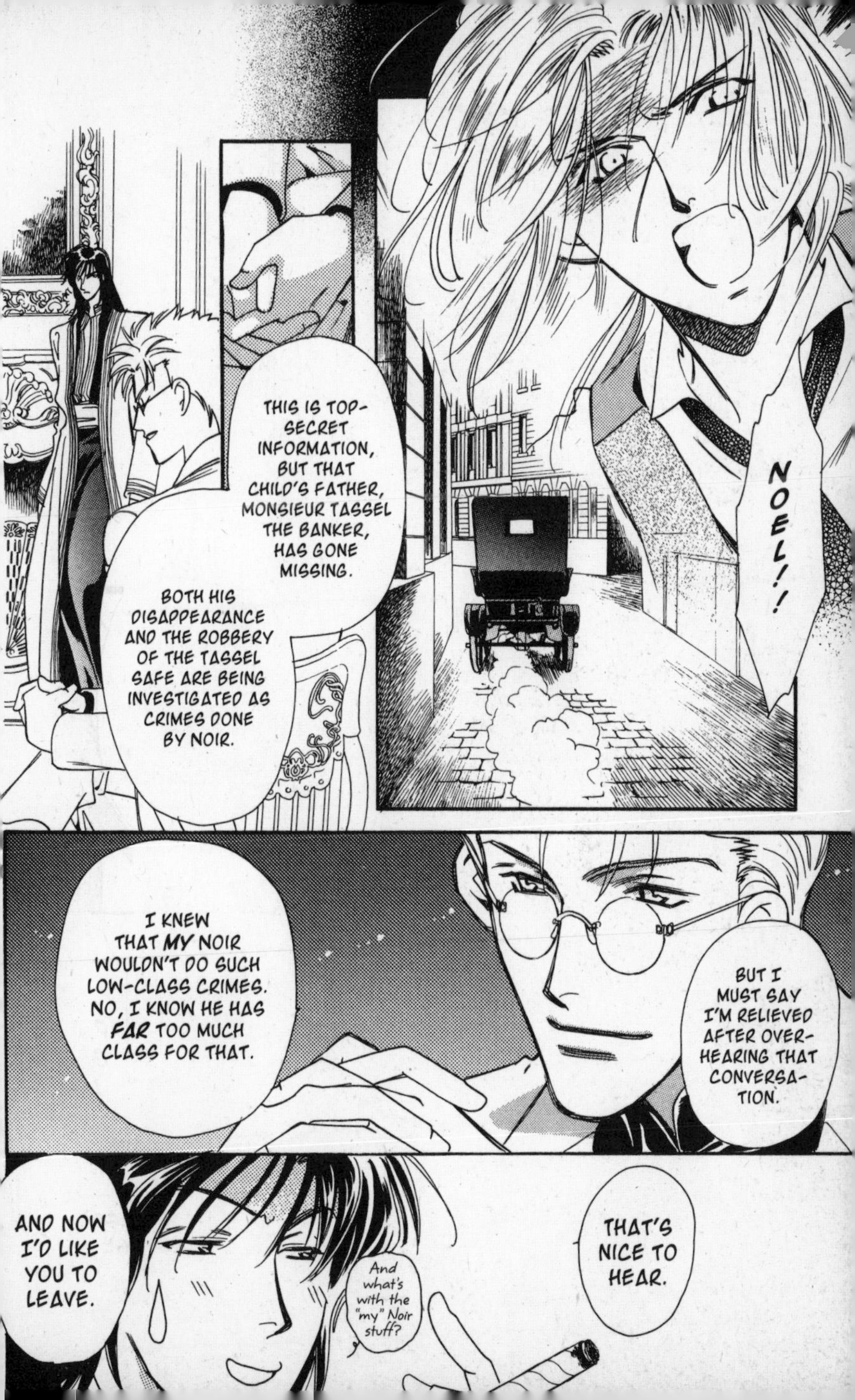
NOEL!!
THIS IS TOP-SECRET INFORMATION, BUT THAT CHILD'S FATHER, MONSIEUR TASSEL THE BANKER, HAS GONE MISSING.
BOTH HIS DISAPPEARANCE AND THE ROBBERY OF THE TASSEL SAFE ARE BEING INVESTIGATED AS CRIMES DONE BY NOIR.
BUT I MUST SAY I'M RELIEVED AFTER OVER-HEARING THAT CONVERSA-TION.
I KNEW THAT MY NOIR WOULDN'T DO SUCH LOW-CLASS CRIMES. NO, I KNOW HE HAS FAR TOO MUCH CLASS FOR THAT.
THAT'S NICE TO HEAR.
And what's with the "my" Noir stuff?
AND NOW I'D LIKE YOU TO LEAVE.

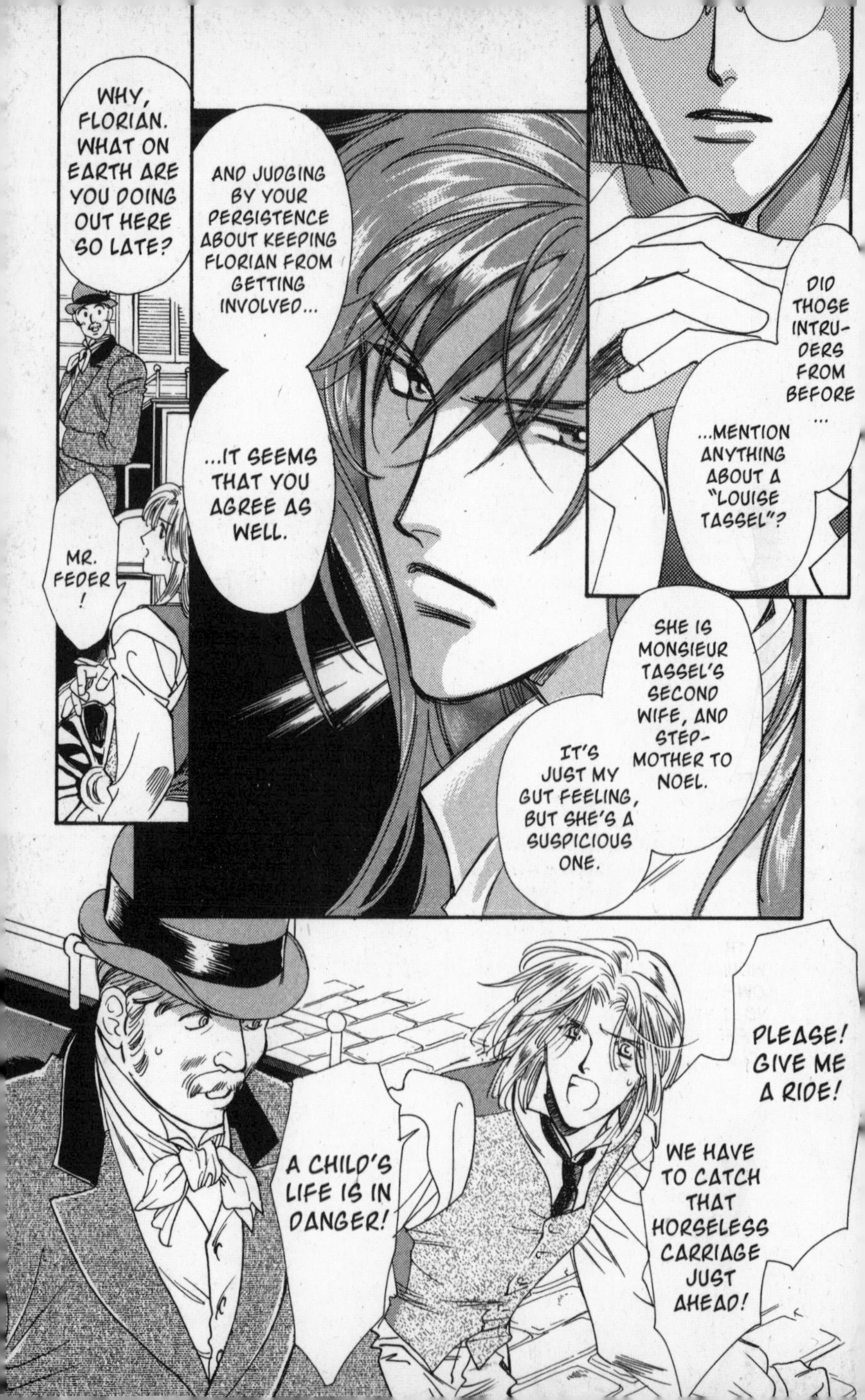
DID THOSE INTRUDERS FROM BEFORE ...
...MENTION ANYTHING ABOUT A "LOUISE TASSEL"?
SHE IS MONSIEUR TASSEL'S SECOND WIFE, AND STEP-MOTHER TO NOEL.
IT'S JUST MY GUT FEELING, BUT SHE'S A SUSPICIOUS ONE.
AND JUDGING BY YOUR PERSISTENCE ABOUT KEEPING FLORIAN FROM GETTING INVOLVED...
...IT SEEMS THAT YOU AGREE AS WELL.
WHY, FLORIAN. WHAT ON EARTH ARE YOU DOING OUT HERE SO LATE?
MR. FEDER!
PLEASE! GIVE ME A RIDE!
WE HAVE TO CATCH THAT HORSELESS CARRIAGE JUST AHEAD!
A CHILD'S LIFE IS IN DANGER!

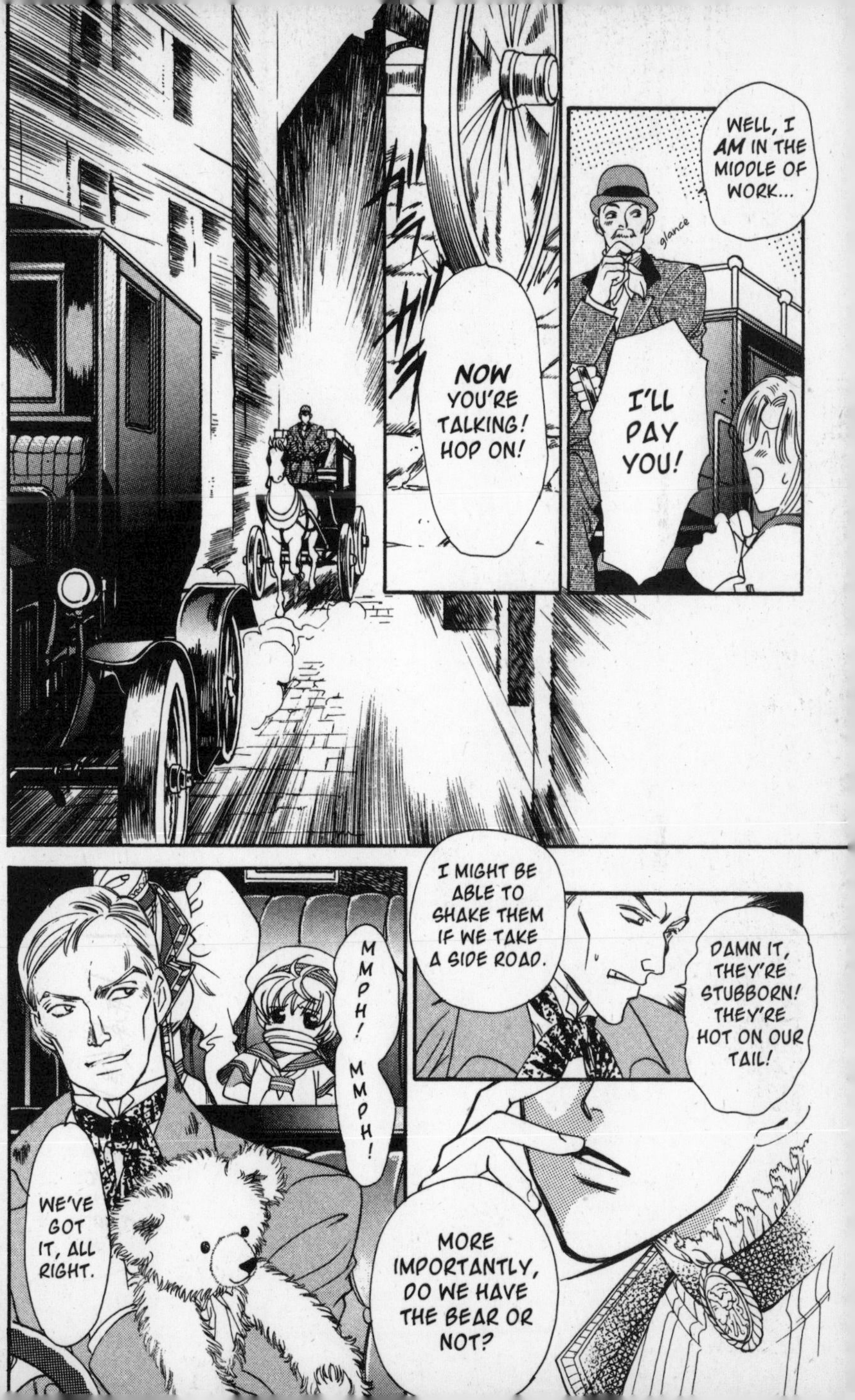
WELL, I AM IN THE MIDDLE OF WORK...
glance
I'LL PAY YOU!
NOW YOU'RE TALKING! HOP ON!
DAMN IT, THEY'RE STUBBORN! THEY'RE HOT ON OUR TAIL!
I MIGHT BE ABLE TO SHAKE THEM IF WE TAKE A SIDE ROAD.
MMPH! MMPH!
MORE IMPORTANTLY, DO WE HAVE THE BEAR OR NOT?
WE'VE GOT IT, ALL RIGHT.

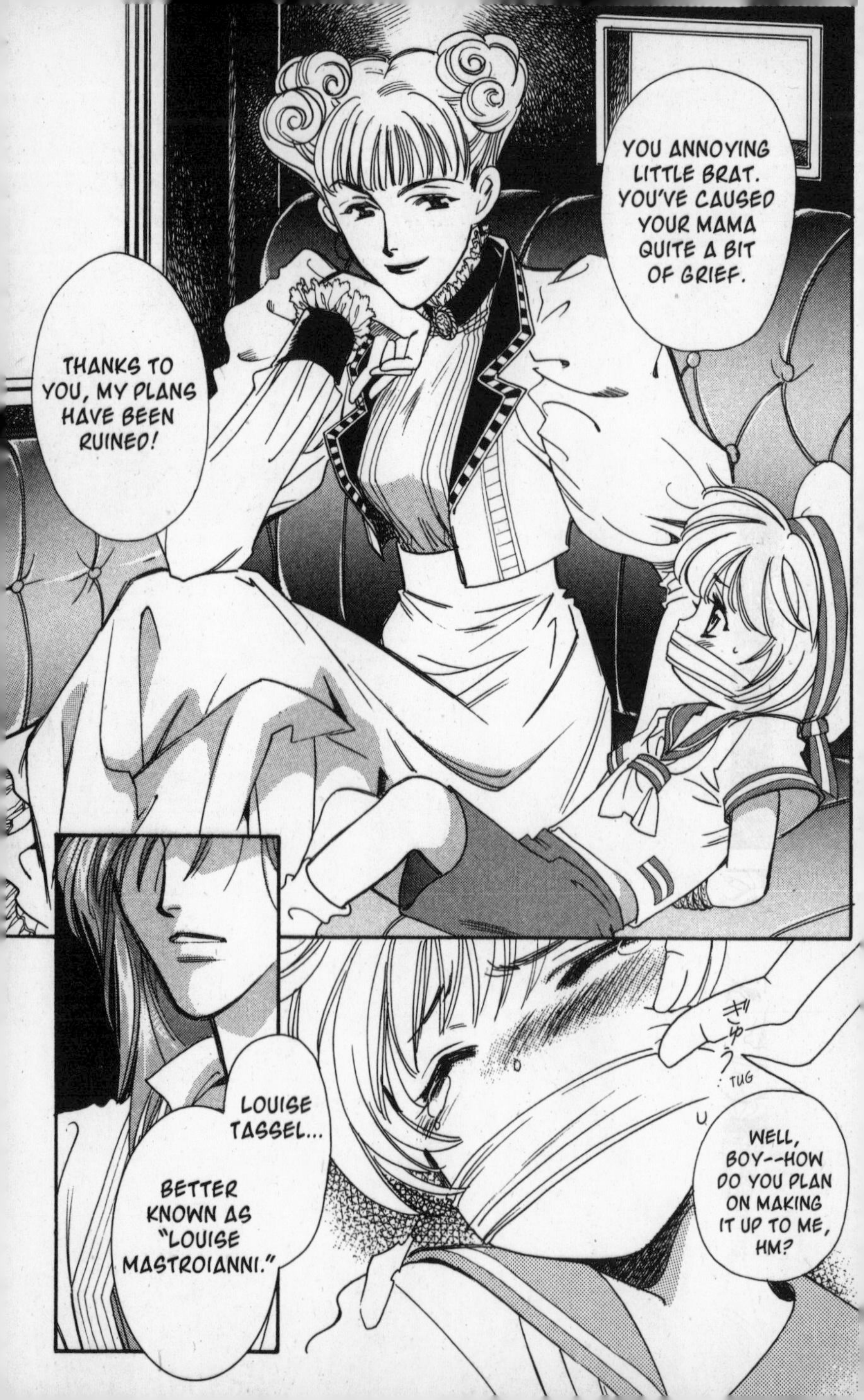
YOU ANNOYING LITTLE BRAT. YOU'VE CAUSED YOUR MAMA QUITE A BIT OF GRIEF.
THANKS TO YOU, MY PLANS HAVE BEEN RUINED!
ぎゅう
TUG
WELL, BOY--HOW DO YOU PLAN ON MAKING IT UP TO ME, HM?
LOUISE TASSEL...
BETTER KNOWN AS "LOUISE MASTROIANNI."

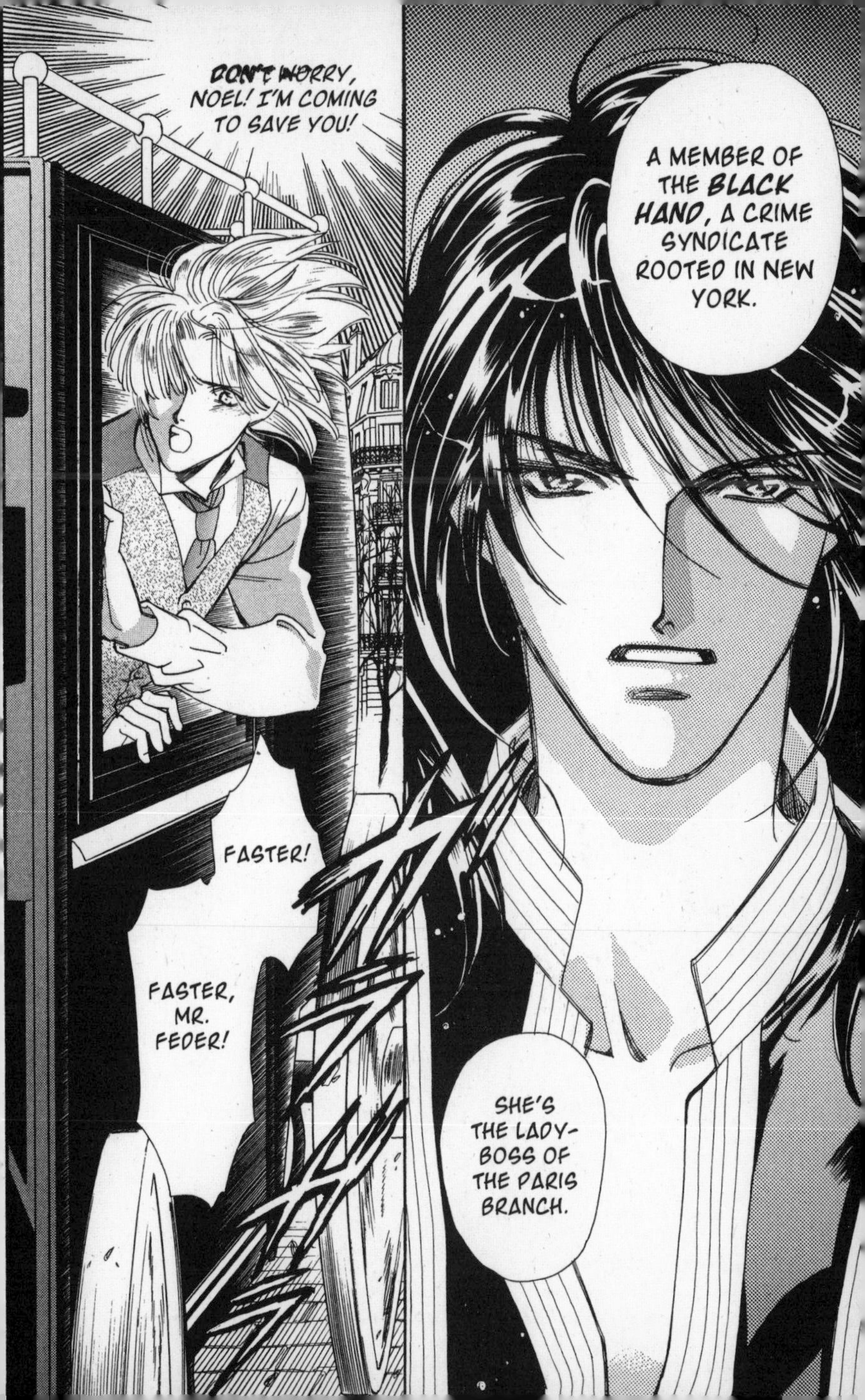
A MEMBER OF THE **BLACK HAND**, A CRIME SYNDICATE ROOTED IN NEW YORK.
SHE'S THE LADY-BOSS OF THE PARIS BRANCH.
DON'T WORRY, NOEL! I'M COMING TO SAVE YOU!
FASTER!
FASTER, MR. FEDER!

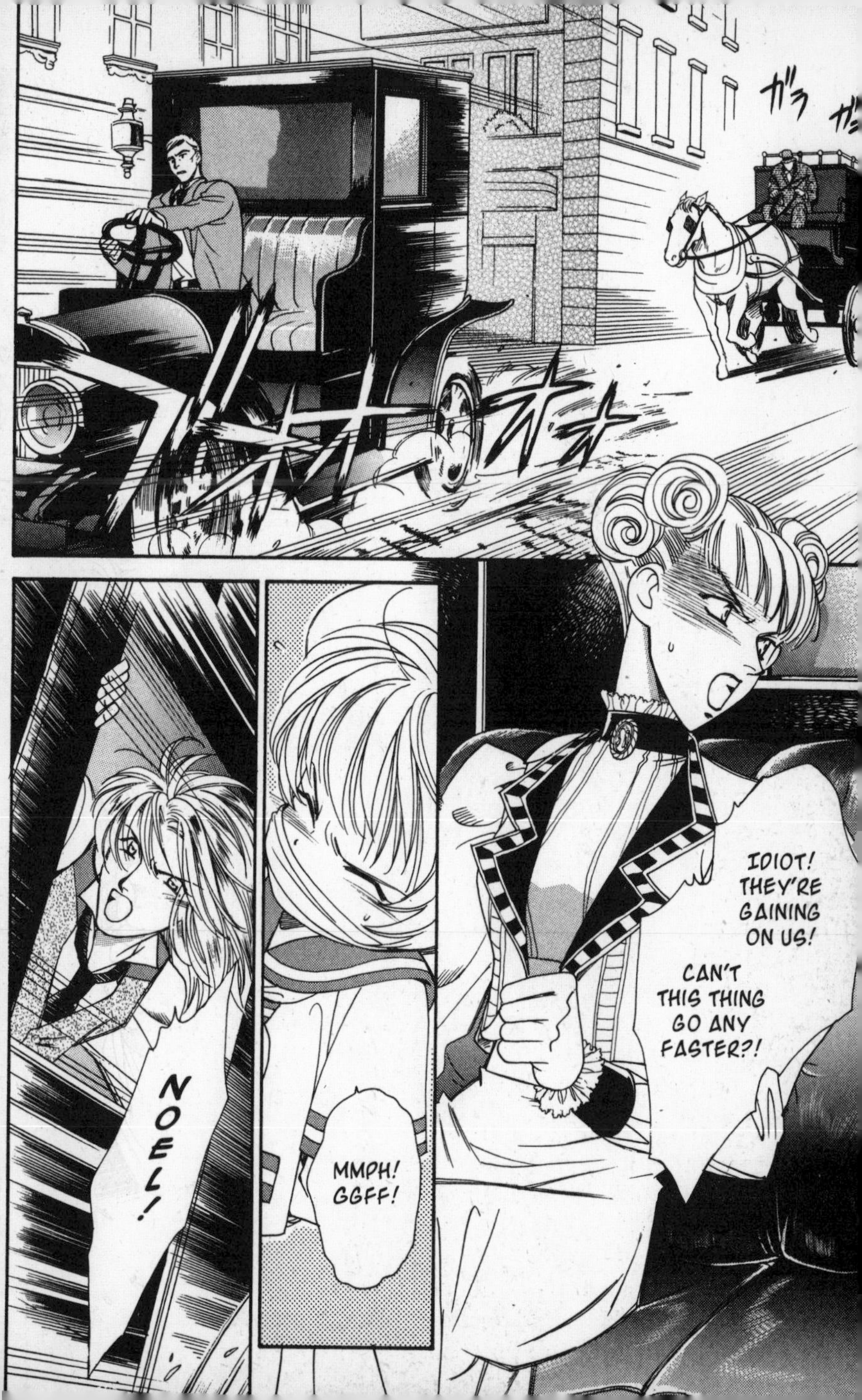
IDIOT! THEY'RE GAINING ON US!
CAN'T THIS THING GO ANY FASTER?!
MMPH! GGFF!
NOEL!

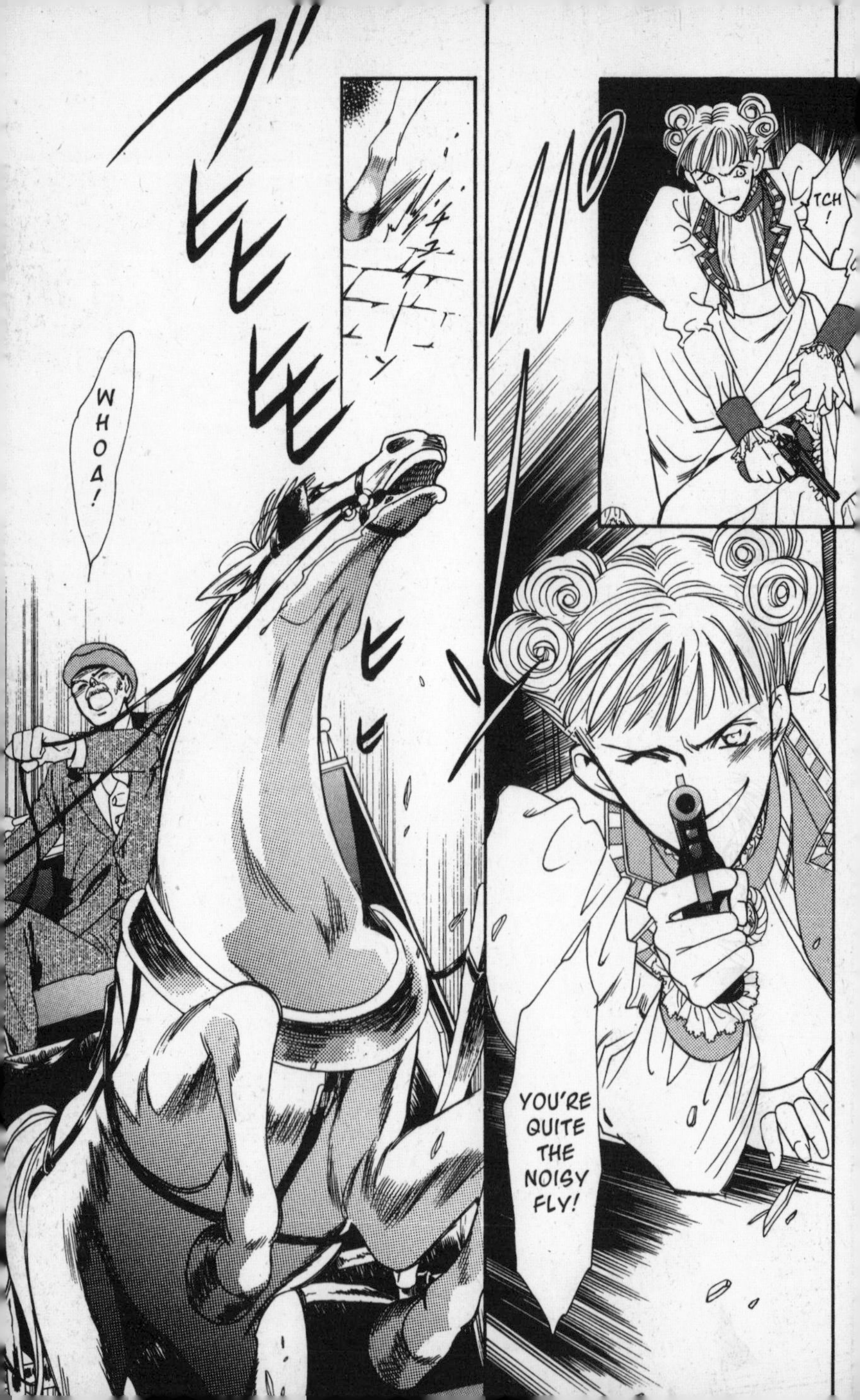
TCH!
YOU'RE QUITE THE NOISY FLY!
WHOA!

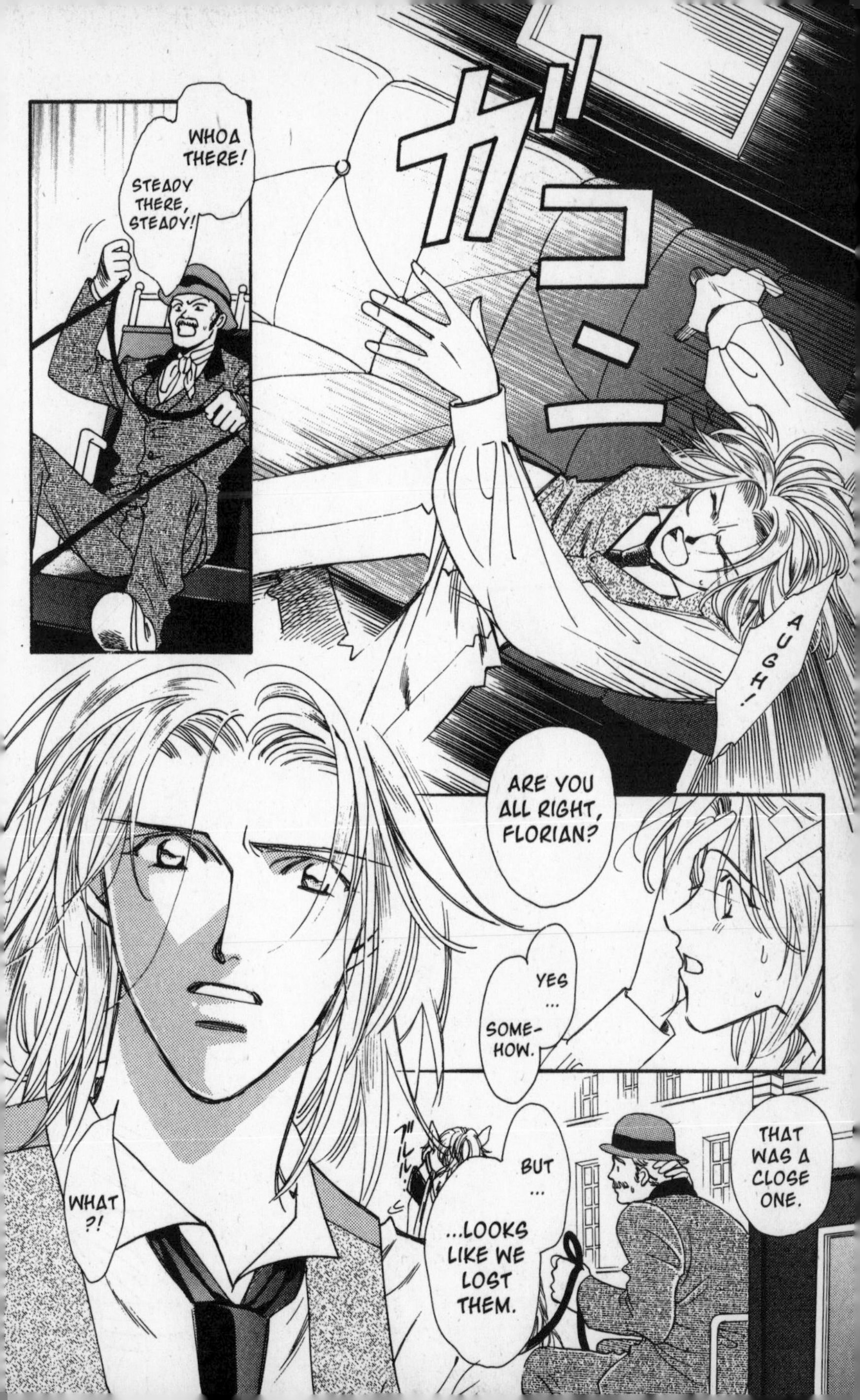
ガコーン
AUGH!
WHOA THERE!
STEADY THERE, STEADY!
ARE YOU ALL RIGHT, FLORIAN?
YES ... SOME-HOW.
THAT WAS A CLOSE ONE.
BUT ...
...LOOKS LIKE WE LOST THEM.
WHAT ?!

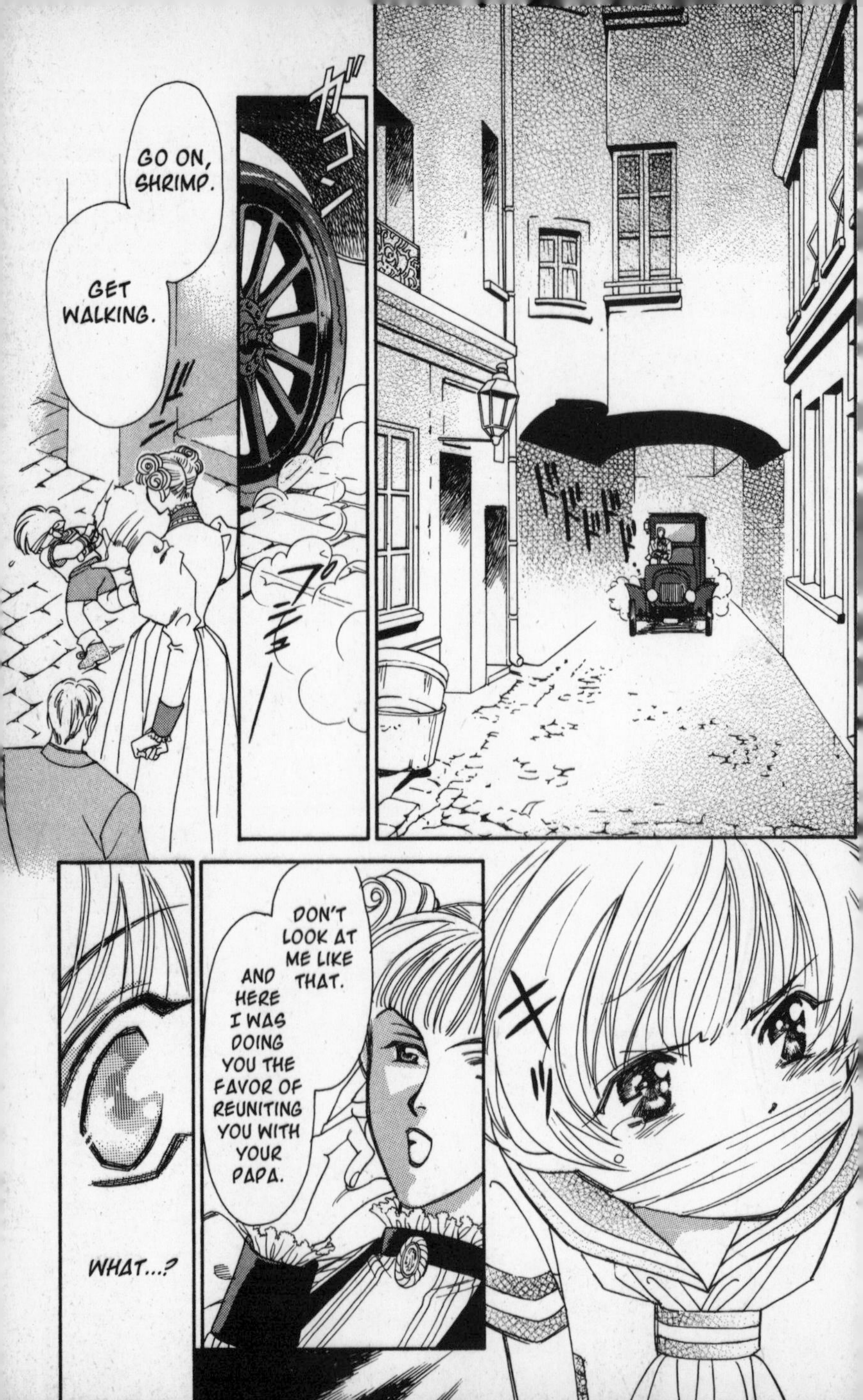
ドドドド
GO ON, SHRIMP.
GET WALKING.
DON'T LOOK AT ME LIKE THAT.
AND HERE I WAS DOING YOU THE FAVOR OF REUNITING YOU WITH YOUR PAPA.
WHAT...?

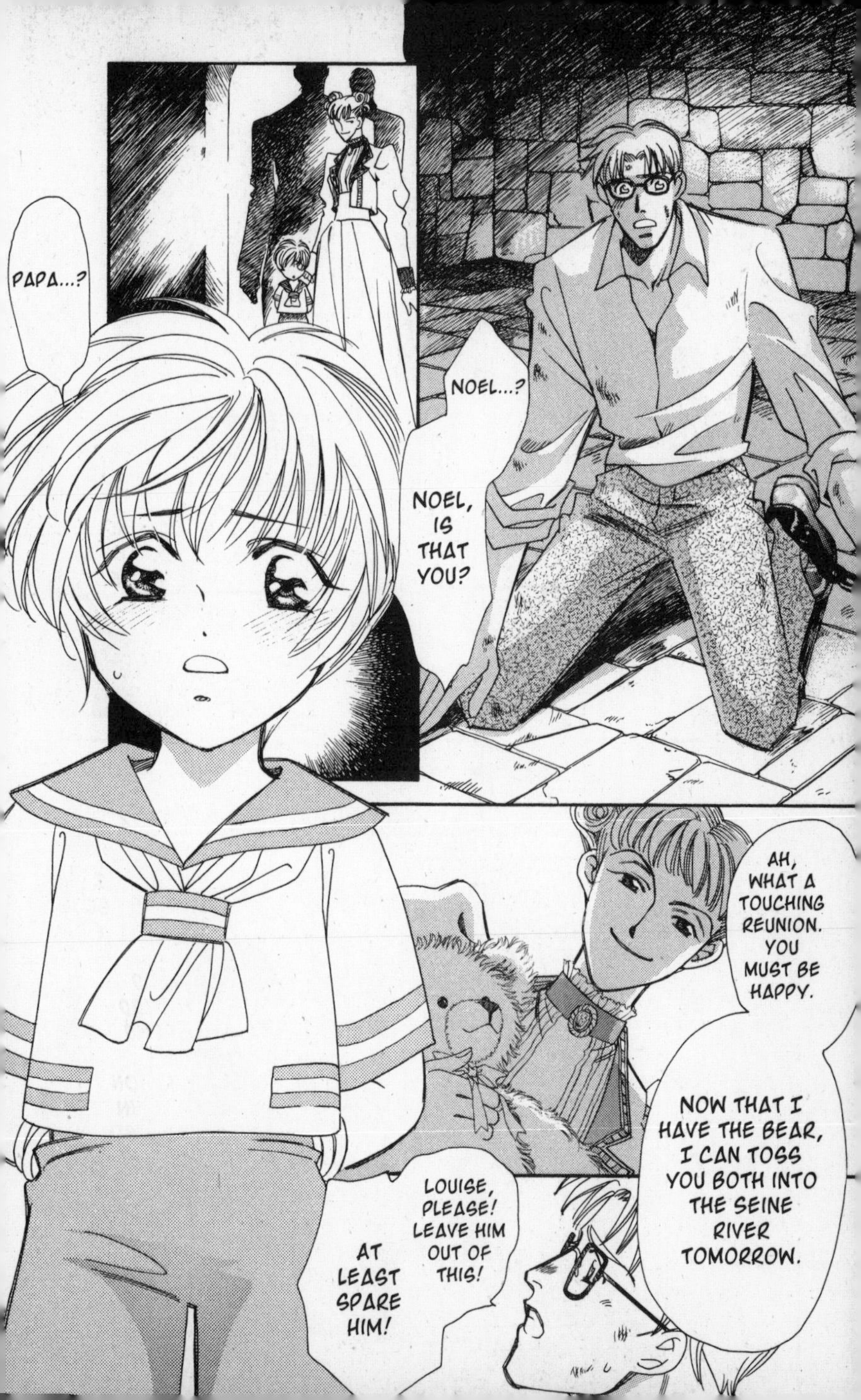
NOEL...?
NOEL, IS THAT YOU?
PAPA...?
AH, WHAT A TOUCHING REUNION. YOU MUST BE HAPPY.
NOW THAT I HAVE THE BEAR, I CAN TOSS YOU BOTH INTO THE SEINE RIVER TOMORROW.
LOUISE, PLEASE! LEAVE HIM OUT OF THIS!
AT LEAST SPARE HIM!

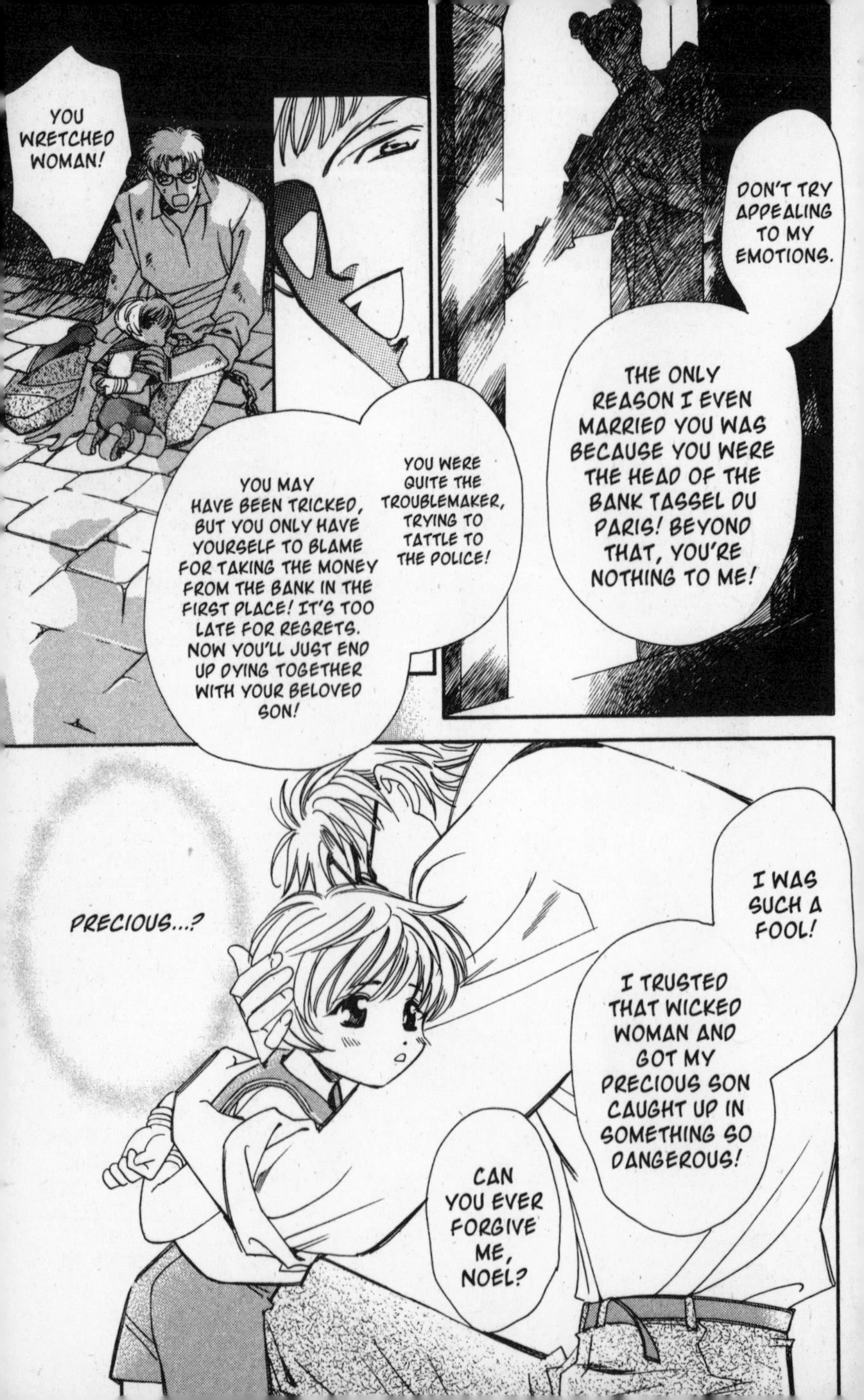

DON'T TRY APPEALING TO MY EMOTIONS.
THE ONLY REASON I EVEN MARRIED YOU WAS BECAUSE YOU WERE THE HEAD OF THE BANK TASSEL DU PARIS! BEYOND THAT, YOU'RE NOTHING TO ME!
YOU WERE QUITE THE TROUBLEMAKER, TRYING TO TATTLE TO THE POLICE!
YOU MAY HAVE BEEN TRICKED, BUT YOU ONLY HAVE YOURSELF TO BLAME FOR TAKING THE MONEY FROM THE BANK IN THE FIRST PLACE! IT'S TOO LATE FOR REGRETS. NOW YOU'LL JUST END UP DYING TOGETHER WITH YOUR BELOVED SON!
YOU WRETCHED WOMAN!
I WAS SUCH A FOOL!
I TRUSTED THAT WICKED WOMAN AND GOT MY PRECIOUS SON CAUGHT UP IN SOMETHING SO DANGEROUS!
CAN YOU EVER FORGIVE ME, NOEL?
PRECIOUS...?

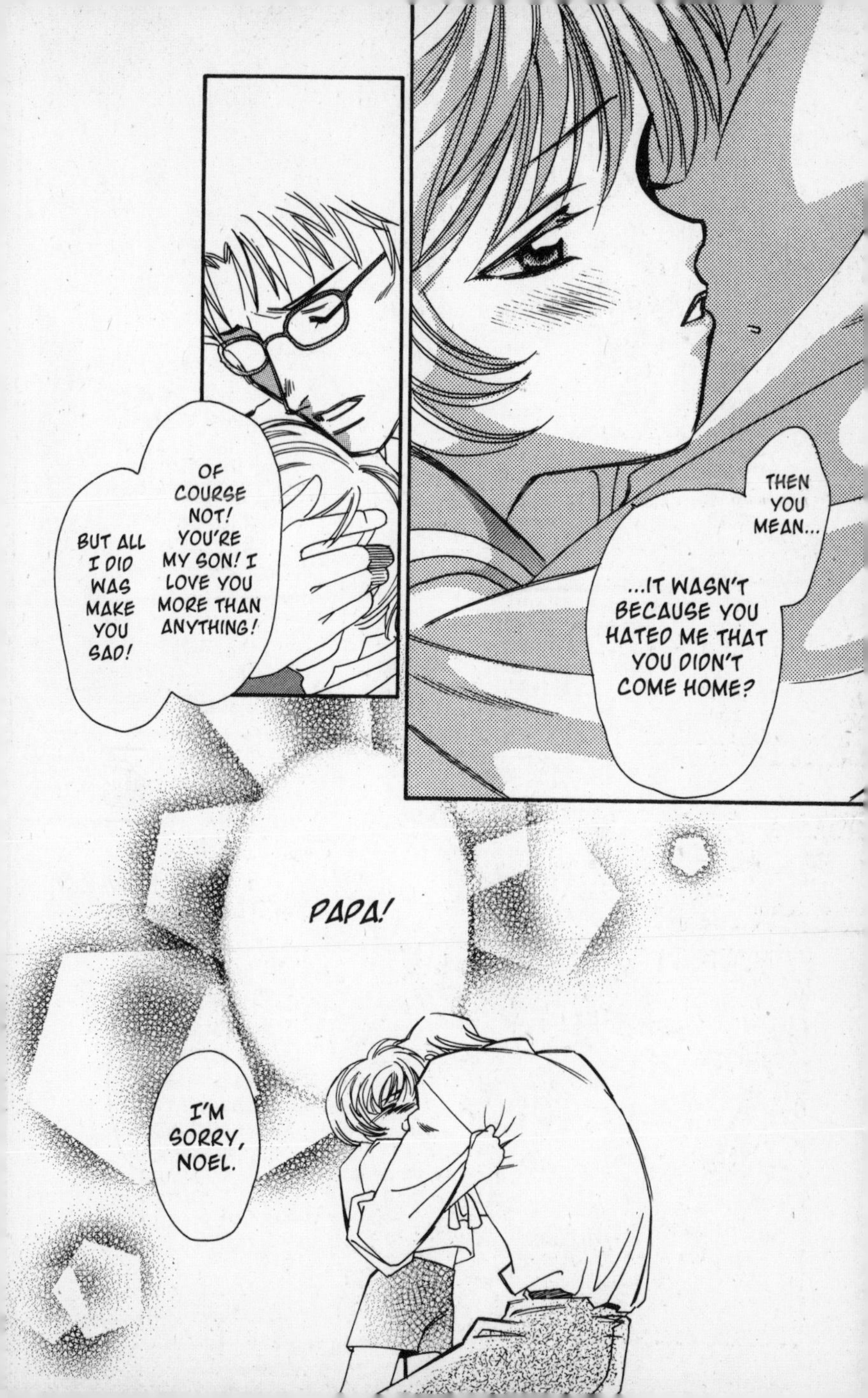
THEN YOU MEAN...
...IT WASN'T BECAUSE YOU HATED ME THAT YOU DIDN'T COME HOME?
OF COURSE NOT! YOU'RE MY SON! I LOVE YOU MORE THAN ANYTHING!
BUT ALL I DID WAS MAKE YOU SAD!
PAPA!
I'M SORRY, NOEL.

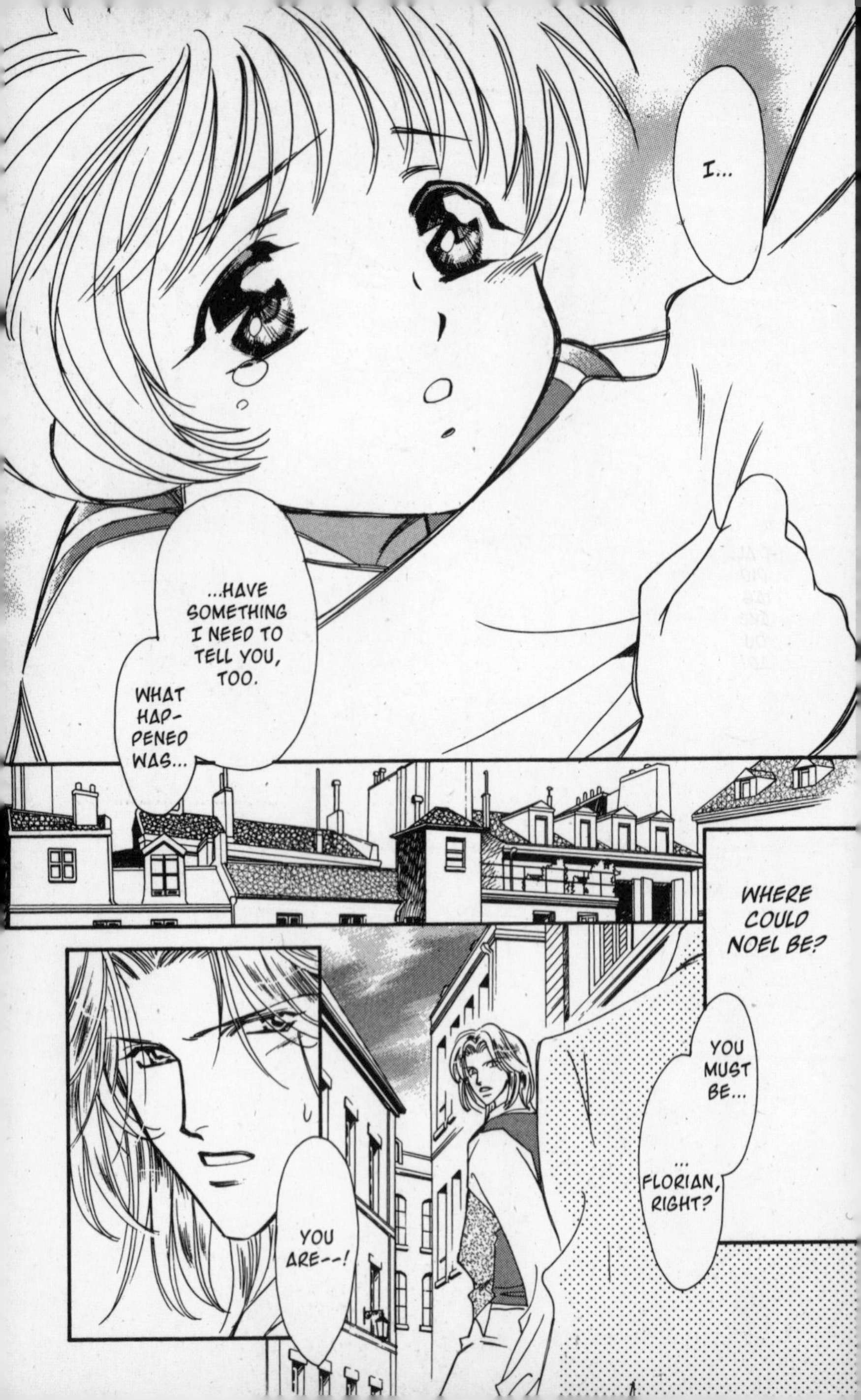
I...
...HAVE SOMETHING I NEED TO TELL YOU, TOO.
WHAT HAP-PENED WAS...
WHERE COULD NOEL BE?
YOU MUST BE...
...FLORIAN, RIGHT?
YOU ARE--!

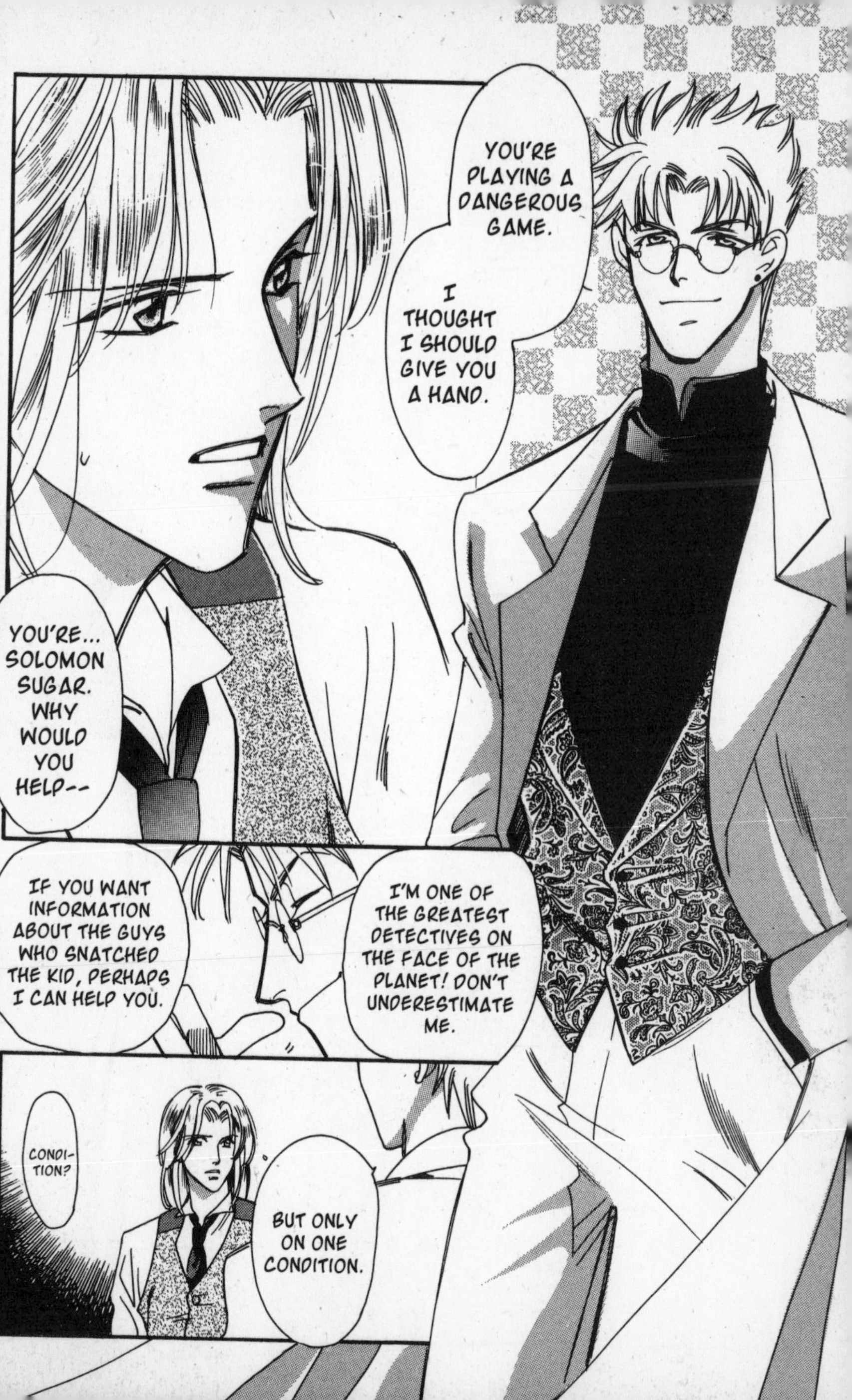
YOU'RE PLAYING A DANGEROUS GAME.
I THOUGHT I SHOULD GIVE YOU A HAND.
YOU'RE... SOLOMON SUGAR. WHY WOULD YOU HELP--
I'M ONE OF THE GREATEST DETECTIVES ON THE FACE OF THE PLANET! DON'T UNDERESTIMATE ME.
IF YOU WANT INFORMATION ABOUT THE GUYS WHO SNATCHED THE KID, PERHAPS I CAN HELP YOU.
BUT ONLY ON ONE CONDITION.
CONDI-TION?

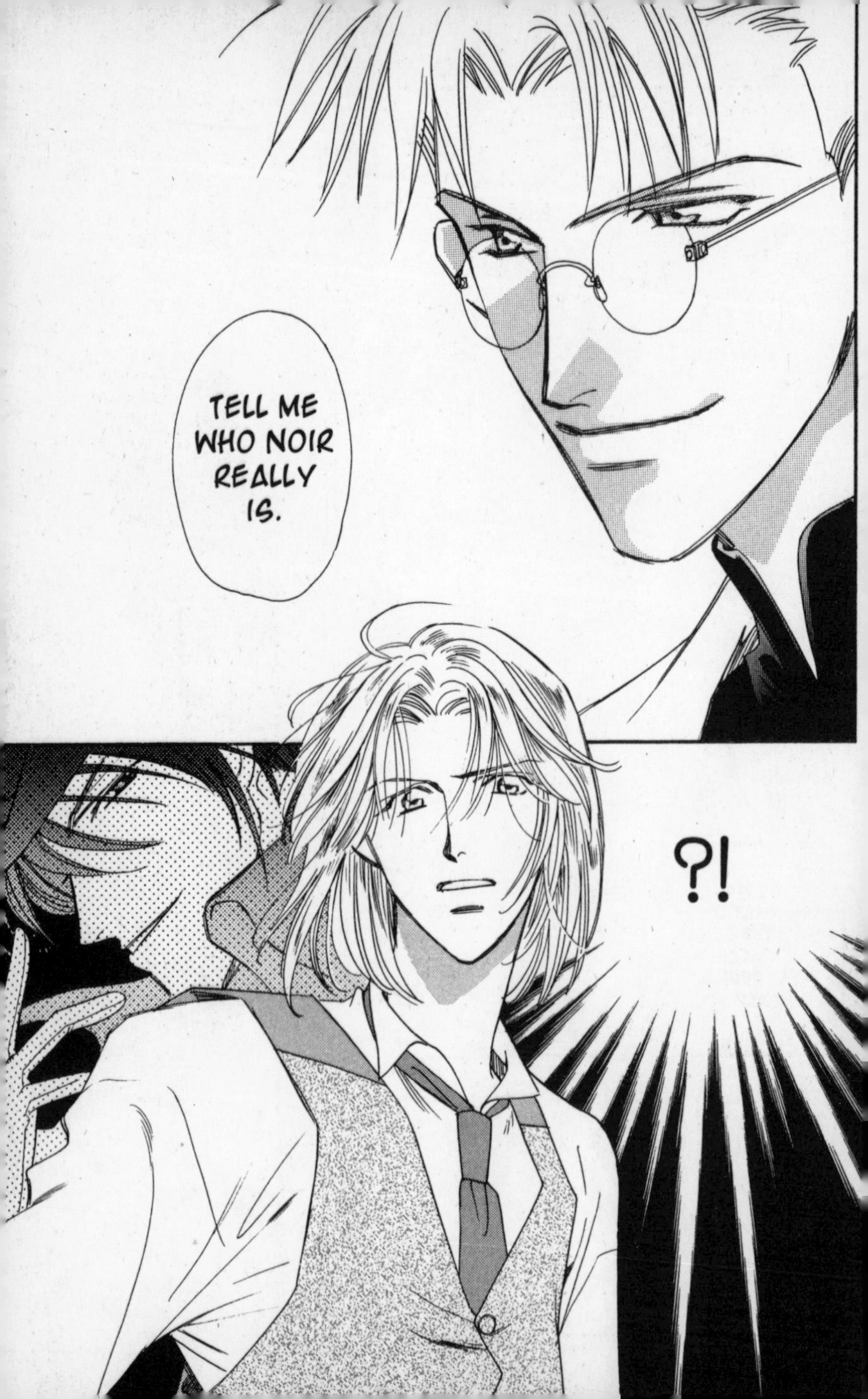
TELL ME WHO NOIR REALLY IS.
?!

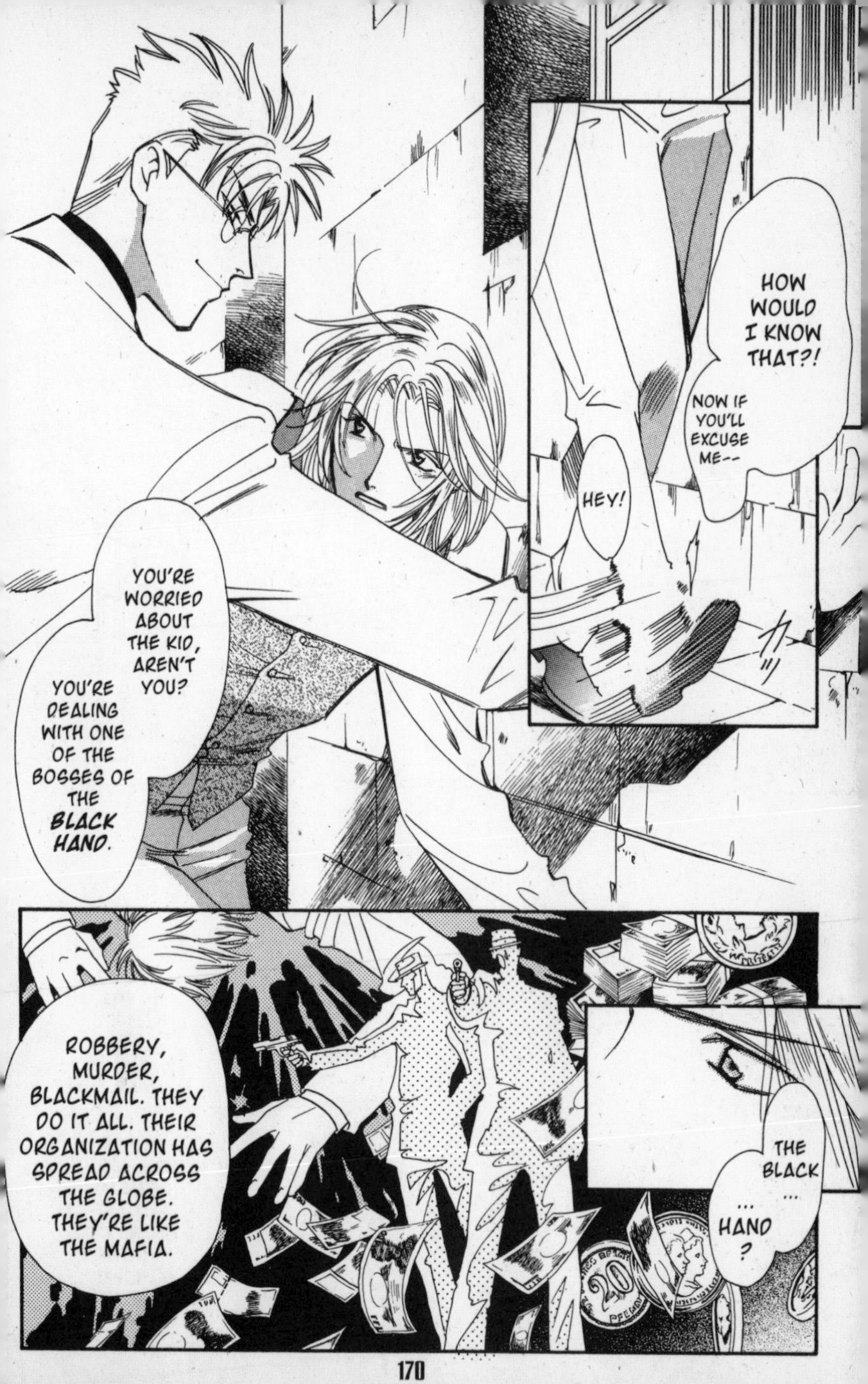
HOW WOULD I KNOW THAT?!
NOW IF YOU'LL EXCUSE ME--
HEY!
YOU'RE WORRIED ABOUT THE KID, AREN'T YOU?
YOU'RE DEALING WITH ONE OF THE BOSSES OF THE **BLACK HAND**.
THE BLACK ... HAND?
ROBBERY, MURDER, BLACKMAIL. THEY DO IT ALL. THEIR ORGANIZATION HAS SPREAD ACROSS THE GLOBE. THEY'RE LIKE THE MAFIA.

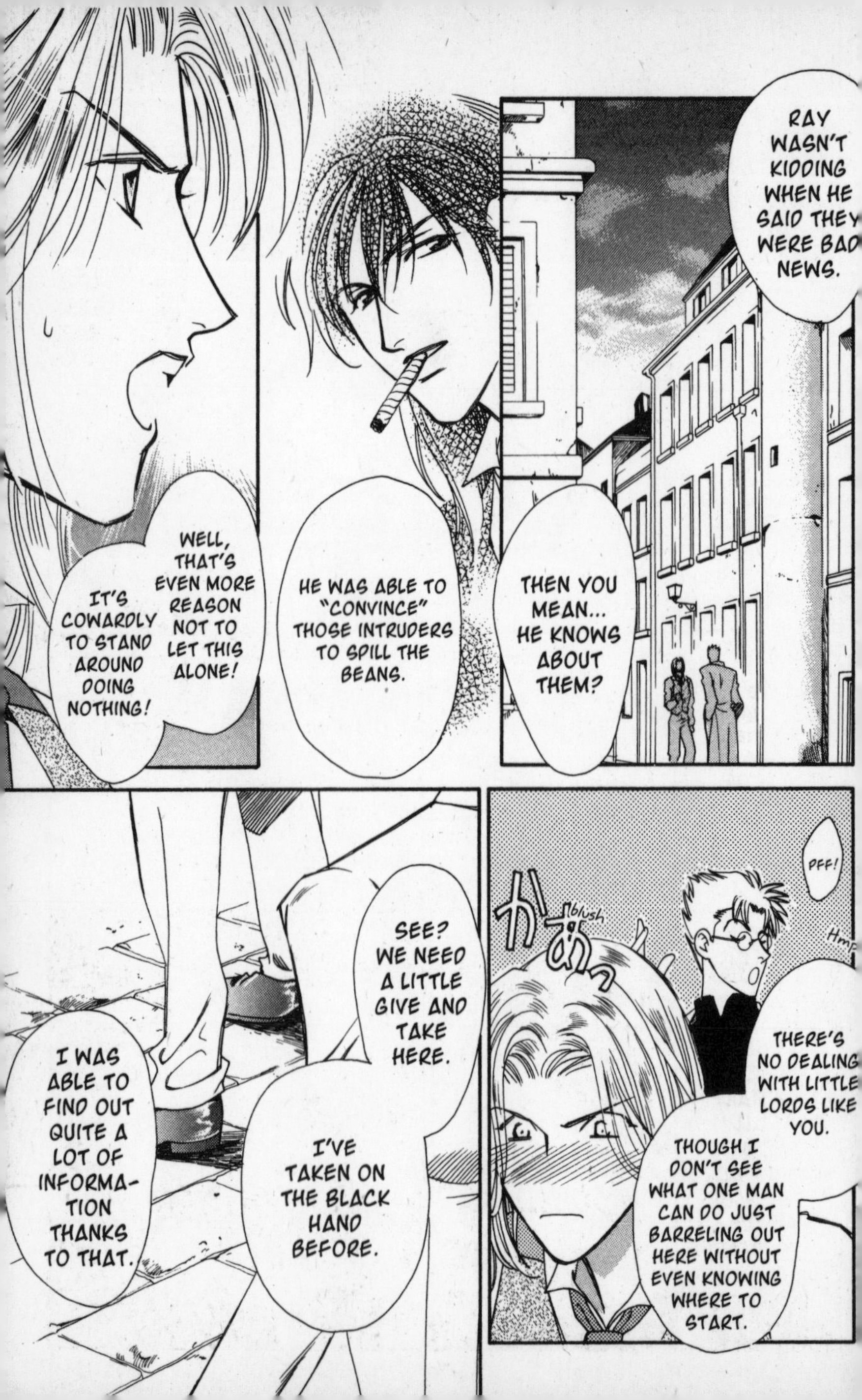

RAY WASN'T KIDDING WHEN HE SAID THEY WERE BAD NEWS.
THEN YOU MEAN... HE KNOWS ABOUT THEM?
HE WAS ABLE TO "CONVINCE" THOSE INTRUDERS TO SPILL THE BEANS.
WELL, THAT'S EVEN MORE REASON NOT TO LET THIS ALONE!
IT'S COWARDLY TO STAND AROUND DOING NOTHING!
PFF!
Hmph
THERE'S NO DEALING WITH LITTLE LORDS LIKE YOU.
かあっ
blush
THOUGH I DON'T SEE WHAT ONE MAN CAN DO JUST BARRELING OUT HERE WITHOUT EVEN KNOWING WHERE TO START.
SEE? WE NEED A LITTLE GIVE AND TAKE HERE.
I'VE TAKEN ON THE BLACK HAND BEFORE.
I WAS ABLE TO FIND OUT QUITE A LOT OF INFORMATION THANKS TO THAT.

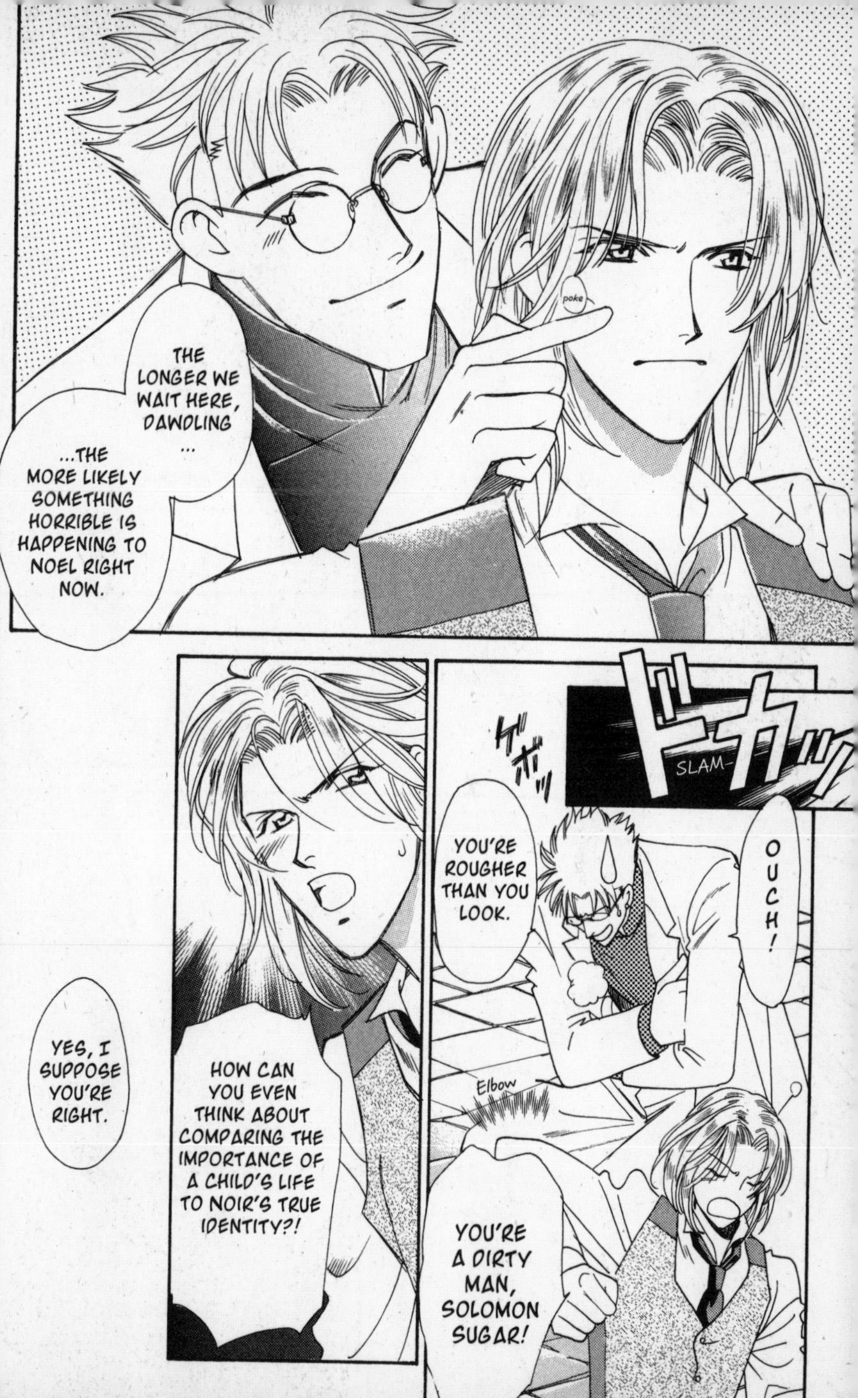
poke
THE LONGER WE WAIT HERE, DAWDLING ...
...THE MORE LIKELY SOMETHING HORRIBLE IS HAPPENING TO NOEL RIGHT NOW.
ドカッ
SLAM
OUCH!
YOU'RE ROUGHER THAN YOU LOOK.
Elbow
YOU'RE A DIRTY MAN, SOLOMON SUGAR!
HOW CAN YOU EVEN THINK ABOUT COMPARING THE IMPORTANCE OF A CHILD'S LIFE TO NOIR'S TRUE IDENTITY?!
YES, I SUPPOSE YOU'RE RIGHT.

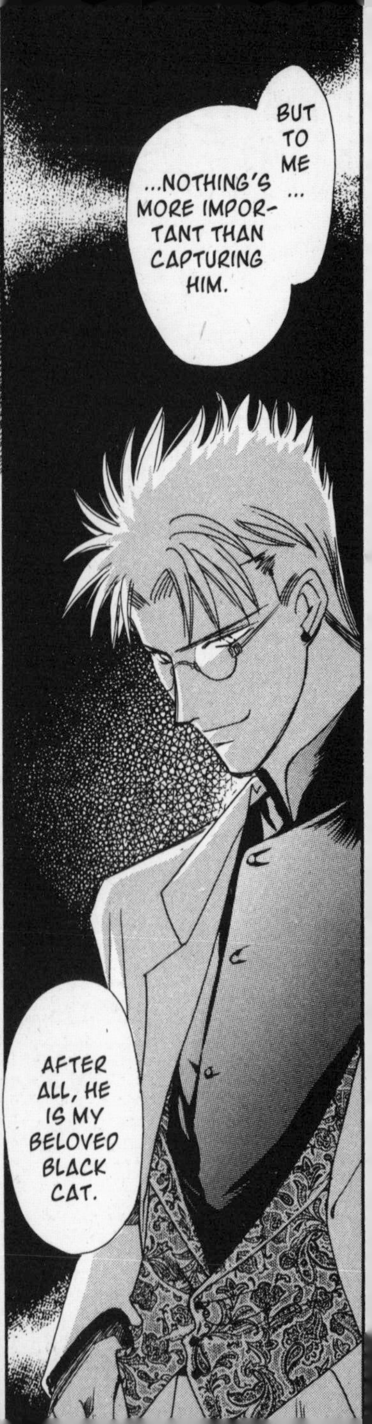
BUT TO ME ...
...NOTHING'S MORE IMPOR-TANT THAN CAPTURING HIM.
AFTER ALL, HE IS MY BELOVED BLACK CAT.
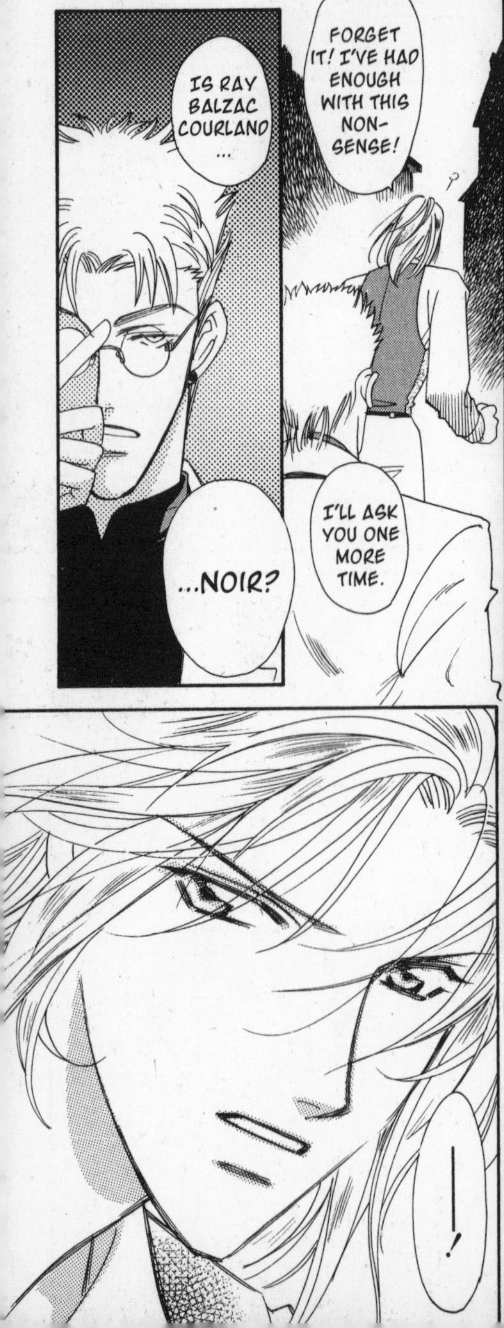
FORGET IT! I'VE HAD ENOUGH WITH THIS NON-SENSE!
I'LL ASK YOU ONE MORE TIME.
IS RAY BALZAC COURLAND ...
...NOIR?
!

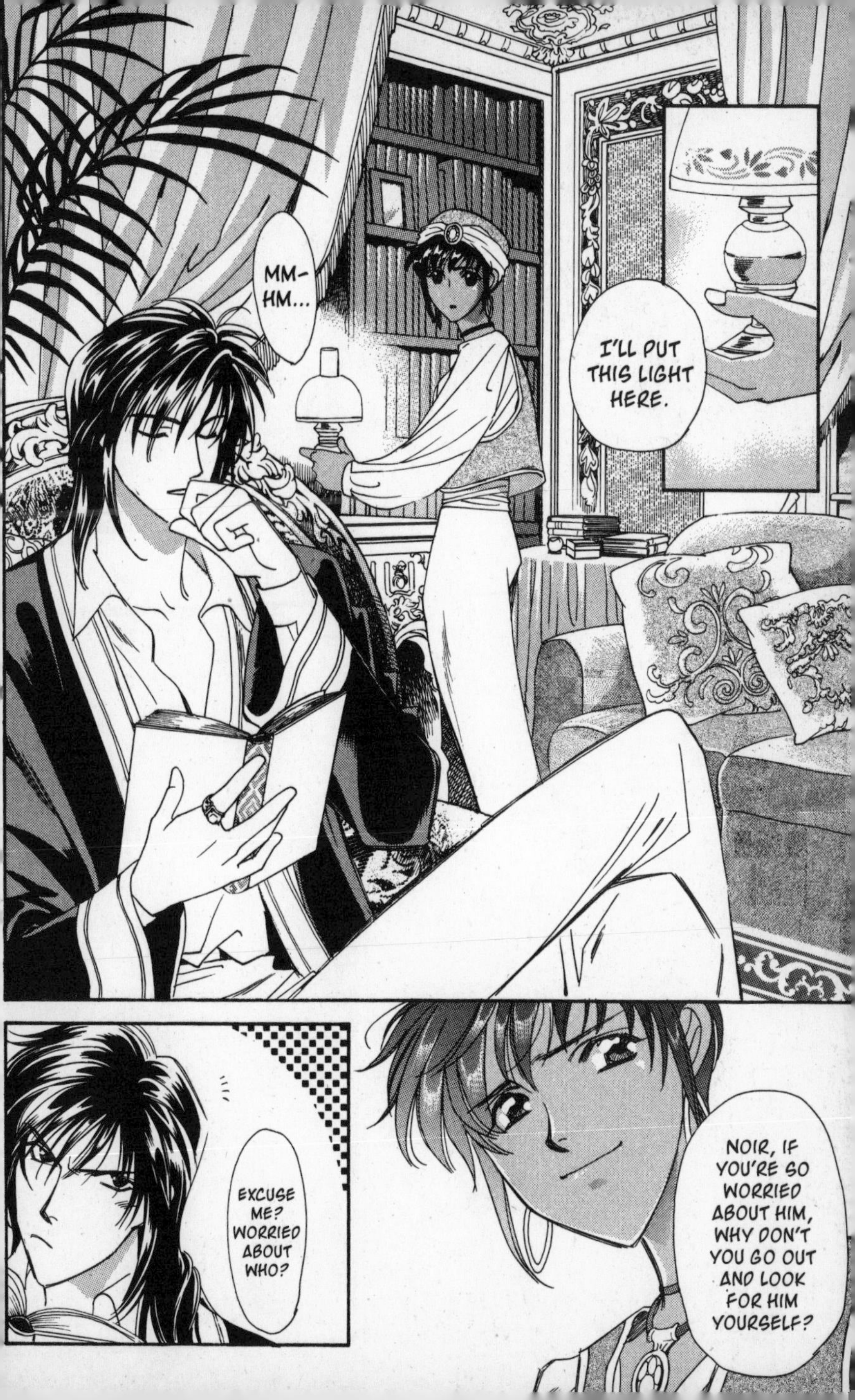

I'LL PUT THIS LIGHT HERE.
MM-HM...
NOIR, IF YOU'RE SO WORRIED ABOUT HIM, WHY DON'T YOU GO OUT AND LOOK FOR HIM YOURSELF?
EXCUSE ME? WORRIED ABOUT WHO?

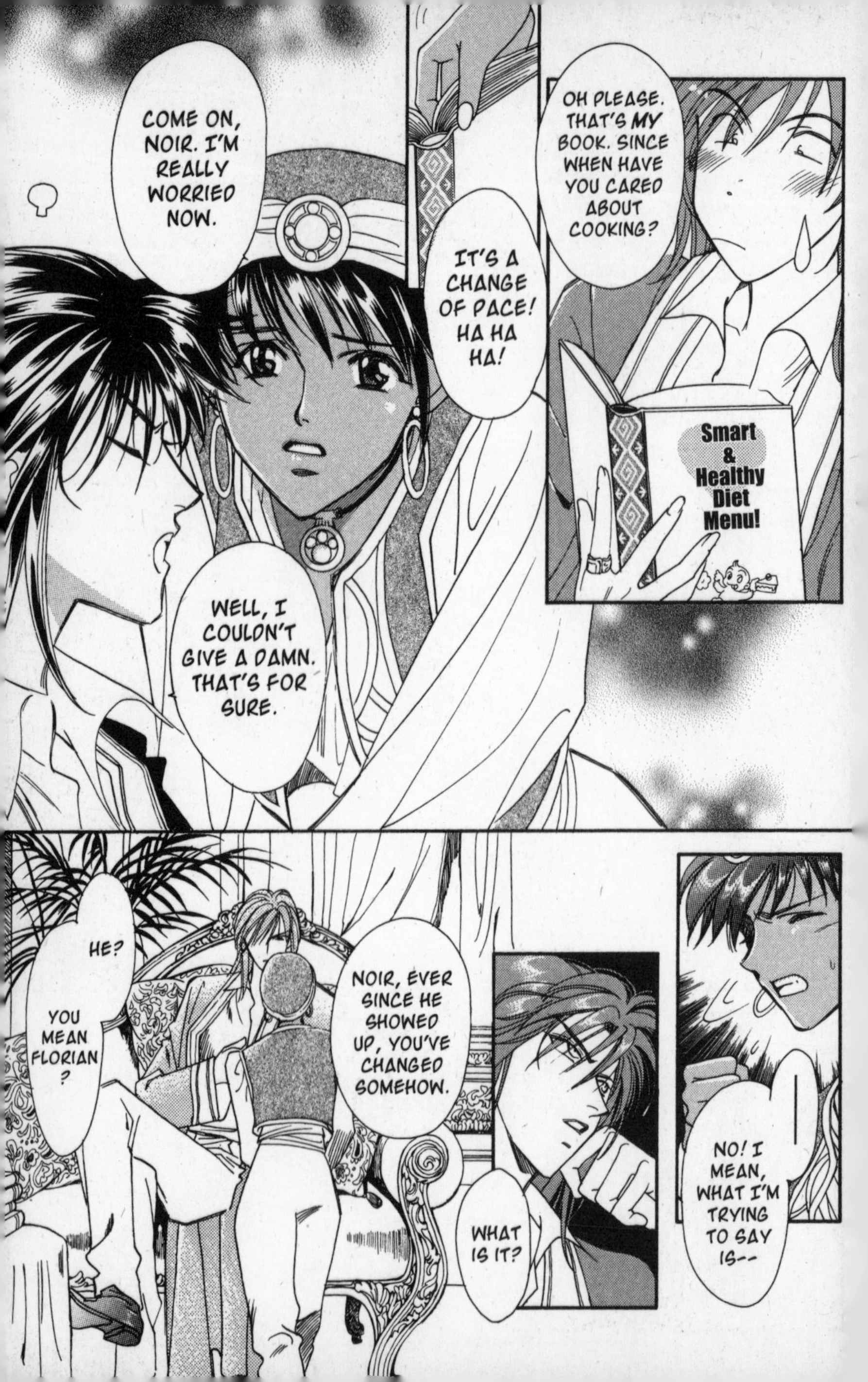
OH PLEASE. THAT'S **MY** BOOK. SINCE WHEN HAVE YOU CARED ABOUT COOKING?
Smart & Healthy Diet Menu!
IT'S A CHANGE OF PACE! HA HA HA!
COME ON, NOIR. I'M REALLY WORRIED NOW.
WELL, I COULDN'T GIVE A DAMN. THAT'S FOR SURE.
NO! I MEAN, WHAT I'M TRYING TO SAY IS--
WHAT IS IT?
NOIR, EVER SINCE HE SHOWED UP, YOU'VE CHANGED SOMEHOW.
HE?
YOU MEAN FLORIAN?

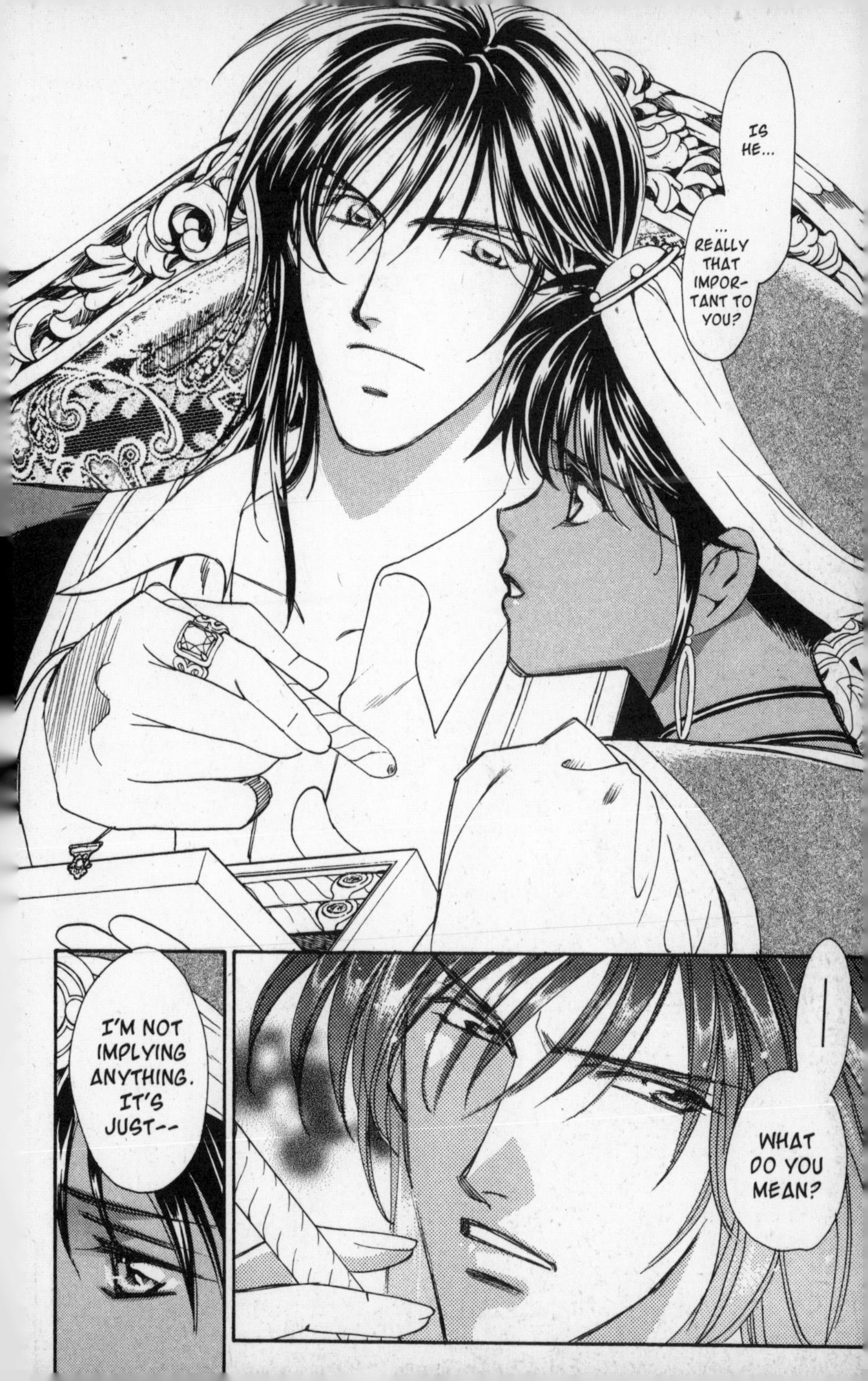
IS HE...
...REALLY THAT IMPORTANT TO YOU?
WHAT DO YOU MEAN?
I'M NOT IMPLYING ANYTHING. IT'S JUST--

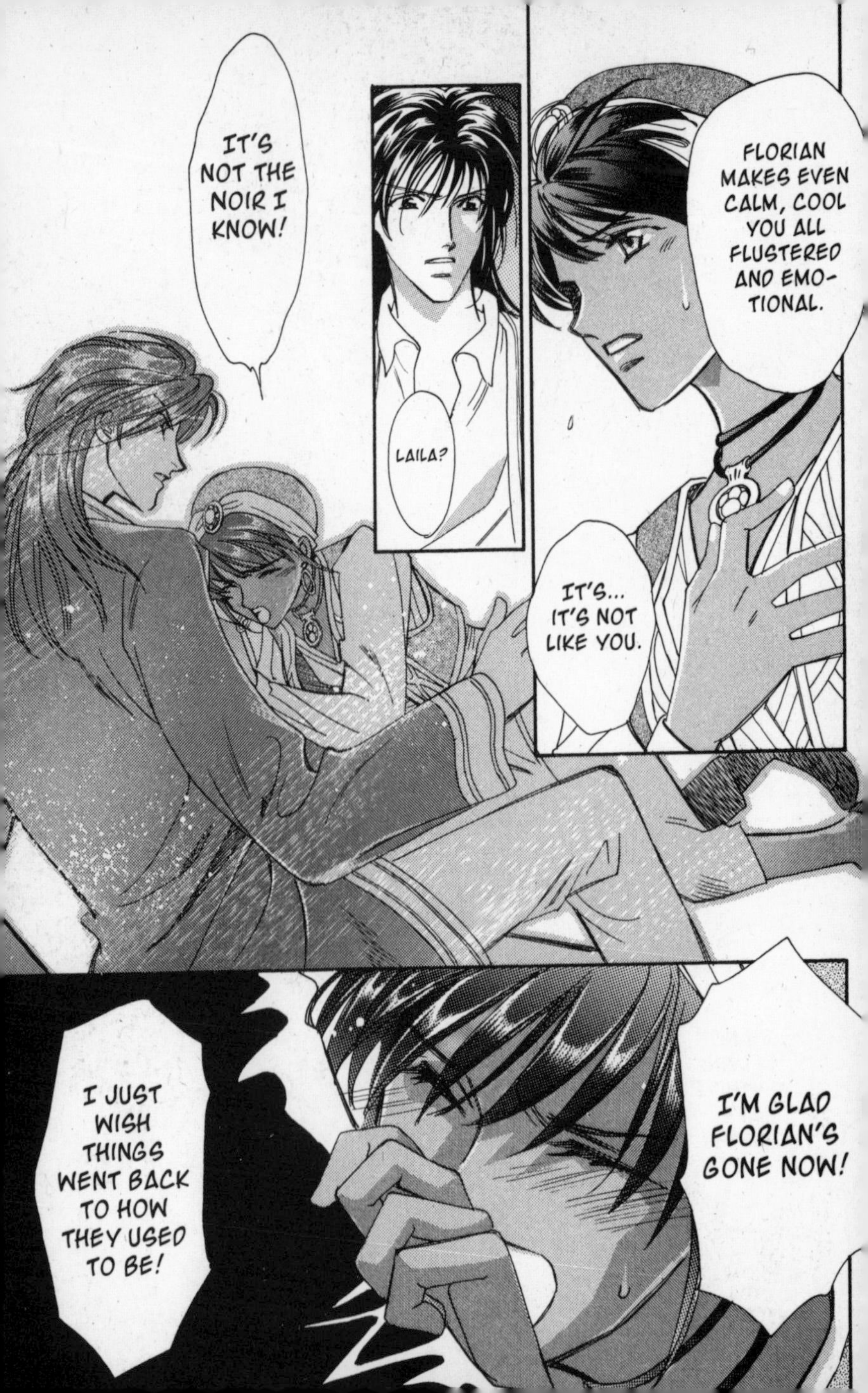
FLORIAN MAKES EVEN CALM, COOL YOU ALL FLUSTERED AND EMO-TIONAL.
IT'S... IT'S NOT LIKE YOU.
LAILA?
IT'S NOT THE NOIR I KNOW!
I'M GLAD FLORIAN'S GONE NOW!
I JUST WISH THINGS WENT BACK TO HOW THEY USED TO BE!

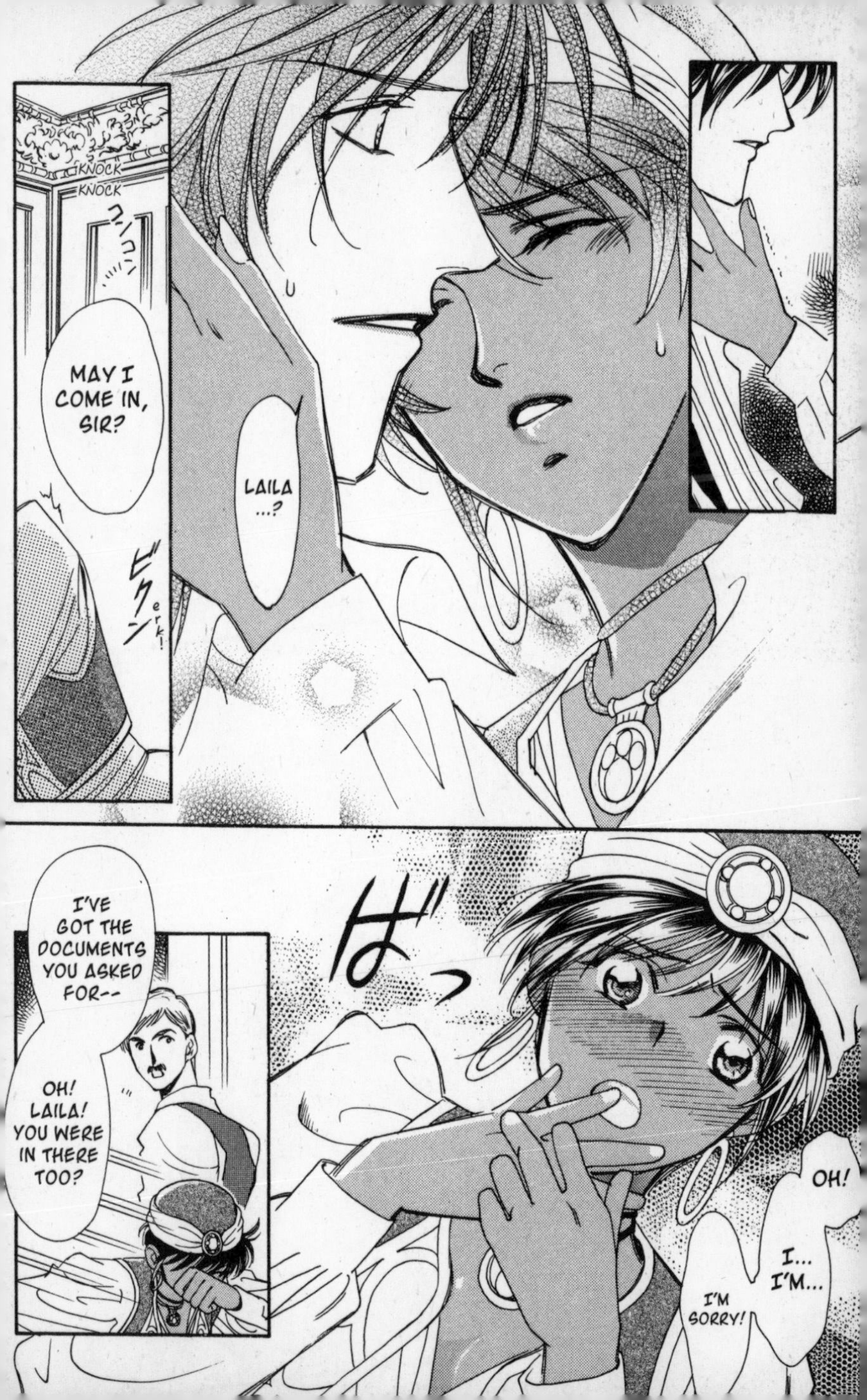

LAILA ...?
KNOCK
KNOCK
MAY I COME IN, SIR?
erk!
OH!
I... I'M...
I'M SORRY!
I'VE GOT THE DOCUMENTS YOU ASKED FOR--
OH! LAILA! YOU WERE IN THERE TOO?

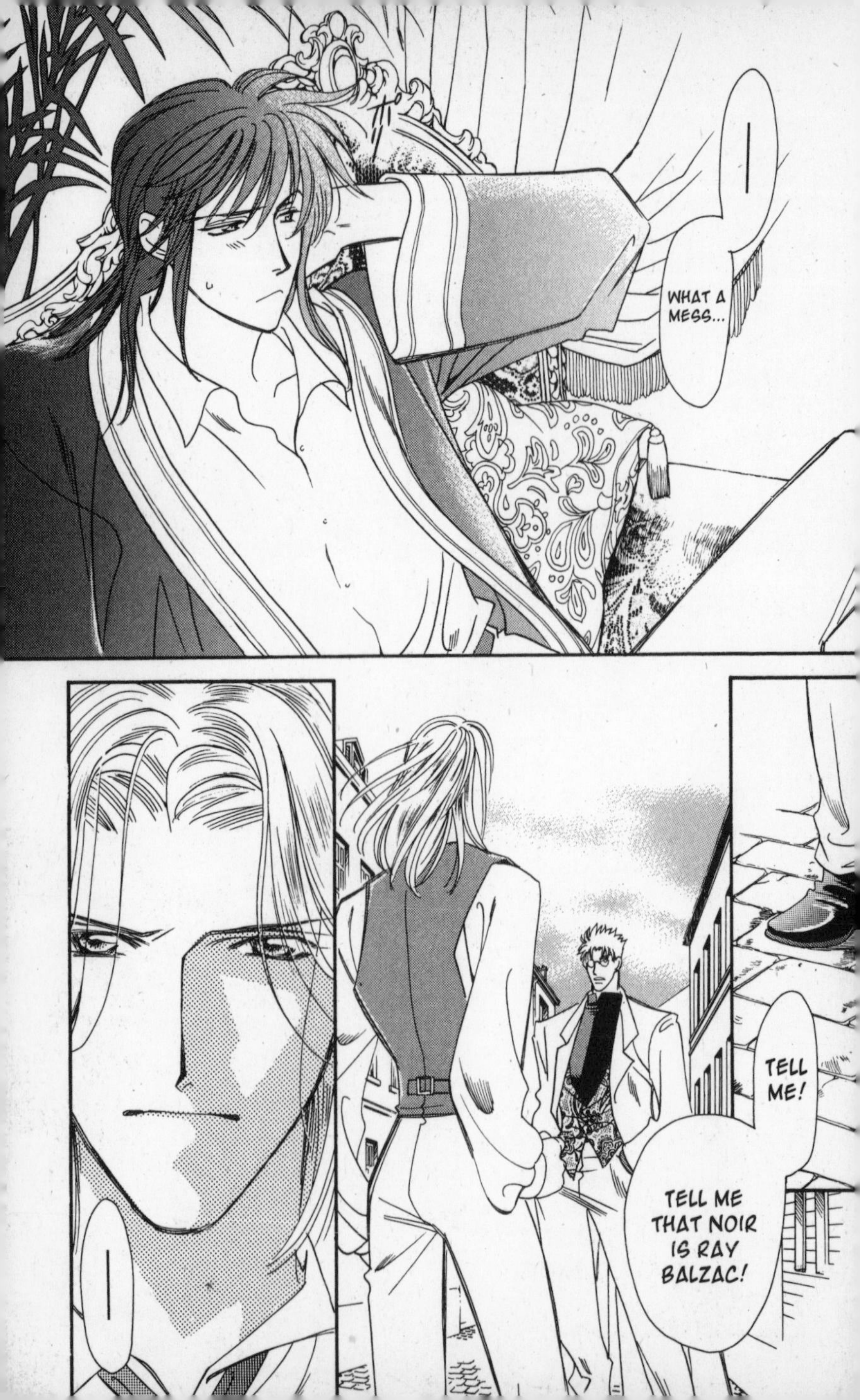
WHAT A MESS...
TELL ME!
TELL ME THAT NOIR IS RAY BALZAC!

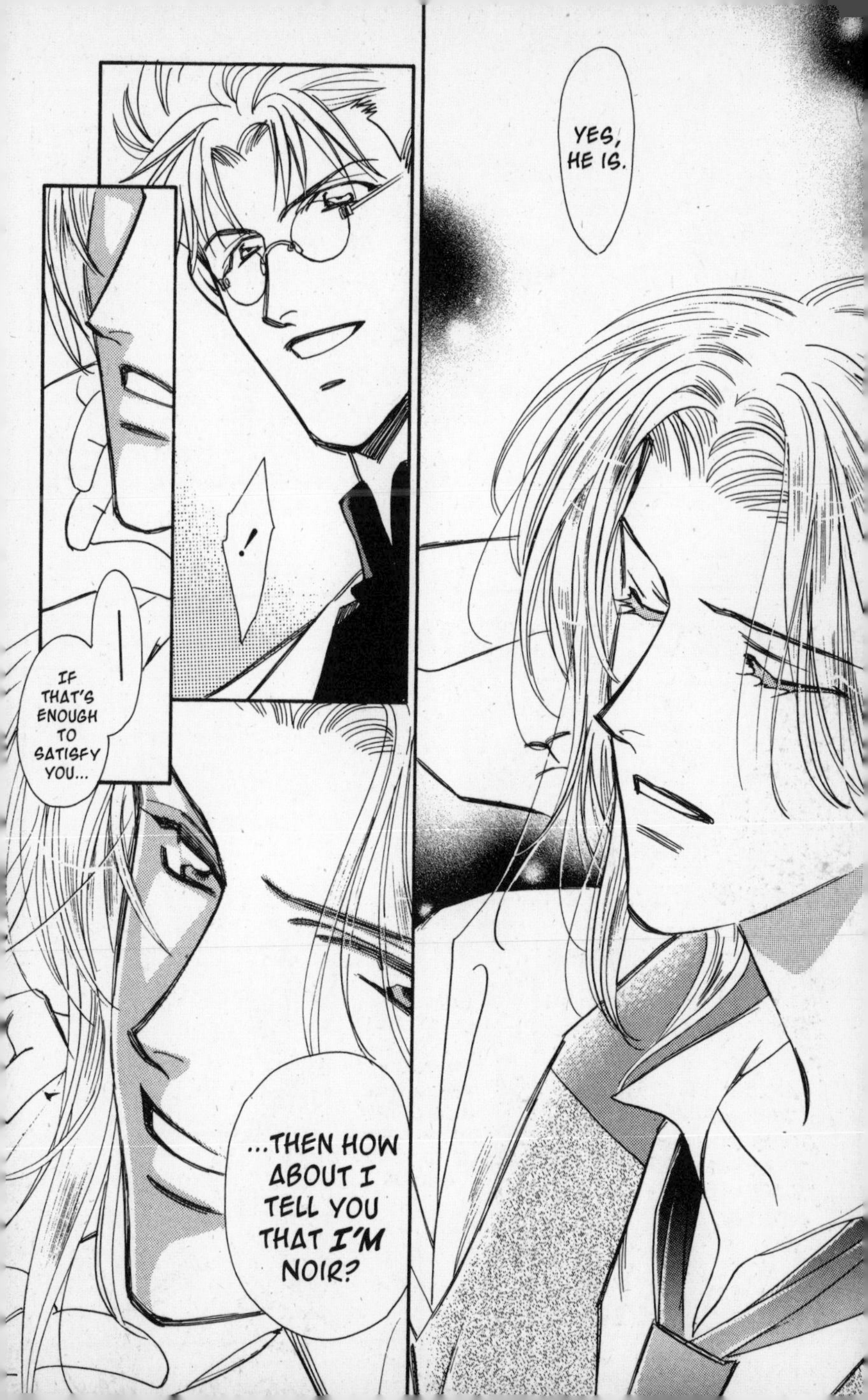
YES, HE IS.
!
IF THAT'S ENOUGH TO SATISFY YOU...
...THEN HOW ABOUT I TELL YOU THAT *I'M* NOIR?

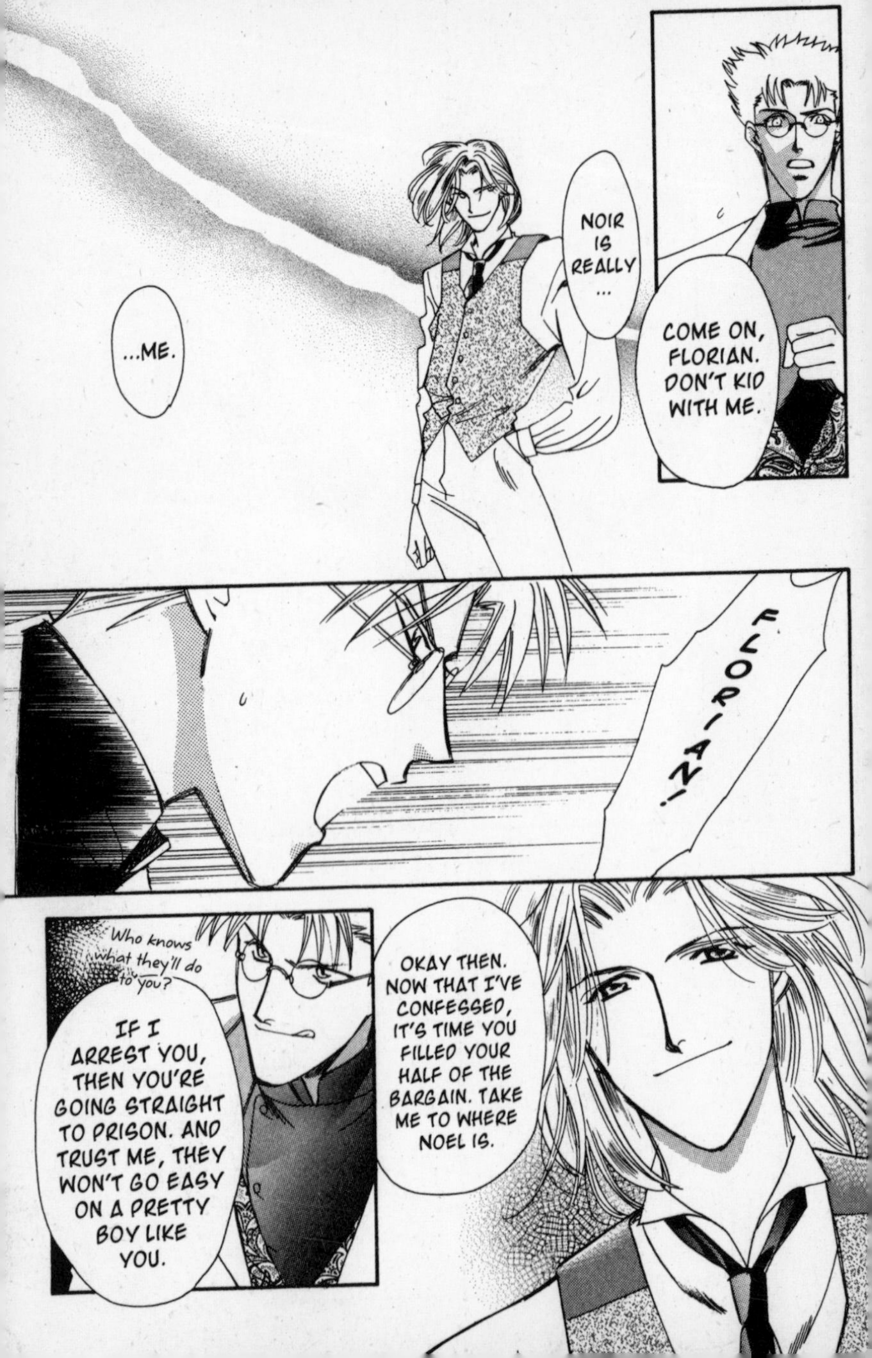
NOIR IS REALLY ...
...ME.
COME ON, FLORIAN. DON'T KID WITH ME.
FLORIAN!
OKAY THEN. NOW THAT I'VE CONFESSED, IT'S TIME YOU FILLED YOUR HALF OF THE BARGAIN. TAKE ME TO WHERE NOEL IS.
IF I ARREST YOU, THEN YOU'RE GOING STRAIGHT TO PRISON. AND TRUST ME, THEY WON'T GO EASY ON A PRETTY BOY LIKE YOU.
Who knows what they'll do to you?

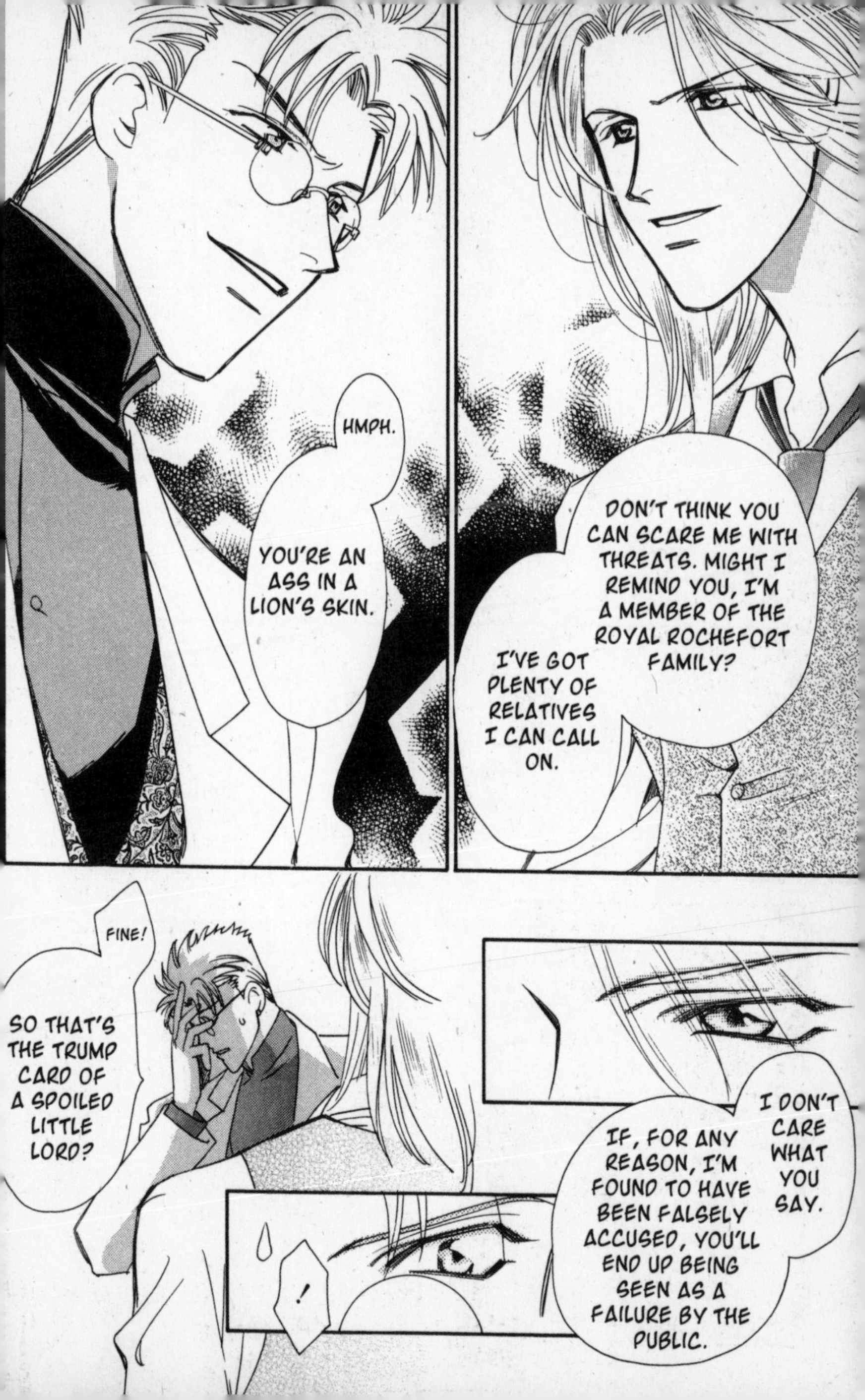
DON'T THINK YOU CAN SCARE ME WITH THREATS. MIGHT I REMIND YOU, I'M A MEMBER OF THE ROYAL ROCHEFORT FAMILY?
I'VE GOT PLENTY OF RELATIVES I CAN CALL ON.
HMPH.
YOU'RE AN ASS IN A LION'S SKIN.
FINE!
SO THAT'S THE TRUMP CARD OF A SPOILED LITTLE LORD?
I DON'T CARE WHAT YOU SAY.
IF, FOR ANY REASON, I'M FOUND TO HAVE BEEN FALSELY ACCUSED, YOU'LL END UP BEING SEEN AS A FAILURE BY THE PUBLIC.
!

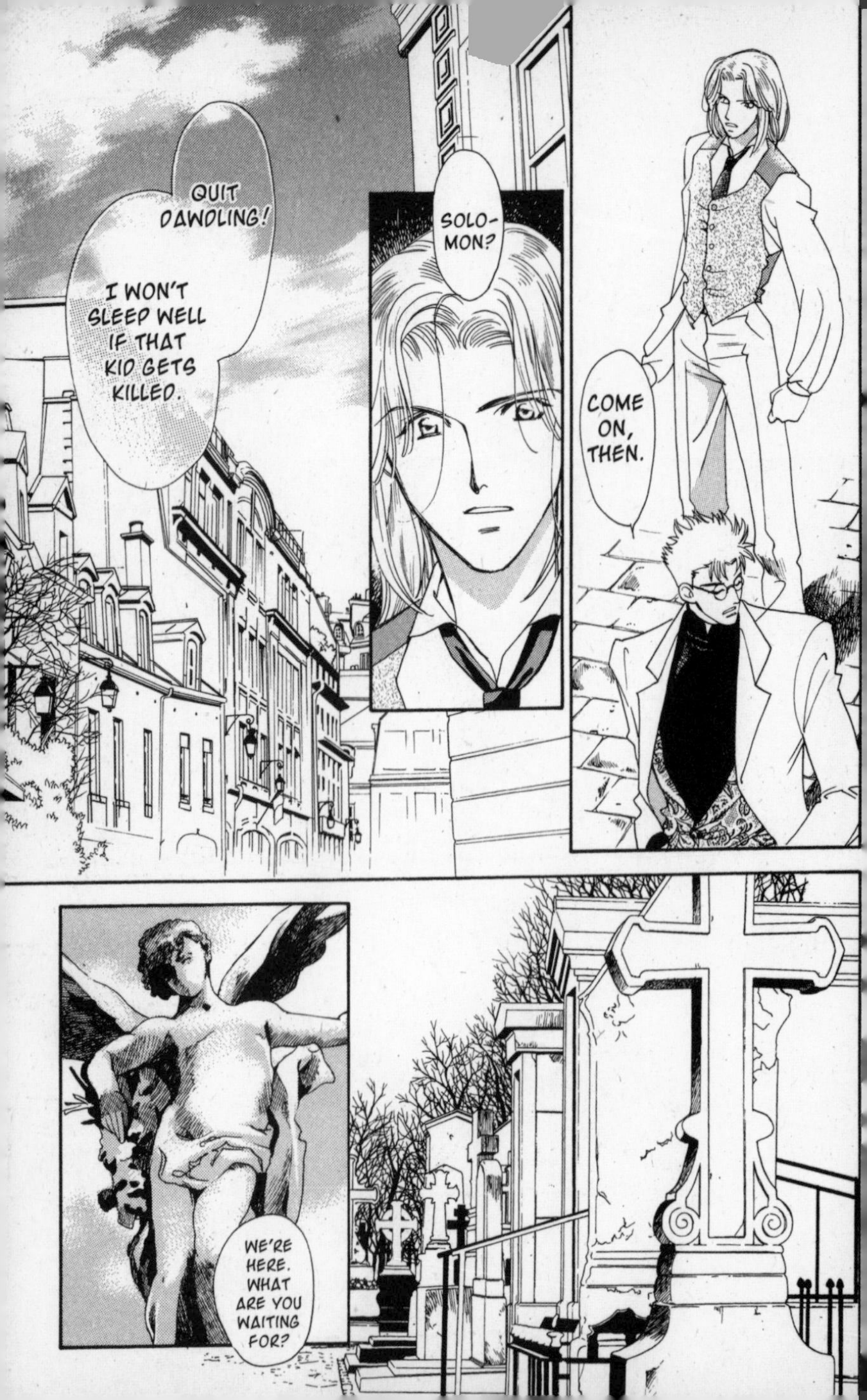
COME ON, THEN.
SOLO-MON?
QUIT DAWDLING!
I WON'T SLEEP WELL IF THAT KID GETS KILLED.
WE'RE HERE. WHAT ARE YOU WAITING FOR?

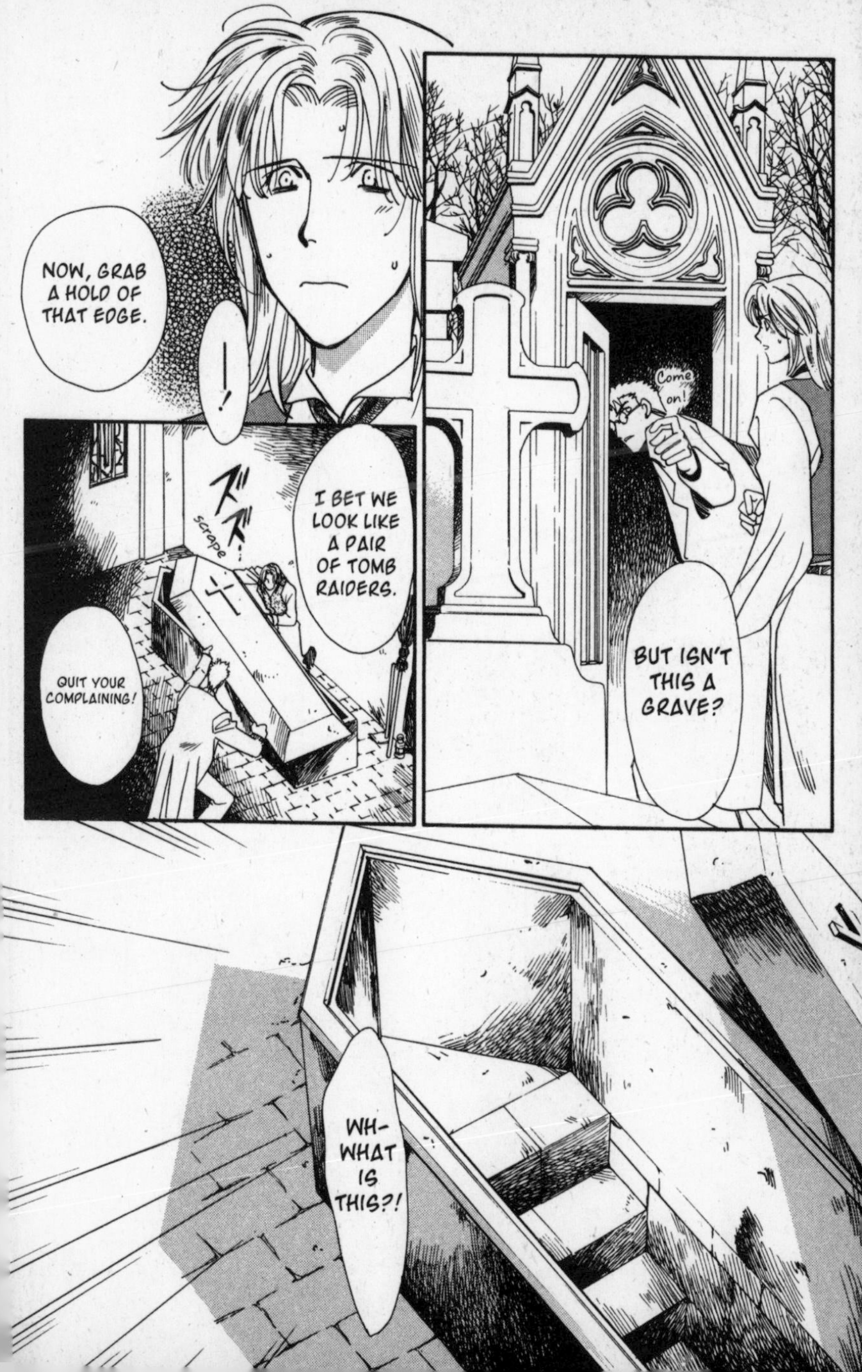
Come on!
BUT ISN'T THIS A GRAVE?
NOW, GRAB A HOLD OF THAT EDGE.
—!
ズズ
scrape
I BET WE LOOK LIKE A PAIR OF TOMB RAIDERS.
QUIT YOUR COMPLAINING!
WH-WHAT IS THIS?!

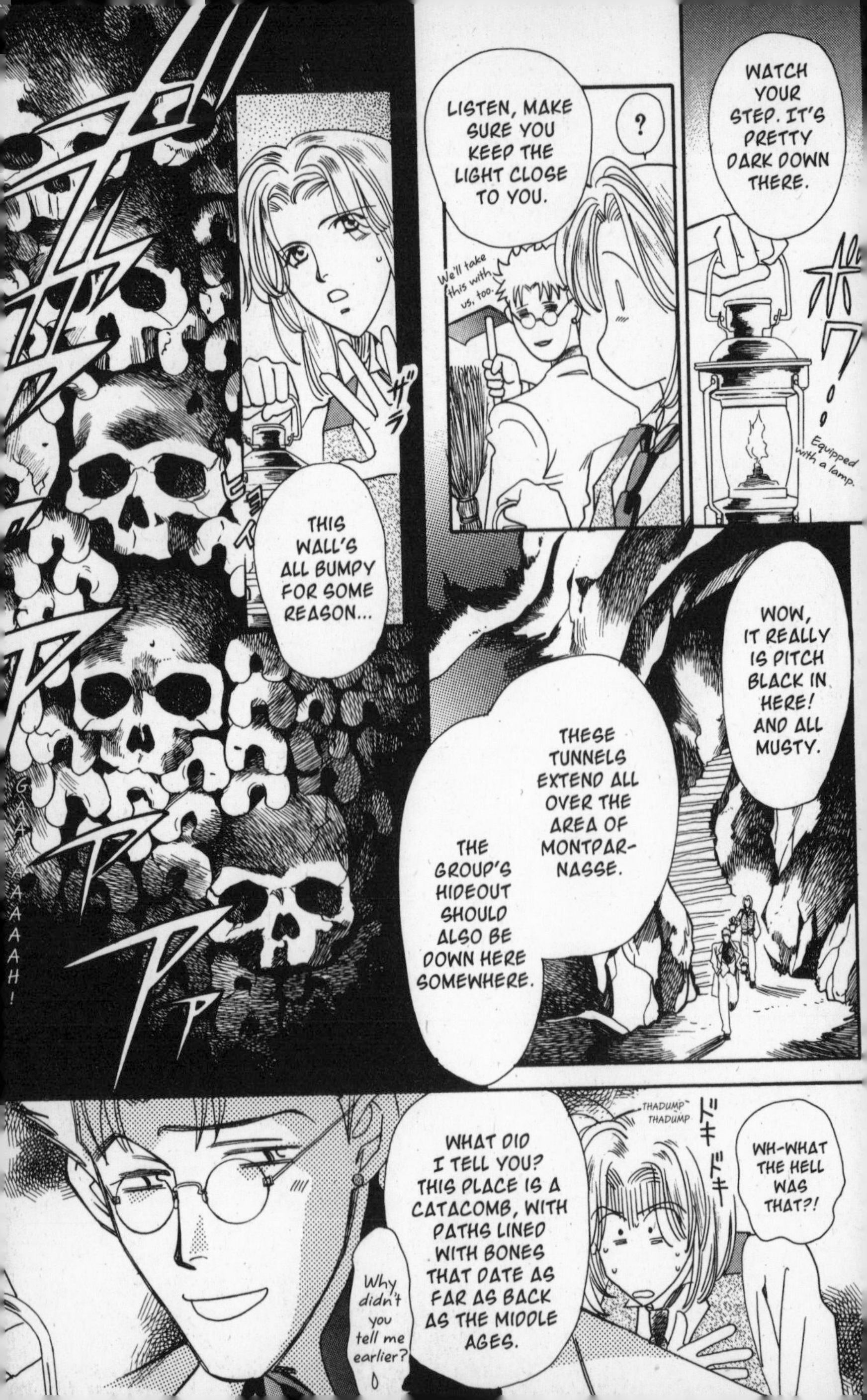
WATCH YOUR STEP. IT'S PRETTY DARK DOWN THERE.
Equipped with a lamp.
?
LISTEN, MAKE SURE YOU KEEP THE LIGHT CLOSE TO YOU.
We'll take this with us, too.
WOW, IT REALLY IS PITCH BLACK IN HERE! AND ALL MUSTY.
THESE TUNNELS EXTEND ALL OVER THE AREA OF MONTPAR-NASSE.
THE GROUP'S HIDEOUT SHOULD ALSO BE DOWN HERE SOMEWHERE.
THIS WALL'S ALL BUMPY FOR SOME REASON...
GAAAAAAAAAH!
WH-WHAT THE HELL WAS THAT?!
THADUMP THADUMP
WHAT DID I TELL YOU? THIS PLACE IS A CATACOMB, WITH PATHS LINED WITH BONES THAT DATE AS FAR AS BACK AS THE MIDDLE AGES.
Why didn't you tell me earlier?

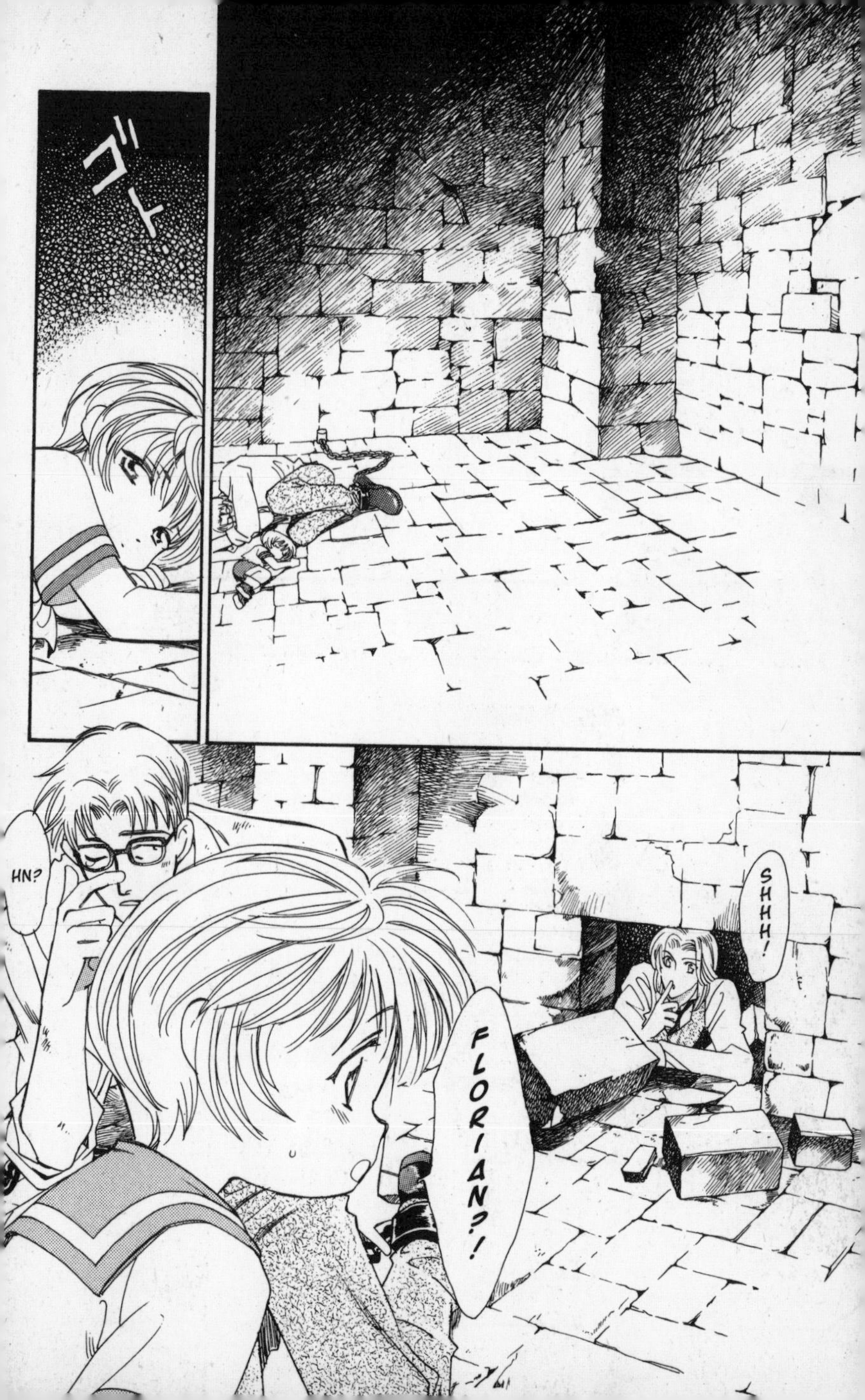
ゴト…
SHHH!
FLORIAN?!
HN?

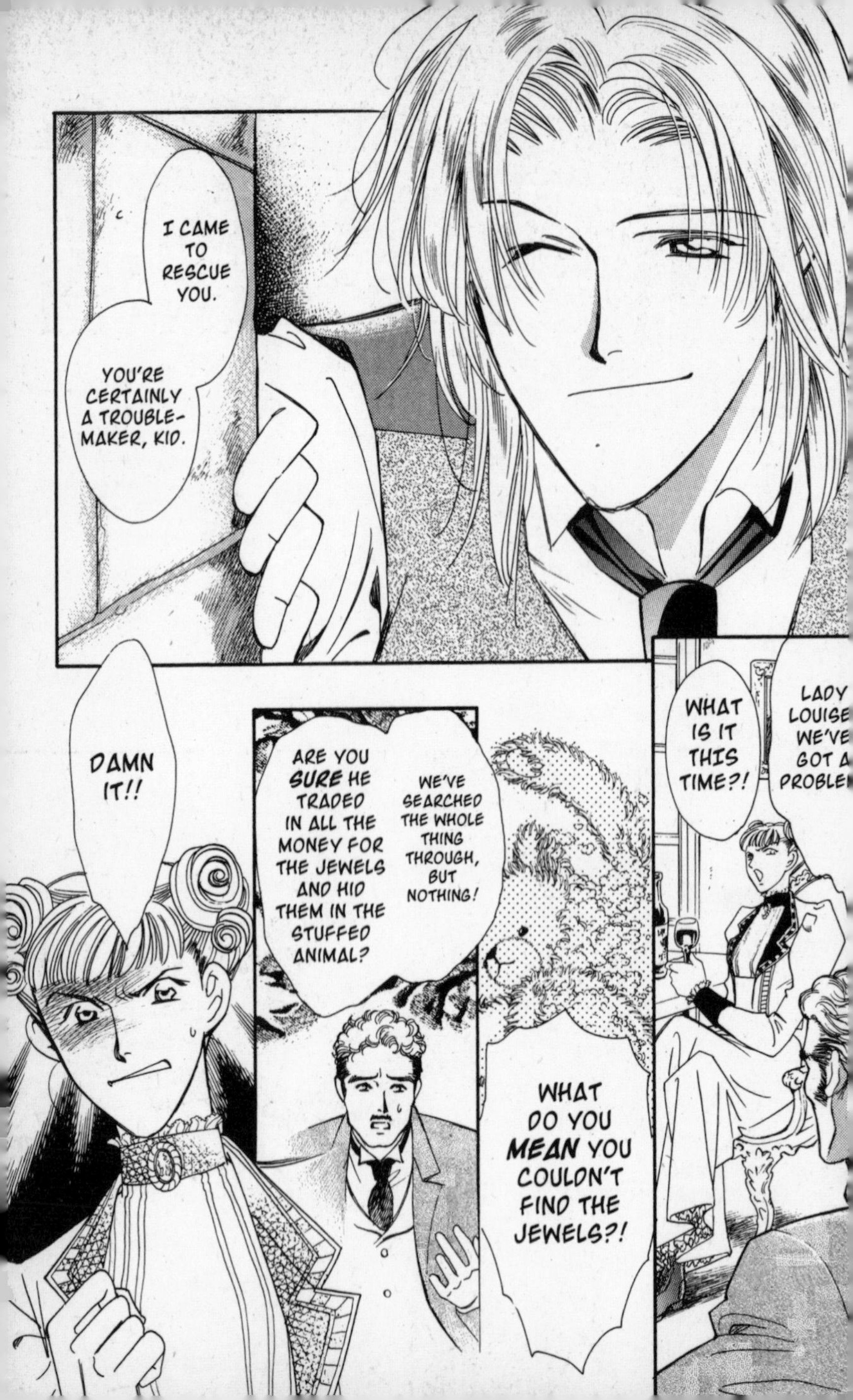
I CAME TO RESCUE YOU.
YOU'RE CERTAINLY A TROUBLE-MAKER, KID.
LADY LOUISE WE'VE GOT A PROBLE
WHAT IS IT THIS TIME?!
WHAT DO YOU MEAN YOU COULDN'T FIND THE JEWELS?!
WE'VE SEARCHED THE WHOLE THING THROUGH, BUT NOTHING!
ARE YOU SURE HE TRADED IN ALL THE MONEY FOR THE JEWELS AND HID THEM IN THE STUFFED ANIMAL?
DAMN IT!!

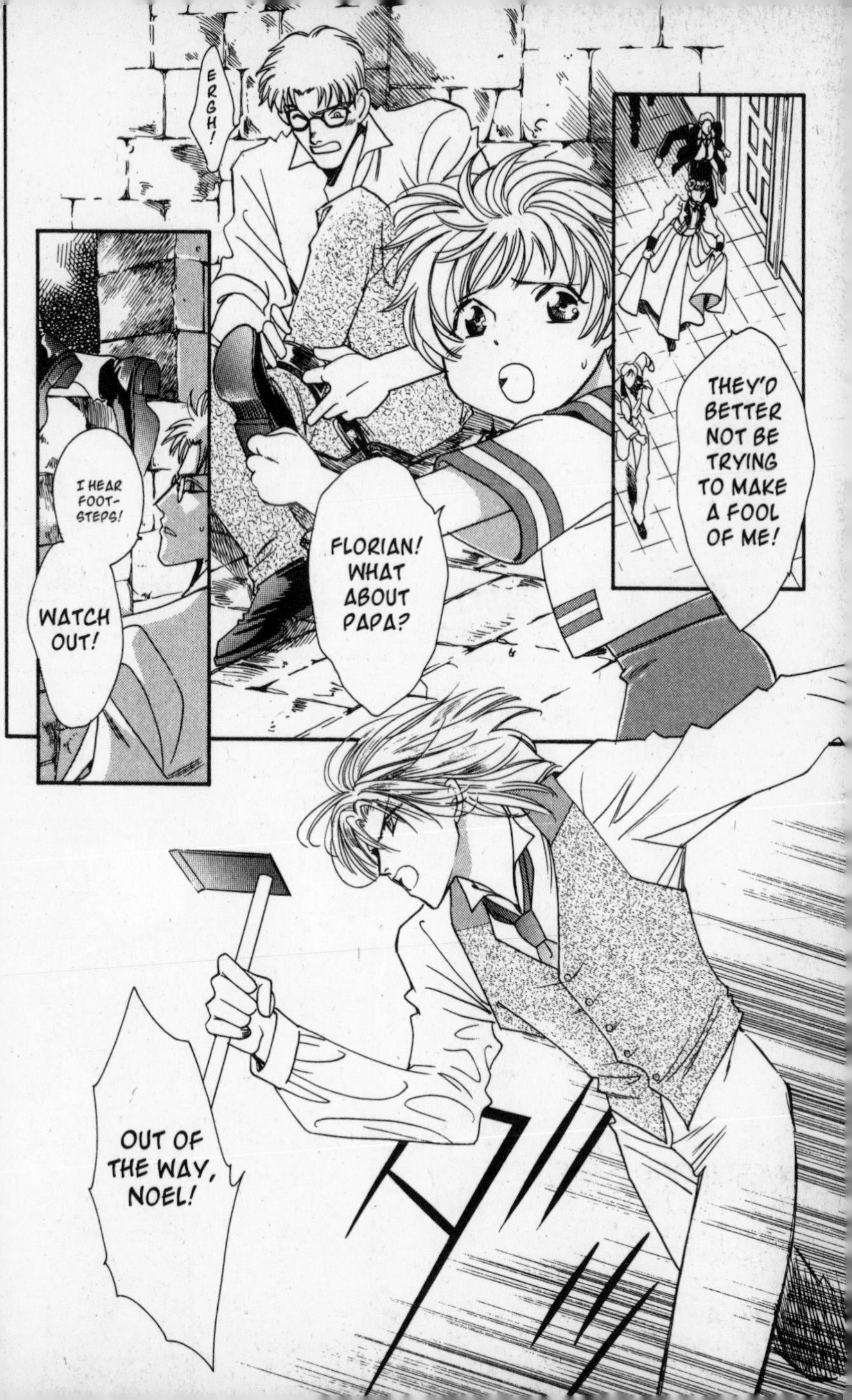
THEY'D BETTER NOT BE TRYING TO MAKE A FOOL OF ME!
ERGH!
FLORIAN! WHAT ABOUT PAPA?
I HEAR FOOT-STEPS!
WATCH OUT!
OUT OF THE WAY, NOEL!

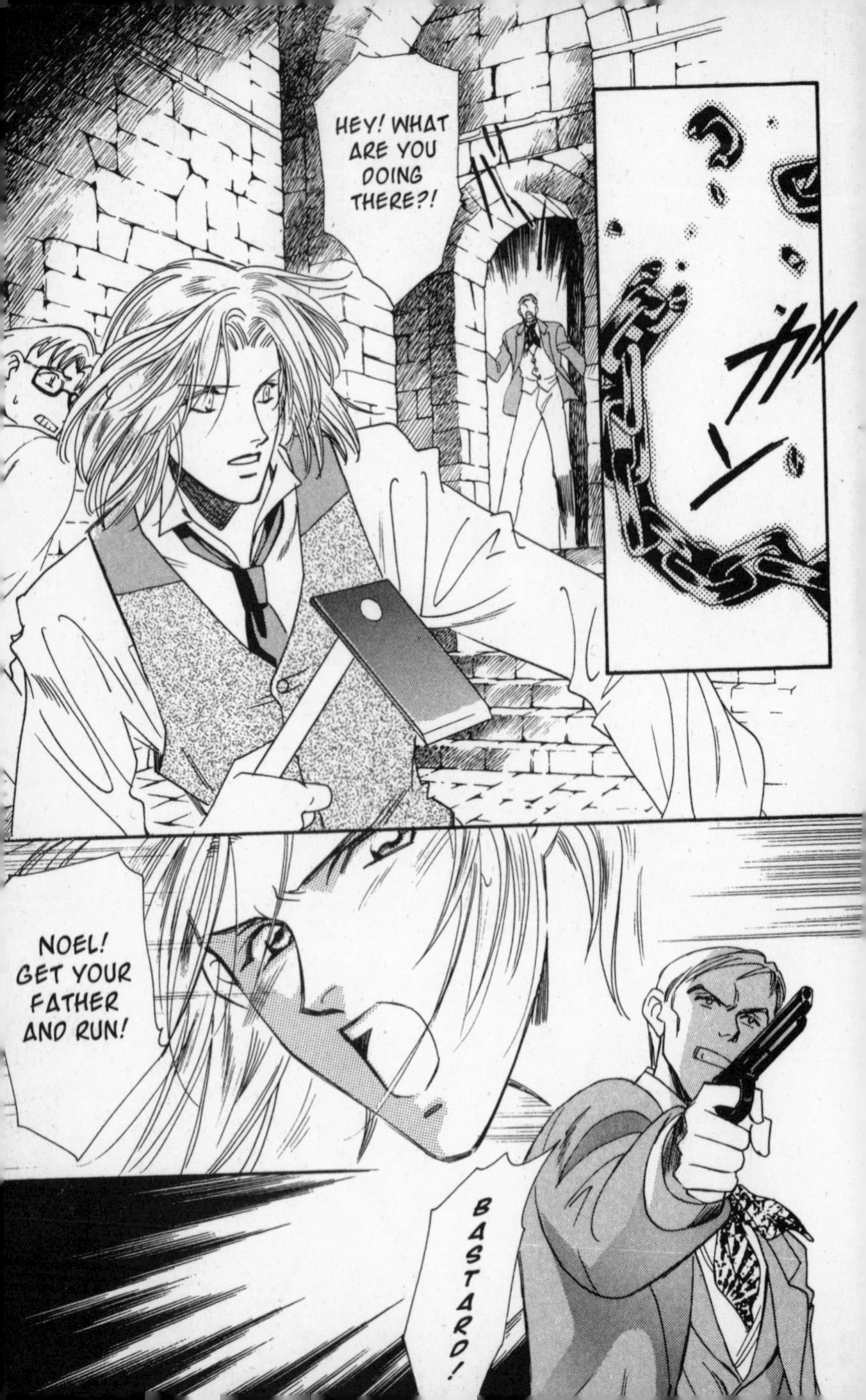
HEY! WHAT ARE YOU DOING THERE?!
NOEL! GET YOUR FATHER AND RUN!
BASTARDO!

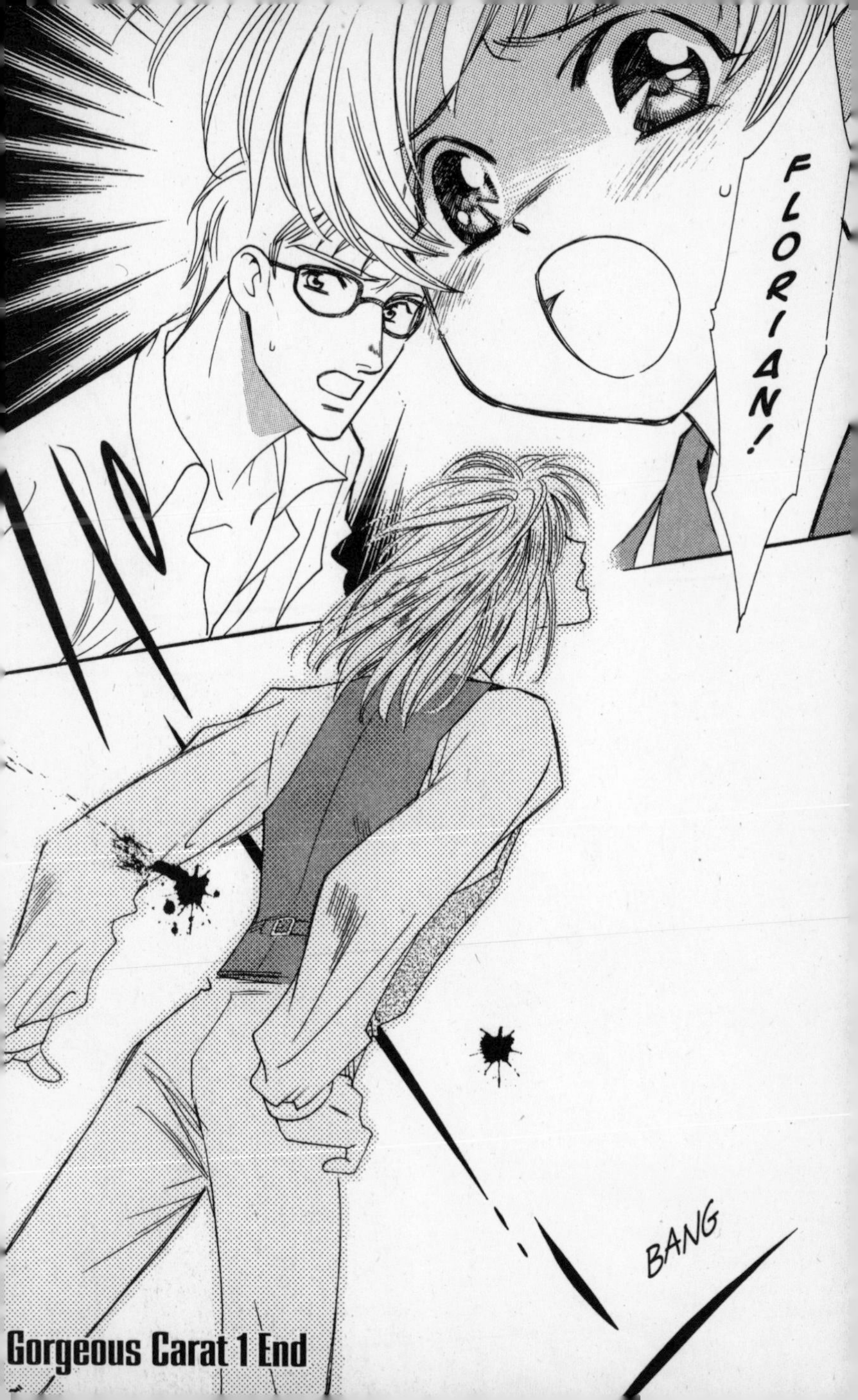
FLORIAN!
BANG

Gorgeous Carat 1 End

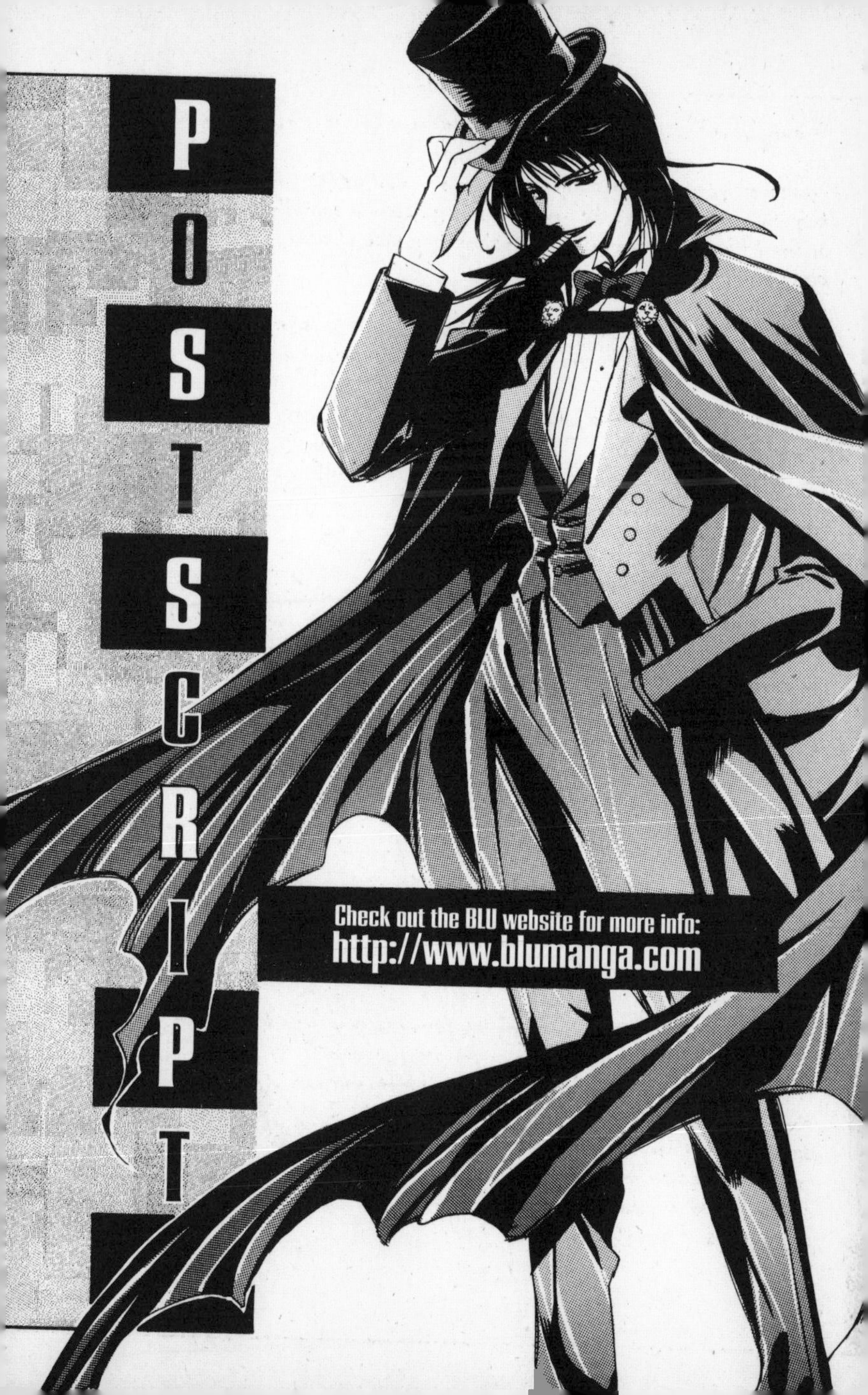
POSTSCRIPT
Check out the BLU website for more info:
http://www.blumanga.com

Thanks to all of you who picked up *Gorgeous Carat: Virtue of Darkness*!

Once again, old but beautiful Europe was used as the setting. I've always known that it was a fashionable and adverse place, but something about the beginning of the 19th-20th century has this inexpressible charm. I should say it has a certain atmosphere.

It was a lovely era, overflowing with beauty and lyricism. I also felt that its moderate "moisture" fit the movements of my characters well.

This is my image of the place and time, so please take it as fantasy. Of course, I'm just doing whatever I wish (who knows, maybe people from those countries would laugh if they saw it). World history is actually not my specialty. This series isn't really too concerned with staying realistic, because I just planned for it to be an adventure/action type.

The subtitle "Virtue of Darkness" was handed down by one of the editors. Originally, I had plans to make this manga more of a freaky torture type manga, but...well...I guess it turned out...a little different. But at least the contents are wholesome. I guess I really like drawing my bishies getting picked on... Guess that means that in the future more of this pattern will come out... Either way, it was by the request of my (male) editor.

I also hope I continue having a good time with *Eyes* magazine.

I'd also like to thank all those that helped me in the creation of this work: Izumi Sei-san, Kitazawa Misaki-san, Nakatsuji Naoko-san, Miyakoshi Wasou-san, Fujikata Moemi-san, Enohara Michiko-san, Kazuki Matsuri-san, Hondou Makoto-san, Iwahashi Mikiko-san, and others.

But above all, I'd like to give my gratitude to my friend, Oda Ryouka, who's raised me in the tough world of a mangaka and helped me to improve myself ten times over. I can't forget my editor, Mr. Yosshi. I'm so sorry for always being a burden! I just hope you don't decide to throw me out. And then, of course, to all my readers. I send you a big wet sloppy kiss of thanks! ♡

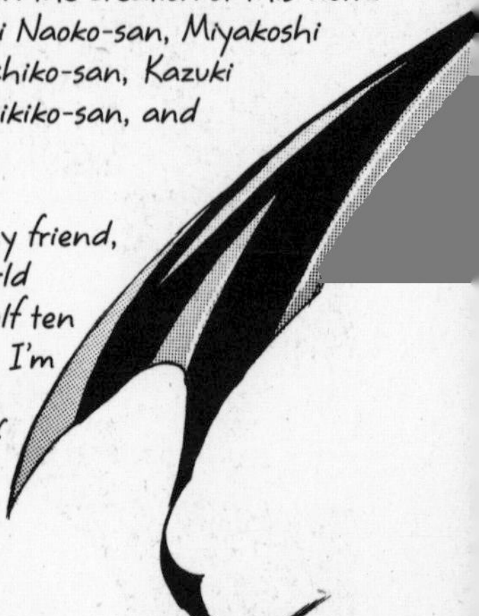

NOIR

FLORIAN

IN THE NEXT VOLUME

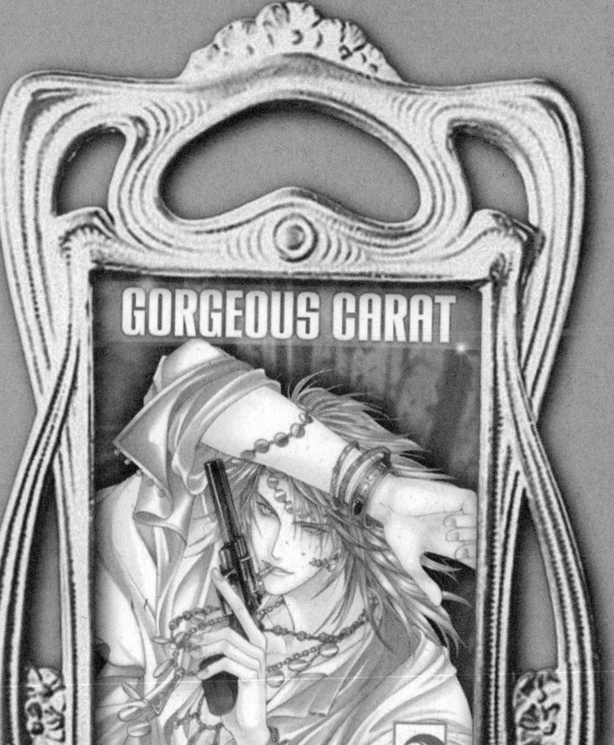
GORGEOUS CARAT
2 YOU HIGURI
青 BLU

Florian has been taken hostage by the evil Black Hand organization. Will Phantom Thief Noir come to the rescue or will he keep the precious jewels for himself? And what adventures await as the gang heads down to Morocco to meet Ray's old friend? Things heat up in book two of *Gorgeous Carat* as Ray and Florian seek out the ancient treasure of the Knights Templar.

GORGEOUS CARAT VOL. 1

Created by You Higuri

First published in Japan by HOME-SHA INC., Tokyo, Japan.

ISBN: 1-59816-102-4

First Printing: February 2006
10 9 8 7 6 5 4 3 2 1
Printed in the USA

*F*ollow the love lives of Izumi, Takamiya and others as they are brought together at a host club called "Blue Boy" that specializes in high-class male escorts. Love lines cross, chances are lost and found, and hearts are broken in this fan favorite boys' love classic.

LOVE MODE
Yuki Shimizu
1

青 BLU

In stores now! $9.99

Hisae Shino is an unemployed anime voice actor who also has to support his son Nakaya, a sophomore in high school. The sweet and naive Shino will take any job he can get—even if it means boys' love radio dramas! When he gets paired up with the supercool Tenryuu, the two bond...to a degree that Shino never intended!

stop

blu manga are published in the original japanese format

go to the other side and begin reading